Sampo: The Magic Mill

Sampo
THE MAGIC MILL

A Collection of Finnish-American Writing

Edited by Michael G. Karni
& Aili Jarvenpa

Graphics by Oili Mäki

Many Minnesotas Project Number 5

NEW RIVERS PRESS

Acknowledgements and credits appear on page 391

Sampo: The Magic Mill has been published with the aid of grants from the Metropolitan Regional Arts Council (with funds provided by the Legislature of the State of Minnesota), the First Bank System Foundation, the Arts Development Fund of the United Arts Council, and the Finnish Ministry of Education.

New Rivers Press books are distributed by

The Talman Company
150-5th Avenue
New York, NY 10011

Sampo: The Magic Mill has been published by New Rivers Press, Inc. (C.W. Truesdale, editor/publisher), 420 North 5th St./Suite 910, Minneapolis, MN 55401 in a first edition of 2,000 copies.

CONTENTS

Introduction
  Michael G. Karni and Aili Jarvenpa...........................xi
What is the Sampo?
  K. Börge Vähämäki..xv

PART I: IN THE BEGINNING

Ilmari Kianto
  Excerpt from *Scenes from Travels in Viena-Karelia*
  translated by Reino Virtanen..................................3
Juhani Aho
  "A Visit to a Sauna" (short story)
  translated by Inkeri Väänänen-Jensen.........................7
Unto Seppänen
  "The Knitting" (short story) translated by Reino Virtanen......12
Jaakko Liukkonen
  "Karhu the Bear" (Finnish folk tales)
  translated by Kathleen Osgood Dana..........................17
Aaro Hellaakoski
  "Song of the Pike" and "Moonlight in the Woods" (poems)
  translated by Aina Swan Cutler..............................21
Anna Perkkiö
  "Grandmother's Wedding Gift" (short story).................23
Juhani Aho
  "Bread" (short story) translated by Inkeri Väänänen-Jensen....28
Eeva Joenpelto
  Excerpts from the novel *A Draft from All the Doors*
  translated by Aili Jarvenpa.................................31

PART II: THE IMMIGRANT STORY

Jim Johnson
  "Getting Off the Train at Brimson" (poem)..................49
Lauri Lemberg
  Excerpts from the novel *St. Croix Avenue*
  translated by Timo Riippa...................................50
William R. Lamppa
  "Finns of the North Country" (poem)........................63
Jane Piirto
  "Grandma You Used To" (poem)...............................64

Annie Ruissalo
"The Floating Caravan" and other sketches (memoir)
translated by Timo Riippa..............................66
Lynn Maria Laitala
"Timo's Team" (short story)...............................73
Marlene Ekola Gerberick
"In Old Photographs of You" and six other poems...........76
Rebecca Cummings
"The Hair Brooch" (short story)...........................83
Sirkka Tuomi Holm
"Stage Recollections Among the Finns" (memoir)............90
Nancy Mattson
"Writing" and six other poems............................99
Glen Kartin
"Hacking Away at the Family Tree" (memoir)..............106
Jim Johnson
"Skeletons" (poem).......................................114
Earl Nurmi
".25-36 Caliber Rifle" and "Trapping Weasel
Near Duluth in Winter" (poems).........................115
Helmi Mavis Hiltunen Biesanz
Exerpts from the memoir *Helmi Mavis:*
A Finnish-American Girlhood............................117
Ruth Pitkanen Johnson
"The Riches in Poverty" (memoir).........................130
Bernhard Hillila
"Yrjö Kaarto" (poem).....................................136
Ernest Hekkanen
"In the New World" (short story).........................139
Gladys Koski Holmes
"Fragments" and "Widows" (poems).........................147
Eila Siren-Perlmutter
"Room and Board" (short story)...........................150
Inkeri Väänänen-Jensen
Excerpts from the memoir *Inkeri's Journey*..............161

PART III: SUCCEEDING GENERATIONS IN FINLAND & AMERICA

Carl Gawboy
"Christmas at Birch Lake" (memoir).......................171
Jim Johnson
"At Eagle Lake" and "Mojakka" (poems)...................176
"The Visit" (prose poem).................................179

Jane Piirto
"Sauna" (poem)..180
Lynn Maria Laitala
"Winter Trip" (short story)................................182
"The Big Wedding" (short story)...........................188
Pierre Delattre
Excerpts from the novel *Korrigan's Wedding*
"Korrigan's Tree"...192
"The Spirit of the Water".................................199
Anselm Hollo
"Gig" and seven other poems...............................203
Jane Piirto
"Blueberry Season" (short story)..........................209
Eeva-Liisa Manner
Selections from *Collected Poems 1956-1977*
translated by Ritva Poom..................................216
Eeva Kilpi
Excerpts from *A Woman's Diary*
translated by Inkeri Väänänen-Jensen......................220
Lauri Anderson
"Hunting Hemingway's Trout" (short story).................224
"Pictures" (short story)..................................236
Timo Koskinen
"Dead Weight" (short story)...............................239
Sheila Packa
"Minnesota Steel 1975" and four other poems...............246
Eeva Kilpi
"At the Cottage" (short story)
translated by Kathleen Osgood Dana........................252
Bernhard Hillila
"Hail Mary" and two other poems...........................258
Kathleen Osgood Dana
"Midsummer" (poem)..260
Aale Tynni
"On Many a Windy Night" and "The Lake" (poems)
translated by Richard A. Impola...........................261
Heikki Turunen
Excerpts from the novel *Children of the Land*
translated by Richard A. Impola...........................264
Diane Jarvenpa
"After the Concert" and five other poems..................275

Jussi Stenvall
"The Last Swim" (short story)............................281
Stephen Kuusisto
"Pentti Saarikoski: Outside the Circle" (essay)...............286
Pentti Saarikoski
Four untitled poems translated by Stephen Kuusisto.........287
Stephen Kuusisto
"Papyrus & Stone" (elegy to Pentti Saarikoski)..............290
Shirley Waisanen Schoonover
Excerpt from the novel *Mountain of Winter*..................292
Gladys Koski Holmes
"While Driving to Work" (poem)...........................298
Mary Jokela Eichholz
"Maia to Orion" and "Cavity" (poems)....................299
Oili Mäki
"Landmark" (poem) translated by Aili Jarvenpa..............301
John Piirto
"Spur" (short story)..302
Carol Staats
"Lapland Bear Song" and two other poems................310
"The Rituals" (short story)................................312
Sara Johnson
"Mixing" and two other poems............................318
Roberta Christine Kulma
"The Immigrant's Grandchild Remembers" (memoir)........321
Marcelle Doby-Williams
"Soul Food" and two other poems........................327
"The Gift" (short story)....................................329
Aili Jarvenpa
"First Lesson" and two other poems......................338
Eeva Kilpi
"The Brides" (poem) translated by Aili Jarvenpa............342

PART IV: A RETROSPECTIVE

Anselm Hollo
"The *Kalevala* Through My Years" (personal essay)..........351
Sara Johnson
"Chickaloon Lumber Company" (poem)....................357
William Lamppa
"Soudan Iron Ore Miner" (poem).........................358

Jane Piirto
"The Company" (poem)................................359
Paula Erkkila
"On the Road to Rock: A Search for Identity" (memoir)......363
Kathleen Halme
"Wool, Bread, Rope" and "Sauna" (poems).................370
Paula Ivaska Robbins
"Impressions of Finland" (memoir)........................373
Mary Jokela Eichholz
"Spinster" and "Happy Birthday, Mother!" (poems).........380
Hazel M. Koskenlinna
" 'Talking Story' – Finnish Style" (memoir).................383
Aili Jarvenpa
"The Spruce" and "To Grandmother's House" (poems).......387
Arlene Renken
"Reunion at Lake Superior" (poem).......................390
Contributor Notes...391
Acknowledgements...404

GRAPHICS BY OILI MÄKI

Tapestry depicting "Forging of the Sampo,"
(Poem X, *Kalevala*).......................................cover
Tapestry depicting "The Creation," (Poem I, *Kalevala*).........xviii
Tapestry depicting "Väinämöinen's Thanks"
(Poem II, *Kalevala*).......................................46
Double weaving entitled "Invitation to a Wedding"............168
Tapestry entitled "The Understanding Angel".................348

INTRODUCTION

*F*OR OVER FIVE centuries Finland was governed by Sweden. From 1809 until 1917, the small nation was a Grand Duchy of Czarist Russia. There seemed little hope for self-identification until 1835 when Elias Lönnrot, a medical doctor and literary scholar, signed the preface to the first edition of the *Kalevala*, a collection of thirty-two cantos that he had compiled from oral poetry of unlettered folk of Karelia and northeast Finland, handed down through centuries by Finno-Karelian singers. During the next half century, Lönnrot's *Kalevala* helped open the doors to education, national identity and literature for the Finnish people.

While few Finns at that time were able to read the *Kalevala* with real comprehension, what was important was that Lönnrot had recovered an ancient literary tradition that was impressive and beautiful, as well as capable, in the right hands, of changing attitudes necessary for the elevation of the Finnish language to equal status with Swedish and Russian. The *Kalevala* awakened the national spirit of the Finnish people and gave them pride and confidence in their own language. The rest is history. From it evolved the literature of the people, written by leading Finnish writers of the nineteenth and early twentieth centuries. They included, among others, Aleksis Kivi, Juhani Aho, Eino Leino, Minna Canth, Ilmari Kianto, and Aaro Hellaakoski. Kianto, Aho, and Hellaakoski are represented in this book. By the time of the first waves of Finnish emigration to America at the end of the nineteenth century, Finns had already become a literate people.

Kalervo Siikala, Director of International Affairs in the Finnish Education Ministry, wrote recently in *Scandinavian Review:*

> Finland and the birthdays of the Republic bring to my mind a picture of a fragment of a people which sought its way from the mists of a Finno-Ugric past to the northeastern corner of Europe and there nursed its flickering flame of life — a modest, unschooled and isolated linguistic community far from the great historical avenues of war and trade.

In a real sense, the experiences of Finnish Americans have paralleled those of Finns in the Old World. Isolated from Americans and other ethnic groups in America by their strange language, living in remote rural areas and small mining communities throughout the northern states of America, they avoided being absorbed into the melting pot. They were not shaped by their experience in America as much as they shaped the American environment to fit their perceived needs. There were church groups, temperance societies, workingmen's associations and cooperatives of all kinds (including boarding houses and mortuaries); gymnastics societies, fraternal orders and mixed choruses; debate societies, drama groups, reading circles and publishing associations. And, of course, every group from the local temperance chapter to the local socialist club had women's guilds and youth leagues to serve as auxiliaries to the larger bodies, which in turn belonged to state, regional and national federations. Throughout the immigrant generation, Finns certainly did nurse a "flickering flame" of literary life, not unschooled, merely isolated behind a language unfathomable to outsiders.

In recent years, Finnish Americans have rediscovered their cultural heritage. This is evident in the wide range of activities in which Finnish Americans are involved, such as language camps, scholarly conferences, festivals, publications, organizations, historical societies, folk dance and vocal groups. Since 1982 Finnish American writers have had the opportunity to participate in literature symposia, workshops and translation forums organized especially for them. In 1986 and 1987, the two Reunion of Sisters conferences held in St. Paul, Minnesota and Kuopio, Finland, for Finnish American women and women of Finland, included literature sessions for writers. We believe efforts such as these have had a great deal to do with providing *Sampo: The Magic Mill* with variety and quality.

Written almost entirely by Finnish Americans, *Sampo* contains poetry, short fiction, personal essays, memoirs and translations that reflect the experiences of Finnish immigrants and subsequent generations. Many of the writers, for example, grew up in rural Finnish communities or small towns in the Upper Midwest to which their parents or grandparents had immigrated. Many have moved to other states and to cities far removed from their childhood roots. Yet from their submissions we learn that their heritage continues as an important part of their lives. Jim Johnson's poem, for example, "Getting Off the Train at Brimson," expresses poignantly the trepidation a young Finnish immigrant felt when she reached her destination in the New World: a remote, cold, heavily forested lowland region in northeastern Minnesota where she felt isolated geographically as well as linguistically. Mavis Biesanz's excerpt from her memoir, *Helmi Mavis: Finnish-American Girlhood*, extols the beauty of farm life in the northwoods, again in Minnesota. And Lynn Laitala's piece of short fiction, "Timo's Team," deals with the hard work and ultimate tragedy of a man and his wife who desperately farm and log in a brutal northern climate.

Sampo includes Finnish American writers whose work has been published by major American publishers. Among these are Shirley

Schoonover whose novel, *Mountain Of Winter*, from which the selection in *Sampo* is taken, deals with the same rural themes described above. It was published in 1965 by Coward-McCann, New York, and has been translated into eighteen languages. She has been the recipient of two O. Henry Awards for her short stories. Pierre Delattre, whose work is also included in this collection, is the author of two novels, *Tales of a Dali Lama* and *Walking On Air*, published by Houghton-Mifflin.

Anselm Hollo and Kathleen Osgood Dana, two of the writer/translators included in *Sampo*, have both been recipients of the annual PEN/ American Scandinavian Foundation Translation Award. Hollo received the award for his translations of the poetry of Pentti Saarikoski, Dana for her translation of a portion of Väinö Linna's trilogy, *Here Beneath the Northern Star*. Several of Hollo's own poems are included in *Sampo*, as well as prose translations by Dana, including Dana's translation of Eeva Kilpi's short story, "At the Cottage." A third award-winning translator, Ritva Poom, is represented in this volume. Poom won the 1988 translation prize from Columbia University's Translation Center for her bilingual poetry book, *Fog Horses*, a collection of Eeva-Liisa Manner's poems. Manner is the leading poet of the Finnish modernist movement of the 'fifties and the late Pentti Saarikoski a major poet of postwar Finland. Saarikoski's poetry is represented in *Sampo* by the translations of Stephen Kuusisto.

Also included in *Sampo* are translations of works written in Finnish in the United States and Canada by immigrant writers. Timo Riippa has translated excerpts from Lauri Lemberg's novel, *Saint Croix Avenue*, which provides for the first time for those who do not understand Finnish a glimpse of early 20th century life in the leading urban settlement of Finns in America, the city of Duluth, Minnesota. Lemberg was a gifted actor and playwright in Finnish socialist theaters in America. Annie Ruissalo, a Finnish Canadian immigrant writer, wrote novels, short stories, and articles which appeared for nearly sixty years in the Finnish language women's newspapers. We include excerpts from her autobiographical writings, also translated by Timo Riippa, that describe everyday life in the backwoods of Ontario.

We have selected *Sampo: The Magic Mill* as the title of this anthology because we see metaphorical similarities between the magic Sampo of the *Kalevala*, which poured forth elements of different kinds (such as grain and salt and precious metals), and our ability, by means of this anthology, to evoke different kinds of literary expression from Finnish Americans the nation over. We include an introductory essay that interprets the term "Sampo," written by K. Börje Vähämäki, Chairman of the Department of Scandinavian Studies at the University of Minnesota.

The cover illustration, a depiction of the forging of the Sampo in the *Kalevala*, is the design of Oili Mäki, a textile artist and writer of Finland. The other illustrations in the volume are also hers.

We wish to thank Kalervo Siikala, Finnish Ministry of Education, for pledging financial support to the publication of *Sampo: The Magic Mill*, the first attempt ever to anthologize the writings of Finnish Americans. We are also deeply grateful for the large number of submissions we received for possible inclusion. And, finally, we wish to thank C. W. Truesdale, Publisher/Editor of New Rivers Press, for providing us with the opportunity to compile this rich collection of work, and we especially thank him for providing Finnish American writers with this opportunity to have their work published.

Michael G. Karni
Aili Jarvenpa
Editors

WHAT IS THE SAMPO?

*T*HE *Sampo Epos*, the poems which deal with creation, with the forging of the Sampo, and with the theft and subsequent strug—gle for and destruction of the Sampo, is the single most studied and explored element of the *Kalevala* itself and of Finnish epic narrative poetry at large.* In addition to capturing the fancy of scholars, the Sampo has also served as an infinite source of inspiration for the Finnish artist, poet and cultural interpreter.

The Sampo is often mentioned in the *Kalevala*. Either it is being created or forged by Ilmarinen, the eternal Smith, or it is being deposited in Louhi's Pohjola, or North Farm (in F. P. Magoun's phrasing). There Louhi, a woman of intimidating powers, reigns.

The Sampo produces a wealth of good things for North Farm, but is ultimately coveted also by the people of the Kaleva District, led by Old Väinämöinen, who set out to claim the Sampo, offering first to share it with Pohjola. When Louhi, as is only to be expected, refuses to share any portion of it with Väinämöinen's clan, they outright steal the Sampo. In the ensuing fight, the Sampo breaks and falls into the ocean. Some areas are blessed with fragments of the broken Sampo; they bring prosperity to the region. For the most part, however, it is lost to the sea, explaining why the sea is more fertile than land, and why the ocean's water is salty.

The great primeval craftsman Ilmarinen was asked, as a qualifying task of courtship, to forge *a* Sampo, *the* Sampo or *a new* Sampo, with a "brightly-coloured cover" (Kirby translation) or a "lid of many colors" (Magoun translation), leaving much confusion as to how the Sampo may have been conceived. The descriptive qualities are confined to such expressions, or to vague (and sometimes confusing) references to the bulkiness of the Sampo itself, and its subsequent secure installation behind nine locks within the Mount of Copper. The cover is said to revolve or grind and there are three sides to it:

> On one side there was a corn-mill,
> On another side a salt-mill,
> And upon the third a coin-mill. (Kirby, X.414-6)

The mill image, most frequently associated with Sampo, derives from this very description and is corroborated by the frequent mentions of grinding and revolving movements.

According to the clues given in the text, Ilmarinen is something more than a blacksmith. He is a central agent in Finnish mythology like

Haephestos or Vulcan (his Greek or Roman equivalent):

> *I will go to forge the Sampo, —*
> *For 'twas I who forged the heavens,*
> *And the vault of air I hammered,*
> *Ere the air had yet beginning,*
> *Or a trace of aught was present.*

As to the Sampo itself, some of the suggestions put forth view it as a chest (maybe a treasure chest or a jewelry box); a mill; a statue (usually a fertility statue); a frog or a turtle or a turtle's back (a purely technical object on which a revolving axis rests); the sun itself; the vault of heaven; or the *axis mundi*, the axle of the world attached at the top to the North Star, sometimes referred to as "the navel of the North," around which the entire world revolves. The options are endless. But the most popular explanation — the mill notion — is strengthened by the similarity between the Sampo descriptions and the Scandinavian story of *Grotti*, a magic mill owned by King Frodi of Denmark.

Most scholars today hold that the Sampo is a fertility symbol, worshipped in order to secure good crops, harvests, safety for livestock, continued prosperity for human beings, magic powers, beauty, and happiness. The image of mini-world pillars with ornately-worked metal tops, in the image of the vault of heaven, symbolizing the pillar of the world which holds up the sky, and which thus upholds life, is quite attractive indeed.

What should be emphasized, however, in the context of the present volume is the central mission the Sampo symbolism carries for Finnish culture. The mission is creativity, imagination, and bold aspirations. The Sampo stands in Finnish consciousness as the symbol of the wonder of life, of the creative powers, which have fueled the Finnish people in its forging of an identity of distinction and dignity.

This volume is a symbol of this very creativity, now in its Finnish-American dimension.

—K. Börje Vähämäki
Department of Scandinavian Studies
University of Minnesota

*The scholars who have made significant contributions to Sampo research are Julius and Kaarle Krohn, E. N. Setälä in his monumental book *Sammon arvoitus* (the Sampo riddle), 1932, Matti Kuusi with his *magnum opus, Sampo-eepos* (The Sampo Epos) of 1949, Uuno Harva-Holmberg, Martti Haavio, Michael Branch, and, most recently Juha Pentikäinen, *The Mythology of the Kalevala*. The works of these scholars as well as others serve as rich and imaginative sources of observations and interpretations of *Kalevala* poetry and the Sampo.

We dedicate this anthology
to
the Finnish immigrant writers
who nurtured a love for literature
and passed it on to succeeding generations

and to
Pentti Saarikoski
a major poet of Finland
(1927-1983).

PART I

In the beginning

Ilmari Kianto

Excerpt from

SCENES FROM TRAVELS IN VIENA-KARELIA
(Translated by Reino Virtanen)

Deep sources, rare things
(Kalevala, III, v. 187-8)

THE BLIND MAN from Likopää village near Uhtua guided me along the lakeshore trail, and I for my part guided him.

"Here it is," he said, when I informed him that we were approaching a red house.

"But there's a prop blocking the outside door," I pointed out.

"Remove it," he urged, and we climbed up some steps.

When we opened the door, I didn't think there was any one in the hut. Not a rustle was heard. The state of the room, like the blocked door, indicated that the regular residents were absent. But as I penetrated deeper into the hut, I noticed an old man sitting motionless beside the window that looked out over the lake, a cane between his legs, a black prayer wreath in his hands and a cuspidor at his feet. He sat there in quiet meditation like a stone image fingering a rosary, and listening to sounds coming from the depths of eternity. In his watery deep-set eyes a melancholy reverie seemed to stir.

He was Jamani Paavila, 108 years of age, the last great singer of northern Karelia. I remembered having seen a photograph of him taken much earlier in one of our Finnish publications on Karelia. I must admit that I had paid little attention to this singer at the time, but now that my travels happened to take me by way of Uhtua and I had learned that he still lived, I naturally wished to satisfy my curiosity.

So I approached the oldster, grasped his hand and shouted a greeting. He appeared greatly surprised. Who in the world could this strange person be, coming to shake the hand of a decrepit old man?

The blind man shouted into his ear, "How are you, Dad?" The old one snapped back, "Who are you?"

"I am Ortto, your son."

"Good!" said the elder, appeased. "And who is this other visitor?"

The blind man knelt and shouted in his ear, "He is a gentleman from Finland. He came to see you because you are so old and still alive. He had read some of your songs in books and knows you from that."

"Fine, fine," said the old man in a trembling voice. "It was good he came. Where did you meet him? Are you coming from church?"

"No," shouted the blind one.

The church bells were ringing just then, for the pastor was engaged in sending off some men called to the colors. Probably the old one sensed instinctively that church bells were ringing, or perhaps his second son, the head of this house, had said on his departure that there were peasants gathered at the church. Wherever the women of the house might be, whether out in the fields or fishing, the old man had been left alone, but it was evident from the orderly condition of the room that he was being well cared for. He was not deserted, that was obvious.

Contemplating the 108-year-old, I drew some sketches of him in my diary, for I had no camera. Of course my drawings had no artistic merit, but I felt that there was something sacred in preserving if only a trace of that man's blouse — a man sitting like a patriarch in the heart of the village, and who might be just then living out the last days of his life. (Only on my return to Finland was I able to get a photograph of him, by writing to the district forester.)

"It was good he came!" the old man had remarked. I asked the blind son to inquire whether he remembered any of his poems. The son shouted the question into Jamani Paavila's ear: "The visitor asks whether you still know those poems, those songs?"

"Poems, songs?" He seemed startled. "I know a lot of them," he replied in a shrill voice.

The blind man pressed his mouth against the oldster's ear: "The visitor asks, could you sing some as a sample?"

"Sing now?" he shrilled, and his weak eyes lit up strangely and turned moist. "You mean about Väinämöinen, or what?" His voice had taken on strength.

I reflected a moment, and the blind man interpreted again for his father: "The visitor would like you to sing, if you would, about that old Väinämöinen."

The 108-year-old became excited. He sighed heavily and his mouth opened, his eyes glistened. But no sound came forth. Only the peals of the bells could be heard from the edge of the village. Otherwise everything was deadly still. Then suddenly it burst out! At first in a quavering tone, groping and stammering, then with increasing animation:

Vako vanha Väinämöini
Iski virkkua visalla.
Tuli nuori Joukahainen,
Ajoi tiellä vastatussen
Puuttui aisa aisan piähän
Rahe rahkehen nenäähän.
Vähä on miehen nuoruuesta.
Kumpi tiiolta parempi.
Sepä tiellä seisokaahan,
Toini tieltä siirtykäänän.

Mitäpä sie enintä tiiät?
Tiiän tervan karkieksi,
Mustan mullan muikieksi,
Tuopa nuori Joukahaini
Murti suuta, viänti päätä,
Sanan virkkoi, noin nimeesi:
Voi se vanaha Väinämöini,
*Pyörrytä pyhät sanasi.**

The stalwart old Väinämöinen
Whipped at his horse.
Young Joukahainen came up,
Drove against him on the road.
Their shafts got stuck together
Their reins got entangled.
Being young doesn't make a difference,
It's which of us knows more.
Let him hold the right of way,
Let the other move aside.

What do you know most about?
I know tar is coarse,
Black mud is bitter.
So that young Joukahainen
Twisted his mouth, tossed his head,
Said the word, spoke thus:
Oh, you old Väinämöinen,
Turn your magic words around.

*Fragments from the singing contest in the *Kalevala* (Poem III), in which Joukahainen is bested by Väinämöinen.

"Well, that's enough," shouted the blind man in the singer's ear. "What's that?" said the old one, and got a new start:

Pyörrytä pyhät sanasi . . .

"The visitor says you needn't sing anymore. Lest you get tired."
"I'm not tired, I'm not tired!" the old man yelled back. "I have a lot of songs. I remember . . . ."

It was hard to stop him when he once got started. Who knows, he might have recited for hours if my conscience had permitted me to encourage him. But making a 108-year-old sing—that was inhuman. I was already content with all I had seen and heard. Therefore, we didn't have him recite anymore.

When I tried to give him money, the son Ortto forbade it, affirming that his father was in no need and that he didn't care for money anyway. Nevertheless, I left a couple of small silver coins on the window-sill. Then I begged the old man for one of his canes as a memento. He replied, "Take this staff. Take it. I won't say no. I can get others from the forest."

Having accepted the staff, I shouted into his ear: "I promise to keep this a hundred years as a sacred heritage."

"Good, good!" he murmured.

He sat lost in thought. And I was also. Finally I posed my usual query to people of advanced age: "Do you fear death, Jamani Paavila?"

The oldster replied in classic style, like all old Karelians: "Why should I fear it? When God wills . . . *when that time comes*, it will be all right."

Imagine a 108-year-old saying, "When that time comes." He does not expect to die tomorrow, nor next month, nor next year. Just sometime, much later. There's plenty of time, for that.

How is it possible that Jamani Paavila, who has worked hard all his life and known the harsh existence of the forest dweller, has attained such an advanced age? That is nature's secret. But it is not a secret that this fortunate man is one of the old stock. Never a drop of spirits. Never smoked. Never a smell of coffee, hardly even a drop of tea! Never broken a fast-day. Throughout his life a man of the old type. Sipped his soup from his own bowl. Fish and greens, mushrooms and wild berries.

Taking my departure, I knew I was seeing him for the last time alive.*
Had I not, in my youth, heard Miihkali Perttunen of Latvajärvi singing his swan songs on his island? Well, this patriarch of Uhtua with his change of Väinämöinen, heard against the blaring sounds of the present day, seemed to voice the final murmur of those heroic ancient lays.

(Summer of 1914)

*Jamani Paavila died at the age of 111 years.

Juhani Aho

A VISIT TO A SAUNA
(Translated by Inkeri Väänänen-Jensen)

NATURE'S GIFTS are countless and for this reason it is entirely possible that everyone has received his share of them. It is true that we often speak about talented and untalented people, but this rises perhaps from the fact that we do not get to see all people in their proper environment. But if each is seen in his own element, then each person's competence is revealed. You have thought someone to be quite an insignificant man, and then suddenly he can appear as one of the most unique in his particular field.

I had always thought that Sasu Punanen was nothing much. Fat, lazy, dull, slow of speech, with no interests, with no zeal. He was studying to be a minister, just an assistant minister, which, one could say, was as high as he seemed to have set his goal. I did not find in him any special talent, not a single original idea, nor any inherent ardor or passion, at least not any about which I would have known, even though we lived in the same house, just a wall between us—unless one would consider as talents the fact that he liked to sleep and that he sometimes went to Kamppi's Restaurant specifically to eat beef. But otherwise there were no signs with which he would have indicated that he was "his own man." He was just nothing—until suddenly he appeared before me with all his talents.

"Let's go for a sauna," he said to me one evening.

"Not now . . . I plan to go to the Finnish Theater."

"Why to the theater?"

"There's a premiere today."

"You'll have time to see that premiere some other time . . . come on, I'll even pay for a sleigh, if you come."

It was the first good sleighing weather, and since I am particularly fond of riding in a sleigh, we set out for the sauna and left the premiere —for another time.

It is said that the samovar is the only thing the Russians have invented. Similarly, it is said the Finns have invented the sauna, that it is probably their only invention. That is why the Finnish people know how to bathe better than any other people. And that is why there are also in this nation the best bathers, the most skilled steam virtuosos. But I have not yet, even in their midst, met another such bather as he, this Sasu Punanen. He is of his talented breed the most talented; he is all sauna virtuosos' sauna virtuoso.

"It is a great inconvenience that the steam cabinet and the steam sauna are not connected," he said, after we had purchased our tickets. This was the first time I had ever heard any opinion from him on anything.

"Is Miina's sauna free?" he then called at the end of the hall.

Miina's sauna was free, and as we walked to it, he explained to me that he did not care for any other sauna attendant—he would rather wait an hour for his turn with Miina.

"Will the gentlemen take a tub bath or a shower after their sauna?"

"Miina should know that I take both a tub bath *and* a shower."

"And bath whisks also?"

"Bath whisks also, but don't put them to soak yet."

"Don't hurry," he advised me when he saw me beginning hurriedly to take off my clothes. "In the sauna one must undress in a leisurely way and not as if one is in a great rush."

And he had a special ritual completely thought out for this purpose.

"You shouldn't toss your clothes helter skelter, here and there, so it is difficult to find them when you dress. I always put my clothes in such an order so I can easily put them on again in that very same order. You can't imagine how pleasant that feels after you've finished with your sauna."

It was enlightening to watch how carefully, for the sake of that future pleasure, he undressed himself. First, he took off his overcoat and placed it on a nail; then he placed his scarf on the same nail and his hat on top of that, for the head was to be covered before the overcoat was put on.

"Why?"

"Because it feels good that way."

"Who showed you that?"

"I thought of it myself."

On another nail he placed his jacket and vest, over which he placed his necktie and shirt. His trousers and his underwear were hung separately on a third nail. But before he finished undressing, he sat and rubbed and massaged his neck, shoulders, back, and under his arms, his face alternating between a strange smile and a grimace during the most strenuous of the massaging. Finally, he took off his shoes and socks.

"Miina, take my socks to be warmed up . . . you give her your socks to be warmed up, too."

Now he was completely undressed. But before going into the sauna he still stood for a long time before the mirror and scrutinized himself from every side. And very round he was, too, on every side.

There are some bodies which appear at their best with clothes on; others which appear to their best advantage in a gymnasium. Sasu Punanen's limbs and body were built so that only in a sauna did they seem to come into their rightful surroundings. If one is to understand the beauty of a man, one has to see him on a sauna bench, in the midst of warm and moist steam.

He had a smallish head, a thick red neck, a long, fleshy back, the beginning of a pot belly, wide hips, stocky legs, flat feet, and was generally of a stout build, with his skin as tough and waterproof as shoe leather.

Before he began to take steam seriously, he wanted to perspire, to get rid of his "drouth," as he said. He threw himself on his back on the bench and lifted his short, chunky legs to the ceiling. But the ceiling was slippery, and his legs kept sliding down from time to time.

"There ought to be notches in the ceiling," he reflected. "It's easier for you, since you have longer legs. One could arrange it so that one would have a rope running around his neck to the bottoms of his feet . . . This is the most enjoyable part of the sauna . . . when you lie like this and slowly begin to perspire . . . Well, now we can put the bath whisks to soak. Whenever you go to the sauna, don't ever let them soak your bath whisk before you yourself are up on the bench . . . otherwise something good is wasted. The fine fragrance from the leaves . . . it is the best part of the whole bath."

When he got his whisk, he switched the backs of his knees several times with it, as if he were testing its bite, and then he called confidently, "Lay on the steam!"

The sauna attendant produced steam.

"More?"

"More, more!"

"That's enough . . . that's enough!"

"Just keep it coming! Are you beginning to feel it?"

"For heaven's sake, Sasu!"

"Why, this isn't anything yet!"

"Stop it, stop it!. . . I'm burning up; I'm burning up!"

I have to run below, but he says most calmly, "Miina, please give me a little more steam."

The stones over the fire hiss like a hundred spitting cats, and I feel that in an instant they will assault me with their sharp claws and tear me to pieces. Yelling and groaning, I flee from them crouching on the floor, but from up near the top of the ceiling Sasu commands, "Now Miina may come to beat me with the whisk."

"First the bottoms of my feet, then my shoulders . . . now my back . . . my calves . . . now back to the bottoms of my feet . . . a little more . . . a little more . . . aah! . . . uh! That's the way . . . that's the way . . . Rub now! Beat with the whisk now! Harder, harder! Can't you beat harder?"

"You're going to burn yourself up, and me too!"

"Why, this is nothing yet . . . how will Miina manage then in hell?" (He even makes jokes, the devil!) "This isn't even a man's steam yet. Miina, please sharpen up the steam some more."

Poor Miina. With her hands protecting her eyes, she throws two more pails of water over the stones on the stove. The stones spit and sizzle; there are a hundred new cats hissing, and, shrieking, I flee to the dressing room.

"Even the stones can no longer take this without splitting!" I hear the sauna attendant complain.

"Well, then, start the shower."

He is like a skinned seal as he stands under the ice cold shower. But the water comes too slowly and there is too little of it, so the attendant must fill two pails, climb to a bench and pour the water over him.

Now he feels that most of the perspiration has left his body and he rises again to the boards.

"Get yourself washed while I still warm myself a little more here."

"Can't we open the damper?"

"Damn it, don't let the heat outdoors . . . heat is one of God's crops, too, you know."

"Does the gentleman want his hair washed?"

"Yes."

"Ville, wait a while . . . I'm a little thirsty . . . Miina, go and get a bottle of beer . . . it'll help me to start perspiring again."

Sitting on the edge of a bench, with one gulp he empties one glass, then another, and generously offers the rest of the bottle to the sauna attendant.

While I am being washed, he lies motionless up there and every now and then blows a long, mighty snort through his nostrils. I didn't know what he was thinking about but, compared to me, he seemed like a genius, a giant of a genius among all other sauna geniuses. If the Finns had a sauna god, if they had a guardian spirit of steam whom they served, then he must have been just such a man.

"So there's a premiere today at the Finnish Theater?"

And a little later, "You know, there's an excellent portrayal of a sauna scene in Minna Canth's play, *The Burglary.*

When I seat myself in the bathtub to rinse off, he finally comes down to be washed.

It is a pleasure to look at him on the washing bench. He is now so softened up that he drops like dough to the bench, like limp dough, which the sauna attendant can knead, mix, and turn however she wishes. The more she turns, rubs, and works on him, the happier he appears. The more vehemently she soaps, kneads, and massages him, the more blissful does his countenance become.

"If Miina would still rub a little along my backbone with her bare hands."

I have long since then taken my bath towel and gone into the dressing room, dried myself, and am already half dressed when I begin to hear water splashing in the sauna.

"What in the world is he doing now?"

I see a wide, red mass of back and shoulders in the tub. He has been washed and now he is taking a tub bath.

"There's just no end to this!" groans the sauna attendant in an exhausted voice.

He puts a towel over his shoulders, and comes into the dressing room. He throws himself on his back on the bed, covers himself with the greatest of care, produces half a bottle of beer, empties it, takes a cigarette from his overcoat pocket, and only then, when he has lit his cigarette, does he sigh, "Hooh! Hooh! This is wonderful!"

I didn't have the patience to wait for him, nor did he care that I left. I went to Kamppi's. An hour later, he appeared there, his cheeks shining and taut, his hair meticulously parted and combed. Calmly he sits beside me and, in an amiable manner, his eyes a little dull, he remarks to me, does Sasu Punanen, "Why did you leave the sauna right in the middle . . . I still used the steam cabinet after my bath."

Unto Seppänen

THE KNITTING
(Translated by Reino Virtanen)

*T*HEY CHANGED THEIR sitting positions a little and moistened their throats very, very carefully. Then Sohvi said, "You tell us a story, Aatami."

Aatami tried to find a comfortable position, finally succeeded in settling himself, and when they had all cut branches from the alder tree nearby, to keep the insects away, he told the following tale—while the others whisked their branches almost in time with his words:

That well over there that I've been looking at all evening reminds me of something that happened at our old home place.

Our sauna had burned down and its well had run dry. The wind had been blowing aspen leaves into the well for a couple of autumns already and other miscellaneous trash had dropped in.

It was just about this time a little before Midsummer Day.

In one of those fine aspens there was a woodpecker's nest, and it sounded as if the trunk were full of grasshoppers, there was such a chirping in it. The hole was almost within reach of a man's hand, and my brother Kalle and I used to keep watch especially in the mornings when the redtop was frantically filling the wide-open mouths of its young. We too managed to get some crumbs and dead flies into the hole to assist the mother bird, but I don't know whether they were much help.

Well, as we were watching the tree one morning, Mamma walked over to call us to breakfast. She was a little odd in that she always had to have her knitting in her hands. She couldn't live without her needles, and if, as they say, knitting needles wear out in one's hands, she must have worn out a good many. If anyone asked her to explain her mania she answered, "It seems to keep down my blood pressure."

Father often laughed at her and once asked how she could even get the milking done without her needles, but after the next milking when Mamma went into the milk shed she had her knitting in one hand and the milk pail in the other. She said to Father, "I guess it can be done all right, milking and knitting."

But at this Father lost his temper and Mamma didn't dare carry her zeal too far.

So then Mamma was coming along with her needles to call us to breakfast. We could see that very well.

We went behind the aspen a second to look at the woodpecker which just then flicked into the hole. We were listening to the hungry cheeping inside when Kalle suddenly burst out, "Where did Mamma disappear to?"

We jumped out from behind the tree to look.

It was true! We couldn't see Mamma anywhere, although a moment ago she had been quite close to us.

We both thought at the same time that the earth had swallowed her; in other words, the old well had gobbled her up.

We dashed over to it and peered in.

Mamma was sitting quietly on the bottom and was finishing a sock just as if she had been seated in her own rocking chair.

We burst into tears and started to yell, "Mamma, come out!"

She looked up, waved her hand calmly, and shouted back, "Go and eat! Your porridge is already poured for you!"

We shouted tearfully into the well, "First we'll get help!"

She shook her head and replied, "Let me finish this sock in peace!"

"But what if you die down there?" shrieked Kalle desperately.

"It's cool and comfortable here, better than anywhere, and there are no wasps here to sting you, as there are up there!" yelled Mamma smiling reassuringly and then waved us away with a commanding gesture.

We started off obediently to breakfast but weeping bitterly as we thought of Mamma left there in the well like in a grave.

But we ran back anyway to ask if she needed anything, and she replied, asking us to get the other sock hanging from the cord in the back room and drop it into the well so that she could get the size. Still there was no hurry, first we should go to eat before the warm milk got filmy.

We sat down at the table still weeping and had trouble getting the porridge to glide down our throats.

A doleful meal it was.

Just then the door flew open and Father stood on the threshold. He looked at us in amazement.

"What are you kids crying for?"

"Mamma fell in the well!" we answered and we let out a fearful wail, as if to show our grief at being left motherless.

Father became very pale, turned, and rushed out of the house. We dashed after him. We got to the porch just in time to see Father reach the well sweep and plunge into our regular well. Splash! And now we really did start wailing, with Mamma in one well and Father in the other. There we two helpless orphans stood caterwauling with all our might. If that had been enough to raise our parents from their pits they would surely have come out flying.

"Let's go see Father," said Kalle at last.

But I was too scared, and so I proposed that we should first bring Mamma the finished sock she wanted for she probably needed it in a hurry now to match the one she was working on.

We ran over to the dry well with the sock, whimpering.

We dropped the sock into the well.

Mamma looked up gratefully and yelled, "Is Father eating yet?"

"No!" we wailed back.

"Why are you crying? I'm all right. The sock is almost done. I'm glad you brought the other one."

"We are crying because of Father" we shouted in reply.

"What about him?"

"He just jumped into the water well!"

Mother sprang up with a jerk that set the leaves under her tossing, and she began screaming so we couldn't stand it. We went off blubbering to see Father in the other well.

It was awful to peer down into our well which threw up cold air like a mountain cranny. There were still icicles along its side walls.

There stood our father up to his neck in water holding on to the bucket and splashing like a logging horse in the river.

We heard a hollow shout, "But Mamma isn't here! I've felt along the whole bottom."

We both started yelling our explanations at once, but they got so scrambled on the way down that Father couldn't make any sense out of them. He shook his fist and bellowed, "One at a time, you little heathens!"

So we took turns howling, "Mamma's in the old sauna well!"

"Knitting a sock!"

"We just tossed her the sock's mate!"

"The sock's almost done!"

It occurred to Kalle to bawl out a question, "Should we throw you anything, or should we go and eat? The porridge is getting cold!"

Thereupon a roar rang out of the well that sounded as if it came from the vaults of the bottomless pit, "Help!"

Kalle and I took fright and ran back sobbing to the dry well.

Mamma seemed to have regained her calm and was knitting away as before but was now standing up to her knees in the rubble.

We bent over to shriek, "Mamma, Father is yelling for help! Can you get out to help?"

Thereupon our usually gentle Mamma started to yell so that it was painful to hear.

We chose to run back to the water well and cried down to Father.

Kalle: "Father! Now Mamma is calling for help."

"That's true!" I affirmed. "She is so angry! I've never heard her like that before."

We noticed Father's cheeks turning strangely purple and his fist lifted more threateningly. Kalle, older and wiser than I, said to me, "You watch lest they get out while I run for help!" And he darted off to the neighbors.

In our yard there were scattered various summer tools, including a loose stick. I picked this up, as Kalle had left me to keep watch, and so I walked back and forth between the wells with the stick in my hand, but I didn't dare to look into either one. I was feeling awfully bad. I kept on whimpering. I don't understand even today why I picked up the stick. Perhaps I was feeling so forsaken with even Kalle gone that I had to have something to hold on to . . . .

Soon our yard was filled with people, and Father was raised first from his well, his teeth chattering, incredibly angry. We didn't understand his growling at all.

He got out easily, for several men had climbed up to hang from the sweep weight, and thus our dear father was pulled out of his chilly hole like a big fish; he was standing up in the bucket.

Our whimpers changed into giggles. Father looked so comical with his pants spurting water like a rainspout in a cloudburst.

Then the whole crowd hurried over to the old well, and everyone marveled aloud at the Creator's purpose in taking away from two helpless boys both father and mother and stowing them into wells, into different wells at that, so that they didn't even have each other's company, and messages had to be carried between them.

A yoke had to be made for Mamma and when it was ready her sock was already finished.

The lifting rig was let down into the well, Mamma stuck the knitting needles in the bun of her hair, sat down on the yoke, and was presently swinging there like a churchbell.

Soon she too was with us on the earth's surface.

We burst out laughing when we sighted her hairknot.

"Mamma has new hairpins!" shouted Kalle.

Father threw us an angry look, but we were feeling very happy.

Suddenly from the midst of the babble of voices arose Mamma's cry, "Oh my stars! The socks got left in the well!"

Father's eyes gleamed and he said, "That's easily fixed — we'll drop the boys down to get them!"

This they did and we thought it was great fun.

But when we got down to the bottom, the men let the ropes fall to the ground of Father's suggestion, and Father cried "Hey, you little rascals! Wait for your father to change into dry clothes and get a pinch of snuff."

Now we were left in the cool pit. Thus in one day the whole family has visited the well bottom on account of Mamma's doings.

Kalle, who was quite ingenious, said, "Let's put the socks on our heads and dig down under the leaves so everybody'll think the earth has swallowed us up."

So we did. Both socks and boys vanished.

When they came after a long while to hoist us up, they were all bewildered.

We could hear as from a distance our dear Mamma screaming, "The well bottom must have caved in a swallowed up the boys!"

Father had himself lowered swiftly into the well. He dug us out and shouted, "Here they are!"

Kalle, who was not only smart but also bold of nature, asked, "Father, which well is more fun to be in?"

Father solemnly set us on the yoke and so we swung, with the gray socks on our heads, like caterpillars, back into the world of woodpecker's nests, which is full of the food calls of all sorts of young creatures. We too began to call for our porridge.

When Father in his turn was hoisted to the surface he snatched the socks from our heads and gave them to Aaton Mikko, who had directed the rescue operations.

Mamma paled and said, "I'll have to start knitting another pair."

In the evening father polished off our backsides a little. Kalle was then in his eighth year and I was going on six.

Even now as two old codgers, we have to laugh when one of us asks the other: "Do you remember when Mamma knit a sock in one well while Father washed his whiskers in the other?"

FINNISH FOLK TALES—
retold by Jaakko Liukkonen

KARHU THE BEAR
(Translated by Kathleen Osgood Dana)

These three Finnish folk tales about Karhu the Bear are based on stories in a collection in the Folk Poetry Archives of the Finnish Literature Society.

THE THRESHING OF THE RYE

O NCE UPON A TIME, Kettu the Fox and Karhu the Bear decided to raise a field of rye together. First they had to clear a spot in the forest and burn it over. The companions found a suitable spot and commenced felling the trees and dragging them into a pile. Kettu let a tall pine fall so that its top just brushed Karhu's back. Said Kettu, "Here, let me hold the trees so they don't fall on your head as that one just did. And you, old chap, you can fell the trees without fear."

Karhu got all the trees felled. Then when it came time to burn the clearing over, Kettu said, "I shall mount guard over there on that rise to be sure the fire will not burn you. And you, old chap, you can toil without fear." Kettu lolled atop a stump and watched Karhu burn the clearing over.

After a while it came time for the companions to plow the field. Kettu said to Karhu, "Since you are the stronger, you draw the plow. And I will guide it so that our furrows are clean and true."

When all the plowing and planting had been done, they set about fencing in the field. Kettu said, "You set the fenceposts in their places, old chap. And I will watch to be sure they go where they should."

The fence was finished and that summer a beautiful crop of rye billowed in their field.

That fall the rye was cut and stood in shocks. The threshing barn was crammed full of sheaves. The barn was warmed and the threshing began. Karhu said to Kettu, "Good friend, go up in the loft and throw the sheaves down to the floor."

Kettu climbed up into the loft and threw down the sheaves. But he also let a beam tumble down on to Karhu's back. In fright Karhu cried out, "Hold on to those beams, good friend, so they won't fall on my head as that one just did. Meanwhile I will thresh the rye."

Karhu threshed and thrashed below. Kettu lolled about above in the loft. When only a few sheaves were still unthreshed, Kettu came down and told Karhu to feel his forehead so that the bear might see how much he had sweated holding on to those beams.

"Those beams will stay there without my holding them now. You take a break and I'll thresh what remains," said Kettu.

When all the threshing was done and the chaff had been separated from the grain, two piles stood on the barn floor—in the smaller pile the grain, in the larger the chaff.

"Well, how shall we divide up our harvest?" asked Karhu.

"The greater pile for the bigger one and the lesser pile for the smaller," responded Kettu.

And it pleased Karhu no end that as the bigger of the two he would get the greater pile.

HOW THE PORRIDGE WAS COOKED

Kettu the Fox and Karhu the Bear went to the mill to have the fruits of their harvest ground. First Kettu ground his rye berries. Then Karhu put his chaff on the millstone. When the stones started turning, Karhu said in surprise, "When you were grinding, the stone went 'crinch, crunch'; but now that I'm grinding, all the stone says is 'mish, mash.'"

"Throw a bit of sand in. That's what I did," advised Kettu.

Karhu threw in some sand. The millstones rattled away and Karhu was satisfied with that.

When they had come home from the mill, the companions set about cooking their porridge. Karhu came over to where Kettu was cooking and asked in surprise, "How on earth did your porridge get so white? Mine is all black."

"I put snow in mine," replied Kettu.

Karhu added some snow to his porridge. But that made it no whiter, only runnier. So now Karhu had to add more meal to thicken it. After his porridge had been cooking a while, Karhu tasted it. Then he went over to Kettu and said, "My porridge isn't sweet. Let me have a little taste of yours and see if that isn't sweet."

Karhu tasted it and asked in amazement, "How did you get your porridge so sweet?"

"I dribbled in a little fat from under my tail. That's what makes my porridge sweet. You try cooking yours with a little dribble of fat from under your tail and your porridge will be sweet, too," advised Kettu.

"I don't know how to. Come and cook my porridge for me and show me how to dribble fat from under my tail," said Karhu.

Kettu told Karhu to sit on the crossbar holding the kettle over the fire, and Kettu said, "You have to sit there as long as you can possibly stand it. Fat doesn't drip easily."

Kettu hastened to put more wood under the kettle. Before long Karhu asked, "Is the fat dripping yet?"

"Not yet. You'll have to sit a while longer," replied Kettu.

Kettu kept piling more wood on the fire and Karhu kept sitting on the crossbar until his backside was scorched. He leaped down off his perch and tried to catch Kettu, but the fox fled hastily for cover. Karhu lost his patience with him and cried out in a fit of rage, "All you did was burn my tail!"

THE BEAR IN THE HAY SLEDGE

Karhu the Bear had curled up for his winter's nap in one of the rectory's hay barns. One winter day the hired man drove out to fetch some hay from that field. He turned his horse around in front of the barn so that the sledge would be right next to the barn door, and he started forking hay into the sledge. When he plunged his pitchfork into the hay, the tines stabbed the bear in the flank.

Karhu charged up in terror thinking he'd been bagged by a hunter. He plunged toward the door and tumbled right into the hay sledge. Startled, the horse took off for home at a full gallop. In bewilderment Karhu stood in the back of the sledge, clinging to its sides with his front paws. The frightened horse ran as fast as it could.

The pastor met up with them on the road. He recognized the rectory's horse, and when he saw a bundle of fur in the back of the sledge, he thought it was the provost himself out for a drive. Politely, the pastor raised his hat and wished him a good afternoon. Karhu didn't reply. This disturbed the pastor no end. He thought, "What do you suppose was wrong with the provost that he disdained my greeting so and had his horse carry on at that pace?"

A bit further along they met up with the choirmaster. He too made the mistake of thinking, "There goes the provost in his new fur coat." The choirmaster bowed deeply in an exceptionally polite greeting. But he didn't get a response either. Rigid with fright, the bear just stood in the back of the sledge, digging his claws ever deeper into the sides of the sledge. In bewilderment, the choirmaster stood by the roadside pondering, "Why do you suppose the provost was in such an all-fired hurry for, dashing about like that and not a civil word in reply?"

Next they met up with the sheriff. And he too raised his hat in greeting as good manners call for. But he didn't get a response either. Karhu just growled as he went by, and the sheriff thought in surprise, "The mighty provost must be in a most particular hurry if he wouldn't even exchange amenities. Imagine driving by like that and grumbling!"

The provost himself was sitting in his study puffing on his pipe and working on his next sermon. Glancing out of his window, he saw his horse come charging into the yard. The provost caught a glimpse of a squat figure muffled in furs in the sledge. He was startled, "Where the devil did the hired man pick up the governor?"

He dashed out onto the porch to welcome his distinguished guest, bowing deeply.

Karhu said nothing. He just sat in the sledge dazed by his mad ride. The provost didn't realize what was really going on and just kept bowing deeper to his worthy guest.

Finally the hired man, who had come running after the horse, reached the rectory steps, and he shouted to the provost who was still bowing away on the porch, "That's a bear in the sledge!"

At that Karhu shook himself out of his stupor and got back on his feet.

And that was how Karhu the Bear tricked all those gentlemen. They took him for the provost and they took him for the governor, but it was only Karhu after all.

Aaro Hellaakoski

THE SONG OF THE PIKE

HAUEN LAULU

(Translated by Aina Swan Cutler)

When the early morning sun
first pierced the grayness in the sky,

a pickerel rose from his watery home
to climb a pine tree, singing.
And high in the branches, he looked upon
the morning's glowing beauty—
the wind-blown ripples on the lake,
dew-freshened flowers and fields below.

He breathed the fragrant summer air
and bit the red-tipped cones in two
to ease his pain, to ease his joy
in the newly wakened day.

    Then opening up his
    heavy jawbones
    he poured out such
    savage singing,

so deep and mournful,
so wild his howling,
that at once all the
birds fell silent,
as though they shared in
the utter sadness,
the desperate longing,
pain-filled, lonely.

MOONLIGHT IN THE WOODS

KUUTAMO METSÄSSÄ

(Translated by Aina Swan Cutler)

In a shadowy, misty wood
under an eerie, flickering light

runs a strange, a secret road
that comes from nowhere and nowhere goes.

Even my shadow flees.
Moonlight dissolves my bones.

Suddenly I am free
floating high over haunted trees,

reaching my hand to nothingness.

Anna Perkkiö

GRANDMOTHER'S WEDDING GIFT

"M AMMA, MAMMA, they are coming," hollered little Otto excitedly running into the *tupa*.

"What now Otto?" asked Mamma, wiping her face with her apron.

"The Russians are coming; a whole regiment of them, marching right in to our yard; come and see for yourself."

"*Herra Jest*," was all Mamma could say running to the only window they had in the *tupa*. "What shall we do Otto, your Papa gone to the market and not expecting to return until the end of the week?"

"Don't you worry Mamma," said little Otto, "I'm here and Antti and Grandma and Anna-Liisa."

Mamma put her arms around little Otto as they stood by the window, but seeing the line of soldiers marching in to the yard, her heart sank. What was she going to do with her husband away? Left alone with Antti the half-witted handyman. True, there was Grandma and Anna-Liisa, but Grandma was so old. This past winter she had taken to her bed more and more. Anna-Liisa was young, just betrothed to John.

John's father had the biggest farm in the county, no hard work for Anna-Liisa, not the way her mother had had to work coming out here as a bride, for this was a new homestead. Big Otto's father had been a hard worker but a lifetime was not enough in these parts.

It was for Anna-Liisa that Mamma was mostly worried. You could house the men in the hay loft, but a young girl was not safe around them. She had heard some wild stories. You couldn't trust the Russians.

"Go out and find Anna-Liisa, Otto."

"Shall I take Grandfather's rifle, Mamma?" asked little Otto anxiously.

Mamma had to laugh. "Better leave the rifle here. Maybe Mamma will be needing it."

Muttering to himself, little Otto ran out. How was he ever going to do anything the way the women folks treated him, just as if he were a child. At his age Grandfather had killed a bear. Winter nights sitting around the fire Grandma would tell tales about him. This was little Otto's chance to prove that he was a man, if Mamma would only let him have the rifle.

After little Otto had left, Mamma went to the *kamari* where Grandma was sleeping after her mid-day meal. Thank goodness she was still snoring. Then she heard someone come in to the *tupa*. Mamma rushed back in. Her heart was pounding so—she didn't know what to expect.

"You're the lady of the house?" It was an officer of the Russian Army. It was not so much the uniform as the way he was greeting her in her own language. He was very clever as he said, "I did surprise you. Not many of us can speak Finnish, but I'm almost your neighbor, born a little ways from the border. I have orders to stay here overnight. It's very unpleasant for you and I'm sorry to put you in any trouble, but my men can stay in the loft. There's plenty of room for them there."

There was nothing that Mamma could say. She knew that the orders were that they should give lodgings to the men in the Russian Army, but why did this have to happen now? Otto would have known how to deal with the situation. She was standing there wondering what to say to the man when the door opened and Anna-Liisa stood there all out of breath. Anna-Liisa with her waxen hair tied in braids around her head. Mamma could see the way the man turned to look at the girl with his beady eyes going over her heaving breast and her full body that was just barely covered with last year's calico dress.

Mamma felt a hatred for this man that she had never known before. Her eyes wandered over to the wall where Grandfather's rifle was hanging on a nail. When she turned around again the man was gone.

Anna-Liisa ran into her mother's arms. There was safety in her soft, wide bosom.

"What are we going to do, Mamma?" she cried, for never before had anyone looked at her like that.

"Hush, child," said Mamma. "We'll think of something. Maybe he'll put up for the night with his men in the loft."

"What are we going to feed them, Mamma?" Anna-Liisa asked.

"We'll give them the food we have for the wedding feast. It's a good thing that we have enough to hide, too. How many men do you think are there?"

"Little Otto says that there are about twenty of them, but I didn't see them myself. He told me to run before they would see me, and then that hateful man had to be in here."

"Don't worry child. Somehow we'll take care of him. Hurry and put on more clothing. Then come and help me. We'll have to hide some of the cheese and bread under Grandma's bed. They won't ever think of looking for anything in there."

Anna-Liisa braided her hair, put on her heaviest skirt and blouse, lacing the blouse up to her neck. She could still feel that look. It made her cheeks flame when she even thought about it. Here she was, engaged to John, the wedding only a month off. He had no right to look at her like that. If it had been some other man, she would have slapped his face good and proper, but she couldn't do that to an officer in His Majesty's Army.

The men were eating out in the yard. They had found the smoked hams and lambs; Mamma had given them bread and cheese. In the *kamari* where Anna-Liisa usually slept with her Grandmother, the officer was eating his supper. With her eyes downcast, Anna-Liisa was serving him. From the yard they could hear the boisterous laugh of the men.

It was a pleasant room overlooking the yard. White homespun curtains were hung on the window. On the windowsill a pot of geraniums were blooming. Anna-Liisa's bed was right by the door. On the other side of the room by the now unused fireplace was Grandmother's big bed, still unmade, for the old woman spent most of her time in there. It didn't take the man long to go over the rest of the room. There was the table where the simple supper lay, the few chairs, Anna-Liisa's things scattered here and there.

"For a small place like this you're well stocked up," he said with a very soft voice. "Perhaps you were fixing for a feast?"

Anna-Liisa couldn't keep the tears out of her eyes, "It was a wedding we were fixing to have," she blurted out in an angry tone.

"Then we were just in time," laughed the stranger, and added, "So you're going to get married." Anna-Liisa couldn't say anything. How she hated this man.

"The lucky fellow! In my country it is a very old custom for someone else to sleep with the bride before the wedding night." He looked at her with a devil's grin and lowered his voice, "I'll come by when the moon is high. I trust the old woman sleeps sound." He stood up wiping his black mustache, then gave her a sly grin and went out. Long after he was gone Anna-Liisa stood there as if she had turned to stone.

"Perhaps he was only joking." Mamma was trying to cheer weeping Anna-Liisa.

"Mamma, let me take the rifle down," begged little Otto. "I'll stay up all night by Anna-Liisa's door, and if he dares to come in, I'll shoot him dead."

"No, Otto, forget the rifle. Won't do us any good to start shooting," said Mamma. "I'll try talking to him."

"No use wasting time talking to any Russian," piped up Grandma, her toothless jaws opening wide. She had been just sitting there eating, not paying any attention to anything, so they all looked up at her in surprise. "There is just one thing left for us to do. I'll sleep in Anna-Liisa's bed tonight."

It was as if lightning had struck them. Even Antti sat there with his mouth wide open, the wooden spoon swinging in the air, the cereal dropping down on the table.

Mamma was the first to find her tongue. "You're too old Grandma. There must be something else we can do."

"I'm not too old," snapped the old woman, "and there is nothing else we can do." Then she turned to Antti and asked, "Anything in the house to drink?"

"The few bottles of wine, but it was to be saved for the wedding feast," Antti muttered.

"You'll take them, Antti, and use them all if you need to. See that the man gets his share. The sauna is nice and cool. You can take him there."

"What about your bed?" asked little Otto. "Who will sleep there?"

"Bless the child," said Grandma. "He's just like his grandfather. We'll have to take a chance and fix the bed so that it looks like someone is sleeping there," and she got up from the table and left the room, leaving the rest of them sitting there in dead silence.

"Mamma, we shouldn't let her do it," said Anna-Liisa when they were getting ready to go to bed.

"When Grandma makes up her mind, there is nothing anyone can do," Mamma said. How well she remembered the times she had had to give in to her. She had almost come to hate the old woman then. After Otto's father had died, Grandma had left everything to Mamma, and she had grown quite fond of her.

"Mamma, I wish that you would let little Otto take the rifle and shoot him," said Anna-Liisa. "Why should they treat us this way. Isn't there any law left in the country?"

"The law of the strongest. It is the lot of the conquered people. But don't worry so, Anna-Liisa. Maybe after Antti gets him drunk, he'll forget the whole idea."

"If anyone gets drunk it will be Antti. It was crazy to give him all those bottles."

"Antti will do as he is told, so get in to the bed before you get cold."

Little Otto was sleeping soundly. Mamma and Anna-Liisa were lying awake straining their ears, waiting and waiting. The nights were dark now for it was after the harvest time. But the moon was coming up. It was long past midnight before they heard the heavy unsteady steps coming towards the house. The door opened up. In the pale light of the moon the stranger had no trouble to find his way across the *tupa*.

It was a long time before his steps went through the *tupa* again. This time the door swung shut with a bang, and soon the sound of them faded and were gone. Out there in the night someone was whistling.

Anna-Liisa shivered. She pressed herself closer to Mamma and started to sob.

The church bells were ringing. To Anna-Liisa it was the sweetest sound as she alighted from the carriage. This was her wedding day. Such a beautiful day, not a cloud in the sky.

"Anna-Liisa," cried little Otto, "nearly everyone in the county is here, look at the carriages, look at the people! What if the Russians should come today? I wish that Mamma had let me take the rifle along."

"Did you ever hear of anyone going to a wedding with a gun?" asked Father, smiling down at his son.

To Anna-Liisa the church was just a sea of faces. She was so happy that she thought her heart would burst, for there was John waiting for her. After the pastor had made them man and wife and she was coming down the church aisle, she saw Mamma sitting there with Grandma on one side and little Otto on the other. She stopped by her Grandma and her eyes met those of the old and wise one. There was no need for words, for what was in their minds they both knew and so they understood.

John was pulling her on and smiling as she went towards the open door.

Grandma sat there with her hands folded on her lap. Gently Mamma laid her hands on top of Grandma's. Grandma didn't pull them away. Perhaps she didn't know, for she sat there looking straight ahead and her old eyes grew soft and mellow and her face spread into a toothless grin.

Juhani Aho

BREAD
(Translated by Inkeri Väänänen-Jensen)

I SAT ONE cold winter evening in a train speeding through the desolate backwoods of Finland. The coach was almost empty. It was dark outside and the snow whipped about as the train sped on. We stopped at some nameless flag station. No one got off, only one man got on. He entered cautiously and timidly, as a hired hand enters his master's drawing room, and when no one asked him to leave nor what he wanted, he chose a narrow bench in a corner near the door, sat down, placed his knapsack on the floor between his legs, and took off his hat.

He was covered with snow and looked tired. It was apparent that he had either come on skis or had waded through the snowdrifted roads. His face was haggard, his cheeks hollow; his look was weary and yet his eyes were bright. I tried to determine what kind of work he did and came to the conclusion that he must be a tenant farmer. He was not a workingman, for workingmen nowadays can afford to dress better than he was dressed and usually wear at least one ready-made garment. All this man's clothes were homemade, no doubt woven by his wife, and full of patches. In fact, all that he wore, particularly his pants, consisted of one patch beside another.

After glancing about, he bent over to open his knapsack. He dug around in the knapsack for a while, then lifted out a small cloth bundle and began to untie the knot. His numbed fingers worked clumsily at the knot, and it appeared to me as if his face became strained, and the look in eyes turned grim as he struggled with the knot. With great curiosity, I watched to see what would appear.

Out of the bundle he pulled out a large, black flatbread. Holding it with shaking hands, he turned the bread around, studying it from all sides. It had already been eaten from and he appeared to be looking for a suitable place to bite into. He seemed almost to caress the flatbread, and his face took on a gentle, contented expression while at the same time the movement of his fingers reminded me of a cat playing with a mouse he has cornered. Suddenly his fingers tightened around the flatbread, his mouth opened wide, he thrust his head forward, his face took on a look of frenzy, his eyes bulged out of their sockets, and he attacked the bread as an animal attacks his prey. He chewed at it as a cat might—I had the feeling that it would be foolhardy to disturb him.

For a long time he kept the bread between his teeth; he gnawed so hard that his eyes closed. He gnawed as a dog gnaws at a bone and then peers about to see if anything is coming to snatch the bone away. Finally the bread broke apart and he got a large piece into his mouth, which he began to chew slowly. After swallowing several times, he lifted a small flagon of buttermilk from his knapsack, took a big gulp from it, and then somewhere in the folds of his bundle he located a piece of salted fish. Gradually he relaxed as his hunger was appeased. He became completely quiet.

But I had seen enough. Having watched him so closely, I now had something to think about.

It had seemed as if the bread was his worst enemy. It was as if a long-suppressed rage had driven him to avenge all the sufferings that bread had caused him.

There are those for whom work is a pleasure and whose daily bread is a reward of that pleasure. There are others for whom work is torment and agony, whose bread is its only reward. For the former, a piece of bread is only a part of his sustenance, which he buys casually or someone buys for him. For the latter, bread is his complete sustenance and providing it consumes his whole life. This man was one of the latter and providing bread was a ceaseless war and torment, his life a never-ending pursuit after bread which, when he finally holds it in his hands, he attacks with ferocity.

And how has he earned that hard, black bread?

He has cleared a field in the unrelenting forest. A poor man cannot choose his land; he must make his field from what others discard. Besides rooting out stumps, he has also had to pry up rocks. He has had to do this work alone, for he has no means with which to pay for help. Then he has grubbed the stony ground with a hoe and plowed it. Years have passed before the rye can be planted, and more years have passed before he can produce his own seed. Of course he must go into debt and must pay a high interest. From the village neither horse nor boat can reach his backwoods cottage, which lies beyond even the poorest of roads. He must carry the seed on his back across swamps and through wilderness. At last the patch of field is sowed. It will take most of the year before the rye will be ready for reaping. He must agonize throughout the fall, winter, and spring, tormented by fears— heavy snow may crush the rye, crusted snow may smother it, hail may shatter it, heavy rains may beat down the heading rye, and, finally, a late frost may kill it. And each of these does take its toll of the poor man's field, of the barren ground, which by itself has no power and to which he has not been able to give power. The meager crop is tied into sheaves, placed in shocks. But a threshing barn must be built for the rye, wood must be chopped so the barn can be heated to dry out the rye, and then the rye must be threshed. He has no watermill nor windmill, the grain must be ground by hand in a corner of the one room of his cottage.

At last he is able to make a dough, but then he realizes that if he wishes to survive through the long winter, the loaves must be kneaded thin and dried into hard crusts so they will not mold.

And this is the hard crust which he can eat at last. This is the reward which he, driven to exhaustion in its pursuit, has finally achieved. This is why he attacks it with such fury, as if to avenge all his suffering.

But now he is very quiet. He has eaten half the bread and folds the other half into his bundle for safekeeping for another time. He handles the bread as if it is a cherished possession, and his face is peaceful. In his eyes there is a gentle glow. He gathers the crumbs which have fallen on his knees, carefully places everything back into his knapsack and sighs, sighs with relief.

I cannot resist speaking with him, I move and sit beside him and ask where he is going. I learn that he is on his way to the provincial prison to discharge with bread and water the delinquent taxes he owes to the Crown. *(1899)*

Eeva Joenpelto

Excerpts from

A DRAFT FROM ALL
THE DOORS
VETÄÄ KAIKISTA OVISTA
(Translated by Aili Jarvenpa)

> *A group of three novels that aroused the most attention in
> Finland in the 1970s is Eeva Joenpelto's renowned Lohja
> trilogy, the first book of which is* A Draft from All the
> Doors. *It begins in the Spring of 1919, the first year of
> Finland's independence. Everyday life of the new nation is
> overcast by recent events. Independence has been gained at the
> expense of a short but harsh civil war, and the "White" victors
> are now the rulers. Many of the defeated "Reds" are shot.
> Others starve in prison camps, and some hide underground.
> The nation is split in two. The war has divided former friends,
> sometimes even relatives, as is revealed in these excerpts from
> Chapters One and Two:*

CHAPTER ONE

SALME HÄNNINEN, a large, peaceful woman, stood at her kitchen
window, one hand resting on her tightly belted waist. With the
other she fussed with the buttons on her blouse and fanned herself.
She was uncomfortably warm and drenched with perspiration. The sun
shone directly on the windowpane, but the window could not be
opened. It was papered over from the past winter. Perhaps also from
the previous winter, since there had been no time to pay much attention to what time of year it was. It was enough to have been able to
stay alive and keep the family together.

The Hänninen family had survived, although there was little for which
to be thankful. They were now among those people whom the general
turmoil had swept up and whirled around.

She intended to say something pleasant to the maid, who was busy
cleaning, but she let it be. Instead, she went over to open the doors
to the entrance hall and to the outside to make sure the aroma of the

coffee bread baking in the oven would spread out into the yard. You had to be so careful these days and take everything into consideration. But it was from her own provisions that she had baked, from the last of the flour hidden under the floor boards. From the very last, since she had read in the newspaper that new rations would be distributed. Who knows from where, probably foreign ships. But Salme Hänninen knew that no matter how little came, a portion would appear in this kitchen, on this table. He would take care of that—Oskari Hänninen, shopkeeper, enterprising man. Hänninen took care of his family. But Salme Hänninen did not sigh with relief. She now knew for sure that when a woman has been married for twenty-eight years, she realizes that she has been sleeping with a total stranger.

It was Hänninen for whom she was now waiting and, of course, her daughters. They would come in about an hour, or even later, but she was used to waiting. She went over to lift up the linen towel that covered the coffee bread, looked at the braids and suddenly remembered the baby pigs at the mill back home years ago. She broke off a piece and nibbled on it. A vague, unusual restlessness took her back to the window.

The yard had an April bareness. The afternoon sun sketched black slashes of birch trunks through it, which moved, as she watched, over to the cover of the well, then to last year's bed of foxglove, now turned into topsy-turvy dried twigs. The maid walked through the yard heading for the shed and returned carrying an empty bucket. Old woman, poor wretch, rescued from her home village sometime in the past. What could she, too, be thinking about, or did she think about anything? Now she clattered around in the cupboard while Salme Hänninen continued to watch the road, which circled behind Pemenof's Clothing Store. It was already dry and dusty this early in the spring.

"Stop that racket," she said to the maid and began removing hairpins from her bun, one at a time, and then started putting them back in again. She straightened her posture, looked stern and matronly.

Like misfortunes that sometimes come half-teasing as one waits, she now saw one coming down the road in payment for all her standing. Not the steady, firm-stepping Oskari Hänninen but, instead, a thin, timid woman as middle-aged as she.

"Oh, Jesus," she exclaimed as the woman came closer and paused at the gate opening. The maid hurried to the window to look, a dust cloth in her hand. She only reached up to Salme Hänninen's shoulder as she blinked up at her. Salme Hänninen drew a deep breath.

"It's not Tilta, Tilta Gröönroos? Lord bless us, is it? Yes, yes, it is." Salme Hänninen watched how the woman stepped inside through the gate and then remained standing in the yard, her pale, bitter, discolored face turned toward the window.

"Why is she standing there? Everyone can see," Salme Hänninen said to herself. It didn't look like Tilta Gröönroos intended to go inside, just stood there in the middle of all the grasses and rubbish of past years. If her face had not been visible, she could have been mistaken for a child communicant brought from the backwoods to the church village for the first time, so helplessly small did she look in the overly large clothes that she wore, clothing that was turning green with age.

"Scrub the floor," Salme Hänninen said to the maid. "I'm going outside. Can you imagine a woman getting to look like that?"

"Mebbe she's suffered," the maid suggested.

"Take a bucket and brush and soap. And don't jabber, not even to yourself. The walls have ears, maybe even eyes. How come you don't learn?"

Salme Hänninen watched to see that the maid got busy, then grabbed a shawl for her shoulders from the back of a chair and went outside. She stopped about three feet from Tilta Gröönroos, her cousin, but they were actually separated by half the world. They both stared at the ground in front of their feet and grew silent. Salme Hänninen bent down, snatched up the dried branch of a tree and threw it farther away. Then she straightened up, her hand moving suddenly to a stay in her corset that was gnawing and stinging her in her side and found herself looking directly at the other woman. Tilta Gröönroos swallowed, tried to speak, but then pressed her lips against a corner of her coat collar.

"You shouldn't have come," Salme said finally. "I'd have sent you food secretly anyway. Are you in need? Oh, if Hänninen finds out now."

An expression flickered briefly in Tilta's sunken eyes. Outside in the fresh air, in the sunlight, one could see that her cheeks were not pale after all. The gray and yellow color came from the other side of hunger and worry.

"Gröönroos died. At the army camp." Her voice came softly, and suddenly the woman lifted her head and looked Salme straight in the eye. "They sez 'twas typhoid."

Salme began to stare up at the tree tops, her eyes blinking. The barren branches swayed without a quiver, as if rustling to themselves eternally until they, too, would die some day from the blow of an axe. She stood, her back to the house of which she was the mistress. In her was all the strength and firmness of the two-story structure. Not downright ashamed, but in a hurry, she headed to the rear of the house, her hands on her hips, to the rear where they could not be seen from the road.

Tilta followed her as soon as she understood. There in the cool shade Salme grasped Tilta's hand and squeezed it.

"Oh, is that how it went? Is that how it went?"

Tilta's face wrinkled all up as she pulled her hand away and shook it as though it had gone numb and she had to revive it.

"An' the shop it went for taxes. Nothin' left but the old cottage. An' Hilja's sick, jus' lays there. Spanish flu, I guess. I put ashes with water in a bucket. She's asoakin' her skinny legs in it now. This mornin' I give 'er some wormwood coffee. Did I say coffee? Twarn't nothin' but old rye meal half burnt. Crap flew everywheres like a flock o' sparrows. An' now I run here with all my troubles."

"Well, you have a lot to bear, and so do we," Salme said as she stood as though to leave. What was there that she could do about past events?

"You has?" Tilta began, drawing in her breath. "Oh, you has? Hänninen a staff officer. Everybody knows that. Yeah, an' Anja, that smart, purty gal. S'pose she's agoin' to the University soon. That's what I hear. Sure looks like all o' you got lots to bear."

"Well," Salme said, "she'll go for sure. What's so bad about that? And while Hänninen has a lot to do otherwise, what's a few days' service on the staff? He hasn't shot anyone or had anyone shot either. But a guard still stands watch at night near our place so you people can't get to hurt us in any way." When the serious trouble first started, Salme had not been able to stand the unruliness, not any of it. "You people raged around so that an ordinary person didn't know where to go. You even threw a bomb in Julin's bedroom, killed his wife, a totally innocent person, and would have killed her husband except he was in the barn. And we were supposed to have peace by then. Last summer it was."

"We and we," Tilta mocked her. "We and we is it? At least I've given everythin' a'ready. His pa went and Vieno's still there. Only Hilja an' me at home. Damn it, what kinda names do they now have? I gave in good faith. Now I'd like to curse the whole world. Hilja an' me, we're no good fer nothin'. You don't need to be 'fraid of us. Look at this here hand. Look. I used to sew onct. You 'member? Dresses an' pillow cases. An' lace on sheets, like you got. Look now. Look how it shakes. What needle can it hold? An' there's Vieno. If Vieno, too, should go—"

"Oh, don't think that. Vieno's a strong, young man. Gröönroos—that's different. Oh dear, oh dear. Do you remember when Hänninen helped him get work at a tannery? Good place it was, learned a trade. At least something about it. But did he stay there? Did he stay anywhere? No, no. Just left. Hänninen even covered his debts. And Hänninen wasn't so well off then. Not that he's now. But Gröönroos just had to get a shoemaker's shop. Was it worth it? Did he resole shoes in the time he had promised? And if he resoled them, how well? Guess he gave it away for a song. And just think, to show his gratitude this same man was shameless enough to come, a rifle, bayonet extended, a red ribbon around his arm. Comes to confiscate harnesses from Hänninen's shop. And as drunk as a cuckoo then too. Therefore, no, no."

"But I liked him. An' at least we lived together. An' had children. Didn't Hänninen get his money out when he right away puts the shop up for sale? Couldn' he have waited a bit so's we coulda figgered somethin' out?"

"Well, all our nerves are shot. But I think Gröönroos was at fault more than many others since he didn't get out. We must believe that justice will prevail. Perhaps he was an agitator or maybe a chief of something."

"You mean Gröönroos?" The widow's jaw dropped. "Chief, you say? God almighty, that's some mouthful, 'tis. If only he'd a been a chief."

"Well, what about Vieno then? Perhaps there's a reason. They wouldn't be providing him with food and drink for nothing."

"You say food and drink? I ain't 'eard. But if there's somethin' to that, then I'd join in asupportin' it. I would. You think about that, that justice could come 'bout. That there'd be a better life for all of us."

"Would there?"

Tilta grew silent, put her hands in front of her and studied them and let Salme look at her shaking fingers as though everything was explained by them, including the outcome of all the battles. Then she dropped them to her sides, stood straight like a man and began hurriedly, in a soft voice, to tell how the week before she had walked through her old neighborhood, in her home town that was also Salme's hometown. She had gone to every home asking, imploring, even praying that any gentleman, head of the house, would send a letter of recommendation to the army staff offering to employ Vieno. But not a single one offered to do so. They had already been able to get their own back, those whom they cared about. She saw them gathered together at long tables, eating, sharing food. There had been potatoes and herring and meat and milk. "Milk," she repeated. No one acknowledged knowing Vieno. Nor did anyone remember Vieno from the time when he attended the same school for two years where Anja also went. But then it had been necessary for him to leave because there just was not enough money, although he had the ability. After that he had just been his father's assistant at the shop. But now, when he had no father, he had no shop in which to work. Even if there had been one, who would have backed him? Vieno was only twenty-two and such a lively, courageous young man.

"Well, since he's so lively and courageous, he no doubt can stay alive."
Salme hardened herself. "He'll probably get out soon since even those
remaining are being pardoned bit by bit."

"Now Hilja had to get sick. We ain't got nothin' salty to lick 'cept some
old herrin' boards. That's the God's truth. So I figgered, we're gonna
lose everythin' now. If I could jus' get Vieno back. From death. Sure
death."

Salme started to go inside, stepping carefully around the scrub pail
on the kitchen floor. She pulled out drawer after drawer, sometimes
forgetting what she was looking for. Then she saw a knife on the dish-
washing table, remembered and cut the coffee bread in half. She looked
at the halves and weighed them in her hands. Mari, the maid, looked
at her from where she knelt on the floor. Then suddenly Salme wrapped
both pieces in a hand towel and again stepped around Mari, went outside and headed toward the back of the house. Her daughters came
in through the gate just as she turned the corner. She nodded to them.

"Take these now," she said, and Tilta put the package inside her
blouse. The bread changed the shape of her figure. It was a though she,
at her advanced age, had just recently given birth and the milk was
swelling her breasts. Tilta did not thank Salme nor did it look like she
would continue to talk either.

"What are you waiting for now," Salme asked.

"Seems useless to say anythin'."

"Speak now that you're here."

"It's Hänninen I was hopin' to see. If he could jus' see his way to be
merciful and write to the army staff that he'll hire Vieno for any kinda
work. Anythin' at all. Jus' so's I could get 'im home alive. Even jus' a
bit alive. I could then nurse 'im back to health."

"Well," Salme said, "it's like this now. Hänninen just won't. There
have been all those matters, and he has straight out forbidden you."

"Like what?"

"That you mustn't associate with Reds or with widows of Reds."

"Ooh." Again Tilta shook all over. Then once more she gathered
together her remaining strength.

"But 'twas Gröönroos who did all those bad things. An' now he's
dead. Lies in some ditch, face full o' dirt. Dirty an' messy like always.
He wasn't even tidy. If I coulda jus' been able to wipe his face the las'
time. But Vieno. What has he ever done to Hänninen? What would he
do now if he lived? Even if he lived. If he didn' know how b'fore, how
could he now? If he could jus' get home alive. He's still alive now. I'd
keep 'im alive."

"Are you making any sense?"

Salme listened to sounds behind her back. She heard people running up and down the steps constantly, causing a continuous noise. Then the door to the second floor veranda opened, and the music from a gramophone could be heard. On the road one team of horses after another went by, the wheels rumbling and hooves clattering. Then people began coming constantly, men and women, on foot. The shift at the mill had ended, and the workers' barracks began to fill up. Children cried, mothers scolded, a dog howled somewhere, a long, steady howl as though caught in the spokes of a wheel. From all the sounds she heard the din of the world, although nothing could be seen from where she was.

Salme scraped some sand with the tip of her shoe and then smoothed it out immediately. She didn't know how to continue the conversation. She had her own worries like everyone else.

"How long you plannin' this to last?" Tilta asked. Then suddenly she tossed her head back as though mimicking someone, grabbed at her slender waist so hard that the bread package shifted to under her arm.

"Do you 'member anythin' we believed in when we was young?" Tilta added. "All those evenin's we sat on the shore o' your pond and watched the water lilies, yellow water lilies an' the water ripplin' away? Was there such a big dif'rence 'tween us then? Perhaps there was if someone hada been smart enough to figger it out. You bein' an only child an' even got 'cepted to the University. You got so uppity an' you even begun to talk uppity. In my fam'ly we had a God awful number o' kids an' we was always hungry. No way at all to get any special schoolin' to learn what to do now. But way back then we didn't know no dif'rence. Do you 'member all the things we 'magined?"

"I guess I remember."

"Yeah, oh yeah. We used to think we could get married, have our pitchers took, an' then life would start. Then we'd have someone's shoulder on which to rest our head. There'd only be silk an' satin. There's not been a sign of silk or satin, not that it makes much dif'rence. Looks like you've had better luck. You married a gentleman. I only got Gröönroos. What's that, a tenant farmer's son, even a bit crippled, even his leg crooked an' both hands not right. An' his whole life no home of his own nowheres. So what could he become? When his pa died, he was left one axe, a razor, and a fiddle. A fiddle. But I'm tellin' you, in a way 'twas good too. 'Twas just kinda sad, but I wouldn't give away one single day. He slept with others, you cert'nly know that. There was every kinda whore. An' he would drink an' carouse an' then howl. Sometimes I thought he'd hurt me so much that death couldn' be any worse. He died many times, or so I thought. An' never a decent word, hardly ever, an' no damn shoulder either. Sometimes that woulda been enuf. But you know, he'd always come back an' was there at the head of the table smellin' o' wine an' booze. At least I got to wash the lout, old wreck. He was an' he lived. But now—"

"Don't, Tilta. I doubt if anybody had any silk or satin. Now don't."

"Like I says, he was an' he lived. But then came such happenin's that even when I'm a clump o' dirt I'll 'member."

Tilta collapsed, wept a bit. Two miserable tears appeared in her sunken eyes and stayed there. She angrily wiped them away.

"I'll send you some food," Salme said. "But don't tell anyone. Promise. Hänninen would beat me black and blue if he found out."

A mocking smile flickered briefly over Tilta's face. Then she turned, left without saying goodbye while Salme sighed. Tilta walked next to her shadow all the way to the gate, hurried out in a fury of despair. Dust whirled around her skirts.

She only has rubbers on her feet, Salme thought in amazement as she watched from the steps. Then she had reason to turn suddenly and seize a nearby broom in her hands. She had glimpsed Hänninen coming around the turn and noticed that the unhappy Tilta had stopped in front of him.

Salme swept the steps and then turned the broom over to shake off the winter's bird leavings. Now and then she would glance quickly toward the road. Hänninen's chest heaved and his hand tugged at the edge of his jacket. She didn't have to hear the words at all. Then Tilta turned, stumbled a bit but left immediately, walking fast.

Salme continued to sweep the steps a while longer since Hänninen had already gone inside without saying a word, his manner revealing intense irritation. She carefully put the broom in its place, adjusted her hair and expression, and stared at the door hinge for a moment while she quieted down. When the gramophone music ended in an angry shriek, she stepped inside looking calm and composed.

CHAPTER TWO

This day, too, had been spent in the company of others. Was it only a year since the Germans marched from the direction of Hanko and destroyed everything on their way? That joyous and bitter, longest of long, twenty-four hour day. Since then the mornings had grown brighter and night had fallen three hundred and sixty-five times and the earth had continued to tremble under one's feet and victory wreaths were as fresh as though they had been woven yesterday and wounds had continued to ooze blood.

Nature, however, seemed totally unaware, as though it were saying "so what." The leafless elms and lindens stood bordering the church yard the same way as before, getting ready for their buds to swell. Cloud banks wandered in the sky as usual. The earth also sprang under heavy boots as before. A certain clergyman spoke in German the other summer and in Finnish the next, and the wind blew from the north as always and chilled the cheekbones. The jackdaws left their nests of twigs in the church attic to fly a small circle every time the bells in the tower began a new clamor.

In honor of the day, schools and all businesses were closed except the drugstore, of course. It was also announced that factory workers would be given the day off. Everyone was expected to be idle, to remember, to sit expressionless on hitching rails or stand at a crossroads, or wander somewhere behind the festival crowd until the band music, hymns, and ever more inspiring speeches would finally wipe the rails clean and the roads empty. It would be unwise to leave too early. Indeed, it had to be heard all the way up to the sky—what grave and turbulent conditions now prevailed throughout the land.

The loud voice of a clergyman could be heard from near the graves of the Whites:

"Like a flash of lightning after a hundred years of suffocating, ghastly pressure, the sound of the war bugle beckoned all free men of Finland to rescue the Fatherland from foreign oppression and cleanse it of the filth brought here from the East. The sign that was observed by hundreds and thousands, the sign that joined together all of Finland's true children, heirs of their fathers' ideals, the beginning of Finland's War of Independence—"

Chilled by the cold, Salme stood with Anja on a moss-covered rock bordering someone's family grave.

"Let's go now," she said quietly to her daughter, but when Anja did not hear, a far-away expression on her face, Salme tugged at her sleeve and said, "Let's go before the parade starts."

The clergyman continued, "The task of the Civil Guard is like that of a psychiatric nurse in a mental hospital. We must stay awake so that a blind fellow creature won't be able to plunge into his own destruction and pull others with him. We must also prepare outwardly. Our arch enemy does not intend lasting peace. He just needs time to prepare. Therefore, hold your rifles tightly in your fists and present a united front against the enemies both within and outside our borders."

"Come now," Salme said. "I thought the pastor was going to talk about God's mercy. So what's that all about?"

Salme stepped down from the rock and began walking toward the gate. Anja followed reluctantly. Others were also beginning to move. Only around one grave did members of the Civil Guard still stand with their flags and rifles.

"Oh, how I wish, how I wish," Salme said as they stepped through the soft sand on their way toward the center of town. "Well, at least he got to help dedicate the flag. Even got to pound one nail. If he can now get at least what he hopes for—your father, that is."

"Papa? Really?" Anja asked.

"Papa. He'd be willing to stand upside down in a well all day and all night if the sheriff and the postmaster and other appointed officials—"

Salme suddenly stopped talking and increased her speed. She had already noticed for some time that she had begun to say whatever she thought. Whether it was right or wrong, it was stupid nevertheless.

"We're still outsiders here. Your father's from far away, and I'm from another parish too. It's always the same. Yet we've lived here almost thirty years. But maybe now, finally."

The parade began to form a line in the churchyard. Words of command could be heard, and positioning of rifles on shoulders.

"Let's go see Inkeri," Salme said as they approached a building from the corner of which stairs rose up to a drugstore. There were glass jars in the window, in one jar dried wormwood, in another yarrow, and in a third blueberries. At the other end of the building there was a casket firm, but its window was completely covered by white drapes. The entire upstairs was the residence of the druggist.

"Let's go in," Salme said as she walked inside. Inkeri stood with her back to the door as she stirred something in a large bowl. The door bell stopped ringing after Anja came inside. A farmer sat on the end of a bench, waiting. He turned his face away. As a reminder of a long ago case of smallpox, his lower eyelids were twisted double and were very red. On the counter sat a bottle of rose drops beautifully arranged in a pale green paper container shaped in the form of a hat.

Inkeri carried the bowl over to the counter and continued to stir. She was expressionless like her father. Salme whispered, asked if Inkeri could leave in about two hours or thereabouts. Inkeri put the bowl under her arm and walked to the back room to ask permission. The man who had been sitting on the bench stood up.

"It's for my horse," he said and sat right down again.

"Yes," said Inkeri as she returned. A strong odor rose up from the bowl. "Liniment," she said, stirring with all her strength. "A big amount."

"Anja will come to get you then," Salme said, and when Inkeri turned her back to her again, Salme lingered and held Anja's sleeve so she could not leave. The man got up again and joined them by the window. The parade was passing by and horns were blaring. The entire Civil Guard marched past them. Also marching was Oskari Hänninen in his handsome new suit and the country doctor in his old one. He had not even had new edging put on. There, in front of them, marched the town's entire elite, including older gentlemen as well as young.

"Look. There goes Lauri," Anja whispered.

"So he does," Salme answered.

"Do you know," the man next to them started to say, "I ran and hid in a potato dugout for three days an' nights when they tried to git me to join the Red Guard. My wife fetched me food, lowered the basket down, told 'em she don't know where I was. Sure's good I knew to do that. I really shouldn't be here now. My wife's got Spanish flu. An' now the horse, old work horse, covered with scabs."

Salme nodded, agreed there was no justice in this world. Those who survived the war or were saved by a potato dugout could be taken away by sickness. How long would her family survive? That's what you thought about first, of course, your own. At least a woman did.

Then came the last of the parade, a noisy group of small boys running pell mell at the tail end. They were sons of both Whites and Reds. The sound of the horns began to fade and the dust settled, and soon the road lay desolate and empty.

"Remember to take the detour then," Salme instructed Anja at home. "Pick up Inkeri at the drugstore like we planned and go together. And take the detour, not past Father's shop, although he's not here today."

We could just as well have chosen another day, Salme thought as she gathered bread, rye flour, a piece of salt pork, and a little wormy oatmeal into a bundle. Into another bundle she folded a piece of cotton fabric she had found on a closet shelf and on top of that she placed an apron pattern for Mari. In another way, it was a good day for them to go since Hänninen would be returning home late in the evening and would be less likely to ask any questions.

Anja combed her hair in front of the kitchen window and tried to view herself from both sides. She adjusted her clipped-on collar and retied one shoe. The hem of her skirt reached exactly to the top of her shoes.

"You look just fine," Salme said. "Even less fixing up would be enough for this kind of a trip. You've done nothing all day but fuss with yourself."

"Did you see Lauri?"

"Yes, yes," Salme said and tied each bundle with twine.

"Lauri rode a horse through the front lines during the night, going north. He always tells me about that. The stars in the sky so big and Reds on every side. He says he'll never forget it."

Salme leaned her hands on the packages and looked outside. There was a suggestion of color on the tops of the birches, a forecast of spring, and it was about time.

"Do you want to know why Julin let Lauri go?" Salme asked. "Julin told him to go because he said it will be time for planting before long, and we should get some kind of order in the land and the men back into the fields. It was as simple as that." Salme didn't look at her daughter, just talked looking straight ahead. "Now those words have come back to haunt Lauri's father. Now he is sad, and no one feels like marching then. And then his youngest boy left home for Aunus that way without saying a thing. Ran off. I suppose he wanted to go to war because Lauri had. He just had to become a hero. It's extraordinary, it really is, how a person finally faces everything. Everyone does, but not right away. Although Julin will get through this. It would be different, of course, if—"

Her daughter came over and cuddled unusually close to her mother.

"Lauri and I really care about each other."

"Yes, yes, and that's probably good. Your father's pleased too. He has business dealings with Julin. Or he'd want to have. Although that shouldn't make any difference. And it doesn't."

"We care for each other." Anja breathed deep and twirled away.

"It's good to hear. You'll be entering the University together too. You just be happy. But leave now and do as I said. And take your woolen jacket."

So Salme Hänninen stood again at the window as she watched her daughter attach the two bundles to either side of her bicycle and ride off. Her collar flapped around her shoulders and the hem of her skirt clung to the frame of the bicycle.

Anja rode back to the drugstore. She decided not to go inside when she saw the other apprentice behind the counter buttoning his coat, a young man who lived there and who was fully supported by the druggist. Anja's chin rose in disdain. The druggist's wife lived in Helsinki in the winter, and the young man was the druggist's drinking partner. During her night shifts Inkeri had been forced to listen to the racket. It could even be heard outside if someone happened to pass by.

Inkeri still had a customer. She reminded him of the prescription sitting on the counter so he wouldn't forget it. Her eyes looked sleepy and were downcast the whole time. Her skin used to break out when she was young, and perhaps she would never be rid of the acne scars. But her hair was like her mother's—thick and dark—and she was as magnificent as an elk. And often just as silent. It was as though she had a dark secret which she had to protect. She probably did, Anja thought. Inkeri was starting to be irreversibly old, already twenty-five.

Inkeri went to the back room to remove her white coat, returned, raised the counter door latch, walked long steps toward the door and outside. She lifted up her bicycle, which was leaning against the wall of the building.

"Why am I needed there?"

"Mother just wanted you to. If anything is said, then at least we were both there. If Papa finds out. Let's go first by way of the Inn and from there down to the shore and then on from there."

The woods began thinning out, and it was difficult to say where the yard began when there was no fence and, therefore, no gate. One of the two windows of the old gray cottage was open, a half curtain in the other. The door was propped open a crack with a short stick. The girls walked their bikes up to the side of the cottage. Anja removed the bundles from her bike, and they turned to go toward the entrance.

It was totally still. Not even the birds sang. In the yard there was a pile of cut up spruce branches and an axe on a block of wood. The sun shone bright in many-layered rays.

Then they saw Tilta. She sat on the steps of an outbuilding together with some man. He was barefoot and held his head in his hands. As they stood there, his hands dropped down, and he slowly revealed his shrunken face, his large, dull eyes staring from within deep sockets. Tilta put her hand on the man's shoulder, removed it, then stood up and started toward the girls.

"Let's go inside," she said. "Why'd you come so late? You shoulda knowed to come sooner."

There was a peculiar odor in the cottage. It probably came from a pot on the stove, the lid of which was not on tight. You had to get used to the odor before you could stay in such a human habitat and then walk over to the table and put your bundles down and start talking. "Mother sent these," Inkeri said, "—and also some cloth so perhaps you could sew aprons for our Mari. There's no hurry."

Tilta settled herself next to the stove. She didn't even look to see what was in the bundles. The old kitchen was full with its cot, table, footstools, cupboards, mugs, and buckets of water. In the corner there was a pile of spruce logs, littered among them dried, broken branches. Three women standing in the small room were way too many.

"My, what high-toned, purty gals to have in this poor shack," Tilta said as she looked at them coldly. "I could ask you into the bedroom. Hilja lays there now on top o' the boards. Like I sez, you come too late.

My gal, she died the other night. Sickness is what took her. Or mebbe not. She jus' gotten so weak."

"Oh, no," Anja said and turned toward Tilta.

"Oh, yeah. She's free o' this bad world. You tell Salme that. Hänninen too. You kin see, there ain't no justice. If the sickness don't take you, hunger will. The Reds are dyin' like fleas. An' what was she, jus' a fifteen year old gal. Hadn't even been confirmed yet. That's what she fussed so 'bout. Over and over. Always atalkin' 'bout religion. We ain't got no God."

Tilta began to toss her head back and forth, but when Inkeri went over and matter-of-factly grasped her hand hanging limp at her side, Tilta calmed down, turned back to the stove to move the pot a bit.

"You wanna see the deceased? No, I guess you don't. Couldn't find stockin's for her nowheres. But I guess she kin lay there without stockin's. This here is where she was born an' grew, played awhile in these corners an' died. Makes no sense, none of it don't."

"Many people are dying from the same sickness," Inkeri said. "Strong, healthy people are dying because there is no medicine for it."

"Mebbe so. I hear the pastor's been kep' very busy." Tilta left her pot and turned around. "But Vieno came. You tell Hänninen that too. I didn't need no help at all. I come home from a-visitin', from tryin' to sell the only silver spoon we got. The first an' only nice thing we've ever had in this house. Hilja died whilst I was gone. I figgered that some way I got to get her buried. So I sold the spoon. When I gets close to home, I found Vieno layin' in a mud puddle near the path. He had limped for four hours, all the way from the station. Jus' couldn't make it all the long way without fallin'. But anyway, I got Vieno back."

"Is that who the old man is," Anja asked.

"Yeah, that old man," Tilta answered. "Old man o' twenty-two. If I don't know how to cry no more, he knows how for both of us. Sez a word or two an' starts bawlin'. I heated the sauna, washed an' scrubbed 'im like a baby, my own flesh and blood. There he now sits, on those steps."

"There's no hurry with the aprons," Inkeri said. "We'll get them sometime."

"Jus' get 'em soon. I needs to get 'em done in a hurry. An' 'member to say at home that my hands don't shake no more. I was weak an' forgettin' things, but that's all over. If I get the aperns an' if I kin get even a little money for Gröönroos's clothes and shoemaker's tools, I could 'ave a nice burial for Hilja."

"We'll tell Mother," Anja promised. "Perhaps she can do something."

"Let 'er do what she wants. I know she'll do everythin' she kin."

The girls could find nothing more to say. Tilta went over to open the bundles, held the bread to her cheek while she looked out the window at the steps where Vieno still sat. Then she carried the food to a cupboard in the entrance and remained by the door. The girls went past her as they left to go outside. Tilta followed them into the yard and remained standing on the bare ground.

Suddenly Anja started walking toward Vieno. She felt she had to. She sat down beside him like Tilta had earlier and planned to touch him. She lifted her hand, lightly brushed the empty-looking sleeve of his worn work shirt, but then returned it to her own knee. Something moved in her stomach, then moved to her throat.

Vieno's hair looked like it had been dusted with flour, and it was parted like a child's. The vertebrae in his neck stood out singly, one by one. He seemed unaware of the girl's presence.

Tilta stood watching as she adjusted her skirt. Inkeri took her bike and started guiding it toward the path.

"Anja," she called softly by the nearest pines, "let's go now."

PART II
The immigrant story

Jim Johnson

GETTING OFF THE TRAIN
AT BRIMSON

When
she got off the train
at Brimson, there was
no one there. she wept.
beside the pulpwood
piled at the crossing
she wept.

the train, the tracks
went on through
swamp and trees;
behind her
frosted cattails, dead firs

placed along the tracks
like poles.
she understood. it was so.
she had not arrived. here
there was no Väinämöinen,
finger tips worn through
knitted mittens
strumming the wind.

Lauri Lemberg

Two excerpts from the novel

SAINT CROIX AVENUE

AN OLD-FASHIONED STORY ABOUT PEOPLE LONG AGO

(Translated by Timo Riippa)

> Lauri Lemberg's Saint Croix Avenue *is a novel about* Hannes Järvinen, *a 17-year-old watchmaker's apprentice who emigrates in 1903 from Tampere, Finland, to Duluth, Minnesota. The first excerpt (which includes most of Chapter One) picks up the story as Hannes has boarded the* S.S. Arcturus *in Helsinki and is about to leave for Hanko. The second excerpt (the beginning of Chapter Two) is a description of the milieu into which Hannes would arrive.*

I

As we hasten away from our homeland,
From its forests and rock-bound shore. . . .

THE STEAMSHIP ARCTURUS left Helsinki harbor in the evening with about twenty passengers bound for America. Hannes found himself in a small, six-person cabin with an interesting group of cabin mates. Holmström, the pharmacist, had a black satchel filled with an amazing variety of medicines for seasickness and other illnesses. Adolf Lindström, an intelligent, but know-it-all University freshman, generously dispensed advice without charge in a loud voice and boasted of the fact that he had been expelled from the sixth grade of the Lyceum for his wild behavior. Wäinö Vaahtera, a young bookkeeper from Porvoo, was fleeing military service. And, finally, there were two very quiet Finns whose names Hannes never found out.

By morning the ship had reached Hanko. Officials checked passports and examined eyes in the offices of the steamship company. One had to have healthy eyes, otherwise they'd never let you into America. So they said. Hannes's passport, ticket, and eyes were all declared to be satisfactory, and when the government official stuck some kind of stamp onto his suitcase, the young man knew he was all set to sail across the sea to the New World.

In Hannes's opinion Hanko was an ugly, small, ramshackle town, at least when compared to the splendors of Tampere. Overcrowded and swarming with activity, it was filled with America-bound emigrants who packed the streets, hotels, offices, and taverns. The majority of them were easy-going southern Ostrobothnians, mostly young farmhands and maids fleeing poverty and drudgery. Some were farmers' sons fleeing military conscription. Others were young men seeking adventures and young women seeking rich husbands. Amid the throng in front of the steamship company, Hannes happened to meet two young men from Tampere who were also going to America. Kusti Helin had been a bookkeeper at the Nasijärvi brewery, and Kalle Lahtinen a machinist at Sommer's machine shop. After the three had talked for a while about the upcoming trip, Kusti and Kalle headed for a nearby tavern to relieve the dryness in their throats. Hannes walked around Hanko's streets and harbor for a bit and then returned to the ship to get ready for departure. He got out his English grammar and became absorbed in conjugating verbs.

Finally everything was set. All of the passengers had been situated. The cabins had already filled up in Helsinki and now the Arcturus' large steerage compartment was full. The large converted cargo hold had double bunks along both sides of the large room, women on one side and men on the other. The corridor was filled with rucksacks, baskets, and suitcases, as were the ends of the bunks.

When the Arcturus' harsh-sounding horn sounded, Hannes interrupted his study and hurried out to watch the departure and bid goodbye to his homeland. All the other passengers had also gathered on the deck for the same purpose. Catching sight of Kusti and Kalle leaning against a railing, Hannes hurried toward them.

"Aha! Here comes the watchmaker," Kalle exclaimed. "Come on over here and join the rest of us as we deliver our fond farewells to Finland's beloved shores!"

He made room for Hannes by shoving aside the Ostrobothnian farmhand standing next to him.

The heavy lines were unfastened from the moorings. As the ship sounded its horn and began to inch away from the pier, Kalle began singing in a strong bass voice. Others joined him and in a few moments a melancholy farewell song echoed from the deck of the Arcturus:

> As we hasten away from our homeland,
> From its forests and rock-bound shore

Though our beautiful Mother we're leaving,
In our thoughts she'll remain evermore.

May she always be blessed with good fortune,
May her children be free from all fear.
In God's care with these prayers we now leave her,
Oh Finland, our birthplace so dear.

Hannes was suddenly gripped by a feeling of home-sickness so overwhelming that it was impossible to keep the tears from his eyes. Mother, Father, home, Tampere's busy main street, the watchmaker's shop, working companions, Mr. Holtti, the Näsijärvi swimming pool— memories of his entire world as it had existed up to that point suddenly flooded his consciousness. He tried his best to sing along with the others, but it was no use. At the same time he felt very ashamed of his emotionalism which wasn't appropriate at all for a young man sailing to America. In his pocket was a clean handkerchief, but he wasn't about to wipe his eyes, not with Kusti and Kalle standing right next to him. He tried to secretly dab at the tears with his sleeve, but Kalle noticed the movement and blurted out:

"Say, Hannes, your eyes look a little watery! Uh, oh, this isn't going to do at all! Crying doesn't help at the market, you know."

"Something flew into my eye," Hannes said quietly, wiping the corners of his eyes with his forefinger.

"Sure," Kalle chuckled. "Into both eyes at the same time."

As the ship drew away from the dock, the waving of handkerchiefs and shouting gradually ceased. The boys from Tampere talked for a long time on deck about the lengthy sea voyage ahead of them and of all the incredible things that they had heard about America. During the course of the conversation, Kusti mentioned that he was on his way to a city named Worcester in the state called Massachusetts. Hannes and Kalle, in turn, were on their way to Minnesota, Kalle to a mining town named Sparta and Hannes to Duluth. It was already getting dark when the three decided to return to the accommodations where they would be spending the next three days and four nights. Hannes went to his cabin, while Kalle and Kusti descended into the steerage quarters, where they had bunks 23 and 24. The room bustled with activity as people arranged their personal belongings and cleared their baggage out of the corridor. One could hear the steady murmur of conversation, occasional bursts of laughter, and soft crying and sobbing.

Hannes's cabin mates had already turned in. Holmström the pharmacist, who had been drinking to a *bon voyage* with friends in Hanko, was sleeping with his clothes on and snoring loudly. Adolf was lounging in his bunk, leafing through a Swedish book, and eating tortes that his mother had made for him.

"Oh, it's you," he said, glancing at Hannes. "Hi."

"Hello, hello. Were you out watching when we left."

"Me? Why should I?" Adolf answered. "I've been out of the country before. It's nothing new to me. Here, have a torte."

"No thank you. I don't think I care for one right now." The pastry looked tempting and tasty, but he didn't want to take something for free and then owe someone a debt of gratitude.

Hannes sat down on the edge of his bunk and tried to continue with the conjugations, but found it difficult to concentrate. A strange feeling of restlessness pressed at him and he didn't know what was causing it. It wasn't homesickness or the thought of leaving Finland, although a deep feeling of sadness had come over him at the moment of departure and he hadn't been able to suppress the tears. Nor did he fear the North Sea or the Atlantic, with their possible storms and seasickness. Perhaps the restlessness was caused by the uncertain future...a new world, new conditions, a new destiny.

Hannes undressed and got ready to spend the second night in his temporary quarters in the Arcturus' third cabin. Remembering his uncle's instructions, he had put his money into a secret pocket sewn into his underwear. His funds were still safe. Then he set his uncle's gold plated pocketwatch under his pillow. The rhythmic waves of the Baltic and the monotonous beating of the ship's engine gradually lulled him into a deep sleep.

Morning dawned. Hannes, who was an early riser, awoke and climbed down from his bunk. The others in the cabin were still asleep. He dressed quickly and rushed out onto the deck for some fresh air. No other passengers were out on the deck yet, only sailors and stewards who were busy with their duties. After staring at the shoreless horizon, he decided to see if Kalle and Kusti were awake yet. He climbed down the stairs into the steerage quarters, but at the bottom he suddenly stopped and quickly covered his nose. His uncle had been right. It smelled. Hannes hurried back up to the deck.

The sun rose ever higher. Passengers began to gradually appear on deck. In dishes made of tin-plate, the ship's cooks served a breakfast of weak coffee and something that faintly resembled porridge.

"You can't survive on this stuff," Kalle complained. "However...I just happen to have a couple of loaves of rye bread and a kilo of lard in my rucksack. Wait here, I'll go get them."

He soon returned. Kalle tore the dark, flat loaf into three pieces and cut two thick slices of lard for Kusti and Hannes.

"There you go. . . ."

Kusti, who was accustomed to more elegant fare, motioned with a wave of his hand for Kalle to keep it. Then he walked away. Hunger had been gnawing away at Hannes, who gladly ate the sandwich. Soon he began to feel much better. Life began smiling again and the sun felt nice and warm on his back as he leaned against a railing. The weather was calm, the ocean was beautiful, his conscience was clear, and the future glowed with promise.

After breakfast the atmosphere on deck turned festive, with contagious laughter, shouting, and loud talking. When a young man from Toholampi appeared on deck with his accordion, the dancing began. Fast polkas alternated with waltzes and mazurkas. The red-cheeked girls in scarves were truly in their element. The exuberance of youth shone on every face. In the entire group there were few over thirty. In fact, the majority were young men and women between twenty-two and twenty-eight. There also wasn't a married couple in the group, although several young wives were joining their husbands in America, and several young husbands were leaving their "widows" at home.

Everywhere there was activity. Those who weren't dancing gathered in small groups and chit-chatted, made predictions about the weather, described terrible storms they had heard about, and told off-color stories. Card games went on continuously down in the steerage compartment. Some gambled, while others played Old Maid and other games. Strictly speaking, gambling was prohibited; but on the Arcturus adherence to the rules wasn't all that strict. Some men just rested in their bunks, taking it easy, recovering from chronic departure hangovers.

Dinner was served in the same fashion as breakfast. Two hefty, tanned, and weatherworn women carried a large cauldron to the dining area. They then ladled out some kind of thin and tasteless potato soup to the passengers, who lined up and filed by with their tin bowls. Several younger women, also tanned and weatherworn, served as assistants. One of them had charge of the tin dishes and the other handed a piece of bread to each person in line.

A short break followed dinner, but soon the dancing started again and the merriment continued at an even higher pitch. A feeling of freedom pervaded the atmosphere. The birds had escaped from their cages. There were no parents giving advice, no masters or mistresses issuing orders, no pastors preaching the Law and the Gospel.

Kusti didn't take part in the dancing. He didn't dance. Kalle, on the other hand, was all over the dance floor. That's where he was really in his element. No wonder then that the long-trussed ladies would look at him longingly and whisper among themselves how they really wanted to polka with that boy from Tampere. Hannes and Kusti leaned against a railing and watched the festivities. Hannes had never been especially interested in dancing. Because of his long hours at work and his studies, he hadn't had time for much socializing, but now he felt a desire to be out jumping around with the rest of the people.

After awhile Adolf stopped beside him.

"Well, why aren't you out there dancing? There's still a couple of girls from Karstula over there waiting," he said with a tinge of sarcasm.

"I don't know how to dance," Hannes answered. "Why don't *you* go? Or don't you know how to dance either?"

"I don't dance with maids," Adolf said. "But if you want, I'll teach you."

"I don't know. . . ," Hannes wondered. "I'm not sure I can learn."

"Anybody can learn. There's no big trick to it," Adolf replied, dragging Hannes into the midst of the dancers.

Adolf was an excellent dancer. He had attended dance school and knew how to add little variations to the steps and movements that embellished the dance and gave it an artistic quality.

"You'll do all right," he finally said to Hannes after several dances. "Tomorrow you can go and ask some girls. Then you'll really enjoy it."

"I don't know if I dare," Hannes answered, but the idea appealed to him.

After supper he went to his cabin and tried to solve some problems with grammar. Articles and prepositions. . . they were hard nuts to crack. Soon he grew tired of it, put the book under his pillow and returned to the deck. The other boys from Tampere were already there and he joined in on the conversation until everyone finally quieted down to watch the beautiful sunset. For Hannes it was something new and spectacular. Finland, home, Tampere, Father, Mother, all were forgotten. As the sun slowly disappeared into the darkness of the boundless sea, he suddenly felt a mysterious and indescribable sense of harmony.

The boys stayed out on the deck of the Arcturus until it got dark and then turned in for the night.

A strong wind gradually arose on the North Sea and the ship began to sway. Seasickness and nausea began to make their way through the ranks of the dancers. It especially seemed to bother the women, who stayed in their bunks in the steerage quarters. When Hannes, who hadn't been affected yet, went to see Kalle and Kusti, he too became nauseated. On every side people moaned and complained, there were trails of vomit in the corridors, and the smell was unbearable. Hannes had to quickly run back up the steps to the deck.

On the fourth day, as the Arcturus approached England, the going was still rough and the northeast gale shook the ship as it steamed across the North Sea, forcing passengers to stay in their cabins and in the steerage compartment. As Hannes walked on the deserted deck, only a few sailors could be seen here and there.

Already for a couple of days he had been curious about the upper deck, where the second class passengers seemed to live in a world of their own. It, too, now seemed empty. Hannes decided to take the opportunity to discover what the ocean looked like from above and how the well-to-do lived. His exploration hadn't lasted very long before he was approached by a Swedish speaking porter who gestured impatiently for him to leave. Hannes tried to apologize and explain what he was doing, but the man didn't understand. Under the porter's impatient gaze, Hannes ran back down the steps to the third class deck. He went straight to his cabin, where the continually intoxicated Holmström was at that very moment dispensing some drops from a small bottle into a teaspoon and spoon-feeding the groaning, seasick Adolf. Sprawled in their bunks, the other passengers in the cabin weren't feeling well either. Holmström medicated each of them in turn in quite a serious and self-important manner. Hannes watched the pharmacist for a while and then returned to the deck. He was thinking about the second class deck, when Kalle, who had climbed up from the steerage compartment, grabbed hold of his shoulder.

"So, watchmaker, how's it going this morning? What's new?"

"Not much. This northeasterly just keeps blowing."

"Well, it sure shook things around last night. I came close to getting seasick myself. But fortunately I have this little bottle of brandy in my suitcase. It sure helps when things start swinging and swaying, I guarantee!"

"I suppose it does. I've never tasted it."

"And it's better that you don't," Kalle said in a fatherly tone. "So then...tonight we arrive in England."

"I guess so. If they keep to the schedule."

The ship arrived safely in Hull, where the Arcturus' passengers were divided into two groups. Those traveling on the Cunard Line were taken to Liverpool, while those on the White Star Line went to Southampton by way of London. Kusti, who was heading for Boston by way of Liverpool, parted company with his two friends. The boys from Tampere shook hands and wished each other well. To get to their waiting train, Kalle and Hannes boarded a wagon that was drawn by huge, muscular horses with tufted hooves. Before long the English train was speeding on its way to London. Its cars were entirely different from those in

Finland and the train traveled much faster. Hannes for the first time also heard spoken English. It sounded awful. Englishmen spoke through their noses, and although he had learned hundreds of English words and phrases, Hannes didn't understand a word he heard.

In Southampton the Finns were taken to an immigrant hostel where they waited for two days, which Kalle and Hannes spent sightseeing in town. Everything was strange and new – and extremely interesting. Hannes was especially intrigued by streetcars and the display windows of watchmakers' shops, but above all, he admired English wagons and the massive horses with tufted hooves. Sometimes there would be *six* horses pulling a giant wagon.

The day of departure finally arrived. The stately S.S. Olympic rested majestically in Southampton harbor ready to transport the waiting immigrants across the Atlantic to the golden West. At the immigration bureau, passports were checked once again and eyes examined. Hannes thought that the eye examination was much too rough. His eyes still stung for several hours afterward.

Compared to the Arcturus, the Olympic was a giant. Hannes wasn't able to find out just how many people it accommodated, but there were many. On board the Arcturus all of the passengers had been Finns, but now the blue-eyed children of the North were hopelessly in the minority. The Olympic's passengers as a whole were quite a colorful group made up of numerous nationalities – Scandinavians, Polish Jews, English, French, Italians, and Slavs, among others. They all looked different, dressed differently, and had come from different circumstances. Yet, all shared in common an optimistic attitude and the same goals. All were making their way toward freedom, toward equality, toward riches.

The Olympic operated under a completely different system from the Arcturus. People from each nationality were lodged together, usually in the same cabins, which held from six to ten people. There were no steerage quarters and meals were served at long tables in a dining room.

The days on the Atlantic went by fast. There was plenty to see, as Hannes walked from one end of the ship to the other, exploring every corner that he could. The weather was also favorable. Only on a few days did it storm so that giant waves swept across the deck, which meant that the passengers spent their time in the cabins or the ship's spacious salon. This gave Holmström, tipsy as ever, the chance to go from cabin to cabin selling his medicines.

Dancing was the main form of entertainment on the Olympic. Starting right after lunch and lasting until late at night, it always occurred in a particularly international manner. Sometimes the musicians were

Slavs from the Balkans with their guitars and mandolins, at other times they would be Italians with their harmonicas and concertinas, but every dance followed its own style and a Slovenian polka beat got the Swedes as well as the Italians tapping their feet. Music and dance seemed to weave their own secret, harmonious magic that brought the different nationalities together. Kalle, in particular, could have cared less about national or racial differences. He scurried about at a breathless pace, dancing with everyone and approaching everyone with the same enthusiasm, even getting a slap in the face from one Slavic belle for being a little too bold. For a couple of days Hannes watched all of this from the sidelines, but on the third day he worked up the courage to ask a young lady from Toholampi for a dance. At the end of the trip he was already dancing with the Italian women.

The same routine lasted for twelve days. On the morning of June 10 the American mainland loomed on the horizon, and by midday the Olympic had sailed into New York harbor. All of the passengers hurried to bring their baggage to the deck. They were heading for different parts of the country, but as they said their good-byes and hugged each other, there were no tears. Instead their faces radiated confidence and self-reliance as each one waited excitedly for the moment to step onto the soil of the New World.

On Bedloe's Island in New York harbor stood the majestic Statue of Liberty, the world's most famous symbol of freedom, who with upraised torch declared to the Old World:

> *Give me your tired, your poor,*
> *Your huddled masses yearning to breathe free,*
> *The wretched refuse of your teeming shore.*
> *Send these, the homeless, tempest-tossed to me,*
> *I lift my lamp beside the golden door.*

As the ship's interpreter translated the words into several languages, how impressive this greeting sounded to the young Finn whose beloved homeland couldn't promise a future...to the father who, as a tenant farmer, was unable to provide for his family...to the factory mother, who worked twelve-hour days just to keep body and spirit together, to the man who had fled from the gendarmes of the East and from the local bureaucrats whose foreign gibberish he couldn't even understand.

To all of these, America opened its golden door, received them warmly, and, pointing to its riches, said: "All of this I offer you. Go where you wish. Do what you want. From now on your success depends entirely on you yourselves."

Ready to disembark, Kalle and Hannes stood with their suitcases on deck, looking at New York's majestic skyscrapers. Kalle, whose attention tended to focus on material things, stared in amazement at the metropolitan skyline and thought of how much work there must have been for masons and carpenters. Hannes, on the other hand, hardly saw the tall buildings. His imagination soared to include everything he had read about America—its enormous deserts, flourishing wheatlands, magnificent Western mountains, primal forests, and dozens of big cities with their industries and highly paid watchmakers. . . .

He snapped out of it when Kalle nudged him in the ribs.

"Hey, stop staring and let's go. We're in America now!"

There were no problems in going through immigration or customs. From Ellis Island they were taken to New York's Grand Central Station and a train left for Minnesota that evening.

When the night train was well on its way, Hannes suddenly remembered something very important. He grabbed Kalle's wrist.

"Kalle, do you know what?"

"Not until you tell me."

"It's my birthday! I'm eighteen today."

"The hell you say! Well, I suppose you'll become a man yet, especially once you start eating white bread and learn American ways!"

Kalle pulled down his cap, closed his eyes, and leaned comfortably against the upholstered seat. He remembered the shaky, vibrating wooden seats on Finnish trains. "Things in this country are certainly something compared to things in the old country!" he muttered to himself. In a short while, he was asleep.

Hannes wasn't at all sleepy. His thoughts hovered in the past as he relived the incredible experiences of the last few weeks. Then he daydreamed of the future. "America is the land of opportunity," Uncle Matti had said.

He opened up his diary and wrote, "On the train—June 10, 1903: Today we arrived in America and I turned eighteen. Now we are on our way to Duluth and the train is going very fast. . . ."

II
ST. CROIX AVENUE, OR, THE WAY OF THE HOLY CROSS

Situated at the western tip of vast and majestic Lake Superior, Duluth has always been a significant staging-area for Finnish immigrants. The city, which at the turn of the century had 50,000 inhabitants, 35 schools, 43 churches, and 100 saloons, is built on a steep, rocky hillside, with a beautiful vista of the blueness of the lake and the bluer horizon. At the turn of the century Duluth became something of a dispersal point for Finnish immigrants, a kind of inn where the job hunters stopped as they came and went. There were dozens of employment offices from which men were recruited to the mines of Michigan and Minnesota, the wheat fields of Dakota, as well as the forests, sawmills, and railroads of the Northwest. Some Finns had even settled permanently in the city, so that between 1900 and 1905 the Finnish population had risen to four figures.

In this unique town there was an unusual street.

It wasn't a main street nor was it economically significant, unless we take into account its taverns and bordellos. In fact, it's puzzling how this slum street ever got such a sublime, romantic and moral-sounding name as St. Croix Avenue, "the Way of the Holy Cross." A more appropriate name probably would have been simply "the way of the cross," since that's what the street became for hundreds of people, Finns as well as many others.

When Nature distributed its splendors, it probably intended for St. Croix Avenue to become a beautiful park along a lakeshore beach. It was located on a peninsula called Minnesota Point and extended along the scenic shoreline of Lake Superior. The Avenue wasn't very long nor was it wide, but it accommodated an enormous number of human beings and countless stories of life, work, joy and sorrow, suffering and tears. The Avenue also encompassed two opposite worlds: the world of work, drudgery, and the daily struggle for existence on the one hand and the world of sin, debauchery, and vice on the other. The unpaved street, which was dusty when dry and a mud hole when wet, divided these two worlds from each other.

On the eastern, lakeshore side of this slum street the Finnish immigrants had built their homes. In humble, mostly two-story wooden structures there were Finnish boarding houses, restaurants, homes, coffee shops, employment agencies, groceries, clothing stores, and some three saloons. On the other side of the street stood the red-light district, thirteen houses in all, ten of which were painted white. Finnish lumberjacks had named the largest of the white houses, "Big Heikkilä." During the day a ghostly silence pervaded these mysterious buildings. Now and then a lady dressed in silks, satin, and plumes could be seen leaving to do her shopping downtown. But in the evenings and at night the houses would bustle with activity, although from the outside they looked dark and quiet. Not even the thin strips of light streaming from the edges of the drawn shades gave any indication of the joys and delights within. The street-side doors were always locked, which meant that all the traffic was in the back.

These pleasure palaces didn't actually disturb the peace of the Finns. In fact, they hardly noticed them. The residents of each side of the Avenue kept to their own wooden sidewalks. The Finns formed their own little world, a kind of society within a society, which the outer winds of turmoil were unable to disturb. The men went to work every day and came home in the evenings. Those with families returned to their small homes or rented houses; and the singles, who comprised the vast majority, returned to the numerous boarding houses. Among them were various kinds of professionals, tailors, machinists, and contractors, but the largest number of men were unskilled workers who found their livelihood working on the docks, in the sawmills, and at various odd jobs for the city. The Avenue also housed an ever-changing group of lumberjacks, who arrived in the city from the dark depths of the northern Minnesota and Wisconsin backwoods. When they came to relax and have a good time, these "carefree Knights of the Forest," as one Finnish newspaper called them, added their own bit of color and life to the everyday routine on St. Croix Avenue. Businessmen and businesswomen on both sides of the street certainly profited from their visits.

Most of the Finnish women on the Avenue were either young housewives or employees in boarding houses or other business establishments. The majority worked as domestic servants for wealthy families on the East End. From these women the young immigrant men chose wives for themselves and established homes along St. Croix Avenue or "the Point," as it was also called. Two large buildings, Wieland Flats and the Lakeshore Block (also known as the Long Building, "Pitkä Piltinki"), were filled with Finnish newlyweds, although some of the more sophisticated and "Yankee-fied" couples left the Avenue and settled on the hillside in the downtown area. In addition to business activity, Finnish organizational and religious life also centered on the Avenue, where, on the lower end at a suitable distance from the red-light district, the Finns had built a church. In its basement was an assembly hall where the Star of Hope Temperance Society and the Gavel Young People's Society held their organizational activities. The church with its hall was built through the united effort of the congregation, temperance society, young people's society, and the Avenue's businessmen. In the early days these groups worked together harmoniously with mutual tolerance. But later, as the population increased and the community became ideologically aligned, the demons of disagreement destroyed the harmony, replacing it with hate and hostility; and each organization wandered off to follow a path of its own.

The church with its hall, Wieland Flats, the Long Building, as well as the surrounding homes, formed a Finnish community of sorts that came to be called the "parish village." Like all other immigrant groups, the Finns of the "village" had their own colloquial language. *Fingliska* was easy to learn, simple to use, practical, and the vocabulary was vast since you simply added the appropriate Finnish case ending to whatever English word you had in mind. Thus, a boarding house was a "poortihaussi," street became "striitti," stove "stouvi," and building "piltinki." A dollar became a "taala" and the earning and amassing of the "taala" formed the most important article of the Immigrant's Creed.

William R. Lamppa

FINNS OF THE
NORTH COUNTRY

They came with eager eyes and
backs and hands to work the land
and down the trees, never forgetting
the placid woods and clearings of Finland
where many surely left their hearts.

Relentlessly they filtered through the pines
to twisted, rocky, hilly places, and
hung on stubbornly while winter winds
swirled around dim little saunas.

Clearing, plowing, cursing (in Finnish),
loving, laughing, singing, dying,
these bushy-headed, unyielding Finns
grappled with the harsh country.

And, by God, they drank their coffee,
made *mojakka*, *viiliä*, ate rice pudding
with sauce, and treading thin snow
under bitter stars on moonless nights,
looked up and shrugged their shoulders,
and decided to stay a while longer.

Jane Piirto

GRANDMA YOU USED TO

keep a boarding house you fed pulp cutters
and ore dock men and railroaders up at 5
each morning packing lunch buckets
changed their beds fed them dinner too
for three bucks a week *work work work*
you called to my mother and aunt at dawn
sleeping behind the draped arch front room
(now my mother feeds you baby food)

Grandma you came over

on the boat to the promised land in '07
from finland to be a maid in the U.P., michigan
they beat you your cousin took you away
to the next town you were 16 you cleaned up
after rich people; work work work
you yelled at my grandfather a handsome lad
dark wavy hair who drank 'til you
divorced him when people didn't get divorced
(now my mother changes you)

Grandma you scrubbed

floors at the hospital a scouring maid
dumb finn crabby lady on your hands
and knees a cow a garden and 4 kids
can't even talk english waiting on people
all your life; work work work
you yelled at your grandchildren whose mother
was having a baby on your hands
and knees scrubbing clean floors
(now my mother sponge bathes you)

Grandma your mother

wouldn't marry your father in finland
she was a weaver traveled then town to town
with you the fatherless child the outcast
laughed at and scorned so when I came to you
pregnant with my new young husband you held
my hand on your knee and said *love each other*
in a language I never learned: *rakastakaa*
before you died you wanted to make for
my mother serve her just one cup of coffee.

Annie Ruissalo

THE FLOATING CARAVAN
and Other Sketches of
Finnish Immigrant Farm Life
(Compiled and Translated by Timo Riippa)

THE FARMER'S OLD LADY

THE FARMER'S old lady is my title of nobility.

As a farmer's old lady I was Commander-in-Chief of the Horned Army, a rank I held for 40 years until I retired. I rose to that esteemed office in the following way:

We began farming with little more than a saw, an ax, and a hoe. We went into the woods to do our destructive deeds, cutting down trees and selling the logs to make a living. They say that "the death of one means bread for the other." Well, that loaf of bread hopped around in the tree tops and teased us with, "Here I am...come and get me...if you can...."

That's where our upward climb began.

Just like the Indians, we pretty much depended on the whims of fate for our daily vittles. We carried supplies home from town in a backpack. We ate our mush without an eye of butter since we didn't have a cow. We cut down trees and burned and cleared the land. And in the fall we enjoyed berries and mushrooms, which was fine, except for the wolves in the woods. They frightened me. Berry picking was women's work, but I was terrified. My partner just laughed.

Once when he went to town to pick up supplies, he bought a cowbell. We had no cow. In the evening when he returned home tired and hungry, the wolves outside began their usual, frightful howling. As I emptied out the backpack onto the kitchen table, there, at the bottom, was a clanging cowbell.

"What's this for?" I asked.

"It's for you," he said.

I was startled. His mind had finally snapped. I glanced at the door, but outside were those wolves and I saw myself as their evening meal. My own wits, such as they were, teetered on the verge of snapping, when my partner noticed that something was wrong.

"Ah, come on now, let me explain," he said. "It'll soon be berry picking time and you're going out there into the thick woods where you could easily get lost. It's best if you tie this cowbell around your neck so if you can't find your way home, just start ringing it and I'll come out and find you. Besides, it'll scare the wolves away."

I got very angry and things soon developed into an all-out argument which almost ended in an all-out fight. Our first family scuffle, by the way.

Anyway, we cleared the land and plowed and sowed and gradually added livestock. The real man, they say, is the one who faces adversity without giving up. And that is how our climb in life began.

SUNDAY MORNING

It's Sunday morning. I get up early just like on any weekday. Work calls to the worker, they say. The farmer's "lady" doesn't have time to lounge around waiting for breakfast in bed. She has to get up to prepare breakfast for her family, which is still fast asleep. This routine continues year after year without rest or vacation. Always harnessed. Always working sixteen-hour days.

I light the fire in the wooden stove, fill the kettle with water, set it on the stove over the open hole, and go outside to clear my head. As I open the door, I'm greeted by a huge flock of chirping, cheerful birds. It warms my heart to hear them. I'm not alone, after all, but among good friends. As I throw them seeds and other food from the granary, I'm amused to watch the eating contest begin. After feeding, the whole flock flies into a large shade tree in the yard where they warble their thanksgiving hymn to me.

A small wren appears on a nearby fence post. Outwardly it seems insignificant with its long and thin beak that looks like a knitting needle split in half. But just listen to its artistry! Its song is so incredible that it melts the frost from my mind. The singing continues and I'm enchanted. This creature has descended to earth from the azure heights, from the Creator's outer court, to comfort the weary. Its singing silences the heavy heart. The song ends and the singer flies off.

The clanging of cowbells awakens me. Work awaits the worker. My cows have come for breakfast and milking. I open the barnyard gate and then the barn door. The cows go to their own stalls and I tie them in. There is salt and feed in their feeding troughs. They don't have to be encouraged to eat.

I hurry back to the house. First of all I make the coffee and drink to the start of the new day. When breakfast is ready, I wake up the "sleepyheads."

The everyday chores are waiting.

THE FUR COAT

The neighbor lady had a fur coat and I didn't.

Back in those days it was fashionable to have a fur coat and they were warm, which gave me an opportunity to bring up the subject with my partner. So I complained about the cold.

"Well," he said, "wait until summer when the prices go down. Then we'll see. Besides, in summer you probably won't want it anyway."

I was irritated, of course. But what are you going to do? If no, then no.

THE FLOATING CARAVAN

Our farmhouse sat near the banks of a muddy-bottomed, narrow stream. In the spring it was a wide and fast flowing little river, but in summer it sank to the level of a meandering brook that quietly flowed between two steep banks. Upstream where the beaver built their dams, groves of young aspen grew on both banks.

We had a little lap dog, named Pusu, who always wanted to kiss the homefolks, but hated strangers, especially men, who usually teased it. When strange men came over, Pusu would jump and bark and shake the living daylights out of their pants cuffs. It had also learned to drive the cows around if they loitered in the barnyard and didn't leave for the pasture where they spent the night. All you had to do was to point your finger and say, "Pusu, go drive those gorillas into the woods." It would be at their heels and the cows would quickly march off to the woods by the straightest path. The little dog brought a lot of joy into an otherwise monotonous farm life.

We also kept a few geese because the stream would've looked dead without some waterfowl, and they helped keep the banks clean of frogs and other little critters. As the brook flowed quietly between the steep banks, the geese would glide along its surface.

The neighbor lady went to visit her relatives in the States. She had a little pig that her husband didn't want to look after, what with having to take care of the whole farm by himself, so she asked me if I would look after it and I gladly agreed. She came over one day with the piglet in a sack and let it out on the kitchen floor. Pusu was puzzled at first, but when the little stranger went over to its food bowl, the dog took after the intruder to teach it a thing or two. The little pig squealed around the room and didn't quiet down until our neighbor picked it up into her lap.

A few days passed. Peace reigned on the farm. I cared for and fed the little visitor, which lived in an elevated wooden crate where it was quite content with its existence. At feeding time, the dog would watch me closely, put its front paws up on the sides of the crate and listen as I talked to my charge. Pusu, of course, didn't care for any of this and would jealously jump around and bark, to which the piglet would reply with a simple "noh, noh."

It was Sunday.

My partner sat smoking a cigarette in the shade of the house while I was busy inside with dinner. The dog sat beside him, waiting anxiously to be asked to do something. I went to get water from the well and my partner asked if he could let the pig out to run around a bit. "Ok," I said and went on my way. The geese were swimming quietly in the brook and a peaceful Sunday morning quiet prevailed on the farm...until it was suddenly interrupted in a strange way when the freed piglet, delighted with its freedom, snorted "noh, noh" a couple of times and ran toward my partner, at which point Pusu attacked, sinking his teeth into its tail.

The race was on. Squealing in fright, the little pig tried to escape and in its haste ran straight into the stream and the startled geese, who honked excitedly and swam off in formation with the piglet close behind, followed by the dog in earnest pursuit.

We laughed as we watched the floating caravan make its way around the edges of the brook with the frightened geese leading the procession. The voyage continued until the little pig as well as the dog showed signs of tiring and started to sink. Suddenly I became very concerned and jumped into the stream to rescue the drowners. Up to my waist in water, I hoisted the piglet onto one shoulder and lifted Pusu onto the other. But my feet were firmly rooted in the sludge on the bottom, and I couldn't move, as the animals on my shoulders struggled to escape. My partner came over to help, but couldn't do anything from the bank. So *he* lowered himself into the stream and for a moment our entire family bobbed about in the brackish water. The pig and the dog were saved, but my partner swore a blue streak about "every kind of stew that a manly man has to get into."

From the direction of the road we heard the sound of an engine.

Guests from town!

We scampered out of the mud and up the bank just as the car came to a halt.

Sweet Jesus!

Our visitors had piled out of the car to admire the beauty of nature in spring.

"What happened?" someone in the group asked.

My legs were covered with mud. So were my partner's pants. As I did my best to hide behind him, I whispered, "Say something!" My own powers of speech had fled.

"You haven't lost your voices, have you?" our guests wondered.

"We. . .we were just taking a mud bath to ward off rheumatism," I heard through the idling of the engine.

"It prevents *rheumatism*?" they asked in unison.

"Absolutely," my partner answered without batting an eyelash.

"Well, that's good to know," the group decided. "We'll have to remember it."

I sighed with relief and admired my partner's boldness, for which he clearly deserved a PhD.

We led our guests over to a long bench under our large shade tree and then went into the house to get cleaned up. While I started dinner again, my partner put on the coffee, got dressed, and then served it to our visitors, who enjoyed our fragrant wild flowers and my coffee with cream immensely.

Pusu and the piglet rested lazily side by side in the sun.

I prepared a hearty farm dinner, knowing from experience what the townsfolk enjoyed. We ate and talked, above all about the beneficial aspects of mud baths, especially with regard to rheumatism. Finally the guests said their good-byes and promised to return. "And then we'll also heat up the sauna," one of them suggested.

Pusu and the piglet made a truce. In days to come, the dog followed the peaceful little pig around like a guardian as it roamed freely on the farm.

TOWNSFOLK AND THE FARMER

There was a lot of traffic on our farm in the summer, especially during berry picking time when the townsfolk often came over by the carload. We entertained them as best we could. Even during the busiest of times, we always at least put on the coffee pot.

One Sunday when haying was finished, we went by horse into town to visit some friends who often came over to sauna.

In front of their house stood a new car. I went around to the kitchen door in back and knocked. The Mrs. came to the door, opened it a bit, and told me, "We have some guests just now, so come back some other time. . ." and shut the door.

"Thank you," I managed to say and left.

THE SPEAKER AT THE HALL

It's been some thirty-five years now since we argued about the theory of evolution, the idea that humans have descended from the ape, a favorite topic among the men.

We women would listen as the men talked.

Out on the farm we followed the debate in the newspapers without making up our minds. We just didn't know about these lofty matters.

It was summer and we were busy with our usual summer work. One Saturday evening the neighbor came over to say that tomorrow night a speaker was coming to the workers' hall. Were we going?

We decided to go get enlightened.

"Would there be room in your car?" my partner asked.

"You bet," the neighbor promised.

On Sunday we did the chores early and had to hurry, my partner with his shaving and me ironing his suit. I didn't even have time to see after my own appearance, there was so much to do, and my dress needed ironing, but never mind.

After shaving, my partner powdered his face with barber's talcum. He looked so handsome. . . and I was torn with jealousy because it was leap year and I'd no doubt lose him to some woman at the hall. . . but I couldn't back out now. We had to go.

As we were leaving, I quickly patted my cheeks with potato flour since I didn't have any other beauty aids.

"What in the world are you doing?" my partner asked. And laughed.

My temper flared. . . and I reluctantly followed him down the road to the neighbor's.

The hall was packed. There were only a few empty seats near the door.

"Comrades!" the speaker began, "Tonight let us talk about the plasma of the soul and its effect on the human being. You all know, of course, what 'the soul' is."

"Of course we know!!!" someone yelled.

"The soul is the inner structure of the human being," the speaker continued. "And how does it operate? Well. . . we do not know."

"Well, explain it!!!" someone else yelled.

So the speaker explained "the plasma of the soul" and he clarified one side of the issue and then the other, and we didn't understand a thing he said. He went on and on with this stuff about the "plasma" and we accepted it unanimously.

Then he started in on the theory of evolution, describing how the human had descended from the ape.

"Our ancestor lived in the trees because it feared the predators that roamed around everywhere. Now...it is true that we also fear predators, but it is very strange nowadays to find anyone living in the trees! (Laughter)

"Our ancestor had a long tail that disappeared as a result of evolution and the proof of this is your tail bone. At the end of your spine is a moving tail-piece, where a long tail once swung. We know this for a fact. But, in the course of evolution the tail disappeared."

Yet, among other things, the speaker didn't mention how we lost our covering of hair.

After the speech, there were comments from all around:

"He sure gave a great talk!!!"

"I tell you, that man has wits that just won't quit!"

"There's no moving tail-piece in his skull, that's for sure!"

"But what about our fur coat!" the smart-aleck neighbor lady exclaimed. "Those barbers back then must have been real busy!" (Laughter)

The country road was winding and bumpy. The Ford performed an artistic dance over the bumps and so did we in our seats. In fact, the evening at the hall ended as usual. With a dance.

EPILOGUE

So I tended the cattle as Commander-in-Chief along with the dog (sounds impressive, doesn't it?) and after forty years I retired.

Here I now sit and remember the past.

It's a known fact that the Commander-in-Chief is entitled to a proper and fitting retirement. I could now buy a chinchilla coat. But as I sit here within these four walls, I guess I really don't need it.

At least not now during summer.

Lynn Maria Laitala

TIMO'S TEAM

*E*ARLY EVERY MORNING, as I walked to the barn, I thanked God. Then I added a short prayer of thanks to Timo Lahti. Everything I had was, in the larger sense, due to the grace of God but, in the smaller sense, inherited from Timo, God rest his soul.

I knew from what he left behind that Timo was a man of great skill and good taste. There was no site in God's creation more beautiful than the little farm he claimed from the forest. His tight square log buildings with their dovetailed corners were built to stand for generations. He'd traveled as far as North Dakota to find a wife as lovely as my sweet Kaija, and even the child closest to my heart was Timo's own.

For all of that, I never ceased to marvel at Timo's team. They were not poor man's horses. Perfectly matched true blacks, with arched necks and prancing feet, they could have pulled the coaches of royalty.

Timo had trained them himself, and they were a joy to work. Pick up the lines and they leaned into their collars. Cluck and they walked out, matching steps. I'd never driven any like them. Timo got all the credit for training them to work as one, because as matched as they were in appearance, they differed in temperament. Kivi was steady and bold. Loistaa was hot tempered, quick to be alarmed, first to feel a slight. Yet they had learned to pull together, to match steps, to halt in unison.

That team made a pleasure of a day's work. I never tired of watching powerful muscles ripple under sleek coats. We plowed the potato patch, grubbed stumps out of the field, cut the hay and raked it and hauled it to the barn—just me and that team. A man couldn't know better companions. Ten years we worked side by side, and I thought we'd be together another ten, fit as they were.

Kaija and I lived like so many others in those days. We milked twelve cows, raised all their hay and some to sell, sold potatoes and a few eggs and chickens. But there still wasn't enough money to get by, so in the winter I would go off to the logging camps to make a little cash. I hated to leave Kaija and little Clara alone with the chores. The big girls had to stay in town to go to school, and Kaija did not even have a horse to go to town with. I needed Loistaa and Kiva in the logging camp— a team earned as much in a day as a man. I can tell you, too, that I did not mind the admiration that I got from the other men as the owner of such a team.

That winter of 1924 I was working at Eino Norha's logging camp. I was put to hauling a bobsled from the landing in the woods across the lake to the railroad tracks. The ice was two feet thick. We'd been working for three weeks in thirty below weather on that road. In one place the road curved around a stream that flowed into the lake, but the current must have shifted under the ice. We didn't know the running water had made the ice thin.

It was near the end of the day. I was hauling my last load, logs piled ten feet high on the bobsled, me sitting up on the load. As always I watched my team with pleasure, but I was thinking ahead to the warm barn, of rubbing them down, feeding them their evening oats. The air was getting even colder. Sitting still as I was, arms outstretched holding the lines, I could feel the chill working through my heavy wool mackinaw. My hands were nearly frozen inside my choppers.

Ahead of me the ice cracked like the sound of gunfire. Kiva dropped out of sight in the gloom. The sled slid toward the hole, but Loistaa scrambled to the side, digging caulked shoes into ice, and the sled stopped. My knife was out of its sheath before I had landed on the ice. I cut through the hame strap on Loistaa's harness and he lunged free. Kiva thrashed in the water. I freed his tugs from the evener on the bobsled, and then lay down on the ice to catch hold of his bridle. If I could hold his head out of the water until another sled came we could haul him out with the other team. My foot slipped into the hole. My boot filled with water. My arms were soaking. I got ahold of the bridle: on the far shore I heard the clink of harness and shoe as the next team came out of the woods on to the ice road.

My arms grew numb. I couldn't feel my hands holding the bridle. Kiva shook himself free with one last plunge, and slipped out of sight under the ice.

Eino Norha brought me to the hospital in Vermilion. The doctor saved my hands but the foot was frozen and he had to cut part of it off. The doctor said I was done with logging. My hands and feet would freeze more easily now, and the next time I would lose them altogether.

I didn't have the heart to go back to work in the logging camp, anyway. Never would I know such a team.

They sent me home to Kaija, hands and feet bound, useless for the winter months. No help at all, just adding to her work. I would go out to the barn and sit with Loistaa. He was mourning. Loistaa, flash of light, had lost his spirit, and so had I. God punishes us for our pride.

I could have gotten another horse to farm with, but unless I went back to the logging camps there never would be enough money.

We stayed on through the summer. Loistaa did the work of two horses, with head bowed and slow step. I limped behind him. Kaija sold some cows.

Late in the summer Kaija came back from town with news.

"Matt, the school janitor left town. They asked if you wanted the job."

"How can I take such a job? How do I plow and plant and tend the farm?"

"We will move to town, Matt."

There was no other way. We sold the rest of the cows. A Yankee family bought our farm. We moved our things to a frame house in Sawyer.

Kaija and I came back one last time to walk the worn paths between the buildings: the house and barn, blacksmith shop and sauna. Timo's dream. Our home.

We drove the wagon as far as the neighbor's house and left Loistaa there with Reino.

Slowly Kaija and I walked to town.

Marlene Ekola Gerberick

Seven selections from a sequence of poems in
homage to Gerberick's paternal grandmother,
Taava Miina Ekola, a traditional folk healer from
Hakojärvi, Finland.

IN OLD PHOTOGRAPHS OF YOU

You look direct, piercing, unwavering;
like this one where you are
standing on the farmhouse steps.
How old were you? Maybe eighty-one or -two.
There's not an extra pound
on your bony frame. You wear
clothing of plain, strong cloth.
Some kind of cap
covers your thin, bunned hair.
You don't smile. Just stand there,
looking straight ahead
as if you were defying the unseen
photographer. Old Finnish curses
seem to hang ominously in the air
so that even now, forty-five
years later,
I look at you and shiver,
like a child.

OF LANGUAGE AND GRANDMA EKOLA

I remember going to Grandma's at Christmas,
practicing all the way there,
Hyvää Joulua, Hyvää Joulua. . .

I would say it first thing.
She would lead me into her bedroom
reeking of strange medicines,
reach into the bottom drawer of her dresser
bring forth a handful
of round pink peppermints
each with four x's pressed in the top,
put them in my hand,
smile.

But there would be tears
running down her cheeks,

for I knew no more of her language than that.
She knew no more of mine.

VANHA ISO-ÄITI

Old Grandmother you haunt me still
your long black skirt
makes for my shoulders a heavy cloak.
Your high button shoes
tramp roughly
over the meadows of my mind.

Here in Bedford, New York, family lineage
is cleaner, finer than it was
in our Peninsula.
These people bequeath bone china,
elegant houses, delicate laces,
old leather bound first editions
to their offspring, along with a certainty
of their Eastern Seaboard Who They Are.

Grandmother, you gave me a rougher cloth
out of which to make my life.
Nubby, dark, homespun, wide
with the strongest warp and weft
I've seen anywhere,

but you do not fade decently away.
No.
Every day you return.
Every day you take my measure still.

ISO KARHU

It was summer
only so dry
you could hardly believe it,
no berries for hungry bears
so this mean, fetid one
had it in mind
to fill his stomach
with calf.

Taava Miina saw
from a long way off
the circle of frightened cows,
the calves
inside that circle,
the bear spiraling
closer, closer;
long claws and squinty
evil eyes.

Taava Miina didn't even
slow down.
She picked up
a big stick
just as if it had been
lying there, just for
that purpose.
She picked up that stick,

gave a good swing,
and, WHACK! She gave
that bear a good crack
on the head.
Iso Karhu saw stars.
And Taava Miina?
She rounded up those cows
even though they bellowed some.
She just rounded up those cows
and led them on home.

BLOODCUPPING

*A folk healing practice, usually done in the sauna,
whereby the patient was rid of superficial, bad blood by
suction (using cow's horns) and tiny, sharp blades.*

A sauna, dimly lit
as a path deep in a dense
forest at twilight

yet strangely red.

Heat weighing down
making the air
a heavy burden

yet red.

On the lowest bench,
her underskirts pulled high,
lies a woman

red.

Taava Miina squats
on a stool
hunched over that woman

red.

Taava Miina's blue eyes
fierce with concentration
her hands

red

move everywhere; here the cow's horns
there the blade.
Something is oozing, running

red.

Red mixes with water
in the old washtub
on the sauna floor

red.

Afterward
the woman says
her legs are as light as two birds

(both red).

They want to fly!
Later, scars like bird tracks.
Yes,

and red.

YES

She'd been dead then
for two years;
I must have been
about twelve or so.
Mother was poking
a fork into the fiercely
boiling potatoes, testing.
I told her that I liked

them on the hard side.
Mother looked at me
long and steadily
and said, "You're
just like Grandma Ekola.
She liked them that way.
You're just like her."

A quiver of recognition
went through me.
It was something
I think I'd always known.
"Yes," I said.
"Yes. I am."

TWIGS, FEATHERS, STONES, MOSS

That summer
when I finally got to your
side of the ocean
when I finally
found your forests
your shore
your lake
your soft moss
covered stones,
your heather
under the blue
blessing of your
skies;
the forests, the air
the wildly fragrant
wildflowers were filled
with the waiting spirit of you.

I went down your forest path,
let my being become filled
with your being
and in this trance-like state
my hands
became your hands.

My hands
your hands recreated signals/
signs of twigs, feathers, stones,
moss. Signals you'd made
once before
just before you left,
when you were young
with tears flowing down
your cheeks, for you knew
you had to leave.
But you also knew I'd come,
your grand-daughter, spirit
of you, someday. You wanted
to show me your way.

So finally that summer
we sat together, you and I
on soft green-covered stones
and with
twigs, feathers, stones, lichen,
feathers, twigs, pebbles,
feathers we made
signs of our blood-
ties. Our oneness
you and I together
at last in the gentle forest
of Hakojärvi.

Rebecca Cummings

THE HAIR BROOCH

R EINO, ESKO, AND my father sent their sister Vappu a ticket so that she also could come to America. At first, Vappu seemed happy enough, setting up housekeeping for them. After a while, though, she slid into bewildering periods of dark silence, broken by bursts of anger, and threatened often to do away with herself. In this way, Vappu ruled until my father said that he was going to get married.

My father met my mother at a temperance meeting in town. I can see why he must have been attracted to her. She was a dark-haired, dark-eyed beauty of Swedish descent, the daughter of a learned clergyman. Even in later years, she was slender and regal in appearance. Father, on the other hand, was short and muscular with the ruddy complexion and dark blond hair that many Finns have. He had a full mustache that he twirled absentmindedly when deep in thought. He told noisy stories that made others laugh, and people liked to be around him. Mother must have known that with him, life would never be dull. He used to tease her, sometimes unmercifully. Although she wouldn't laugh, she did smile, secretly pleased, I think.

When my father broke the news to his two brothers and sister that he was going to marry, Aunt Vappu threw herself into a violent rage. She had grown used to doing for them and didn't want to change. She had seen change enough for a lifetime. The three brothers, who were playing cards at the table that rainy Saturday, made light of her words. Becoming more incensed, she said she would kill herself. They had heard these threats before, though, and only laughed.

She tied her kerchief under her chin and blundered from the house, leaving the doors wide open to the pouring rain and the cheerful singing of spring peepers. While the brothers continued to play at cards in the warm dry kitchen, Vappu crossed the rocky cow pasture to the pond that in early spring overflowed its banks but in summer was no more than a mudhole where the cow and its heifer wallowed. The water was deep and cold, but it wasn't deep enough for her to drown. She got only chest high before it started to level off. Finally, her dress and shoes wet and covered with mud, she went back home, furious that not one of her brothers thought enough to save her.

When Father finally left to get married, she refused to go to the wedding. She remained behind and put a match to the sauna so that Reino and Esko had to rebuild it when they returned.

A few years later, a tree fell on Reino, and he died. Vappu blamed Esko for Reino's untimely death, for not being quick enough. Esko knew that he had done all he could, but still he carried a burden of guilt. Now there were only the two, brother and sister, locked in silence.

Esko, like my father, was easy prey for any traveling man with a new invention who found his way to the end of the long winding road. Maybe it was that Esko was starved for the quick moment of companionship, or maybe it was that he thought he had need for whatever it was that was for sale. One time he bought a milk separator, the latest thing, even though he had only one milking cow and could have continued to do the separating by hand. And then he bought the telephone.

Esko liked the idea of turning the crank and getting Central. He liked the lifeline of the telephone wire stretching from some unknown spot, from pole to pole, right into his own house. Vappu, however, hated the telephone, a constant reminder that her privacy had been invaded. Because she was also tight with money, she hated the cost as much as the instrument itself. Esko reassured her that they'd soon make up the cost, for when the neighbors came to use it — as they were bound to — she could charge for the call.

Just as Esko predicted, the neighbors did come — walking a mile or more to talk to an ailing sister or to send a message to a son in town. Vappu usually hid when the neighbor lady or child came, for she had no desire to associate with folks, even with those who spoke Finnish. If Vappu heard the crunch of a footstep outside or the dog's bark, she would scurry to some private place and peer through a crack in the woodshed wall or the swallow hole in the hay loft. If Esko was at home, he would invite the neighbor inside. Otherwise, the caller would walk in and go to the second room, where the telephone hung on the wall. When Vappu could at last see the neighbor trudging back down the lane, she would go to see what had been left in payment on the kitchen table — five cents, if the money was to be had, otherwise a couple of eggs or a few potatoes. She would then count the rusks in the crock, to make sure none were missing.

As much as Vappu refused to associate with folks who came to her house, she would go to theirs if summoned for medical reasons. She knew about healing and could make remedies from comfrey and lady's mantle and poultices from mustard and pine tar. She dried strange smelling herbs in the rafters over the woodstove. She could do massage, for her hands were strong and nimble, and she practiced cupping or blood letting. Father told me she had a set of polished cow horns and a sharp little knife with an ivory handle in a velvet-lined wooden box which she kept on top of the wardrobe.

She would go out in any kind of weather or at any time of day or night with her cloth bag of remedies and her box of cupping instruments. She expected payment but would take a swatch of cloth as readily as a half dollar.

We always heard how Vappu loved money. She had a fortune, they said, hidden away in the eaves or beneath the floor boards. After she died, some money was found, three hundred dollars or so. But who wouldn't love money, after all, if you had to go out and beg the way Vappu had? Her father, who was a stone cutter, died of lung disease, and there were the four children. Her mother, a laundress, was sickly and weak. Since Vappu was a small girl, she was the one sent out to beg. I wonder how she did it? Did she whine and make her eyes pathetic? Did her hand dart out from under her shawl?

I met Aunt Vappu only one time. My father wanted to visit his brother Esko and perhaps make amends with his sister. He chose me, the youngest, to go with him. On the way, he remembered one thing and another, how she tried to drown herself and was furious when no one rescued her, and he told me about her skills as a healer and about her cupping tools. He laughed a lot, and I was in high spirits because we had embarked on a great adventure.

The house with its rough plank siding in the middle of the clearing looked stark to me. There were fruit trees, apple and pear, and thick growths of raspberry and blackberry bushes. To one side and to the front of the house, down a grassy rise, were a tool shed and a sauna. As we approached, a yellow dog raced toward us, barking.

We drove up the lane and around to the back of the house, for the door—with a bright red geranium on either side of the stone stoop— was at the back, not the front. Father parked the Model A close to a patch of leafy rhubarb by the barn, all rough and bleak. He went into the house without knocking.

Aunt Vappu's eyes pierced through us from where she sat knitting in an armless rocker on the far side of the woodstove. Her hair was parted in the middle and was pulled back into a tight thin bun. Her face was sunken because she had no teeth. At the neck of her dress, she wore an ornament, an oval silver-rimmed brooch with a pale blond knot under a curve of glass. A black and white cat with long white whiskers slept curled near her feet in the dusty stream of sunlight that poured through the single window. It was warm and very close in the room.

The knitting needles clicked.

"This is your niece—Kirsti," Father said, making his voice loud and jovial.

"Christine," I corrected, saying the name the teacher at school had given me.

"KIRSTI," he repeated.

I shrank behind him.

We sat at a table that was small because its leaves were folded down. There were two chairs, one at either end, and Father sat in the one in front of the sunny window. The big black and white cat stretched. I wondered how we would all fit to eat. Maybe we'd take turns sitting in the chairs. The cat, its tail twitching, watched me and suddenly jumped onto my lap. I was surprised at its weight. It kneaded its claws into my dress and purred as I patted it.

Father asked for coffee. My aunt sighed and pushed herself out of the chair to get up to make it. She put some small round sticks into the stove, and the coffee boiled reluctantly. He commented on the weather and the long drive from Massachusetts—a whole day. He fingered his mustache and drummed his fingers on the table as we waited for my uncle to come in.

There was little in the kitchen to make it cheerful. Along one wall was a chipped work cabinet with cans and jars of household goods— baking powder, flour, and coffee. On the top shelf were three sand- colored bowls with bright blue rims, one with a deep crack. Behind Father's head was a calendar with a photograph of Niagara Falls. I had never been to Niagara Falls, but I had seen pictures of it in my geography book so I recognized it. Wilton Home and Farm Insurance, the calen- dar said. Dusty bunches of dried things like witch's claws hung overhead with spidery threads connecting them.

From where I sat, I could see the telephone on the wall in the other room. I wondered if I were to use it, whether my aunt would charge me five cents for the call. Glancing at her, I thought she probably would. The light reflected from her oval brooch as she rocked. Perhaps she had worn the ornament because we were company. The room was warm, and I wished I could go outside, but I continued to stroke the cat, not daring to speak or move.

At last my uncle came in. He strongly resembled my father except that he was thinner and, like my aunt, had no teeth. I was proud my father earned so much money that he could buy his own teeth. "Hello. Hello," Esko said.

My father stood and offered his hand. I hung behind him.

That night, Father went ahead of my uncle up three steps to a closed door and then climbed a creaking stairway to the attic. I slept in a big oak bed beside my aunt in the other room downstairs, the one with the telephone on the wall. I pretended to fall asleep but lay awake with my head boosted on a hard round bolster. I could hear crickets and an owl and, at last, my aunt's snores. She didn't stir all night, nor did I. In the morning, she was already in the kitchen when I woke up. As I lay in bed, I could see the wooden box on top of the wardrobe and wanted to look inside at her instruments but, of course, could not. As I dressed, I peeped behind a long white cloth with a Bible verse embroidered on it, hanging against the wall. Behind it, her nightgown hung on a hook. I hung my nightgown over hers.

As we ate breakfast, I tried to speak to my father in English, but he was brusque with me and wouldn't answer except to say that I was to speak in Finnish. I struggled to understand what they talked about. We had a porridge which looked thin and unappetizing but, with a dot of butter on it, was very tasty. Every day for breakfast and supper we had the same porridge, and I grew to love it and asked my mother to make it when we got home.

My uncle showed me how the yellow dog did tricks. She would beg for a scrap of bread in a pretty way with her ears cocked up. After the count of three, which my uncle said she would understand only in Finnish, she would roll over. I counted in English and, sure enough, she didn't understand. She would fetch wood from the woodshed when my uncle gave the command and carry the stick in her mouth and drop it in the woodbox behind the stove. She seemed happy to have a little girl to play with instead of just the big black and white cat and waited outside the door for me. When she heard my step, her tail thumped against the geraniums, whisking their scent into the air.

My father spent the days with Uncle Esko, helping him hay and rebuild the hen house that was falling in. They stopped often to rest and drink coffee and tell stories. They went fishing, two or three times early in the morning, to the brook way back in the woods. They took me with them once. Tiny black flies caught in my hair and burrowed into my ears and the corners of my eyes. The back of my neck became so infected that my aunt treated me in the steaming sauna by switching my neck with springy birch twigs and then rubbing ointment on me. I worried because I though she would get her cupping instruments and would want to bleed me.

The trout that we caught were small and beautiful. I remember how delicious they were, dipped in crumbs and fried in butter in the big black frying pan.

I played with the dog behind the sauna, finding secret caverns in the tangle of grape vines, and I picked wild strawberries in a clearing that Uncle Esko showed me. I left the bowl of small red berries on the kitchen table and was surprised that night when we had stewed strawberries for dessert. I tried to pick more the next day, but I had already picked most of them, so I just ate what I had in my dish. They had been warmed by the sun and were fragrant and sweet.

In the late afternoons, I fetched the cow. I went barefoot through the rocky pasture, avoiding the thistles and cowflaps that were so dry I could have picked them up and thrown them. I listened carefully for the cowbell to know where she was. I carried a long stick so that I could tap her bony rump to make her move along, but I never hit her hard nor did I make her hurry.

One night I woke up, for the moonlight was shining onto the bed. It was very quiet, and I realized that my aunt was also awake and was looking at me. At first when I turned and saw her eyes on me, I was frightened, but she said something that I couldn't hear and touched me lightly on the hair. For a while, I lay very still, but then I put my hand in hers. Her hand was dry and warm. I heard a rooster crow. Perhaps he thought it was morning, it was so bright. I must have gone back to sleep, and it was late the next day when I thought about it. Maybe it didn't really happen, though, and it was only a dream.

On the morning that we were to leave, Aunt Vappu told me to follow her. She went through the woodshed and door, beyond the rocky pasture to the marshy pond. I had to run to keep up with her. I wanted to ask her if that was the pond where she had tried to drown herself, but I didn't. I followed her along a swampy path through thick alders. She spread aside some leafy bushes to show me a nest of four baby birds.

I don't know what kind they were. They were so small, but their open mouths and beaks were huge. My aunt was watching me closely. I started to reach for one, but she caught my hand and told me not to touch it, or I would leave my scent and the mother would abandon it. I wouldn't want that to happen, would I? It surprised me to hear her talking so much, and I pulled my hand back.

She fumbled at her neck for the heavy silver-rimmed brooch with the blond knot under the curve of glass. "You must remember your Aunt Vappu," she said, folding my fingers around the solid metal of the brooch. She walked away, so fast that she outdistanced me.

I heard the honk of the horn and my father calling me. I ran over the rocky pasture to the house. Our suitcases were already in the back, and my father had the engine running. Now he sat behind the wheel, his elbow on the open window, talking to his brother.

"Kirsti!" he shouted again, but I was already there.

"Where's Vappu?" he asked. "What a strange one she is. All these years and she still carries a grudge." He shrugged and said to Esko, "Tell her good-bye."

Then we were off. The yellow dog chased the car for a while down the lane and then hung back as we sped away. I sat on my knees, the upholstery prickly against my legs, and watched through the rear window, the house with its rough plank siding, the tool shed, and the sauna disappearing behind us. I imagined Aunt Vappu, one eye to a crack in the wall, watching.

An hour or so later, when we were on the open road, I said, "Look, Father. Look what Aunt Vappu gave me." I still spoke in Finnish.

He looked at the brooch in the palm of my hand. "Vappu gave that to you?" he said in surprise. "You know what it is, don't you?"

I shook my head.

"Hair." He was silent for a long time, and I examined the pale blond lock, seeing how fine it was, wondering where it had come from. We drove past a crumbling farmhouse where a little girl was pushing a boy in a wheelbarrow. They both waved, and I waved back.

It was years later when I was grown and had three children of my own that I found Aunt Vappu's brooch. I examined the pale blond knot in the silver oval, remembering my aunt and thinking that the hair was the same color as Margaret's, my own little girl.

"Whose hair do you suppose it was?" I asked my mother who sat crocheting in the corner chair of the guest bedroom.

"Her daughter's, of course," she replied, glancing at me, her dark eyes sharp above wire-framed eyeglasses. White thread danced from her knobbed finger to the hook as she worked. "Don't look so surprised. Didn't you know?"

"No one ever told me—"

"No, I guess not—it was her shame, and no one spoke of it, but I suppose it doesn't matter anymore. She gave the child away. To the family she worked for. Poor thing. No wonder she was so strange." Her thread swirled from the ball to the hook to the snowflake pattern.

I rubbed my thumb over the smudged glass, cleaning it. Then, standing in front of the wide mirror over the dresser, I pinned the hair brooch to the neck of my navy blue dress.

Sirkka Tuomi Holm

STAGE RECOLLECTIONS AMONG THE FINNS

*A*s THE OLD saying goes, get ten or twelve Finns together in one area and before you know it, there's a theater group. This love of theater and literature, including poetry, is as old as the Finns themselves, as evidenced by the survival of the *Kalevala* tales which were handed down orally from generation to generation over hundreds of years. And, as we all know, the Finnish language has survived despite being ignored by the educated classes who spoke and read Swedish, considering it a more civilized tongue. The stubborn and tenacious nature of the Finns in clinging to their own tongue not only saved the language but reinforced a love and respect for literature and theater among the ordinary people. Coupled with this heritage was the church's insistence that everyone should be able to read. There were schools set up every spring just to teach the youngsters how to read, *rippi kouluja* (confirmation schools). I remember my mother saying that *rippi koulu* whetted her appetite for learning, and the rest of her life she constantly read and studied on her own, being especially fond of theater and poetry.

Having been born into a family in which both my father and mother were heavily involved in plays, choruses, orchestras and bands, I made my debut on the amateur stage of the Socialist Opera in Virginia, Minnesota, at the tender age of three months. I might add that, in my debut, I lay in a cradle while the leading lady sang to me. I've been told that I gurgled happily during her entire song and stole the show, thus reinforcing the old show biz warning never to act with children or dogs — they'll steal the show every time.

There are plenty of funny stories and some not so funny; but amusing stories by themselves cannot explain the spirit of the Finnish-American theater movement in the United States and Canada. Funny stories cannot explain why a man who spent ten to twelve hours a day digging iron ore in an open pit hundreds of feet down in the earth, arriving home afterwards so exhausted he could hardly eat his dinner, would wash up afterwards and walk through the cold in the winter-

time and sweltering heat in the summertime to go to a hall—to a bare
stage—and rehearse a play over and over again. He might have been
a farm hand, a *renki*, in Finland with only enough education to be able
to read a little. Perhaps his accent was that of a Hämäläinen or an
Eteläpohjanmaanlainen and his movements were not graceful. But this
man learned; he learned to overcome his accent and make his Finnish
more universal; he learned to move on a stage and how to work with
other actors; and he learned how to take direction from a director and
even how to make up his face and help others with makeup. And he
still continued to dig in the mine day after day, year after year, and performed in play after play. Sometimes he even began directing plays
himself. Those of us who fall under the category of white-collar workers
or professionals cannot understand the complete physical exhaustion
that only a manual laborer can know; it takes a strong person indeed
to overcome the exhaustion of physical labor and yet be able to cross
that great divide into the realm of the cultural world and self-expression.

The women were the same. Most of them were domestic workers who
worked long hours and had the same type of background in Finland,
many of them almost illiterate, coming from crofters' or sharecroppers'
families. These were the people who created the Finnish theater movement in the United States and Canada, and they brought great joy to
thousands of other Finns, the shyer ones who could not be persuaded
to take part in a play. They brought their children up to appreciate theater,
poetry, and literature, and taught them how to speak clearly and even
to express their thoughts.

During the first sixty years of this century, the Finns established halls
and theater groups in the United States and Canada and were frequently
involved in athletic groups and political organizations as well. For awhile
they were able to bring some directors from Finland, and there were
some professional companies in some areas, depending on the size of
the Finnish population. These directors taught the immigrants acting
and speech and even directing. Then, when funds ran out or the directors returned to Finland, the students became the teachers and directors. I can recall from my mother some of the tales of these impresarios
who took "greenhorns" from the farms of Finland—people who had,
in some instances, never been near a city or a theater but who were
eager to learn—and shaped them and made them become aware of
speech, of enunciation, and of how to move on the stage. My mother
said they had a play in Worcester, Massachusetts, where the director
was tearing his hair out with frustration. The play was about one
family—the parents, the grandparents, and children—and each actor
came from a different part of Finland and had a dialect which he or she

struggled to overcome in order to speak general Finnish. There was a Porilainen, a Hämäläinen, a Karjalainen, an Eteläpohjanmaanlainen. Came the night of the performance and each one reverted to his native dialect. But the audience—those wonderful, understanding audiences—saw and listened to the play and enjoyed it immensely, accepting this unique family with its various dialects.

Then there was the time when a particularly shy man was asked to be in a play and only consented when he found out he had one line. He was to make an entrance and say something like, "The carriage is here." He studied his one line assiduously, going over each inflection—the *carriage* is here—the carriage *is* here—the carriage is *here*. The night of the performance arrived and he stood by the doorway, patiently waiting to go on stage, palms in a sweat, but alert and ready. He thought it was longer than usual but waited. Finally the curtain came down and the actors walked off the stage. He asked one of them when he was supposed to come on and the actor said, "Oh, we missed some lines including your cue, but that's all right—we got the gist of the thing."

Finns did not give just two or three plays a year, but gave them once and even twice a month. Some were one-act plays and some were five acts with prologues *and* epilogues. Some were musicals and some were heavy historical dramas. Consequently, they had to rely on the most important person in the Finnish theater, namely the prompter or *kuiskari*, who sat in a little box, covered with a rounded lid, under the stage, his or her eyes level with the actors' knees or ankles. The prompter was usually one of the actors who was gifted with a loud stage whisper, clear enunciation, and fortitude—who could sit scrunched up in a little hole under the stage for hours in the heat of the summer and the cold of the winter, and, with the aid of a little light bulb and a quick eye, prompt the actors line by line. Since plays were held so frequently, it was impossible to memorize them because of the time constraints. As I remember very clearly from both my parents, there were never enough rehearsals because of the varied shift work of the actors, so, of necessity a technique was developed where the prompter, while the actor was saying his line, would be whispering the next line. And he, while saying his line, would be listening for the next. When it worked, it worked well and could be very smooth indeed. But when the actors were not attuned to the prompter, dead spaces developed with occasionally someone from the audience yelling out the line for the now panicked actor who had drawn a blank. I can recall sitting in the audience in Baltimore and watching one of the actors who had forgotten every line he ever knew. He stood there with a glassy look in his eye and in a profusion of sweat and finally leaned down to the prompter and said,

"What did you say?" A man behind me yelled, "The prompter said to exit right." My father told me of the time in Virginia, Minnesota, when a prompter, a stage veteran who was quick and very capable, all of a sudden discovered that the actors were saying lines not in the script. She leafed through the pages, trying to find out where they were, and then, like a light bulb going off over her head, she remembered a play given the previous week with the same dialogue. It took a great deal of desperate whispering to get the cast back on track.

In Baltimore, the prompter always took the curtain calls with the rest of the cast. The curtains would close at the end of the play, and we could hear a scrambling for position taking place behind the curtain. Then the curtain would bulge out with someone trying to keep it closed while the lid was taken off the prompter's box or *koppi*. Occasionally we would get a glimpse of a couple of the men dragging out the lady prompter who, as she got older, got stiffer, and there would be great noise and puffing and exclamations. All would settle down and the curtains would part. The audience, which had stopped applauding by now, renewed the applause, and there in the middle of the stage stood the prompter, beaming happily, with the performers.

Next in importance to the prompter was the stage hand, or *kulissi mies*, who frequently created a hazard with his habit of tippling on the job. Perhaps he did it to bolster himself for the evening's work. Who could blame him, for he often couldn't get to rehearsals and learn the cues of when to open and close the curtains, or roll a piece of metal to make it sound like thunder. So there would be a last-minute briefing. Some stage hands were better than others and more alert, but it was not unusual to see a play end with the actors standing woodenly as a couple of them, perhaps thinking the audience couldn't see, whispered loudly from the upstage corner of their mouths, "Curtain, curtain." The stage hand had quite a job. He would have to change the heavy flats with the back metal props and also drop a corresponding scenery roller curtain in the back, or lift them — and they were heavy. He would lug furniture around and carry on make-believe rocks and even for some scenes hammer a fence to the floor. One time in Warren, Ohio, the stage hand forgot to put a door in the center at the back of the stage. The actor said his lines, turned, and walked into the flat. He stood there and then, desperately seeking an exit, climbed out of a window next to where the door was supposed to be. This brought the audience more than a little amusement since just two lines previously one of the characters had looked out the window and mentioned being on the third floor.

Another time in Worcester, Massachusetts, a couple had a touching love scene on the stage, and, to make it more dramatic, a snowfall was arranged. The snow came down in spurts (as it was thrown by the stage hand) but the audience was tolerant as usual and accepted it. However, they were a little startled when the entire bushel of snow together with the basket, fell down on the stage beside the couple. But the actors were troopers. They continued with their touching scene, holding hands and going on with their lines. In a few moments, the stage hand came staggering out of the "woods," bent over, picked up the "snow," dumped it in the basket and staggered off stage. Then, in another few moments, the clumps of snow began descending and the actors didn't even bat an eyelash. Now that's stage presence!

It was the job of the wardrobe mistress not only to costume the actors but also to look after makeup and the set design as well. In some areas, three people did this one job. However, my mother did all three jobs for at least twenty years in Baltimore, and I would help her with the makeup. Habit is hard to overcome. When the Finns were young, some of them were character actors and frequently played older people. They got used to the makeup artist asking them how old they were supposed to be. I can recall when I made up the face of a 65-year-old stage veteran and started to put the base on. He looked me in the eye and seriously said he was supposed to be an older person and would need liner on his face for lines! I gently said that he wouldn't be needing it — all he would have to do is to act old.

The women who made costumes were often talented in sewing. There was a distinct advantage to working as a domestic in a wealthy home, for when there was a play that showed rich people, the women knew what type of clothing was correct. There was one play I can recall in Baltimore when the cast from another city presented a play. This was done frequently. A group would "go on the road," visiting another Finnish community and everyone would have a wonderful time renewing old acquaintances. At any rate, in one scene, an actor came out munching on what was very obviously a bologna sandwich, and announced how good the caviar was — after all, it was *supposed* to be caviar. One could immediately tell that no woman in that cast ever worked in a *piika paikka* (a domestic job)!

I can recall when we lived in Warren, Ohio, in the twenties and we went on the road with a play. One of the women had an old car with isinglass windows, and it was a windy snowy day when we drove off to the neighboring Finnish community of Conneaut. Actually, it turned into a blizzard, but we made it to the hall, gave the show, and came back that same night. But spirits were high coming back, and I slept very warmly in the crush of human bodies — there must have been six or seven of us in that old car. Now when I read biographies of people in show business who talk about their times on the road, I think those brave Finns were every bit as professional in going on with the show!

Then there were the quick-thinking actors, as at the time in Lanesville, Massachusetts, when one of the actors had to stab someone in the play. He came to the moment when he was supposed to stab the other actor and he froze – he had forgotten his knife! However, being a real trooper he lunged forward and started to choke his fellow actor who, although startled, sensed that he should respond, gurgled appropriately, and dramatically sank to the floor, dying beautifully. All would have been well and the audience never would have known the difference, except that the two other actors on the stage were not as imaginative and did not rise to the occasion. They were to scream, "He's been stabbed, he's been stabbed!" They could have quickly changed it to, "He's been choked, he's been choked!" But, alas, they stuck with the lines they had rehearsed.

In Baltimore, where all the men worked at the steel mill on three shifts, there were many occasions when they had to rehearse at midnight since that was the only time they could all get together. I can recall many times in the winter when members of the cast would huddle around a pot-bellied stove trying to get warm and waiting for their cue to go on the stage. As a child, I can remember going to endless rehearsals, and when not in the show, sleeping on benches, and listening to good-natured kidding of the theaterfolk. Very often those who were most active in theater were looked upon as bohemians by the rest of the Finns; and being show biz folk, they were more free in their speech and actions than the Finns who were never in plays. It was a miniature of the entire world where people in theater are sometimes frowned upon because they are, to use an old-fashioned word, "loose."

The children were included in all theatrical enterprises and we had our own festivals where some of us got up on the stage, scared to death: some played the violin, or piano, some sang in quavering voices, some recited a poem, very fast, and some danced. I shall never forget in one melodrama when a union leader had been murdered and his body was lying on the stage while the soloist was reciting very dramatically to piano accompaniment. We got our cue and another girl and I came running out in white cheesecloth and flower bands in our hair and we skipped around the "corpse" tossing flowers on it. There wasn't a dry eye in the house, and after we got off the stage, we cried and cried, carried away with our own performance. My father then lectured to me as a fellow performer and said that no actor should ever lose control of himself – let the audience do the crying. He was a good actor, particularly at comedy, and had a real respect and love for theater, and he was to teach me about going on with the show at a future time.

Frequently, there would be a dramatic moment when one of the actors would whip out a gun and shoot someone, with blanks of course. The first two or three rows were traditionally saved for the children. However, all we had to do was to see a gun and we would stampede to the back of the hall to the ladies' and gentlemen's cloakrooms where we huddled in the corners, fingers in our ears waiting for the loud shot. After the bang, we'd run back to our seats, giggling nervously, and the adults would whisper loudly, "*Kakarat, olkaa hiljaa*" (Children, be quiet). On a busy night in some of the shows, there were several stampedes and occasionally an adult would grab a child, any child as he or she flew by, and make him or her sit down. The most difficult moment for me when I was in a play was when my father was to be shot. He warned me ahead of time that I was to behave, and not to panic on the stage. The actor whipped out his gun and from the corner of my eye I could see all my friends scurrying to the back. Just as I was about to leap over the footlights and join the stampede, I saw my father give me a look (with his upstage eye) that reminded me of his lecture that a good actress fears nothing and the show must go on. I stood my ground and stayed on the stage acting appropriately.

As for other theatrical forms of expression, poetry was close to plays. And frequently the poems were very long indeed. As a child, I remember trying to keep track of how many pages there were to go before the poem was concluded. There was always one of the reciters whose hands shook, and this was universal in each Finnish community. Actually, in retrospect, I wish we had tapes of these artists, because most of them were remarkably good and held their audiences spellbound. The most effective way to bring poetry as an art to the people was through group poetry presentations or *joukko runoja*. This was truly an art which, unfortunately, has not been developed in English. A group would recite in unison and have soloists, like a chorus, and could give a very effective dramatic presentation. For instance, the poem, "*Jaakko Ilkka*," may be too dramatic in today's world for some people but, when recited, it could raise the hairs of your neck and give you goose bumps if done well.

A unique form of entertainment was that of the balladeer or the *kupletti* singer, the *kupletti* being derived from couplet. The *kupletti* singer made up dozens of humorous verses to the accompaniment of a popular song of the time, the theme based on what was going on in the Finnish community or the nation or even the world. However, there was an occupational failing tied to these singers; once they started, they were reluctant to stop. I can remember many times in Baltimore, after the *kupletti* singer had done his ballad and done it well, I would loudly applaud his performance and his creativity. One of the elder women in front of me would invariably turn around and say, "Don't applaud too loud. You'll encourage him to go on." She was right.

We had two of these singers in our community, and they were really talented. The trick for the audience was to applaud just enough to let the singer know they appreciated him but not enough to encourage him to favor us with another long presentation.

My mother had an ability to write short humorous monologues about events in the Finnish community and make some comments about the political scene. She wrote these in an Eteläpohjanmaan dialect, being inspired by the funny tales of Vaasan Jaakko. She would struggle for weeks to get a running motif for the monologues, then write them over and over, and after each one read it to my father and me, and we would make suggestions accordingly. And when she got up on the stage, both my father and I would sit there in a nervous state going over each word mentally and suffering along with her.

Then there were the newspaper reviews. No matter which Finnish-American paper one subscribed to, I am sure they were all the same. After there was a play or a program at the hall, one of the people in the community would send a long review to the Finnish newspaper, and all the cast members would wait anxiously to read what was said about their performances. They didn't sit up all night as they do in New York to get the *New York Time*'s and other newspapers' reviews, but the principle was the same. Sometimes there were hard feelings when someone was overly criticized, and that would create a great deal of argument. We all had our favorite critics and tried to urge the "soft" ones to be sure to send in a review.

Each hall had its own theater committee, and individuals would choose plays to be presented during the year and direct them. An aggressive director could persuade reluctant actors to take a part, and this could be a chore because, as with all efforts, some of the actors got just plain tired of doing nothing but attending rehearsals. Occasionally a person who didn't know how to act at all would be drafted into a play, and at the performance the audience would quietly mumble what a dreadful performance but still give the actor credit for trying. Then there were the really talented actors who, just by their presence on the stage, created an electric spark and made the evening come alive. We had a woman in Baltimore who was truly talented at both acting and directing. Whenever she was to appear, there was bound to be a full house. She could do any type of role and had such a magnetic personality that people couldn't take their eyes off her. She could have recited the telephone book and people would have remained under her spell.

Just a brief word about music. The Finns had choruses, orchestras, and bands, and frequently performed operettas. And often the person who was a musician was also an actor. I recall my father telling me how he studied the violin in Finland as a child and paid for his lessons by working for a shoemaker. He directed our orchestra at the hall in Warren, Ohio, and played for shows and dance music at our hall. He finally had to discontinue playing the violin when his fingers became too thick from doing manual work in the steel mill. But he was still able to conduct the chorus. He is typical of a great many of the Finns in their cultural expression, in their unbelievably hard work and sacrifice in developing their own group's culture.

Each hall had its own library with books on politics, theater, sports, child care, and art, and they even had encyclopedias. There was a constant eagerness to learn, and that is the essence of what I acquired from my background among the progressive and radical Finns. I venture to state that, despite ideological differences, all the Finns in the United States and Canada who were active in theater shared the same types of experiences, so there is a commonality here that transcends differences.

None of this, however, is mentioned in any textbook. There is no comprehensive material available to the average schoolchild, let alone the average citizen. They do not know of the wonderful theater movement among the Finns, their poetry, their music.

We of the second generation, as we grew up, performed at the hall and worked with the first generation, and as our children grew, they participated as well. But it was never the same, because the interests of the second and third generations became more dispersed into general community activities. We have no hall left in Baltimore and the elders are dying off. But for over sixty years the immigrant Finns gathered at halls and created their own culture—a many-faceted culture at that.

The record is there—it is something to be proud of—and it is our duty and privilege to record and hand it down so future generations will know that there were cultural expressions of the highest order amongst our forebears, the immigrant Finns.

Nancy Mattson

A sequence of seven "Maria" poems from Mattson's poetry collection, Maria Breaks Her Silence

WRITING

a poem about a famous man
is one thing:
    Socrates
    Blake
    Picasso

but how to hymn a woman
whose voice was lost
as she shifted
    continents
    languages
    husbands
    names
one dying into another

whose letters were lost in
    oceans
    furrows
    decades

whose thoughts were lost in
    sewing
    washing
    making do

from under a tangle of genealogies
    rosebushes
    cloudberries
    nettles

your voice, maria, whispering
growing stronger

MARIA LEARNS RESENTMENT

From the last batch of yeast buns
that David baked in her kitchen
before he sneaked away from Kauhava
Maria gave twelve   fresh   to her husband

but wrapped the thirteenth in a white cloth
woven fine on her mother's loom
     linen edged in lace
     embroidered with snowdrops
     never a knot

put the wrapped loaf
into her own oval basket
fashioned as a girl
from the bark of a fresh birch
     with a deft clasp
     never a seam

hid the basket in her father's chest
of smooth white birch
     with carved handles
     mortised corners
     never a nail

After sweaty rituals with her husband
Maria waited until he snored
washed herself with scalded water
rocked herself dry
naked beside the cast-iron stove

Inside the closed chest
under layers of birch and linen
aromas of yeast, cardamom, cloves
hardened to a fist

MATT BREAKS HIS SILENCE

Matt has not spoken in four days.
On the first, Maria respected his silence
offered hopeful glances to his glares
waited her turn. Simply waited.

On the second, she sparrowed her words
as she hopped from stove to sideboard
his woman, making his meals on time
serving them up with gossip and plans
balancing towards him on the edge of her chair.

On the third, the pleading began
small at first, then growing larger and more embarrassing
like a pregnant woman's belly
swollen with purple stretch marks
and a sore-apple navel.
She thrust herself at him.
He turned his head.

On the fourth day.
She bars his exit from their bedroom.
Fills the doorway with her need.
Acknowledge me.
The fist arrives.
She is grateful.
Tastes his knuckles.
Hears the force of the backhand to her ear.
Welcomes his curse.

TIETÄJÄ: ONE WHO KNOWS

When Paavo, the seasoned lumberman
strikes his foot with an axe
the devil's axe seeking a tree root
finding instead Paavo's ankle
through layers of boot and heavy sock

When Paavo's blood is soaking earth and wood
his eyes swimming
in branches and clouds
what can he do but send for Maria,
village blood-stopper?
Run, little helper
to the cottage of the *tietäjä*
we all despise her except in distress
now that her husband has left her

Three heavy lumbermen carry Paavo
a log filled with pain
his leg wrapped in sodden shirts
to Maria's kitchen
her children standing around

She unwraps his foot
dips her hands in the stream of blood
seeks out the edges of his wound
presses the slippery flesh together
    skin to skin
threads the rivers of blood
    vein to vein
lifts her head to Ahto
utters these words:

    Blood, blood, become a wall
    thicken, thicken, like a fence
    stay, stay, behind my hands
    stop, stop, beneath my thumbs!

As Maria chants what she knows, chanting softly
the lumberman Paavo, fearful as a wounded bear
falls quiet under her hands
When the sun falls, his blood sleeps
dries in thick threads and wooden scabs

Maria rises, her hair matted
blood crusting on her arms
she hears his breathing, listens
to the cracked whispers of blood
the secrets of knowing

MARIA'S HOUSE

I've bought a house for you, Maria
here in Ishpeming, a fine house
a big house, *varmasti isotalo*
bigger than your father's

He led her up the steps
across the verandah
held open the door
took her hand
to show her the rooms

She saw the long dining table
such a big table for a family of five
with long benches on either side
the two big stoves in the kitchen
and knew the house was big for a reason

Many rooms upstairs to shelter men
many plates in the cupboard to feed men
miners, loggers, anyone who could pay
drunkards, laggards, anyone who could drag
his feet up the stairs
anyone who could gamble, argue, swear
and pay his weekly board and room

Not like her father's house in Kauhava
with its many bedrooms for guests
many children, many servants
here she was to be the servant
to many strangers
paljon muukalaisia
cooking men's meals
washing men's coveralls
stripping men's beds
washing men's floors with lye soap

I'll fix you some coffee
you look tired after your long journey
sit down in this rocking chair
I'm so glad you're here, Maria

MARIA SEWS A WEDDING DRESS

With this needle
splinter of a reindeer bone
whittled and pierced
I sewed for you the tawny skin
of a southern deer
to wear on your wedding day

The treadle under my foot
guides the needle
through gathers of ivory lawn
that will billow out
from the sinews of your waist

My dress when I married your father
was heavy and black
in the old style of the *vanha maa*
tight at the throat
I wore a crown of brass filigree
polished bright as gold

May you be blessed with a daughter
as wild and bright as you
the deer we saw in the forest
gazing down the hillside

If I ever marry again
I will weave the linen myself
the fit will be loose
I will walk barefoot
through the wolf willow
to the bottom of the hill
and all the guests will be strangers

KANADALAINEN

To have left behind the language
that flowed like spring water
the easy seepage
of fresh words every hour

To have come to a land
of thorough drought
with a dry tongue

To have to pump the handle
like a child again
lifted off the platform
by every upstroke
the pump so stiff
the well so dark
you doubt the alkali earth
will ever release its sour water

To hang a new pail
from the knuckle
on the pump mouth
watching the water trickle
slowly at first
then slowly faster
until the pail is overflowing,
only to stumble on a root
on the path to the house

To watch the pumped water
settle and seep
into insatiable
Canadian earth

To have believed the words
would ever flow together
into sentences

Glen Kartin

HACKING AWAY
AT THE FAMILY TREE

M ANY OF US researching our genealogies more than likely remember an incident in our lives which provided the enthusiasm necessary to find out all we could about our ancestors. The spark kindling the flame of curiosity in me happened shortly after my eleventh birthday when I was shown a large, tinted portrait of my grandmother whom I never knew. The ancient Chinese proverb of one picture being worth 1,000 words could, in my case, be amended to include 1,000 questions. A fifth grader inquiring about his long deceased relatives a generation before Alex Haley's *Roots* popularized the genealogy craze probably caused a few eyebrows in our neighborhood to be raised.

Mother, a second generation Finnish-American, rarely spoke of her parents, Elizabeth and Erkki Soronen, whose marriage dissolved during her childhood. At the turn of the century, the stigma attached to dishonoring marriage vows through divorce was borne by the entire family. Whatever feelings Mother had concerning her family, she kept to herself. Needless to say, it came as quite a surprise to discover her stepfather was old Kalle Louha, our nearest neighbor. Our connection with the Louha family was common knowledge among the surviving early settlers around the Gowan, Minnesota, area where we farmed, but neither they nor my parents ever mentioned Kalle being related to us. After Grandmother died, Kalle remarried and raised a second family.

Annie, the Louha's unmarried daughter, was my favorite grown-up friend. In addition to being kind, witty, and full of fun, she always found time to listen patiently to what I had to say. One sunny April afternoon in 1948 on the way home from school, Annie yoo-hooed from the kitchen door to get my attention, then asked if she could "borrow my muscles" to help carry some cardboard boxes upstairs. She didn't have to repeat her request; I was more than willing to give her a hand and share a "Knock-knock, who is there" joke I heard during recess that morning.

Our task didn't take long. After our last trip to the storeroom, which originally had been sleeping quarters, some tinted portraits in square and oval frames lining the walls caught my eye. While Annie cleared a place for the boxes, I questioned, "Annie, why are all the people in the pictures dressed so funny?"

"That was the style in the olden days," she answered, a tiny smile pulling at the corners of her mouth. "Can you picture your sisters dressed like that?" The thought of seeing my teenage, tomboy sisters, Vienna and Mamie, in anything frilly made me chuckle. Their usual everyday dress consisted of worn out jeans and our older brother's T-shirts.

"Who are these people?" I asked.

"Most of them are Mother's relatives from the Iron Range towns." Pointing to a portrait in the middle of the grouping, she questioned, "Do you know who this couple is?" I studied the faces for a few seconds. The lady wore a high-necked dress ornamented with a small star-shaped brooch. Her dark, upswept hair was held in place by a shiny comb. The man's suit was nearly identical to those seen in the current Sears, Roebuck catalog. Only the stiff, rounded collar seemed out of place.

"Gee, I don't know who they are," I replied. "The lady looks a little like Katharine Hepburn."

"Well, Glen," Annie began in a serious tone, "this is your mother's mother. She was married to my father."

Perhaps it was Grandmother's aristocratic bearing or Mona Lisa smile, or a combination of both, that awed me. Whatever the reason, I was determined to know more about her. Of the many questions going through my mind, the first was if Annie was my aunt and if she had known Grandmother. Annie explained that Elizabeth died four years before her parents married and there were no blood ties between the Louha family and ours. To her knowledge, Mother's closest relative, a bachelor brother named Erick Soronen, whom I'd never met, still lived on their old homeplace near Menahga, Minnesota.

While I continued gaping at the portrait, Annie looked through the contents of a dresser drawer until she found a postcard photograph of a handsome, smiling soldier dressed in a World War I uniform. He had the same twinkly eyes and high cheekbones as Grandmother.

"Is this my Uncle Erick?" I questioned in a voice slightly louder than a whisper. She nodded. Before Annie could tell me her recollections of Uncle Erick, Mother phoned to remind me my chores were waiting at home. My chat with Annie was the first of many inquiries I made regarding Mother's family, which led to unknown relatives, unsettled grudges and, eventually, my roots.

Before beginning chores, I asked Mother if we were related to the Louhas. Giving me a quizzical look, she replied, "Only by marriage.

Mr. Louha was married to my mother at one time," then in the same breath added, "the woodbox needs filling," which ended our conversation. From the tone of her voice, I thought it best to wait until later to pursue the matter further.

During supper that evening, Mother's curiosity bothered her. She wanted to know how I found out about Grandmother and why I was suddenly so interested in anyone dead and buried. I explained how I helped Annie bring some stuff upstairs, saw the picture of a beautiful lady and wondered what kind of person she was.

"I don't want you bothering the Louhas with your foolish questions," Mother insisted.

"But," I hesitated, "why did she get a divorce?"

Seeing Mother's lips compress into a hard line, Father directed one of his well known looks to my end of the table which told me it would be wise to keep quiet or change the subject. Never one to embroider facts, he snapped, "Your grandfather was a drunkard." No one spoke. After a few minutes of absolute silence, he stated, "We can't pick our relatives like apples from a barrel. Some are good, others rotten."

Unless money or celebrities were involved for purposes of name-dropping in casual conversations with their friends, my brothers and sisters cared less about our Finnish heritage and looked upon my efforts to compile our history as a family joke. As a last resort, I questioned our married brother Vilhart if he had ever met any of Mother's relatives. "Meeting them once was enough," he replied after little thought. "Them people we can do without." After asking why he felt that way, he muttered, "They told me to stay away from their car because my buttons would scratch the paint." Being the oldest, Vilhart was favored by my parents and in their eyes could do nothing wrong. I suspected there was more to what he told and hinted at this possibility. For even suggesting this, he responded gruffly, "You're gettin' too big for your britches, boy."

To find out more about Mother's family, I'd have to use a different approach. A week later, I wrote a few questions on a sheet of paper torn from my copy book and would wait until Mother was in a better mood before asking if she would fill in the blanks. Listening to Lux Radio Theater on Monday nights was a "must" in our family. A few minutes to eight we gathered in the living room to wait for Cecil B. deMille to announce the program. We used this time for relaxing or doing projects which didn't distract us from enjoying the dramatic offering. During the commercial break, I told Mother I was trying to compile our family tree, handed her paper and pencil, and asked her if she would write down what she knew about her parents. Mamie and Vienna, playing a heated game of gin rummy, looked at each other and burst into shrieks of girlish laughter.

"Let us ha-ha-ha know if we're related to any crowned heads," Vienna snickered.

"Crowned heads? More like A-tee-hee-hee-'hilla the ha-ha-ha-Hun," Mamie giggled.

"Why don't both of you try out for the football team," I suggested forcefully, "They need some tackling dummies."

"Enough!" Mother interrupted, "or the neighbors will think there's a war going on over here."

After something resembling peace and quiet was restored, Mother handed me the paper. Her father, also named Erick, was born in Finland. After living around the then territory of Deadwood, South Dakota, he homesteaded a farm near Menahga, Minnesota, where Mother was born. Being a fan of the cowboy movies, this bit of information provided my overactive eleven-year-old imagination with images of Wild Bill Hickok and Calamity Jane.

"Was Grandfather an outlaw totin' a six-shooter?" I blurted out.

"No," Mother sighed, "he was a prospector or worked in the gold mines."

"Annie said Uncle Erick lives in Menahga. Can we contact him to see if he has any old pictures and information?" I pleaded.

"NO!" Mother said emphatically. After a few clicks of her knitting needles, she suggested writing to Velma Passo, her girlhood friend, who still lived near Uncle Erick, for pictures. Within a week of mailing my carefully composed letter, a photograph of Grandmother, Mother, Uncle Erick, and their friends arrived with a long letter and recent snapshot of the Passo family. Not one word was mentioned about Uncle Erick, which I thought strange.

Several weeks later, old Kalle Louha passed away in his sleep. Mother was among the relatives Annie summoned to the Louha home to pay their last respects before Kalle's remains were removed by the funeral directors. After politely refusing, she was told Kalle left her something which was to be given after he died. In the same tone of voice Mother used when she ordered groceries, Annie was informed she wanted nothing from the estate. Mother attended the funeral, but refused to be seated with the mourners. Her name was not included in the obituary. Whatever bad feelings there were between Mother and her stepfather, she had the final word.

Over the summer months I questioned some of our neighbors who knew Grandmother as to how they remembered her. Many commented on her endless energy and fine manners. All agreed she was an enterprising, knowledgeable lady who could be relied upon to unselfishly help others in their time of need. I was told Grandmother had one of the first restaurants in Floodwood, Minnesota. She befriended and won the confidence of many Chippewa Indians who lived around Prairie Lake some eight miles from her home. They taught her which plants native to the area could be used for healing, how to predict weather by changes in animal appearance and behavior, and many other secrets then unknown to the white man.

Having used every available resource, I wrote what I had learned about Grandmother in a notebook which I put aside until one frosty December night two years later when Mother received a long distance call informing us of her brother's death. As Uncle Erick had been a member of the American Legion, my parents made arrangements for a military funeral complete with honor guard.

My parents, Vilhart, and I arrived in Menahga one hour before the funeral. While we were seated in the car, an elderly gentleman walked slowly by glancing at us. Halfway down the block, he paused for a minute, returned, and stopped by the car. After Father cranked the window halfway open, he timidly inquired if Mother was Erick Soronen's sister and wondered if Elizabeth was still among the living. Mother recognized her old neighbor, Kalle Saakala, but looked ahead and said nothing. To discourage lengthy conversation, Father minced few words with his one line responses. Given the opportunity, the friendly old man would have enjoyed reminiscing about the experiences he shared with my grandparents while pioneering. The possibility of a fourteen-year-old boy entering into grown-up conversation was as remote as stopping the earth from revolving on its axis. The older family members did the talking while we youngsters were cautioned to keep quiet. I'm sure Mr. Saakala could have added meat and muscle to the family skeletons.

After the funeral, several ladies introduced themselves by mentioning they were related to us through Grandfather. As no obituary was ever published in the local papers listing Uncle Erick's next of kin, our relationship remains unknown. Father, who was similar in stature and appearance to Charles de Gaulle, was congenial to the point of being downright charming. Mother, on the other hand, gave them a down-the-nose-glance that seemed to lower the room temperature by ten degrees.

"I've never seen Ma treat anyone so rudely before," I told Vilhart when they were out of hearing range.

"There's always somebody crawling out from under a rock claiming to be related just to get a few bucks," he philosophized.

Mother promptly hired an attorney to initiate probate proceedings. Vilhart, never one to let a dollar slip through his fingers, insisted on being appointed administrator for the estate. In exchange for his services, my parents agreed to compensate him for time lost from work, traveling expenses, and miscellaneous sundry items not in the least connected to the proceedings. Prior to the farm being sold, we drove out to Erick's place to dispose of the machinery and anything else that could be converted into cash.

The farm bore witness to Grandfather's industriousness. He hacked the farm out of the wilderness with nothing but a strong back, his two hands, and an axe. While Father and Vilhart were inventorying the farm implements, Mother and I went in the house to see if there was anything worth saving. I tried to visualize the parties and crowds of people engaged in threshing and barn raising activities so common among our pioneer immigrants. What sadness and joy the old place must have known. Mother didn't speak until she discovered a dust-covered violin case on a shelf. "This was my father's," she said while gently running her fingers over the strings, "and wouldn't you know, damn Erick didn't keep it tuned."

Rummaging through an army footlocker, she found a moth-eaten uniform among other souvenirs from Uncle Erick's World War I days in France. She packed his steel helmet, gas mask, a few battalion books, and other small items in a box. Having three sons who served in World War II, Mother always had a soft spot in her heart for veterans.

A massive, oak Morris chair with lion heads carved on the back dominated one corner of the room. "Can we take this home?" I asked hopefully.

"Absolutely not," Mother said, eyeing the chair with scorn. "Whatever would we do with it?" and continued looking over some pressed glass dishes in the kitchen. I went through the papers in the footlocker and found an old letter from the Minnesota Historical Society listing my grandparents' birthplaces and birthdates. "WOW!!" I whooped. "What now?" Mother yelled over the clatter of falling dishes. "Did you hurt yourself?"

"No," I shouted. "Here's something about your family history."

"Is it necessary to frighten me half to death? Now stay out of that trunk and carry these boxes out to the car."

I picked up the box of Uncle Erick's keepsakes while Mother tucked the violin under her arm. "I'll have to make another trip for the dishes," I said, eyeing the footlocker.

"Close the door when you leave," Mother said walking out of the house without giving her childhood home a last look.

I placed the box in the trunk next to the violin, ran back to the house, and glanced over the papers. I found several old photos, Uncle Erick's World War I diary, and a yellowing obituary notice in Finnish with "Gustave Soronen" printed on the heading. The honking of the car horn put an abrupt end to my search. I crammed the papers in my pocket.

During the ride home, the conversation centered around disposal of the property, with Vilhart doing most of the talking. At one point I thought I heard cash register bells accenting his words. Nothing was said regarding Grandfather being a man of determination and vision, nor the hardship and privation he must have endured while making a home for his family in the wilderness. I thought of the kindly Mr. Saakala who wanted to renew old family friendships.

After studying the papers in the privacy of my room that evening, I discovered my grandfather was the son of *Talonpoika* Jaakko Soronen, who arrived in New York in July 1880 and filed a 160-acre homestead in 1891, which was the property Mother inherited. He died in 1908 and was buried in Wolf Lake Cemetery near his home. I wondered if as many came to bid their old friend and neighbor farewell as attended Uncle Erick's funeral. Every pew in the small chapel was filled. Apparently the Soronen family was well known in the community.

Having been on my grandparents' homeplace, my curiosity regarding our family history appeased and it was soon replaced by high school extracurricular activities. After graduation I attended college, traveled around the country before settling in Minnesota, and read Alex Haley's best selling novel, *Roots*, which inspired me to continue hacking away at the family tree.

Going over the notes compiled during adolescence, I found the only tangible lead to follow up was the old Gustave Soronen obituary published in the Finnish newspaper *Uusi Kotimaa*. With assistance from a Finnish-English dictionary, I discovered he died in the Calumet, Michigan, area, and his survivors included four sons. On this shred of evidence, I checked the Upper Michigan telephone directories and found a "W. Soronen" listed, whom, I assumed, was Gustave's descendant.

I wrote a brief letter of introduction, explaining my connection with the Soronen family, and requested information which could be used in our family history. Three weeks later I received a friendly letter from Hilda Paarta, Gustave's niece, informing me that we were related through my great-grandfather. She suggested writing to the Oulu parish archives in Finland where vital statistics kept by the church for over 300 years were preserved on microfilm. Hilda included the addresses of her cousins whom I could contact for data on their immediate families.

I set aside a few minutes each evening for writing Hilda's cousins, many of whom were interested in our family tree and wished me luck in my efforts. Not only did these thoughtful people send their individual histories, they also referred me to other relatives. At times it seemed as if I had created another uncontrollable Frankenstein's monster or started a chain reaction with no visible end in sight.

On the advice of friends who were doing their genealogies, I wrote to the Clerk of Court in various counties where my grandparents were known to have resided to ask if copies of family births, marriages, death records, and wills were on file. My inquiries resulted in obtaining Grandfather's death certificate and a xerox copy of his last will and testament made six months before he died. Both documents answered many questions regarding the bad blood between Mother and her relatives. Reading between the lines, I speculated how Grandfather, bedridden with dropsy and cancer, was being cared for by neighbors and other relatives living nearby. Mother was left the sum of one dollar to be paid by Uncle Erick. When Mother became twenty-one, she contested her inheritance. The results of the probate proceedings weren't available.

After six months, the Oulu archives sent the names of Grandfather's ancestors going back six generations to the 1600s. Included were their birth, death, marriage dates, places of residences, and the names of his brothers and sisters. The charge for this service totaled only $15.00. The archive director informed me that Grandmother's maiden name and year of birth were insufficient data for researching her pedigree and that they could offer no assistance. Perhaps this was meant to be. I have my private image of her that I wouldn't want distorted. She will always remain my favorite, unsolved mystery.

Now, to begin hacking away at Father's side of the tree. From what I was told, his forefathers, originally surnamed "Cardin" of French nobility, migrated to Scandinavia, fought with the Danes against the Swedes during the 1500s, and later were granted land in what is now Soviet Karelia, where Father was born. With my luck, their side would be stronger than oak. I hope my axe has retained its cutting edge.

Jim Johnson

SKELETONS

In the photograph
a thin and mustached Gusti Johnson
stiff in suit and tie,
as if he would rather be
excused and raking hay.
beside him
his heavy-set wife Hilda,
his strong blond sons,
his daughters
dark-haired Hildas.
behind him
the house
made of squared logs, dovetailed corners. and
behind it
prairie. everything

seems to balance on
the handlebar mustache.
yet Hilda's eyes
want to wander.
the fields are rolling.
the cross on
the tall church steeple
becomes the masts of a wooden ship
and takes her home again.

Earl Nurmi

.25-36 CALIBER RIFLE

It is the hexagonal barrel
that makes you valuable, an expert told me.
75 year old marling lever action.
What curious tales your mute steel could tell
I know not, but can imagine. You belonged to my father.
He bought you for three dollars in the thirties. You fed
our family more than once, in league
with my father's skill. I remember
how he could move through thick brush
for hours without stopping, bellowing
somber Finnish folk songs in a minor key.
Gun you've killed nothing for over twenty years.
You're more of an anachronism than I am.
You're a handsome instrument with your blued steel barrel
and aged walnut stock, almost alive. You stand in a corner
among stereo speakers and bookcases, sharing a shag carpet
with volumes of Proust and Neruda. One expects to see a tag
attached to you, ".25-36 rifle, 75 years old. File
in immigrant archives." My father and a friend
trekked 100 miles in three days once, in Michigan's
Porcupine Mountains. How like a fantasy
do those days seem now! His voice grows more faint
with each year. Is our heritage as distant and as fragile,
gun, as your steel is immediate and harsh?

TRAPPING WEASEL NEAR DULUTH IN WINTER

The cold was bad. You would breathe
cautiously or sear your lungs.
I moved on snowshoes
through thickets, streams frozen
to their bottom, and the silence
of that country in winter.
I would place traps in dead logs, woodpiles
briefly removing my mittens and quickly
replacing them. I would get as much as a dollar
for each pelt, good money for a boy then

One moved as an astronaut across some alien, frozen land
encased in layers of scarves, heavy boots.
The rare birds would rattle at you indignantly
you were an interloper in their realm. Get lost
and you would perish, not survive a single night

In March of '56 my father died working beneath a car.
He had been a trapper of the first rank, he could trap mink.
My apprenticeship to him was thus brief.
I return only to visit Duluth
and have hunted nothing since.

Helmi Mavis Hiltunen Biesanz

Excerpts from the Memoir

HELMI MAVIS: A FINNISH-AMERICAN GIRLHOOD

INTRODUCTION

I WAS BORN in a small immigrant farm community in northeastern Minnesota. After four boys, Mother wanted a girl, and chose the name "Mavis" from a story in *Woman's World Magazine*, and my middle name, "Helmi," after a sister. But "Helmi" is pronounced so badly in English that, following Aunt Pearl's example, I signed all my school papers "Mavis Pearl Hiltunen."

When I was eighteen I needed a birth certificate and drove to the town clerk's house. Holger put his finger on a line in an old ledger and laughed. "Only a Helmi Hiltunen was born on July 27, 1919." Sure enough, there it was, in Father's flowing script. He had forgotten that "crazy" name on the four-mile trip to register my birth.

Now that split-level name may symbolize my life. On the one hand, I absorbed the difficult language, the songs, food, customs, traditions, and values of an Old World culture—and I still treasure them. On the other, I was eager to be a good American, for early in the century the pressure for "Americanization" was very strong, particularly in school. I am Finnish Helmi and American Mavis.

Going "home" now, I marvel that those immigrants were able to raise large families on that rockstrewn soil, where killing frosts may come in June and August. Most of their children have long since scattered to nearby cities, far-off states, and foreign countries. On a quiet hilltop surrounded by woods, tombstones bear such names as Lempia, Lampi, Holappa, Salmela—and Hiltunen.

School 40 was torn down years ago. Alder bushes and poplars cover the site of Vermilion Hall. The Co-op has been boarded up for many years. Ranch-style houses and mobile homes with strange names on the mailboxes now stand along the roads. Only here and there a neighbor clings to the old homestead, the remodeled sauna still a ritual gathering place on a Saturday night.

The cabin where I was born still stands, leaning and sagging a bit, a summer cottage and hunting lodge for my brothers. Sauna and privy serve their ancient purposes. When you pull open the warped and creaking door of stable and wagonshed, you find a crude museum of a time gone by. In a shadowy corner the bulbous silvery bowl of the old cream separator gleams softly. Several scythes with beautifully curved oak handles and wicked blades lean against the old axe-hewn log walls. A pair of Father's shoepacks, with upturned toes and sturdy leather uppers, on which he trod lightly over the crusted snow, his feet warm in wool felt liners and woolen socks, brings a lump to the throat.

Nostalgia is sweet, but painful. Sitting in the old rocking chair in the kitchen, sleeping in Mother and Father's marriage bed, is almost more than I can bear. Though I drink deep of the light air of summer, sweet and pure as spring water, I cannot stay long. Memories overwhelm me.

And I never go "home" in winter. No one does. The road remains unplowed. Snow weighs down the branches of the pines that seemed so tall to me, but were second growth, naturally reforested after the lumber barons slashed through virgin timberland. It covers the fields where we made hay and planted potatoes, and the barren sites where stood the red barn, the ice house, the chicken coop, the haymows, the blacksmith shop, the woodshed. The brook is frozen solid under the snow. Deer and rabbits and squirrels embroider the blue and lavender shadows with dainty tracks. But in winter no one else is there.

Sixty years ago smoke poured from the chimneys of house and sauna the year around. Half a dozen cows, several calves, and a few sheep shared the barn. A team of horses stamped and neighed in the stable. Cars and snowplows and schoolbuses came and went along the roads, sleighs and wagons over the fields.

Images of my childhood home are still vivid to me, even at my desk in tropical Costa Rica. Summers were magically long and wonderful when I was eight. In memory, the long June days were blissful.

JUNE 1928

June was the best month of the year. Potatoes were already planted but blueberries were not yet ripe nor hay ready for scythe and mower. Right through the Fourth of July, life was especially sweet and wonderful, lived almost entirely out of doors in the high clear light of the north woods.

Mabel and I felt like the new calves frisking in the barnyard. When Mother didn't need us for chores, we were free to roam. Our bare feet were tickled by pine needles in the woods on the hill and new grass in the fields, cooled by the squishy mud of the golden-weedy brook, hardened by the gravel roads, and dusty from the soft powdery paths that cut through the farm in all directions. The sun bleached our hair to platinum blonde and turned our skin brown where our overalls left it bare.

The first good day after school was out—usually near Decoration Day—everyone had pitched in to plant potatoes. No one had to be reminded that we ate potatoes at least once a day all year round. Hour after hour we set the carefully cut pieces with an "eye"—a potential plant—right side up in furrows prepared by the plow. By evening the smoke rising from the sauna chimney beckoned us to wash off the dust and the potato smell and bake out the aches from bending over all day long. We wolfed down Mother's hearty *mojakka* stew and rhubarb pie, and before long, snores, gentle and sonorous, chorused a fugue in the moonlit house.

For two days a week the everlasting washing also had priority over play, but out in the fresh air by the sauna it seemed like pure pleasure compared to a winter washday. The boys started a fire in the small cast-iron stove of the sauna dressing room, set the big copper boiler on top and filled it with water they carried from pump to sauna, pailful after pailful. Then they filled the two big galvanized iron tubs on the stand that looked like two huge wooden chairs back to back, with the upright wringer in between, that stood in the grass near the sauna door.

Mother shaved slices from a bar of Fels-Naphtha soap, so strong it stung my nose, into the boiler. She stirred the clothes in the boiling water with a thick wooden pole like a short baseball bat. She lifted the steaming clothes into a tub and showed us how to scrub them on the metal washboard with another bar of the golden-yellow soap. We scrubbed till our arms grew tired and Mother took pity on us.

I turned the wringer handle while Mabel fed the soapy clothes between the thick rubber rollers into the other tub for the first rinse. I tossed my head in annoyance as Leo went by and from his superior masculine height—now a chunky twelve years—scoffed, "Yeah, girls, that's the way to build muscles!" "Oh, shut up, you baldheaded. . . ." Already aware of girls, Vic and Ray no longer clipped their hair to the scalp the moment school was out, but Leo was still young enough to prefer coolness and freedom.

Through the wringer once more, into the second rinse water, a rich blue from a generous dollop of French's Bluing, and again through the wringer before we shook them out and hung them on the lines stretched from the sauna wall to a T-post.

We laughed as the wind flapped wet diapers into our faces. The sky was so blue, the breeze so alive, and the sun so warm that work became play, and I didn't even mind Father's joking that if I stretched enough to pin the clothes on the line I would grow faster. (Brothers were another story.) Besides, while each lineful dried, Mother let us off to explore the woods behind the house, wade in the brook, or push each other in the swing under a tall pine tree.

Or to fetch the mail. If it was very close to mailtime, Mother handed us a small bundle of penny postcards and letters with two-cent stamps stuck in the corner and told us to run like sixty. Miksi at our heels, we clambered over the Near Gate, ran over the Little Hill through the swamp to the Far Gate, turned left on the township road along the edge of Miettunen's farm, and climbed the steep Big Hill. From its top we could see the row of three mailboxes on the county road. If the mailman's car was there, we waved our letters and ran to give them to him. If he hadn't come yet, we skipped down the sharp dip before the last hill and stopped to sniff the wild roses and notice where columbine grew to pick for Mother on the way home, and to nibble a few of the round points full of nectar. If we wanted to explore the woods, we left the letters in the box and turned up the red metal flag so the mailman would know there were letters inside.

Father was usually waiting impatiently in the rocking chair for his newspapers—*Päivälehti* and *Duluth Herald* and *Co-op Builder*—which he read over mid-morning coffee. Bathed and changed, Bobby was playing in the clever enclosure Vic had concocted in the shade of the house, and rarely needed attention. We knew we had to take down the sweet fresh diapers and fold them into the bushel basket before we could play. Perhaps we also had to fetch "about five sifters of whole wheat flour and three of white" from the cool dark shed. Mabel stood on a stool and reached down into the bins where hundred-pound sacks of flour had been emptied, and counted the sifterfuls into the huge tin pan I held.

Then we escaped to the light shade of the budding, blossoming woods on the hill behind the house. We found fragile velvety mauve hepaticas and delicate pink and white anemones, mayflowers, ordinary purple violets, and the rarer fragrant white ones almost hidden under last year's leaves.

Day by day we watched the small white blossoms of wild strawberries in the low thin grass on the hillside shed their petals and give way to hard greenish-white balls that ripened to bright red. For a few days there were only enough to pop straight into our mouths. Then there were enough to fill a coffee cup or two, and eat with cream and sugar. We shared them with Mother and Father; the boys could find their own. When they were even more plentiful, Mother made rhubarb-strawberry jam, and we saved most of it for special winter occasions. For hours after we had picked strawberries, our hands remained pink and perfumed, no matter how often we washed them.

Mother sometimes straightened up from thinning out a bed of carrots or lettuce, rubbed her back, looked up at the scudding white clouds in the bright blue sky, and recited,

> *What is so rare as a day in June?*
> *Then, if ever, come perfect days.*

Or sang, in her sweet uncertain voice,

> *Sing, bird, up in the apple tree,*
> *Hum, bee, over the rose,*
> *Laugh, brook, ripple in melody,*
> *Sweet little buds, unclose.*
> *Wave, grass, up in the valley wide,*
> *Leap high, grasshopper gay,*
> *Dear flowers, never one chalice hide,*
> *Summer will never stay.*

To us, however, summer seemed to stretch on and on into the future, each day more full of delight and wonder than the last. We knew every cherry tree and sugar-plum bush in the woods, every promising blueberry patch in the pastures and cutover land, every brambly tangle of blossoming raspberry vines. Dandelions were bright golden treasures to weave into crowns or carry in sap-stained hands to Mother, who put them in glasses of water where their glory soon faded. When their heads turned downy white in the grass, we would pick one and say, "Tell me, pretty maiden, does my mother want me home?" Then we had to give one hard puff; it wasn't fair to blow gently. If all the seeds blew away, it was time to go home. If not, we lay a while longer in the grass, imagined monsters and castles and angels in the clouds, or watched ants, bees, and butterflies go about their business.

Mabel liked to climb to the top of the tallest Norway pine on the hill behind the house and shout down to me as I stood timidly below, "I can see Tower and Ely and Virginia and Duluth."

"Aw, you liar, liar, pants on fire, nose as long as a telephone wire! All you can see is Miettunen's house and the potato field and the haylofts in the meadow."

But I didn't tattle on her when she lost her hold on a branch, slipped on the rough bark coming down, and tore her overalls and scraped her skin so it bled; Mother had forbidden us to climb trees. It was all right for boys; they not only climbed sturdy straight pines but swung from the topmost branches of flexible birches and shouted as they let go and hit the ground. Mabel practiced on young birches when the boys weren't around. I tried it too, but preferred to hunt for toadstools and imagine little elves and fairies sheltered under them.

The long twilights invited visiting and games and romping and gossip. After milking time a car or two loaded with whole families would turn down our road. While the ladies helped Mother fix coffee, the men played horseshoes or sat on the grass until the mosquitoes drove them indoors. We children played wild games of hide-and-seek and tag. We threw a softball over the house, yelling "Anti-Anti-I-Over!" to the team on the other side. The boys played catch and softball far enough away from the house to avoid warnings about windows.

Mabel and I held hands in a circle; then, leaning farther and farther away from each other, turned in dizzying circles, hair flying, feet close together, until our hands pulled apart and we fell down in the grass, panting and laughing, flushed, and conscious of our young bodies only as instruments we used and enjoyed. We rolled over and over down the slope, sniffed the camomile blossoms and clover, laughed and squealed. We screamed as it grew dark and bats swooped low, and went in to ask Mother for jars in which to trap fireflies.

One afternoon Mabel and I wandered along the road, making crowns of the sticky vines starred with tiny white flowers that grew in the ditches. "Let's go see Elsie," Mabel suggested, "and take her a crown." We ran up the hill to Miettunen's, where Elsie showed us newborn kittens and her mother gave us milk and cookies.

Before we knew it the sun had slipped behind the trees, and we ran home, sure of a scolding. Mother was flushed with anger and tearful with worry. She whacked each overalled bottom and pulled an ear apiece as she said firmly, "You know you can't go away from home without permission! Now say you're sorry and promise never to do it again. I was worried, and I needed you to take care of Bobby while I milk. No one else is around."

We sat on the front steps with Bobby and pouted to each other. "Yeah, where are the boys? *They* don't have to ask permission every time they turn around."

"No, they go fishing and poling the boat on Pike River and play ball and visit any old time," said Mabel enviously.

The mosquitoes hummed around our legs more and more furiously.

Mabel took the baby in and I ran down to the barn. I pushed aside the gunnysack curtain at the door that was supposed to keep horseflies away from the cows. Mother was sitting on a three-legged stool, her kerchiefed head bent against Kirjonen's flank, and I heard alternating streams of milk striking the sides of the pail with a rhythmic hiss and plink. Trying not to breathe too deeply of the urine-manure-hay scented air, I crossed the straw-strewn concrete floor and stood beside Mother until she looked up.

"Oh, I'm glad you came. I was just going to call and ask you to bring my other shoes and a clean dress and apron in case company comes before I'm through. Would you get them for me?"

I lingered. "Mother, I'm sorry about what we did; we just forgot. But why is it bad for us to go visiting when the boys are out having fun?"

"Well, they're bigger and tougher, and they're boys, and it's not so dangerous for them as for little girls. You have to watch out for bad men who might hurt you."

"But it's dangerous for them too. Remember, Eino Anderson fell in the river and got chilled and died, and the county nurse said the germs were so dangerous she wouldn't even come in our house after she had been there to fumigate. Spinal meningitis; that must be terrible. Mrs. Anderson cried and cried."

"Oh, my goodness, are you still worrying about that? Everyone dies some time, and if they are saved they go straight to Heaven. Now, do you want a squirt of *lämmiä*?" And she aimed a stream of warm milk at my mouth, which I had opened obediently for our old game.

"Now run along, and get those things, and cheer up. You'll grow up fast enough." She smiled, pushed out her false teeth, sucked them back in, and bent her head to the cow's round brown side once more. As I slipped between the poles of the barnyard gate and trudged up the short slope to the house, I wished we had never laughed at Mother's joke with her teeth. It was comical, but what if she forgot and did it when someone else was around? She really looked nice when she combed her hair and was happy.

Next day Andrew Kahtava, who was a clever carpenter, began to put wood siding on the house, with Victor as his helper. I was glad we wouldn't live in an old-fashioned log cabin any more, but I would miss seeing the cabin Mother had lived in on the homestead land, much of the time alone with Victor. Though it was moved to the farm and three rooms were added, all of us except Victor had been born in that very cabin, which was now "the bedroom." With white siding covering the logs, it just wouldn't feel the same. I went around to the back of the house and leaned my head against a silvery log, picked at a sliver of wood, and wondered how I could be both happy and sad about the same thing.

Vic came around the corner with a sawhorse. He always seemed to know just what I was thinking. He glanced at me, smiled, and then looked serious.

"It's really a shame to cover up this old work. These pioneer cabins are made the old Finnish way. See how the logs are squared off with broad axes and fitted so tightly you need hardly any mortar. But Maw wants the house to look more modern, like those in town, and we have to paint it white when we get this siding on. Hey, I hear her calling you!"

Churning time. Mother licked the finger she had dipped into the cream can to see that it was just right—not too sweet and not yet turning sour. "It's going to be very hot today so I want to make the butter early. You girls take turns churning."

She set the big red barrel churn on its stand, locked it into place, poured in the cream, and made sure she snapped the lid tightly shut. I found a fat red book to read during the boring chore and sat down to turn the wooden handle round and round. The cream sloshed and splashed with each turn. The book, I noticed, was one Vic had borrowed from the Virginia library—Zane Grey's *The Vanishing American*. Soon I was so engrossed in it that I turned the handle more and more slowly, stopped to turn pages and forgot to churn for a while, until Mother noticed and took the book away.

When my arm was tired, Mabel took her turn. The day was warm, and it wasn't long before the liquid splashing was punctuated by the thud of lumps, and small yellow balls of butter stuck to the little glass window in the lid. "Mother, now it's kerplunking and not just sloshing around," said Mabel. Her arms were tired, and I took over. It was a little harder to turn the handle now, but I persisted until Mother decided the lumps were big enough to work. Several times she dipped out as much butter as she could with a long-handled strainer and plopped it into the huge shallow wooden bowl that smelled of countless weeks of butter-making. Then she tipped the churn to drain the buttermilk and capture any remaining butter. She rewarded us with glasses of buttermilk and slabs of bread and jam.

We watched her rinse the butter until the water ran clear, and work it with her flat wooden paddle between rinses. When it was free of water, we liked to watch her shape it into deep rippled folds; she turned and turned the bowl and tilted out every last drop of water. As she worked the butter, she worked and pursed her lips in rhythm too, and when she heard our giggles, she caught us mocking her and pushed out her teeth at us.

Last of all, she carefully poured salt into the palm of her hand, sprinkled it on the butter, worked it in, and tasted it several times until she was satisfied that it was just salty enough. We were proud of Mother's expert way with butter. In some homes, the butter tasted strong and sour, but hers was always mild and sweet.

Saturday was cream day. We were very busy until Mother got off to town. We had to scrub pint and quart bottles with a brush in soapy water, scald them, fill them carefully with rich yellow cream, wipe off the drips, and firmly stick a cardboard cap in each opening. We were too small to be trusted with the five-pound stoneware crocks for butter, or even the smaller ones, but we liked watching Mother deftly work the butter into every bit of space before she tied a double layer of wax paper on top.

If the hens had laid enough, we washed eggs and carefully put them into cartons. If there was fresh buttermilk left over, we bottled that too, for there was no dairy in Tower and every drop was welcome.

One Saturday Aunt Hilma was at the farm and offered to look after Bobby so Mabel and I could go to town too. We hurried to change into our new sandals and sundresses, because Father, impatient as always, was already honking the horn.

We sat in back, carefully holding the eggs, and watched for the moment when we crossed a little bridge in the long meadow between Hendricksons' and Wahlstens'. Its high bump gave us a roller-coaster thrill as the car swooped and settled and our stomachs seemed to flip over. Then we were in the pine forest and chorused, "Pretty soon downtown!"

The sign at the edge of town boasted that the Incorporated City of Tower had 700 inhabitants. For Mabel and me it was civilization. Its eight-block-long Main Street looked almost exactly like the town in a cowboy movie we had seen. False-fronted business buildings lined it: the Rex Theater, grocery and hardware stores, the post office, the office of the *Tower Weekly News*, a couple of gas station-garages, and the small hotel-restaurant where Vic had worked. A block off Main Street were the Immanuel Lutheran Church and the Catholic Church, both of which looked huge compared to our little white church near the river. And the red brick schools looked enormous to us! The Tower-Soudan High School had to be large enough to serve not only Tower but also Soudan, only a mile away, near the deepest underground iron mine in the world, where Uncles Ray and Felix worked.

At one end of Main Street there still stands a small gray obelisk with a plaque honoring President William McKinley. When I was handing nails to Vic the day before, he had told me, "You may not think so much of Tower now that you've been to Minneapolis, but it was the first town in the United States to put up a monument to President McKinley after he was assassinated." Then of course he had to explain assassinations, and Abraham Lincoln, and plead coffee time to escape my interminable questions.

Tower stands at one end of huge Lake Vermilion, pine-fringed and island-dotted, and this June day a few out-of-state licenses signaled that the tourist season had begun. Lake cottage owners had arrived for the summer, and fisherman were hauling boats to their favorite camps. A few farmers were shopping for things they couldn't find at the rural co-op, and women were planning their Sunday dinners.

For a while Father took Mother around to various customers, and at one house he carried out a small table she had paid for with cream. When the racks of bottles were light enough for Mother and us girls to carry, he told us to meet him at the IGA grocery store in an hour and went off on his own errands.

I liked to visit the city ladies with their electric lights and indoor bathrooms, their uncluttered glassed-in porches that were inviting places to relax and visit rather than to store the overflow of a farmhouse — and especially their fine English, which sounded almost affected to my ears, but which I did my best to imitate when I was alone. But I felt bashful around them.

Mother, however, appeared perfectly happy and at home with them. She knew just what to say and how to say it, I thought, with the same tone and inflection, and not a trace of Finnish accent. She considered all her customers her friends. During her erratic periods of schooling, many had been her classmates, and they seemed glad to see her and buy her wares. Mrs. Pryor had been airing and sunning winter clothes and getting summer ones ready.

"I put aside a few that Billy and Betty have outgrown. I wonder if any of your children might be able to use them?"

I was proud of the dignified way Mother answered, smiling, "Oh, thank you, Amanda. I'm sure they can."

On Main Street, a woman approached, and Mother greeted her, "Why, hello, Elsie." The woman apparently found the dusty jumble of goods in the hardware store window so fascinating that she didn't hear her. For a moment Mother's face looked like a storm cloud. Then she walked briskly on.

I asked, "Is that lady deaf, Mother?"

"No, she's *not* deaf! She's someone I knew when we were girls, and she doesn't like to admit that she's Finnish. And she was so *mad* at me for marrying a greenhorn!"

"What's a greenhorn?"

She was still angry. "Oh, somebody dumb, I guess!"

"But Father's not one bit dumb. He's smart!"

"Well, I mean she looked down on him because he was so fresh from the Old Country and his English was so poor. Hmmph! She's just *too proud!*"

Although bright red spots still burned on Mother's cheeks, she held her head high as she greeted Mrs. Kitto, her next customer. During sixth grade, Mother had lived with her and helped with the baby and the housework to earn her room and board, and they were close friends.

Her bottle racks empty, Mother headed for her old friend Celia Soper's, where she knew a good coffee awaited her. "Here's a nickel for each of my good helpers. Be back in fifteen minutes."

We ran to Marttila's Drug Store and used up five of those minutes agonizing over which flavor of ice cream we should buy—vanilla, chocolate, or strawberry. How luscious each tongueful! How precious each drip that had to be licked up quickly from the side of the cone on this hot day! Was there ever ice cream as good as old Konst Marttila's?

At the grocery store Father stuck his hands deep in his pockets and looked away while Mother shopped for delicacies he thought foolish, like canned pineapple and coconut, walnuts and chocolate, and the gooey marshmallow-filled cookies with pink or white or chocolate icing sprinkled with chopped coconut that we kids considered a great treat. I was glad that here he couldn't scold her for her extravagance, as he sometimes did at the Co-op. She asked him to pay only for the cans of Campbell's Pork and Beans and the wienies for supper.

Mother managed to provide us with all kinds of things we would never have had without her business—not only goodies to eat, but secondhand furniture like that table, an organ she got for ten dollars, and eventually a radio. The leather sofa in the bedroom. And later, an occasional lifesaver of a five-dollar bill in her letters to me at college. Best of all, I am sure, it gave her a sense of pride in her own accomplishments and a legitimate excuse to go to town and see her old friends.

Bible School interrupted our long June days. Every morning for a week, we walked to School 40, Finnish catechisms in hand. The Reverend Mr. Aho drilled us in such basics of Lutheranism as the Lord's Prayer, the Ten Commandments, and the Apostles' Creed. He taught us proper Finnish as seriously as the catechism; only reluctantly did he explain a difficult point in English.

Not all the school kids were there. Some went to the Apostolic Lutheran Church, whose pastors were usually far from mild-mannered like ours, but shouted and threatened with hellfire anyone who danced or played cards or went to the movies. Some kids, like my friend

Hilma, didn't go at all. Mother sometimes shook her head and tightened her lips about that, but it didn't bother me—perhaps because I had grown up knowing that Finns were alike in many ways but insisted on their right to be different in many others.

Vic's friend Eino, who Mother thought was a bad influence, didn't go either, and one day when he walked part way with us, he teased Vic. "You still going to Bible School like a little kid?"

Vic answered, "You know I'll never hear the end of it if I don't get confirmed next year. Father thinks everyone's just a kid until he's been through *rippi koulu* (confirmation school). And you know how religious Mother is."

"Your hair is so long it's way down to your eyes," Mother remarked on Saturday. "You've got to look nicer for the program tomorrow." She gave Mabel and me each a dime to run over to Charlie Niemi's for haircuts.

"Niemi Kalle" often came to sauna, and I liked to watch him clamber out of his 1922 Model T roadster, walk slowly around it twice, and kick each tire as he made the circuit. Despite his shyness, he never failed to come out with a modest proposal over sauna coffee. Speaking very deliberately, but with a slight smile, he looked into his cup and said, "Pekka, if you ever leave your wife a widow, I'll marry her; she's so clean and such a good cook." Mother winked at us and tried not to laugh, but we thought she was a bit flattered just the same.

One evening in sauna she explained why there were so many bachelors in the neighborhood. "Charlie was quite good-looking when he was younger, with that red hair, those blue eyes, and that dimple in his chin," she said. "But many more young men came from Finland than girls, and not all of them found wives here, especially when they didn't know any English—and you know how poor Charlie's English is. And he's so shy and quiet—and a little slow." Our carpenter, Andrew, drank a lot, and Elias Keranen, though he was as clean as any housewife, was a loner who preferred to read and meditate, and never showed up at social functions. And Matt Mattson—well, Matt tried marriage twice, which is another story.

Charlie's four-room house was clapboarded and painted, and the inside was spacious and light. We marveled that it was so nice and clean for a bachelor's place. It was a bit stuffy, though. Charlie was mortally afraid of drafts. People said he put on suit after suit of long underwear as the weather got colder and peeled them off one by one in the spring.

The smells of yellowing newspapers piled on the Finnish-style benches around the walls, and of chewing tobacco and spittoons, were inoffensive compared to Matt's sour dark cabin. Besides, Charlie played the violin, a much more elegant instrument than Matt's accordion.

Charlie hummed softly as he plied scissors and clippers, walking around and around the chair until he was satisfied with the Dutch bob he had created. We were impatient with his slowness and his shaky hands. We surrendered our dimes and ran homeward, shaking our heads; they felt so light! We stopped to blow away the tickly hairs on each other's necks that had escaped Charlie's towel and brush. And to savor a few strawberries and note where they grew most thickly.

The Bible School program on Sunday afternoon was solemn and low-key. We showed off what we had learned to our smiling parents, who were happy to hear us speaking good old-fashioned Finnish. We tried to sing the *virsis*, slow chants printed in Gothic letters in the small old hymnals, while Elsie Dahl played the organ.

After the usual coffee in the church kitchen and a little visiting on the church lawn, we headed home. Father started another *virsi*, and since the tunes were all about the same, we chanted as best we could. The oft-repeated words mingled sadness and thankfulness. I concentrated on the vowels, which stretched out especially long in these chants. "God" became *Juu-maa-laa* and "in Heaven" was *taai-vaaas-saaa*. When the sun shone out in wide golden rays from behind a gray-blue cloud, radiating like the halos in pictures of white-bearded Old Man God sitting on a throne in the heavens, I thought God must be happy to hear us praising Him.

But the holy mood did not last. While Mother was changing into barn clothes and we undressed Bobby, Vic also changed clothes and headed for Matt's camp, where a few boys would doubtless play cards and drink home brew. Getting what Mother called a "lap" of firewood to make supper,I heard her singing "Oh Happy Day, that fixed my choice, On Thee, my Savior and my God," while she milked the cows. Despite the words, her singing sounded melancholy, and I wondered if Mother ever felt lonely, even with the whole family around, the way I sometimes did.

Ruth Pitkanen Johnson

THE RICHES IN POVERTY

*I*F YOU HAD asked me when I was growing up, would I rather be rich or poor, I would have said I would rather be rich. Ask me that today and I would still say rich, but with qualifications. If not being poor could have some of the richness of the life we created for ourselves because we were poor and if not being poor could have some of the richness of family involvement, then I would say it would be better to be rich.

Every summer my father would find ways to take us to the country. My father was what in earlier days would have been called a circuit rider if he had been an American. He was a Methodist minister, but in reality he was a missionary administering to the small clusters of Finnish people who had settled in the upper peninsula of Michigan and in Wisconsin. Many Finnish-speaking people had settled on sparse farms or near the lake to fish for a livelihood.

During the summer months my father would hold Bible classes and confirmation classes at these various places where no ministers would make the rounds during the cold, bitter winter months. He would hold church services, perform weddings, some overdue, baptisms and burials, and, of course, Sunday School every Sunday, which we had to attend. My whole family would stay with one farm family for one month and another family for another month. My parents helped as much as they could with farm chores—my mother, especially, worked very hard at chores she was physically not equipped to do. These families we stayed with were usually the ones with larger farms and larger houses. For town children these farms were enchantment, so we had a great time. The farm children knew so much more about the exciting things to do. Things like milking cows, turning the separator, haying, finding eggs, even teaching the chickens to fly, to mention only a few of the delicious pursuits.

When I was about ten, we started coming to an area that once had been a small mining operation. Now the pits were all overgrown with grass and weeds, but a few of the old log buildings remained. We stayed in the old mine office which was a log building. Most of the windows were long gone. My mother tacked mosquito netting over the windows. We carried water from a shared well about a quarter of a mile away.

My brother and I did this daily. Occasionally we used a wagon to haul the pails, but the ground was so bumpy we would spill half the water. We didn't spill quite so much by carrying the pails.

For warmth we had a small kerosene stove or we wore more clothes. My younger brother and I built an outdoor cooking stove with rocks and clay over which we placed a large sheet of iron we found in the old engine house. We were just lucky that it was a piece of heat conducting iron. In rainy weather we would hold an umbrella over our mother while she cooked and canned the berries we had picked that day. Our beds were wooden platforms on which we had the most heavenly fragrant mattresses. My mother had sewn large cloth bags from linen she had brought from Finland, and our first chore when we got there was to go to the farmer's barn to fill these bags with fresh hay.

I remember building a fabulous chair from small trees I cut. It grew much bigger than I had planned, so two of us could sit in it. Many years later my brother drove through this area and found this old log shack. He said the chair was still there. At the doorstep we had a welcome mat made of cedar boughs carefully piled and spread, on which we had to wipe our feet. These boughs were replenished each week.

An open field stretched out in front about the size of a football field. It was the greatest playground. My mother devised games for us to play; one was a game of quoits. She made a hoop of twisted branches. The hoop was twirled through the air and was caught with a forked stick. Imagine my delight a few years ago when I visited the hunting lodge of Czar Nicholas of Russia to see the identical kind of willow hoop and forked stick on the wall among the preserved treasures. The hunting lodge is in Finland near the town where my mother grew up. This field, unfortunately, was the browsing ground for the farmer's horses and cows, as they roamed freely. We had to be very observant as to where we stepped, especially when we were barefoot, which we were most of the time. The horses were quite wild and they terrified us. My mother was really terrified by them because they would come to the house and try to poke their heads through the netting covering the windows. They often woke us up butting against the wall.

In the woods at the far end of this field, my brother and I had built a lean-to with branches and twigs carefully laced and secured between two trees. It was a good job, very sound and secure but not rainproof. Before the day ended, it began to rain heavily, so my mother forbade us to sleep outside. The next morning we found our lean-to demolished and tramped on. The wild horses had been there and had romped all over it. That ended any desire on our part to sleep out again. Now I can imagine what my mother must have felt.

We would leave town as soon as school closed for the summer. It was about thirty miles from town. We would arrive there just in time to gather all the wild strawberries that grew in profusion in the abandoned mine pits. Later would come the raspberries, the thimbleberries, blackberries and the blueberries. My father saw to it that we did not suffer from boredom and laziness. We never had to say we had nothing to do. We would all go to the picking areas. One of the farmer's daughters knew all the best places and she would take us to them. She would never tell others where these places were. We would stay until all the buckets were filled or until rain drove us home. My sister was a baby and she came along. We took turns watching and playing with her on a blanket spread on the ground under a large shade tree. It was tricky business picking blackberries near an old logging trail where the black bears competed for the berries. I can't say that I enjoyed this routine of picking berries, but my father kept on prodding and reminding us how much we enjoyed eating the canned berries in the wintertime. We helped to clean the berries and helped my mother preserve these berries over our outdoor stove. At the end of the summer we would take home about two hundred quarts of canned berries. Raspberries are still my very favorite berry.

Now that I look back to this time, I realize what a strenuous time this must have been for my mother. No dishwasher, let alone running water, no washer and drier, no vacuum cleaner nor even a store-bought broom, instead a broom made of twigs fastened together, no convenient bathroom but an outdoor privy a good hundred feet away. Our clothes were hardy and simple—shirts, jeans or rather overalls—and most of the time we were barefoot. I'm sure that this is why my feet grew so big. To do the laundry we would all go to the lakeshore. There were three shores on this lake that were accessible, the closest one about a quarter mile away. The laundry shore had several large boulders near the shore's edge on which we soaped and rubbed the clothes and then rinsed in the lake. Here we never had to worry about not having enough water. To dry the clothes, we used the hot rays of the sun as they beamed on the garments spread over the meadow and the bushes. We would go fishing or take a nap while the clothes dried—they smelled so good.

We had a boat powered by feet and oars. It wasn't in the best shape, but it managed to stay on the surface if we could bail out water faster than it seeped in. It was a good-sized old wooden row boat. Many years later when I was vacationing at our summer home, I bought a wooden row boat for sentimental reasons. My father usually rowed the boat when he was there. On weekends he was back in town to hold church services. When he was gone, my brother and I often sat together and rowed the boat. Our mother usually sat in the front holding our baby sister in her lap. When my father rowed, he would let us sit backwards, dangling our legs in the water. On trips coming back from picking blackberries, the water would soothe the scratches we got from the thorns. We loved these rides. My father sang hymns in a sweet tenor voice while he rowed the boat, and we knew that berry picking was over for that day.

The third shore had the ruins of two log houses long past usefulness. Rumor had it that they had been the hideaway for a Chicago gangster, maybe even Al Capone's gang. The pine-pitch and bark used for chinking had fallen away from the logs. The windows and doors were gone, and the winds whistled through, disturbing the ghosts of those long gone, disturbing the snakes that had nested in the crevices. One day one of the farm boys, who was older than we were, caught a snake and held its head tight between his thumb and fingers until its mouth opened wide. He took a pinch of snuff and put it into the snake's mouth. He let the snake loose but held it to the ground with a stick. In a few minutes the snake puffed to about twice its size and died. We found sluffed-off snake skins all around the place. This was one place that held all the terror we needed. To get to this shore, we went along a narrow path through dark, towering pine trees and heavily leafed shade trees that made a gloomy passage. At one point we came out of this dark forest into a realm of sunlight—a forest of birch trees—tall, white, slender, swaying and glowing with the warmth of reflected sunshine that shone through the windows of quivering leaves overhead. A cathedral of peace and quiet. My mother would stop and whisper, "Don't whistle or the snakes will dance." Many years later when I told my husband about it, he wrote a story about the dancing snake.

The swimming beach was a long stretch of clean white sand and shallow water so we could wade a long way out before we were waist deep. The outlet of the lake went under a bridge over which the road ran that paralleled the shore. The water at this end was turgid and shallow, solid with water lilies and weeds, the lovely, fragrant, white, quivering water lilies. One day I made a wreath of water lilies and placed it on my head, with my long hair wafting in the breeze, much like poor Ophelia. By the time I got home, I was deathly sick. The fragrance was so heady it had given me a headache. Only years later, I learned that these lilies contain some kind of pollen and allergen that can be dangerous.

We were always cautioned to leave the swimming shore before it started to get dark because we had a long walk on a dirt road bordered by tall, dense woods, wild virgin timber. However, one day we stayed too long, and by the time we reached an open clearing near the farmer's field, it was almost dark and we had about a half mile to go. Just as we got alongside the field we saw a big black bear staring at us. My older brother took my hand and my younger brother's hand and he whispered, "Don't run, don't talk, just walk quickly." The bear didn't move but we did, and when we were well past the bear, we ran as fast as our legs could go. The fright must have drained every drop of red blood from our faces. We never overstayed our swimming sessions after that. Now I am surprised that we ever went swimming again.

Now we are told that fish are a desirable item in our diet. Then all we knew was that it was an essential item if we were to eat, so we had fish daily. The boys from the farm families took my brothers fishing with them. They had favorite fishing spots where they caught rock bass, perch, sunfish, and sometimes a big crappie. So we had fish and more fish—fried fish, boiled fish, fish chowder, fish cakes, and cold fish sandwiches. The fish stories belong to my brothers, and they had many adventures keeping the supply plentiful.

My mother loved flowers, so we tried to gather as many as we could find. Wild roses were especially desirable. This lake was dotted with many small islands, some of them no more than an outcropping of rock and scrubble, with a few hardy bushes growing. One was the cedar island where we went to get cedar boughs for the doorstep, another was the wild rose island. This last one was ringed with riotous bushes covered with roses whose fragrance carried over the water a long way.

My younger brother was eight at this time and I was twelve. He was my adventurous partner with far more courage and daring than I had. One day we set off with a supply of food to gather cedar boughs and wild roses. The day started out as crisp and clear as only a northern summer morning can be. We rowed from island to island exploring each in turn. These islands were not near our shore but out in the wider and further expanse of the lake, so we were a long way off from our starting point. After hours of rowing, roaming and eating our food, we had filled the front of the boat with cedar boughs, on top of which we had piled the branches of lovely wild roses.

It was time to cross the water for home. In the north woods a storm can hit before you can lift an oar. We were no sooner out from the shore a ways when wind and rain pelted us with a fury. The lake was shallow so the waves were wild and choppy. My brother was rowing and there was no way we could change places so I could row. To row straight across would have been the shortest way, but to do so would have brought the waves broadside and, without a doubt, would have capsized us. We were good swimmers but we could not have survived that rough water. We had enough water experience to know that you head into the waves and pray. The rain came down in torrents, filling the boat, and the waves tried to outdo the rain. I bailed with a bucket in each hand as fast as I could while my brother rowed. An eight-year-old hero was what he was that day. It seemed forever before we reached calmer water to quickly turn the boat and veer back with the waves behind us. We made our shore and pulled the boat out of the water. The rain and wind were still at gale force. Nevertheless, we gathered the cedar boughs and wild roses and headed for home. We were so wet. Our hair hung over our faces, our clothes were glued to our skin, and we were cold.

My mother had been watching for us at the door. When she saw us coming, she ran out through the rain crying, hugged us both and pulled us into the shelter of the house. She quickly got us dried and into dry clothes, all the time scolding and crying. She thought she would never see us again. The storm was so severe, and she knew we were out on the water. My brother and I didn't have enough time to be frightened while we were in it. We were too busy trying to save ourselves.

Those growing-up summers were full of such experiences, experiences of fun, love, joy, fears and tears. The wonders and terrors of nature and the many dangers added up to a richness that no amount of wealth could buy. We were living a charmed poverty, not a deprivation, richly protected and sheltered in the aura of warmth and security emanating from sources greater than us but predictable and reliable because our parents believed and cared.

Bernhard Hillila

YRJÖ KAARTO

GROWING UP IN THE 1920s

In that Upper Michigan town,
    there were Finnish clerks at the stores
    and Finnish tellers at the banks.
Dad, of course, spoke English
       at the mine
and Mom, with hesitation,
       to the neighbors.
At home the growing Yrjö
       heard only Finnish.
When he went to kindergarten,
    he was uni-lingual
        except for a few essential words
    he'd picked up from neighbor kids.
When Miss McPherson spoke,
    he'd ask his buddy Antti,
       who knew a *lot* of English,
    Mitä se nyt sanoi? –
       "What did she say now?"
Once when he found out
    the teacher had asked for stories,
       he told Antti to let her know
    he knew a really good one –
and so he told the story
    of *Väkevä Matti*, in Finnish.
Later in the year
    he told the story again –
       this time "Mighty Matti," in English.

When he got to second grade,
    Yrjö announced that he was "George."
Antti had told him solemnly
    there weren't supposed to be
       any Yrjös in America.
       nor even Yllis, as his parents called him.
That was the year that Tyyne Pantti, grade four,

asked that her last name
   be spelled with an "o,"
so she wouldn't be Tiny Panty any more.

Now finished with grade six,
   set for grammar school in the fall,
      George savored his summer.
He'd watch the teamster
   drive up with the groceries,
follow the iceman tonging
   a huge 25-cent piece of ice
      to the icebox,
hand the clothespins to his mother
   as she hung the wash
      out on the lines,
focus on the mysteries of radio
   after family supper
and play kick-the-can
   or "pump, pump, pull away"
   or "work-up" baseball
      with his chums.
On rainy days there was
      the Carnegie Public Library
   with the Hardy boys,
      Popular Mechanics
      and *Boy's Life.*

About once a week he'd go down
      to the station to watch
   the Duluth, South Shore and Atlantic
      train come in.
From around the bend it came,
      whistle first,
   then the engine
      with its pointed cowcatcher,
      belching stack,
      swinging bronze bell,

                      awesome drive wheels
                      and the fireman waving from the cab,
                 next the coal tender,
                 mail car,
                 passenger car,
                 and finally the Pullman
                      with the only Negro
                           he had ever seen
                      except in pictures—
                           black-faced,
                           white-eyed,
                           white-jacketed—
                 swinging down from the stair
                      to place a square step
                      on the depot platform.
          After the train pulled out,
                      engine snorting,
                      whistle whoo-ing,
                 George would check the nail
                      or—once in a long while—
                 the penny he'd left on the track,
                      to see how flat it had gotten.

Ernest Hekkanen

IN THE NEW WORLD

*E*VEN THEN he seemed ancient, a mythical itinerant who arrived by train to spend the summer. What remains is a mosaic. A short man with large, enfolding hands who ate raw fish while I watched from the willow tree. A man whose single passion was to conquer; a joyless, stern, work-hardened man whose strange tongue I could not fathom.

Ensti Maallinen. He arrived in search of work in 1904 and how he found his way to southwestern Wyoming and the coal mines can only be guessed. Perhaps he was in the company of men who heard there was work in that land. Someone proffered the ticket, he paid currency he did not know the worth of and soon he was there, siderailed in a dry, hot country so unlike the swampland he had come from that he felt newly terrestrial.

A man who paid his dues. At midnight he would get up to cough phlegm from lungs riddled with coal dust. Embedded in his cheeks and forehead were specks of rock. He worked as a blacksmith, a man with a trade when he was not sinking charges in the mine. Then there was an explosion. A ceiling fell in. He was trapped seventy-eight hours underground in what became a grave for men whose luck had run out. A militant in his day, he was paid in full to the I.W.W. His last contribution was in 1929, and even now when the man no longer lives, the labor newspaper arrives in the mail to keep his ghost informed that the Union is still strong.

The tale. He fled eastern Finland rather than being recruited into the Russian army. He came to America where he worked hard, saved his money and married. He returned to Finland where two children were born and then, dissatisfied with his luck, where he lived in the city, in Helsinki, he came back with his family to the States, to Wyoming and the coal mines. The third child, my father, was the first Maallinen to be born in the New World.

In the family portrait my grandfather looks a handsome man. Doubtlessly strong. His hands rest like huge ornaments on his knees as he sits in the straightback chair with his family around him. Three children: a dark-haired girl, a tall, ungainly son, and a tow-headed boy in knee britches. The wife, my grandmother. She had heavy, bovine features and the husky build of a peasant, but she was kind, you get that feeling. I never knew her. She died three days after I was born.

But the tale. He was an enterprising man and a good provider. Besides working in the mine he ran a small dairy and worked as a bartender in a saloon. It was said that he could use his massive fists if provoked and once he nearly beat a man to death. Or so the tale goes. I have the *puukko* he carried sheathed on his belt: a deadly, fine instrument that was honed to sting like a thistle.

That first trip to the Northwest. We picked him up at the railroad station in Seattle. He had one suitcase and a valise. And he was old. He seemed ancient, as though dust had permanently settled on his features. A stranger. I kept my distance. And he kept his.

"Call him *vaari*," my father said. "Grandpa."

My mother balked. She was an O'Connel. She had black, lustrous hair and needle features, and she didn't approve of her children fraternizing with the foreign and unfamiliar. I was two years younger than my sister, and my brother was still riding my mother's hip. Her face became suspicious whenever Finnish was spoken in the house.

"What are they saying, Mother?'

"It's idiot-talk. Don't listen. It doesn't mean anything."

My grandfather cleared the land. Cut trees and cleared the land. "I bring down light," he said. "Not enough light on this house."

The five acres. My father couldn't have made the down payment without my grandfather's help. Call it an advance against inheritance, anyway my grandfather had legitimate claim on the woods. He took over as though master. He determined which trees would fall and he would have fallen them outward to the horizons of the property had he not been pushing sixty. My father worked as a civil engineer in Seattle; he would leave the house early in the morning and arrive back late at night, in a '39 Plymouth we brush painted one summer to forestall rust. My father could devote little time to decimating the woods and, therefore, the woods survived, although sorely depleted. But the woods. To my sister and me it seemed endless, thick forest. Bears came out of it to topple the garbage can, deer emerged to nibble at the garden, and once there was a wolf. I can remember being roused to witness that gaunt apparition sitting in the snow looking into our windows. My father pitched food, but the wolf, an arrogant fellow, simply watched it drop in the snow. After sitting a while he got up and walked away, past the chicken house with the hens locked securely inside, along the path leading to a neighbor and forever out of our sight.

The house, a cottage. A pre-manufactured, easy-to-assemble cracker box my father ordered through the catalogue. Friends gathered to raise it. The sections bolted together and in two days it was done, all except for tar papering the roof. My father was laying the patio when I made my final thrust into the world. He will relive that moment with my mother. My mother was impatient to go because her water had broken, but my father, a meticulous man who sought perfection in small things, was determined to rake and smooth the concrete before it hardened.

It was to this outpost that my grandfather came with his traditions, his peculiarities, and his foreign tongue. I can remember him climbing out of the car and stretching. The first thing he remarked was his fatigue and his need of a sauna. There was no sauna, my father informed him. But there was a tub. A tub would get you clean. My grandfather was indignant. A sauna must be built. The next day he started work on it. He was a good carpenter in addition to his other skills. He built the sauna to stand against time. A good, concrete floor on good hardpan. Walls with studs every sixteen inches. A firebox made of wrought iron, a metal ring to enclose rocks. When the sauna was done we dug two tremendous holes outside the door and filled them with sod and chicken manure before planting birch trees.

"For the future," my father translated. My mother would have nothing to do with the sauna. Only heathens went in for such practices. Only uncivilized people. Only Finns. She would continue to bathe in a tub, thank you. And so would the children.

"You're letting your blarney get the best of you," my father said.

"That might be so, but I don't see how anyone can get clean soaking in his own sweat. The very idea of it sounds filthy."

"Anyway Lee will sauna with us," my father said. The dinner table became a battleground, but in the end I would sauna with the men.

Then, of course, there was the episode of the lye-fish. We drove into Seattle to the public market, an all-day trip in the hot confines of a car, while my grandfather spat tobacco juice out the window. I remember food stalls, oranges piled high in beautiful pyramids, and the barking of vendors. We went straight to the fish market. My grandfather tried to dicker with a man who wouldn't dicker, relying on my father to translate.

"A,a. Too high, price too high." We walked away. My father removed his billfold and gave my grandfather several bills. We returned to the fish market. My grandfather waved his finger at the dry lye-fish hanging upside down in loops of twine. We bought what seemed a cord of the stiff, board-like fish, parading it back to the car in our arms.

In this way my grandfather brought tradition to the dinner table. It was an involved route. First the lye-fish must be soaked, the water changed daily until the fish became pliable and the lye released. My mother refused to cooperate. She said the lye would eat holes in our stomachs. She sat with folded arms while my father prepared the meal. The fish became jelly that slid on our plates.

"I can still taste the lye," my mother said, pleased that her suspicions had been borne out. "I won't let the children eat this. You two can rot your stomachs, but we'll have sandwiches."

My father translated. My grandfather raised his head to listen. He looked at my mother and grunted. He was a dedicated man at meal-times. He attacked his food noisily, sucking in mouthfuls and releasing his satisfaction. I became afraid watching him, his appetite was so boundless and fierce.

Those days glitter now. The spangled mornings endured until late afternoon. I can picture the chicken house on the hill, the fenced-in yard where the hens scratched. The tang of manure and lime pinches my nostrils. I carry buckets of feed and water, and the chickens, anxious to be fed, form a red sea at my knees. I remember the rite of rolling heads and severed necks, and burying my hands in damp feathers while my mother singed the white bodies over flaming newspapers. And I can remember my grandfather keeping his distance, sitting at a picnic table, the sun at his back, methodically pawing at a raw salt-fish.

When we finished butchering the hens my father crossed the yard and sat down at the picnic table with my grandfather, while my mother scowled. Later I went with the men to the sauna. The heat choked me. I remained on the bottom step while my father sat with my grandfather on the top step conversing in Finn. I was the water boy, in this case a privilege. I liked making the steam that gushed against the ceiling and came floating down around us, erasing our visibility.

That summer with my grandfather ended with another car ride. I shook hands with him when he boarded the train, and to this day I retain the impression of that monstrous hand taking mine into it. Several years later we drove to Wyoming to visit him in Superior. He was sixty-five and he was pitching old photographs into an incinerator in the backyard when we arrived. He had been pensioned and he was about to move to Florida. We drove him to Rock Springs to place flowers on his wife's grave, a last grand gesture before we put him on the train to the land of oranges and coconut palms.

Eventually we moved from the prefab cottage to a larger, more comfortable house designed by an architect. My father had become prosperous, and the city had encroached on our preserve. These were the days of angry chainsaws. Trees fell to make way for suburbs. Bulldozers and earth-movers leveled the land and contractors built houses, the basements of which flooded in the winter. Even now there is little beauty in these subdivisions, although trees, deciduous trees, help to hide the thoughtlessness and the scars. I can remember fighting city children whenever I was called hick or farmer. We were no longer part of the community. The community was big and amorphous. Churches and gas stations vied for diminishing land, as did schools and shopping centers. And the forest retreated, leaving small stands here and there that first-comers clung to despite rising property taxes.

We learned by long distance that my grandfather had remarried. He drove an old Desoto all the way from Florida to show off the bride, a small, plump Finnish lady with delicate features and manners that contrasted sharply with my grandfather's. Her name was Helmi and she had a flair for making plump, round piglets out of clay. I was in high school and I was intolerant of older people. My grandfather spoke less English than he had ten years before and I coveted a secret disgust each time I saw his dentures soaking in a glass of water. His body had become fragile, after all, he was eighty-two. His joints had slowed his momentum and his face had become hollow, especially without his teeth. I was young and I was arrogant and I was proud of my physique, as he must have been in his youth. I was overhauling an old jalopy and to demonstrate my strength I hoisted the engine block in my bare hands.

"Someday make good blacksmith," he said, and for twenty minutes he rambled on in Finnish while I nodded dumbly, grinding my greasy fingers. I looked a young Irishman, curly, black hair, an up-turned nose. But in my body and my gestures I was his grandson. There was a tether as indefinable as time. I remember being impressed by his hands. There was no lack of strength in those meaty, thick, gnarled appendages. Mine would never measure up. They would never have such weight. They would never grasp the world as his had, in deep passageways in the earth.

But what am I trying to say? I grew up as he got older. He returned to Florida where he lived with his newly taken wife. He lived in the midst of his garden, where grapefruit, lemons, oranges, and coconut palms abounded, while the mood of the land got nasty. The time was the late sixties. I gave up my barbells in order to heft weighty ideals. While my grandfather grew old among his flowers. An old Wobbly puttering with his flowers, supported by Old Age pension, Black Lung pension, and Miner's pension. He frowned at the photograph of me with long hair, my father said. He disagreed with my flight north, an old Wobbly amid his flowers. And now it is 1977 and my grandfather is dead. I received the news yesterday by long distance. I will attend the funeral but first I must attend to this. The last years.

At ninety-four, when the Department of Motor Vehicles finally refused to grant him a license, when he was no longer able to take care of himself and his wife, who had become senile, my father brought him north by plane to Seattle and installed him in the tiny pre-fab cottage next door to the big house. For nearly three years the old people lived in those confines, the temperature kept at eighty-five because their bodies were weak and would not adjust to the colder climate.

"We give him pills," my father said. "For his lungs and for his lapses."

An old man with a hearing aid stuck in his ear, which he kept turned off in order to silence his wife's voice. She spoke incessantly of going home. She could stand at the window and see across the country to Minnesota. "I must go home. Why don't you let me go? Why are you holding me? They won't like it if I don't get home for supper." My grandfather tuned out the deterioration of her mind. If brought to his attention he would say, using the male pronoun, "He's old. He doesn't know what he's saying." But she would outlive him, a young girl lost in her old age.

At ninety-four my grandfather had learned the worth of currency in the New World, and he had learned how to manipulate his children by promising to give or withhold. This began as an old man's mischievousness, but in the end it became paranoia, in the last years, when he could no longer feel secure in his sleep unless his bankbook was under his pillow. But he was old. The restraints were going, and thirty-five years in the mines, and the constant need to be frugal, had exaggerated his character.

I returned for a visit in 1976, allowed into the country because of a legal loophole. It was spring and the occasion was my grandfather's birthday. His children were there and you could see by the furtive glances that they regarded one another with suspicion, especially the daughter, my aunt, whose dyed hair and sharp features were an eternal declaration of war. My uncle, an urbane man who spent his winters by the Mediterranean, living in pensiones, vascillated in an anguished sort of way. He did not require the inheritance but he was easily persuaded. And my father. With all deference to his ideals, his love of Emerson and Thoreau, he desired his father's blessing too much not to wish its reward.

Both my brother and sister had arrived with their spouses. We sat apart, drinking, exclaiming our virtues insofar as we were not vying for the old man's inheritance.

"I feel the money should be used to put the old people in a home," my sister said. "It's wearing Mom and Dad out taking care of them."

"You saw the way Mother's hands shook." My brother had the mark of a Finn. He was blond and he had the large, thick nose of the

Maallinens, while I looked a story-book O'Connel.

I said, yes, they did appear tired, run-down. My mother's hair was white and my father's cheeks hung slack. But I had not been close to them for ten years. I had not witnessed their aging. In a way, it frightened me. I was made to feel my impermanence.

My grandfather had become a shriveled old man with a wren's face. His movements were ponderous and slow. But his hands. His hands were large and powerful, incongruous paws hanging from bony arms. I went up to shake hands, making myself heard with a shout. He clutched my hand as he spoke in Finn. His eyes were large and watery behind the bifocals.

"He wants to know if you remember helping him build the sauna?" my father translated. "You had one of those little tool sets. He tried to show you how to use the saw. You didn't want to be shown. Instead you told him you didn't like him and went back to the house. He says you were a stubborn resister even then."

"Tell him I inherited that streak from him," I said, knowing he should be flattered on his ninety-seventh. But I had become cynical. I no longer toted ideals as much as I desired to be blameless.

The real celebration came a week later. My father and I went down to the woods to cut firewood. Later my grandfather, walking painfully slow with his cane, came to help us. He dragged branches and tossed them in a pile.

"He likes doing this," my father said. "I'll have to move the branches out from under the trees to burn them, but that doesn't matter. The work makes him feel useful."

I looked at my father, the thick, unhandsome face, the short, sturdy build. I looked at my grandfather, the manual laborer. You could see the legacy in our hands, the diminishing size from one generation to the next. We had come up from the mines.

We finished cutting firewood and climbed the hill to the house. I suggested we take a sauna. "Ensti might enjoy it," I said. "The tradition. It will be passed on."

My father cut the birch switches while I built the fire. My grandfather looked on with approval, clacking his dentures. It was a bright spring day, and warm, but he shivered on being undressed. He had almost no musculature and no fat. My father was heavy and carried a paunch. I had kept trim being on the road, working at seasonal jobs such as tossing hay. My father brought a bottle of whiskey from the house and we sat drinking while we bathed. Again I was the water boy. I made the steam that erased our visibility. Then we beat ourselves with the birch switches.

"I'm an old man," my grandfather said. My father and I were dressing him. He cleared his throat and went on, "I haven't much life. All, everything is gone. Pretty soon I die," and then he spoke in Finn.

I waited for my father to translate. The way he firmed his face, I knew it was an emotional moment for him.

"He says it will make his passing easier knowing he has such a grandson. He can die happily, he says."

"Tell him he has a lot of years left," I said.

I learned that night that my father was going to put the five acres up for sale.

"We'll keep the house, but we'll give up the land. The taxes are too high." He paused. "You know, it was really his land. I couldn't have bought it without his help. I won't tell him until the sale is confirmed. Perhaps by then—"

"I understand you," I said.

But I was thinking of myself, the fact that I was lost to motion, a Maallinen, whose very name was earthly, a man on the road in the New World.

Gladys Koski Holmes

FRAGMENTS

Grandma is on a trip again,
    In another building, upstairs, or in her house in the woods.
    The nursing home has no second floor.

She is happiest in her house in the woods;
    Once one person has one, every person wants one.

She says hers holds:
    lost recipes, her favorites, Canadian Banana Spice Cake,
    Russian Rocks, Washboards, and Queen Elizabeth Cake;

    her rocking chair *he* sold when they moved
    to the state of Washington in 1929;

    the mantel clock that sat on a shelf
    because they had no mantel
    and chimed the hour and half hour
    and has a thermometer and barometer on each side
    of the round face, glassed in
    that shows the minute, hour and day of the month;

    black and white mittens in a Finnish star pattern
    her mother made her in 1932, tightly knit;

    the rayon pillow top her son sent her
    during World War II that says
    MOTHER and IWO JIMA:

    magazines, *Mother's Home Companion*
    with issues dating back to 1931
    and *Ladies' Home Journal* and *Good Housekeeping*
    and *McCall's* that have really good stories
    about Life and Love;

stacks of white cotton flour sacks for dish towels
to be ripped open and stamped with
SUNDAY through SATURDAY
ready for the embroidery needle;

hand towels and pillow cases bought on sale,
unused until crocheted edgings band each end
in turquoise, hot pink or yellow-orange;

the wooden butter paddle hand-carved with a hook
two-thirds of the way up on the handle
so it won't slide into the bowl
bought at the Farmer's Market
during the Depression Days
she still uses;
a pink depression glass cake plate, eight-sided,
with three glass knobs for feet
and creamer and sugar to match;

and always on her table the pressed glass, fluted-edged
half-way-between-a-bowl-and-vase container
made for holding teaspoons, handles up;

Can't you stay while she cooks coffee?
    well maybe next time,
    the pot is half full of grounds
    and she'd have to clean it out first.

Besides, the walk always tires her.

WIDOWS

I speak of the mettle of

    old women;
    rural women

Whose strengths annealed by

    time and trial,
    crystallize inside

Glass-clear under wrinkled skin.

Of steel and glass a core

    pit-hard
    hidden inside

Outside aging peach flesh

    soft sags
    against life alone,

Belying multi-layers of inner world.

Eila Siren-Perlmutter

ROOM AND BOARD

Sirkka Kallio Suomalainen
Anno Anno Domini
Nineteen hundred thirty three
Anno Anno Domini—

S HE RAN crazily down the pebbled hill, chanting. (Finns still chant in this New World.) Stopped transfixed in front of Barber Otto's shiny-new, red-and-white barber pole down at the bottom of Finn Hill, across the road from the Fire Hall. Watched it spinning, spinning, spinning in the dazzle-bright, Minnesota noon sunshine. In the changeable way of northern weathers, a cool, brisk breeze was beginning to kick up its heels. Sirkka turned around anxiously to the comfort of the familiar and more comprehensible sights and sounds of Winton Falls. But the early morning's usual sights and sounds were long over with: of men off to the woods with packsacks, twenty-twos, saws and axes; of high-school kids toting books and lunch bags, off in the yellow bus; and of younger kids running or dragging off to the brick schoolhouse by the river. Winton Falls was left to spring winds and the sunshine life of small animals and their life-sustaining flutterings and squeekings; and to jealously land reclaiming second-growth pines, implacable in the wake of the human plunderings—inevitable in these border wildernesses.

Yet to Sirkka's quickened senses there was something else. Something incongruent, disconcerting, even formidable. It was a particular groaning and grinding sound that the wind gusts carried to her, a sound peculiar to rusty metal rubbing rusty metal, it seemed to her, that was followed by an echoless thud of dead wood hitting dead wood. She had heard the groans and the thumps before, but never with such an incessant beat, such intransigent frenzy. She turned her head towards the source of the sounds, a half-hinged wooden sign, hanging on twisted lengths of broken chain that with each gust of wind beat on "Carlson's Hotel"—which, with a tinge of mockery, this clapboard building was called in Winton Falls. It was a large and dilapidated structure, moldy green in color, a true tombstone, to mark the vanishing Finn-immigrant boarding house. Window-darkened and begloomed, it sprawled only five false fronts up the road from the barber shop.

The sign was printed up in puritanically narrow and straight letters, that had once in some dim—to the child unknown—past advertised "Carlson's Room and Board." Now only a mocking "Carlson's Roo" remained of it. Kids of course called the place Carlson's Roost. Kids are like that—mean—without knowing just how mean.

Carlson's Hotel had been, as Winton Falls had been, long since denuded of turn-of-the-century necessaries like a wooden sidewalk, hitching posts, and the sprawling porch that encircled such larger buildings—all those marks of frontier hotel affluence. There remained only some now-ugly reminders like the broken sign itself, a painful sigh torn out of the past; a reminder of the days when Carlson's had dominated one of the busiest corners of the village, when on its way to becoming a real town of some 2,000 inhabitants. And its cracked plate-glass windows on the very side of the house that had once faced other thriving businesses—harness maker, livery stable, mill-owned general store, and saloon—now stared disconsolately at a barbed-wire fence enclosing Tuuri Pelto's dairy farm. The cows sometimes stared back questioningly at Carlson's Hotel, between slow sideways jaw movements on their cuds.

The some-time hotel had a strange fascination for Sirkka. It seemed wrapped in a cloud of mysteries of the past, the present, perhaps even the future. She had often tried to imagine the colorful bustle of lumber-jacks about the place in years like 1905 or 1910, for instance—scenes that Barber Otto had often so vividly described to her, of times remote and otherwise unimaginable to her. But just then Carlson's Roost seemed resistant to her imaginings. It was as if lost in some brooding, angry hurt deep in its House Soul. And now, for the first time in her life, Sirkka felt a gloom that somehow had little to do with herself, but rather to originate outside of herself. As though from the house itself, or about to enter the house. She had no words for it then—words like *imminent, determinate. . .inexorable.* So she, as always in a crisis, thought in the Finn's language, deliberate—

I think I am afraid of what it will do—that house. If I turn my back to it, then it will go away. It won't be there any more, and I won't have to think about it any more.

But the groaning and the thumping continued, its cadence accentuating the throbbing pain of an infected boil that nestled in and distorted one small, Finno-Ugric cheek. She turned and walked towards the shelter of Barber Otto's back yard.

Otto Jarvi-called Barber Otto for obvious reasons—was in the very small and very neat backyard of his very white and very neat home-

and-barber shop, building a boat. He was there a lot, building boats, unless some one of the two hundred Finn heads wanted cutting, or that he was out on the lakes. He waved a piece of sandpaper at her. Considering this an invitation, Sirkka turned happily through the wire gate, and sat down on a familiar step of the back stoop. They said nothing to each other. They never did, unless there was something important to say. Sirkka considered Barber Otto her own and special friend. He had two daughters, one younger than she was and one slightly older. His wife—called Barber Otto's Missus, also for obvious reasons—was a homey woman, motherly and sweet.

Barber Otto was famous all over the Mesabi Iron Range for his graceful rowboats and canoes, that no one but an occasional rich tourist could afford to buy, however. As he made the boards out of wilderness cedars, they cost him next to nothing to build. Except in time. And Otto valued his time. As well he might, Sirkka thought. He worked next to his garage, a converted barn, which housed the Essex touring car he, himself, never drove. He claimed that too much technology depraved mankind. He allowed Mrs. Jarvi to take it out in berry-picking time, though, provided the girls and Sirkka and her mother were along. "Good luck, Girls!" he would call out after them, referring to their finding good berry patches. Then again, he may have been referring to his wife's driving, which was unique. Barber Otto's Missus understood only two speeds—fast and stationary.

Well, there he was, working over a cedar strip with a piece of sandpaper. After a time—"No school for you today, eh Sirkka," he suddenly said, positioning a screw into a narrow slat of wood. She pointed to the boil on her puffed-up cheek. Otto's leathery skin cracked a little as his facial muscles spilled into a smile.

"Hurts like a son-of-a-gun, I know," he said then, sympathetically.

For some time the child Sirkka and the man Otto were lost in their private thoughts and rememberings though aware, still, of one another. She liked particularly to be with Otto while he was working on a boat because it seemed to inspire in him certain reminiscences and observations. Otto was not the proverbially taciturn Finn. He was often jovial—at times even witty. Everyone in Winton Falls considered the barber to be a man of uncommon abilities. Sirkka and Alec certainly did—her mother (Martha) had some reservations. He could make boats, cut hair, hunt and trap and fish—all of it better than anyone else in the village. And he could even cook (like any woman, Martha said). Sirkka was most impressed, however, by his house-cleaning techniques. Between haircuts he liked coming into the kitchen to help out his "girls," especially when they were canning bushels of blueberries or whatever else was in season. He would take the broom, not only to the floor, but to counter tops, stove top, chairs, table; in fact, to every flat surface of the kitchen— "Well, why not?" he asked, addressing her shock, "We eat off plates, don't we?" Sirkka could only nod. Alec roared when she told him; Martha was not at all amused.

Yet it wasn't Barber Otto's resourcefulness that attracted her most. He was to her a priceless storehouse of facts and details about a colorful Winton Falls past of more than three decades ago. When men trapped for mink and muskrat in the distant and often tempestuous northern waters. When lumberjacks felled the giant red and white pine and hauled them to waterways on horse-drawn sleighs. Well, Barber Otto had done it all and knew it all. And all this the Kallios had missed, being latecomers to the New World in 1928.

Sirkka knew precisely how to turn Otto on to that lore. Today, the saloons. How many there had been in the old days—though she already knew—

"Five, Sirkka. We used to have five saloons in Winton Falls once," the barber said, the reminiscence lighting him up like a 100-watt lightbulb. "But look over there," he added, pointing towards Pipestone Lake to a row of crumbling cement foundations. "Most of the houses that stood there were rolled away to Shagawa after the lumber boom was over—behind horse teams and, later, tractors. Oh yes, beautiful little homes they were, too, when Winton Falls had more people than Shagawa even." He sighed. "But that was before men began dying in those iron mines!" And then he spat. "That devil ore! It's that devil-red ore that gets into a man's clothes and under his skin and then in his lungs—finally into his very soul." Otto had worked in the mines for two weeks, and fifteen years later would still, he claimed, cough up the red ore.

Sirkka felt the usual frightened wrench in her stomach. Because she was thinking about her father—about Alec. Alec who now worked in the mines for three days a month like most of them did—"to keep sugar, flour, coffee, and dignity on the table," he said. Despite the Depression, two of the Shagawa mines were again in limited operation. The three days of "work available" had been agreed upon in a caucus (according to Otto) representing U.S. Steel, the A.F. of L., the U.S. Government, and two of the five Shagawa mines—mysteriously, Otto said. And that three days was enough for Alec to aggravate his persistent cough for thirty more, Martha said. Alec had an undiagnosed respiratory ailment. Sirkka worried about it a lot. But at ten the heavinesses of life can flit by in a matter of seconds sometimes.

"How dying, Mr. Jarvi?" mechanically, then, she asked. She already knew that answer too. Everybody knew. He however ignored the question, wanting to change the subject. Sensitive.

Talk between the man and the child flowed more easily then, as it turned to pleasanter things, and soon shifted into the stream of timelessness known only by those congenial spirits who can escape all barriers of age and sex and class and race.

Then their easy talk broke off – abruptly – as a long shadow fell across the boat-makings, blocking off a brilliant stream of light from just above the Town Hall bell tower. Otto, no less than Sirkka, was startled by the appearance of Leif Carlson, the Norsk owner of the sometime-hotel. The two men exchanged brief, scarcely audible, greetings – the "hallo" and "howsta" Finns of Minnesota use a lot. For a long while there was no conversation beyond that, as the hotel keeper watched the boat maker. It seemed to Sirkka that Mr. Jarvi paid more than common attention, though, to every board he screwed into place, while Mr. Carlson was so casually looking on. And it seemed to her that Mr. Carlson leaned too heavily on the wire fence as he smoked one after another of some limp and scraggly cigarettes – homemade, like Alec's. Then threw the short and battered butts into the road, where wandering chickens ran innocently and expectantly after each butt. Never learning, they cackled disappointedly at the object and wandered mindlessly off again.

She had been staring fixedly at Carlson since he first appeared. She had what Martha called the "terrible habit" of staring fixedly at persons, unconscious that they were sometimes embarrassed by it. But Mr. Carlson didn't seem to notice the staring. She was fascinated by his down-pointed smile – tried it herself – and by his very freckled lips, fleshy and broad. She watched him intently. He was a big, raw-boned, open-faced man.

"You're Alec Kallio's little girl, aren't you?" he asked in English, turning suddenly to her, but looking through and past her, so that she felt like looking behind herself to see if someone else was there. Recovered enough to nod though. "You're my Bertta's friend," he said then, smiling broadly and making his big lips look beautiful, she thought. She liked the way he spoke the English words. There was none of the heavy Finn-English accent. But then he as suddenly turned away from her again, seeming to forget her; and the corners of his mouth settled once more into that downward pose, as his eyes again followed every movement of Otto's hands.

She knew that nearly everyone in Winton Falls wondered a lot about Leif Carlson. And that no one seemed to know very much about him; that he drank himself unconscious once or twice a week at Haapala's

Pool Hall; that Haapala always, somehow, got him home to the hotel two false fronts up the road; and that he talked a lot to Haapala and rarely to anyone else. But then Haapala was a good listener, not saying much ever, except to quote the prices of his bootlegged liquors – which was not often necessary because the Finns around could afford beer mostly. Except on paydays – if there were paydays – when they went hell-bent for his whiskey. Some said Haapala was too dumb to talk much; others that he was too smart to.

Because of Bertta, Sirkka too thought a lot about the Carlson family. There were three young daughters; Bertta, her friend, was the youngest. Bertta sometimes invited her into the green hotel, but Sirkka had never seen Mr. Carlson there. Privately, she thought of the hotel as a haunted house though this she never uttered to a soul for fear of hurting Bertta's feelings – recalling the day they had peeked at the old Carlson limousine now reposing in a converted horse-barn attached to the hotel. This limousine was a long, black, grim-looking Buick which, judging from the dust and cobwebs shrouding it, hadn't left its stall in ten years.

"Is it a hearse?" Sirkka had – wittily, she thought – asked Bertta. She had forgotten that to be friends with Bertta you had to be careful. There were those taboo subjects. You couldn't ask questions about her parents, or about the hotel. You couldn't even talk to Mrs. Carlson if Bertta or her two sisters were around. They cut you off. You were only expected to say "Hallo" to her.

People said things about Mrs. Carlson – that she was *omituinen*. Sirkka thought she was sadly beautiful.

Well, right after the hearse witticism, Bertta yanked her out of the garage. Then, relenting for reasons of her own, did take her into the house and through the kitchen, where Mrs. Carlson was stirring some good-smelling stuff in a pot on the biggest and blackest cast-iron cook stove Sirkka had ever seen. But before Sirkka even had time to shape her mouth into a "hallo," Bertta pushed her into a darkened hallway where the wall paper was torn and hanging loose all over; then past rows of doors, some of which were ajar, revealing bulky and mirrorless bureau bottoms and rusted, iron bedsteads with those striped mattresses – thin, soiled, lumpy masses they were. Sirkka assumed that the two or three rooms with closed doors had occupants in them.

They passed a dark and narrow staircase leading to the second floor before they reached the large living room which the family still kept private and apart from most of Winton Falls. Sirkka thought living in this room must have been difficult at times, though, because it was so cold and drafty, being so big and high-ceilinged; it seemed doubtful to her that the potbelly stove could ever have heated it into the coziness her own parents achieved in their tiny five-room house on Finn Hill — she felt happy and warm thinking of it. But then, here the Carlsons' beautiful red mahogany piano was, and there were some other interesting massy pieces of mahogany furniture too.

Certainly no one in Winton Falls seemed to know what the family Carlson lived on, in these days. Some guessed at it, some thought they knew, some just shook their heads mysteriously — not knowing. Sure, Leif Carlson had never found, or even looked for, another occupation after the lumber boom was spent. These were the early days of the work shift from lumbering to mining — when Winton Falls metamorphosed from a town back to village status again, a village of miners then, commuting to the five mines in Shagawa — and when the men also metamorphosed into the over-worked and tired-out of this world, begrimed by the red ore-wash. It was said that Lempi Carlson had declared she would leave the Norsk before you would catch her washing one pair of a miner's ore-red underwear. She would go back to Finland first.

It was also said that three or four trappers, former lumberjacks — drinking now their primary occupation and trapping secondary — paid cash for room and board at Carlson's. And, it was said, Lempi Carlson was a lot nicer to them than she had ever been to Leif, whatever that meant.

How, with all that history whirling about Mr. Carlson's head, could Sirkka help staring at him? He was a strange and interesting man to her. She had difficulty imagining him living in that house with his family — the way he was and the way Mrs. Carlson was. The girls never talked about him, never even mentioned him. And kids talked a lot about fathers in Winton Falls.

She looked first at one man then the other: the boat builder, screwing on long and slender boards, saying nothing; the hotel keeper, leaning on the fence, smoking and smiling — well kind of —

Wonder what Mr. Carlson is thinking about, watching like that, not saying anything and just smoking — must be twenty cigarettes already — more than even Alec would. Funny he was never around the house when Bertta and I played in the cold front room, on the beautiful sounding, deep-red piano, harmonizing our favorite song, "Where Would I Be?" That was the time of the horrible laughing from upstairs — must have been Mr. Carlson. Positively scary. We both ran outside. Bertta looked glad to.

She gazed even more intently into Leif Carlson's face.

"You're a lucky man, Otto Jarvi!" abruptly then Carlson said, in his fine American accent. "You make a good boat, and you make yourself a good life. Lucky man."

Otto smiled uneasily, looking first at Carlson then at her, Sirkka. She wondered was that a signal for her to go home or to go inside to visit Mrs. Jarvi, that she wouldn't hear more of the conversation. So, more to prevent his pursuing either one of these possibilities, she quickly addressed Mr. Carlson—

"Would you like to make boats too, Mr. Carlson?"

"Out of the mouths of babes," he answered, smiling with that down-pointed smile again. But he wasn't looking at her when he said it. Up the road rather. Then he said, looking directly at her, "Don't ask me any more questions like that, little girl, or I might insult your tender years and tell you why I don't make boats—or anything else, for that matter, little Swollen Face!" And he began to laugh some more and turn his face up the road towards the hotel. Barber Otto didn't look amused though, pointing and motioning to Sirkka to go into the house. But which sign language she pretended not to see.

Still laughing —or is it a kind of crying, unchildlike, the child thought— Carlson moved slowly off, heading towards the green hotel. Then he started it—

"Rings on her fingers and bells on her toes, / And she shall have music wherever she goes."

He repeated it over and over again, and again there was the strange laugh. Sirkka wanted to put her hands over her ears—

I know there's more to it. About a white horse. . . a white horse . . . a white horse . . .

Carlson didn't go to the hotel. She noticed that. Three false fronts past the barber shop was Haapala's Pool Hall. Its door yawned expectantly, and he disappeared into the beery fumes.

It was already 4:15, and kids were coming home from school in small groups of twos and threes. Sirkka's friend, Aino Peltonen, passed down the alley behind the barber shop and shouted at the top of her shrill little voice, "Jussi Tamminen—highest mark in reading today!" The girls made nose-wrinkling faces, expressing what they thought of Jussi anyway.

The chill of late afternoon shade and the polar bite of an early spring breeze caused Sirkka's ailing cheek to twinge painfully, so she said good-bye to her friend Otto and scampered like a chipmunk up Finn Hill, and home. The kitchen smelled deliciously sweet from baking rutabaga. Two enormous and delighted blue-bottle flies preceded her through the screen door. But what the dumb flies don't know, she thought with a sigh, is that with the rutabaga Mamma would serve sickening-same venison from last winter's stock of rows and rows of Mason jars. These were stored on the shelves of a small earth cellar under the house, that you had to crawl on your belly to get into. The jars were her particular enemies.

She hoped they would blow each other up like the bottles of beet wine Alec had put up the year before.

Mrs. Kallio entered the kitchen briskly, then, carefully bearing the day's egg harvest in her apron. "Good!" she said, giving her daughter's cheek a quick scrutiny. "Now go and lie on the couch until supper."

On the leatherette, wooden-armed couch, Sirkka soon began to feel drowsily comfortable. She felt her mother tucking a blanket about her and placing the family hot water bottle on a pillow next to her swollen cheek. It felt wonderful. But the strange words of the song—if song it was—kept whirling in her mind—*Rings on her . . . bells on her . . . bells on her toes . . . rings on her fingers . . . how did it go again?*

Then the blast! A gunshot! She was certain that it was a gunshot; and that there had been only one shot—not too close, but close enough. She was sitting bolt upright now. She doubted having slept at all, but a blue-dimness, that moments ago wasn't there, had settled over the world about her.

Any kid in Winton Falls could have told you that the blast was from a real shotgun, heavy gauge, not from just any twenty-two. But no one ever fired guns in the village. Well, yes, once on Finn Hill Mr. V. Rauma, next-door neighbor to the south of them, had, according to her friend Mrs. Rauma, shot a black bear in the outhouse. She had been on a rampage, looking for her lost cub, and was about to uproot the outhouse. Little Billy Rauma (age eight) was in it at the time.

But now this shot came from the bottom of Finn Hill, less than a city block away, about where the clapboard homes ended and the false fronts began—a block again from the whirling, crazy barber pole.

Then banging screen doors. And Sirkka muttered, "Curious people flying out to see what's up."

Then a shout next door—Mr. Rauma's. And she heard their own screen door bang once. And once more. She put her hand to her cheek and felt a strange tickling sensation and a stickiness, but no swelling, no pain. Then the Kallio screen door banged yet a third time.

There was a small crowd of people, neighbors mostly, around the main door of Carlson's hotel, so Sirkka pressed in there too. She spotted Alec and Martha. More people were collecting, and it seemed that the whole village was there, crowding in.

She began, slowly, to know and yet not want to know. To feel a clutching dryness in her throat. She saw Ruth, Bertta's twelve-year-old sister. Ruth was on her knees in the road, sobbing and screaming alternately—"Oh merciful, heavenly Father! Oh God, help him. God . . . God . . . God!"

Mr. and Mrs. Jarvi moved in then. The barber picked Ruth up from the dust and carried the now whimpering girl away. And through her tears Sirkka saw Bertta there. There was Bertta, looking straight ahead, white and open-mouthed, holding fast to the hand of her eldest sister, Elizabeth, who was a junior in high school. Elizabeth looked scared and shivered as though cold. Sirkka suddenly wanted to run away, not to think about any of it—

To go backwards—if time would go backwards. If by walking backwards up Finn Hill and doing everything backwards, I could time-take me to the morning again. To the swinging sign that was beating so fast in the wind. But not again to the spinning, spinning, spinning of the crazy barber pole, not that— the on-and-on. Like the knowing-and-the-not-knowing-what-terrible-thing-has-happened-here.

Then, from an open upstairs window of the hotel, a woman's screeching voice—"How could you do this to us! How could you do this to your family! Get up. Get up, goddamn you! Oh poor, beautiful Leif." Then loud sobbing. Then laughing. Then loud sobbing again.

The crowd moved closer to the door as Old Man Koivunen, neighbor to the Carlsons, limped out of the house.

"Jesus!" he said. "He's shot himself through the mouth. Blood and brains all over the place. God help them all. She's up there beating him on the chest. Kallio! Heino!" he called, picking out two of the younger men from the crowd, "Come help!"

Arvo Lintula ran toward his grocery store, shouting something about telephoning the sheriff at Shagawa.

"Go to your homes now," Mrs. Rauma said quietly, taking over the situation outside—Sirkka admired her tremendously at that moment— she, as usual, somehow on top of the situation. Mrs. Rauma repeated her words in calm, firm tones, and whispered something to Mrs. Jarvi and Mrs. Karhula. The two women put their arms around Bertta, crying unrestrainedly now; and around Elizabeth, trembling visibly still. And they led them into the barber's house.

Sirkka felt her hand grasped firmly by her mother, and they were galloping up Finn Hill, very fast—

A white horse . . . a white horse . . . a white horse. The rest of the words! I remember now—

Ride a cock-horse to Banbury Cross
To see a fine lady upon a white horse,
Rings on her fingers and bells on her toes,
And she shall have music wherever she goes.

And years later, Sirkka, thinking of that dry-hot Minnesota noon—

Would it have made a difference, I wonder, if I had remembered all the words then? And if the day had started differently, altogether differently in every way, for me—then for him too? But I didn't know—then—what a cock-horse was.

Inkeri Väänänen-Jensen

Excerpt from the Memoir

INKERI'S JOURNEY

O UR PARENTS DIDN'T TALK VERY MUCH about their lives in the Old
Country. Perhaps they felt we weren't interested, that we were
interested in being Americans, not Finns. And so we were. We resisted
their attempts to talk about Finland; we closed our ears and minds to
talk about Finland. Their attachment to the Old Country became boring to us. For nowhere, except among the Finns themselves, did we
in our childhood ever hear of values attached to our foreign
backgrounds, not even to those of the Greek and Italian kids, whose
backgrounds, however long ago, *had*, after all, been the glories of Greece
and Rome. In school, the varied immigrant backgrounds of most of the
Iron Range students were simply ignored, if not ridiculed.

When in the fall of 1908, a young St. Paul woman went to teach in
Eveleth in northeastern Minnesota, she wrote this to her parents about
Eveleth: "The children in this third grade belong to the foreign population with the exception of one child. They say there are 10,000 people
here, but only about 2,000 civilized folk—of the others the Austrians
and Finns are the majority."

She also wrote the following to her parents: "Mrs. Samuelson, my
landlady, is a strange creature. Her Finnish name is Mikki Koukkari.
She is a rabid Socialist and all the Socialists who come here to speak
stay at her house. One came Saturday night, and they had a grand to-do
down in the kitchen till two in the morning. Socialism is rampant here
among the miners."

When I was among Finns, I was proud to be a Finn; yet, when I was
among Americans, I was ashamed of being a Finn—ashamed even of
my Finnish name. What kind of a name was Inkeri Väänänen for an
American girl? I have read that Leonard Woolf, the husband of the
famous British writer, Virginia Woolf, was proud of being Jewish but
also ashamed of it. He loved his family yet he hated them too.

As a child, and even as an adult, I looked upon myself not as an
American but as a Finn who lived in America. The term, Finnish-
American, was not known to us. We were not Finnish-Americans,

Swedish-Americans, Polish-Americans, Italian-Americans, Croatian-Americans. We were Finns, Swedes, Poles, Italians, Croatians. We did not look upon ourselves as hyphenated Americans.

We were, most of us, immigrant laborers' children, whose parents, seeking lives better than the ones they had in the Old Country, had come to America during the time when immigration to the United States was essentially unrestricted, unrestricted at least until the early 1920s, when immigration quota laws were passed which effectively cut off immigration from eastern and southern Europe. But by that time many of us were already here.

The immigrant parents of all the nationalities I knew as a child were, for the most part, young, hardworking, family oriented, filled with a desire to succeed in this strange new land, wanting education and opportunities for their children so their children's lives would be better than theirs had been in the Old Country, better than their lives were here in this new country. These parents were willing to work at menial jobs.

Many Finns, because English was such an extremely difficult language for most of them, worked for many years at low level jobs in the iron mines, the forests, the sawmills, the railroads, or slaved on their meager soil-poor, cutover farms. Because of this language barrier, most of them were estranged from the culture of the American society. But their families, their friends, their churches, their halls, their many societies provided opportunities for enriching their lives. In my memory at least, it seemed that among the immigrants on the iron Range, the Finns particularly drew much strength from all the groups they belonged to: the church congregations, the temperance societies, the cooperative societies, the Socialist Federation, the Industrial Workers of the World, the Communist groups, the church ladies aids, the cooperative guilds, and within these organizations the many choirs and choruses, orchestras and bands, athletic teams, drama groups, poetry and reading clubs, lending libraries, summer camps, and their numerous festivals. Besides churches, in many parts of the United States the Finns built hundreds of other buildings to house all these activities, halls that came to be known as Finn Halls. These all served as a second home to the Finnish immigrants—here they could speak their own language freely, find friends, exchange ideas, listen to speeches, see plays, hear poetry read, borrow books to read, sing, dance, eat Finnish foods, and drink coffee— and they drank a lot of coffee. Sometimes these social and cultural activities seemed more important to the immigrants than the ideologies of the groups they joined. But here they found release from the pressures of the alien American world. Here they were secure among their own.

None of us knew then that someday all of this would be explained away by historians and sociologists as "life in a Finnish subculture."

Somehow we children were made aware that we were in a melting pot; that we, the children of immigrants, were expected to become Americans even if our parents could not. In the 1920s it seemed as if the language we spoke at home, our foreign customs, our family's emotional ties to the Old Country were better abandoned, that we should turn into Americans, or at least make the attempt. We immigrant children learned early that not only were we different but also that we were inferior to the Americans. However, we were to be made into genuine members of the American society.

And we did try hard to be what Americans wanted us to be, or what in our minds we *thought* Americans wanted us to be. We knew, of course, that *real* American kids had handsome, tall, slender, well-dressed, English-speaking mothers and fathers, with no foreign accents or "broken" English, that they had easy-to-pronounce last names like Brown, Jones, Smith, Richards, Roberts, and first names like Bobby, Jack, Jimmy, Mary Jane, Phyllis, Nancy. To us, these were the *native* Americans, not the Indians in northern Minnesota, who were, to us, just another displaced group, like us. Most of our Finnish names, both first and last, were a dead giveaway about our foreign and humble origins—the majority of Finnish immigrants were unskilled rural people who had fled land-poor Finland. Our last names—Vainionpää, Pylvälä, Väyrynen, Särkipato, Hirvivaara—were unpronounceable by the American tongue. Our first names—Orvokki, Lahja, Kyllikki, Veikko, Väinö—were also strange to the American ear.

Without perhaps being consciously aware of it, we thought of ourselves, and most certainly of our parents, as marginal people in America, not really Americans, or at least not what we perceived *real* Americans to be—white, Anglo-Saxon, English-speaking, Protestant (but certainly *not* Lutheran) Americans. I felt honored when someone said, "But you don't *look* Finnish." We hated it when someone remarked, "She's got the map of Finland on her face." We wanted so to pass into the American stream—as we construed that stream.

Among the immigrant groups, the Finns had an extra burden to carry. For a long time the Finns were looked upon as Mongolians on the basis of a book written as long ago as 1775 by the German anthropologist, J.F. Blumenbach, who had divided the world's people into five races, based on color of skin. Since the Finns didn't easily fit into any of the five races, he lumped them in with the Mongols. Blumenbach's work had been the basis for all subsequent racial classifications and had been passed from one reference work to another, until anthropologists finally realized something was wrong.

The court case of the Finn, *John Svan v. the U.S. Government*, threatened to prevent any Finn from becoming an American citizen on the grounds that Finns were Mongolians, not "white persons" within the meaning of Section 2169, United States Revised Statutes. They were ineligible for citizenship based on a series of Oriental Exclusion Acts passed in 1882, 1892, and 1902. On January 4, 1908, Svan and sixteen other Finns were denied citizenship by District Attorney John C. Sweet of St. Paul. However, on January 17 of that same year, Judge William A. Cant at the U.S. District Court sitting in Duluth officially declared that the Finns were not of the yellow race, that though perhaps the Finns had been "Mongols" in the remote past, their blood had been so tempered by that of the Teutonic and other races that they "are now among the whitest people in Europe." Evidently this relieved the Finns greatly, for they had adopted Western attitudes toward the yellow race. Reverberations from this controversy on Mongolianism were still in the air during my childhood. In fact, as late as 1957, the issue of Mongolianism still bothered many Finns. In that year, the Knights and Ladies of Kaleva, a middle-class fraternal group of Finns, commissioned an amateur anthropologist to write a book "scientifically" disproving once and for all the theory that Finns are Asians.

In a 1938 issue of the *Päivälehti*, the Finnish daily newspaper published in Duluth, Kaarina Leino-Olli wrote about her experiences as a Finnish child growing up in Ely, Minnesota:

> *Why did we Finns who were growing up around 1915 feel ourselves so inferior? First of all, because we belonged to a small nationality group, which in addition to everything else had come from a country of which nobody knew anything at all or only so much, perhaps, that it was some North Russian province. If the name of Finland meant anything at all to an average American, it brought to mind images of a frozen wilderness of reindeer and of Lapps peering out of their leather hoods with slanting eyes. If someone said, "My parents were born in Finland," he was usually asked, "Where's that?" And although we children were born in America, we were usually called foreigners just the same. The irony of it was that those who accused us of being foreigners or worse, were frequently foreigners themselves, but from England or Ireland, and since they spoke the language of the country they considered themselves very superior, even though they often were very simple people.*
>
> *Yes, they called us foreigners, and in less charitable moments they called us bums or dirty Finns. Geography books, encyclopedias, and social studies always used to state that Finns were Mongolians. It is difficult to*

describe to you who have been able to avoid these labels, how it froze the heart and how it could crush a child. I shall never forget what happened to me once when I was about ten years old. Near us lived an Irish family, with a daughter named Kathleen—who also had a nickname, Sunny. One afternoon we had been playing together with our dolls, and when suppertime approached I said, "Goodbye, Sunny, I guess I have to go home now." To my horror she replied to me angrily, "Don't you call me Sunny. You're a dirty Finn, you must call me Kathleen."

I was left speechless with humiliation after this unexpected retort. I went home, bitter and depressed, wondering what really was the matter with Finns and why I had been born one.

I remember how a Finnish girl, whose name was Sirkka, used to be teased in school. Somehow or other the rest of the children had found out that sirkka derived from heinäsirkka, meaning grasshopper, and so that is what they sarcastically called her from that time on, grasshopper. Impi became Imp, Tyyne became Tiny, Tellervo became Telephone. You may be smiling, as I am now, at these childish cruelties, but to those children whose names were twisted about and laughed at, it was no joking matter. Some were so hurt by it that they anglicized their names whenever possible. It must be noted that these same Finnish children growing up and becoming parents gave their own children English names. Among their children you will not find any named Toivo, Impi, or Lempi. And considering the situation, they can hardly be blamed for it.

On the Range, where so many nationalities existed side by side, one of the questions many of us asked when we met someone new was, "What nationality are you?" It seemed such a natural question to ask a newcomer. Later, when I lived in the state of Kentucky, I came to realize that this question had absolutely no meaning for most of the people we met there, people whose Anglo-Saxon ancestors had come to this country long ago. They simply didn't understand what the question meant. "Why, what do you mean, 'What nationality am I?' I'm an American, of course!"

Many of the various Range nationalities engaged to some degree in name-calling, in using offensive names to refer to each other's nationalities: Italians were Wops or Dagos (wine was Dago red); Jews were Kikes, Sheenies, Yids; Slavs were Bohunks or Hunkies; Poles were dumb Polacks; Cornish miners, Cousin Jacks; Danes, Squareheads; Swedes were dumb Swedes; Norwegians, Herring Chokers or Norskies; Chinese were Chinks, Coolies; the Irish were Shanty Irish or Lace Curtain Irish; the black man was a Coon or a Nigger. (We called Brazil nuts niggertoes, without ever realizing what we were actually saying.) In our neighborhood the members of a Polish family named *Ciez* were simply called *The Cheeses*.

As Finns we were often referred to as *those dumb Finlanders, those dirty Finlanders*. As a result, *Finlander* became a deprecating, belittling term in my mind. To this day, even though I know that *Finlander* is an appropriate term designating inhabitants of Finland, I still bridle a little when I read it or hear it since its first meaning for me was a disparaging one. Not so long ago, in fact in the February 9, 1981, issue of the *Minneapolis Tribune* newspaper, the little rural community of Embarrass, where many Finns have lived and still live, and which has gained some notoriety in recent years as having the country's lowest winter temperature readings for many days, was summarily dismissed by the general manager of the *International Falls Journal*, to whom Embarrass was just a pinprick on a roadmap, with the statement, "They're just interlopers, a bunch of Finlanders. Heck, Embarrass is only a grocery store and a gas station. They don't even have a bar."

Two Finnish men's names, Toivo (Hope) and Urho (Hero or Champion) were frequently the names of characters in disparaging jokes about Finns—jokes which the Finns seemed to enjoy as much as anyone, but usually only if they were told by a fellow Finn. If someone not a Finn told a disparaging joke about Finns, not only did we feel he was making fun of us and we were being insulted, but we also felt as if an outsider was usurping something that really belonged to us Finns.

We felt the purpose of these jokes was to subject us to ridicule—especially when they were told by an "outsider" imitating a Finnish accent. And if a child lives with ridicule, he learns to be shy, and we Finnish kids, most of us, *were* shy. These jokes seemed to be a measure of how we were regarded by others—they denigrated us, they created an inferiority complex in us, and we Finns had that in full enough measure without the added pain from these jokes. We cringed and were helpless before them, and we were made even more insecure about our Finnish roots. We weren't sophisticated enough to recognize that the jokes were an assault on the dignity of the human spirit, that bigotry lay just under the surface. And yet, when a Finn told a joke about Finns, perhaps even the same joke that was told by an "outsider," we could laugh and be healed.

After spending the last fifteen years studying the history, language, and literature of Finland, after making four visits to the land of my ancestors, after once again having the opportunity to spend precious time with both Finland Finns and American Finns, after becoming involved with the Minnesota Finnish-American Historical Society, the Finnish language camp called Salolampi, the Finnish-American Cultural Activities group, and then struggling and agonizing through the almost impossible task of reviewing my life and writing about it as clearly as I could, I have finally come to terms with my own identity, something that had eluded me for so many years.

For too long I did not recognize or accept the values in the culture of the Old Country; in trying to become "American" in one fell swoop, in one generation, I ignored many of the folkways and traditions brought to this country by my parents and other Finns. Too late, I apologize to them for this cruelty. For too long, in trying to blend into the mainstream American culture, I had denied my own identity. But it has proved to be an identity that would not go away even though I had abandoned it for most of my adult life, ever since I had left the Iron Range of Minnesota, that gathering place of people who spoke in forty-three different languages.

All of my experiences during these past fifteen years within the Finnish-American and the Finland milieus have provided me with a new perspective on being a Finn; it has been almost like being born again, like becoming a different person, coming at last face to face with the kind of person I really was—am. I am no longer ashamed of being Finnish in America. I have finally been able to find security in my identity as the child of Finnish immigrants. I seemed to have a need to justify my existence as a Finn and through this process have come to recognize myself as a Finnish-American, a member of pluralistic America, where it's all right to be both Finnish *and* American, loyal to both my foreign origins *and* the land of my birth, the United States. Finally I have come to terms with the dichotomy that has plagued me during so much of my life. I have at last found security in this dualism. I am richer for having shared in two cultures.

PART III

Succeeding generations in Finland & America

Carl Gawboy

CHRISTMAS AT BIRCH LAKE

*I*T WAS COLD. There were great columns of icicles from the eaves to the snowbanks piled high against walls. There were brothers and sisters there, and heaps of cinnamon rolls, puddles on the floor, light and noise.

It wasn't always that way, of course. Between 1946 and 1954 there were many Christmases. There were the spare Christmases of the hard years, but others when Pa had work. Sometimes the siblings all came home from college but sometimes they only called on Christmas Eve. There were mild winters, too, and one with rain. But in my memory, the Christmases blend to a Christmas that always was.

On the day before vacation, the sidewalk in front of Washington School thronged with children—galoshes flapping unbuckled (a forbidden fashion), wool coats, aviator caps, and clanking lunch pails, piles of papers from cleaned-out desks, bags of treats from classroom parties. The White Iron-Birch Lake bus pulled up to its place between the one for Spaulding Location and the Tomahawk Timber Company bus bound for Forest Center. As the bus door opened, children large and small elbowed for a place in line. Shorty Lenich sat at the wheel, beside a great cardboard box. As each child stepped in, Shorty handed him a tinseled box covered with images of Santa Claus and Christmas toys. Inside was candy of all stripes and colors. The bus filled and children stood in the aisle from front to back. It smelled of wet wool, leather, rubber, and candied breath. The windows went opaque with frost, and those lucky enough to have a seat made imitation footprints with their clenched hands. Woe to anyone who dropped a book or paper on the floor. Melting snow from boots and snowpants made the floor a cold winter stream complete with ice chunks and mud.

The bus pulled away from the curb and headed south on Highway One. Each stop relieved pressure. The Rodich, Weijo, Shroeder, and Kisrow families all departed with their bundles of treasure. When Chubs Johnson vacated his seat, we gathered around, marveling at the great crater his bulk imprinted in the leatherette. (I remember that pit remained as his memorial long after he graduated.) By the time the Esterbergs, Dojans, and Starkmans departed, the aisle was clear and everyone remaining enjoyed the luxury of a seat.

The bus turned onto the Babbitt cutoff. After the Korppi place was the long stretch of highway past the Buski farm, people too mean to have children. The winter night had come by the time we rounded the curve and climbed the hill to the Birch Lake Road. A circle of mailboxes mounted on a wagon wheel was our stop. The Bischoffs and Jon Wilmunen got off with us. The Tuomala kids were already moving into our seats as we ran down the trail shortcut that Jim kept tramped along the old tote road.

We thundered into the house with our booty. It was chore time, and Jim and Ma went to milk the cows. My sister Pat and I hauled water for the cows and for Nellie, the old horse. We forked hay and bedded them down for the night. We carried wood by the armfuls into the house. Pa came in from the woods and it was time for supper.

From the oven of the great black kitchen range, Ma pulled out the large four-loaf bread pan topped with mounds of golden biscuit. A dipper broke the crust and ladled out chunks of venison, carrot, potato, and rutabaga swimming in a dark brown broth. The older kids wedged around the kitchen table while Pat and I shared the woodbox. We cast a covetous eye at the table. When Jim went off to college we would sit at his place and eat like grownups.

In the days before Christmas, Ma drove the jeep to town, meeting trains and buses as the older siblings came home for the holidays. Irene and Bob taught us the Harvard fight song and "Hail Our Dear Cornell," even though they attended Milwaukee Downer College and the University of Minnesota. They also sang off-color lyrics and told jokes daring us younger children to understand. They swaggered, these college siblings. They talked like college people talked in Donald O'Connor movies. Jim and Pa brought home a tree wedged on the top of a load of logs old Nellie pulled in with the bobsled. The tree was hauled in with pomp and ceremony. One year we bought our first lights. We hung them on the tree first. Extension cords of various gauges connected into our light socket in the middle of the ceiling. The magic moment arrived. The lights came on. I nearly fell over backwards with the loveliness of it all.

"Wait, wait," Ma said.

"Wait, wait," Jim said.

Each light had a tube of glass filled with a colored liquid. A bubble rose in one.

"Look, look," Ma said.

"Look, look," Jim said.

Soon another bubble, then another. The whole tree was filled with light and glass tubes bubbling away. I embraced the wonders of the modern age.

Pat and I believed in Santa Claus, of course. We knew he came over the back field from the Tuomala's, and we knew that at our house he came in through the door. Ma and Pa had known him for years, and he would visit with them in the kitchen and drink coffee. We knew we must never interrupt their visit, not even for a drink of water.

Pat told me that she saw Santa Claus once. She was sleeping in the top bunk next to Irene. She heard the jingle bells and listened to the voices. She peeked through the ventilator hole between the two rooms and saw the tree in all its glory. There was Santa, setting out presents. He threw his head back and laughed heartily. Pat had never told anyone about this before and she told me I must keep this terrible secret. I have kept it—until now.

Most of the time our house was filled with clutter. There were books and magazines piled everywhere. On winter days, sheets hung dripping from clotheslines strung across the living room. Papers, games, school projects, guns, traps, and an occasional muskrat carcass in the process of being skinned filled the small room. But on the days before Christmas our house got a thorough cleaning. All the girls were put to the task. With kerosene soaked rags they dusted the stove, the tables and all the woodwork. The men were kept out of the house while the floors dried from their scrubbing. The rag rugs, beaten and laundered and fresh from the out of doors, were laid down.

Ma and girls swung into action in the kitchen. Pans of fruitcake, great golden cinnamon rolls with candied bottoms, doughnuts deep-fried in oil, and wild rice candy, made by popping wild rice like popcorn.

In the evenings we read or drew, listening to the Christmas episodes of our favorite radio shows. Gene Autrey and his Melody Ranch gang always did "Santa Claus is Coming to Town," and I wondered why no one applauded in the old west. After a song the cowboys just said, "that was real nice, Gene." On "Amos and Andy," Amos would tell the Christmas story to his little niece as she fell asleep. I was very impressed when the announcer told us that the show was beamed to our Armed Forces around the world. The world seemed secure, protected: and those protectors could gather around their radios and feel good, too. Gabriel Heater and Edward R. Morrow brought us the news. Lionel Barrymore played Scrooge in "A Christmas Carol." I wasn't happy with Marley's ghost. I didn't think a Christmas story should scare little kids.

Christmas Eve was the most memorable of nights. We took our

saunas, two at a time, and made the dash through the porch to the house. Jim and Bob slept upstairs under piles of quilts, where the arctic wind blew through the walls. The girls were in the bunks, two to a bed. Ma and Pa stayed up late reading or talking. I lay awake on a mattress on the floor, thinking about my world. We all were clean, the house was clean, there was a fire in the stove throwing its flickering light on the wall. In the barn, I knew, the horse stomped, the cows munched, and the chickens chirped sleepily on their roosts. Outside in the night sky the magical star of Christmas shone over the spruce and birch woods, over the Wilmunens to the south and the Tuomalas to the west. And somewhere in the arctic gloom was the Jolly Old Elf, winging his way to Birch Lake Township.

We children got up first, and gathered around the tree to gaze at the presents. Ma lit the fire, put the coffee on, and started the oatmeal cooking. The presents were unwrapped. I got a ship that exploded with a wooden torpedo, or a toy truck with a picture of the driver in full face on the windshield and in profile in the side window. Jim and Irene told me gravely that when they were my age all there would be for toys were two blocks of wood nailed together. How I wished I could have been there, during the Depression.

The best gift I got, and one I always received, was a full box of sharp new crayons. Sometimes it was a forty-color set with colors like Flesh and Veridian. There was a ream of clean white paper to go with them.

With the opening of the presents, the clutter miraculously reappeared.

Christmas dinner consisted of an entire venison haunch roasting in the great oven in the wood range, mounds of mashed potatoes and rutabagas, hand parched wild rice, home canned pickles and beets, cranberry sauce, and rolls and bread fresh from the oven.

After dinner, Nellie was harnessed to the bobsled, and off we went to bring back hay from the hayshed on the other side of the farm. We made a great load, the older kids pitching the hay with Pat and me tramping. Nellie hauled it home and we forked it from the load into the barn. (Hay scattered on snow always reminded me of milk curdled in rhubarb sauce.) Afterwards, when we came back into the house, the older kids played Chinese Checkers and I colored. That is, I colored as well as I could with my numb and thawing fingers.

Then Christmas was over, and it was time to bring the older kids back to town, to catch their train or bus to the world outside. They seemed excited to go. Those older siblings had an arrogance, a sense of belonging to new culture, one that was alien to me. I felt that perhaps they were chosen for greatness, maybe the cover of *Time* magazine. This house on a rock and swamp farm was a backward place, a Dogpatch, compared to what was in store for them. They told me so. What didn't occur to me then was, if they felt that way, why did they come home? I didn't understand it until a decade went by and my world changed. I was at college in a bleak boarding house. My roommates from small towns and farms did the Donald O'Connor role in their school sweaters. It was then that the vision came to me: a vision of black spruce swamps, snowy fields, venison stew, a kitchen filled with smells of canning and baking, a father smelling of tobacco and pine pitch, and a short round mother with flour dusting her apron and her arms.

Jim Johnson

AT EAGLE LAKE

An east wind blows
off Lake Superior.
birch burns
in the basement fireplace.
Hjalmer Hoglund takes
up the fiddle, turns
up his hearing aid.
Sulo Astedt, retired from
Minnesota Power and Light,
is without a right arm.
he plays
the accordion,
the harmonica (held
with a brace like Bob Dylan's)
and taps an Arco coffee can
with his boot. together
they play a fine *Kulkurin Valssi*.
three generations of blue eyes
have gathered around. only one,
a two-year-old, dances:
the music makes
translations in her feet.

MOJAKKA

Use heavy-bodied
orange-finned pike.
the head is the best.
cut it off.
put it in the pot.
add milk, potatoes.
cook slowly all afternoon.

those who have eaten
this soup know
how the meat
falls easily off the bone,
flakes easily off the cheeks.
they know too
the eyes that shrivel,
come apart from their sockets
and stare up at you are
like lakes, the same lakes where

at the edges of the reeds
the rocks
drop off into
blackwater. there
the pike swims,
its orange fins
finning. vicious its teeth,
its eyes,

as it eyes everything,
glances at anything
that moves:
snails slow as rock,
crawfish pinching along,
young perch, young pike.
then it slashes!
at the flash of tin
fashioned from an Arco
coffee can. then

with thumb and forefinger
grip the eyes that stare,
the lakes that glare.
a quick paralysis,
a turn off of teeth. then

cut off the head.
from the shreds of veins
the blood streams
like the rose-colored dusk
rising
steaming into the blue
twenty-below-zero
winter sky. so
you who have eaten this soup
know the pike swims on.

Jim Johnson

THE VISIT

You must not be late. spit your snoose out (if you chew) into the snow. at the door take off your boots even if your host tells you you do not need to. his family will have placed theirs neatly on the braided rug by the door. place yours there also. many who visit bring along wool socks to wear on linoleum floors.

inside sit down as the host directs. be careful not to sit in his chair. in the living room it will be the one that has the crumpled knitted throw, or in the kitchen it will be the one not squarely facing the table like all the others but will be slightly askew. after sitting down do not talk of grown sons or daughters or socialism or the mines. instead talk of wooden spoons of moonlight or of frogs. do not pretend to know all about these things.

eventually the hostess will announce that coffee will be served. it is considered rude to serve coffee too soon. but if it is not served after a reasonable time a guest may wonder what time it is or switch the conversation to milking or the chickens.

the table will be spread with biscuit and breads and pieces of cake and cookies. coffee will be served in the finest cups either from the old country or from the Miller Hill Mall. there will be a bread and butter plate, a cup and saucer, and a small spoon. there will be a bowl of sugar lumps, a pitcher of cream (bachelors may serve Carnation milk from a can with two holes pegged with wooden pegs), and a vase of lilacs, wild roses, daisies, or violets.

when the hostess pours the first cup of coffee take a piece of the biscuit, with the second cup take a piece of unfrosted cake, and with the third either a piece of berry pie or a piece of fancy frosted cake. a fourth cup may be taken with cookies or a sugar lump (sipping coffee from a saucer with a lump of sugar held between the teeth is acceptable if you are used to doing this at home) or whatever else has not been tasted. it is better to take too much than too little making sure all items have been tasted.

after coffee it will be time to leave. tell the host and hostess the coffee pot is always on at your house. but for now there are many chores to do and our lives are so short and it is a pity we must always be in such a hurry and it is too bad we are not all rich.

Jane Piirto

SAUNA

our feet in buckets we sit
on the top bench in a row
the little kids sit
near the floor

mother throws *löylyä*
on with the ladle
steam rushes from the rocks.
we sting.
we put noses in washcloths.
we talk and sweat.

the urgency takes
over our thumping hearts
we run out barefoot
leap in a group
prance down the hill
through raspberry thorn

dive stumble on pebbles
flail in splashes
the water receives us
our shouts and whoops
force us to relief
to skin eskimo warm

we glow in perfect awareness

cool, we climb the hill
to the sauna again
soap up wash each other's backs
run in lather to the lake
and back again this time
thist time for the real steam
and back to our holy lake
then pop rolls cold cuts
the ritual of our ancestors
ruddy and calm

Lynn Maria Laitala

WINTER TRIP

S ETÄ ANTTI *on kuollut. Voitko te tulla?"* Cousin Laura's call woke me.
So the old man finally died. I hated to take time off work for a
funeral, but I'd do it for Laura.

"I'll leave early tomorrow."

We started from the Cities at 4:30 a.m. and we got to Vermilion
by ten. I brought Emily along. Uncle Antti would be sent off by all the
kin he had.

First we stopped in at the farm to see Mother. The dazzling white
world blinded me when I stepped from the car. Clear air, clean snow.
In the bright sunshine the air felt much warmer than the official ten
below we'd heard on the radio. I smelled wood smoke.

Mother and the scent of cardamom welcomed us into the warm kitchen. Finnish biscuit baked in the wood stove.

She fussed and worried over us, son and granddaughter; I looked
tired. Emily was too thin. It was such a long trip. She set out wild
strawberry jam and took the biscuit from the oven.

"How do you manage here by yourself, *Äiti?"* I asked her.

"It's all right. Johnny comes to cut wood — and I could always hire
someone. Laura brings my groceries and takes me to the doctor. I set
up my loom in the parlor. Come and see."

Tidy piles of rags lay about. On the loom, Mother was finishing a
brightly patterned rug of reds and blues.

Emily chattered in Finnish while we had our biscuit and coffee. She
seldom spoke it at home with Ida and me. She'd learned it when she
lived here as a young child.

"We should go to see about Antti," I said. Emily's eyes questioned
me. She wanted to stay with her grandmother.

"No, Emily. You better come along with me. We'll be back by suppertime. Should I bring groceries, *Äiti?"*

"No, that's all right. I have peas soaking for soup."

We traveled on to Sawyer. Laura's ancient pickup truck was parked
in front of her house. I walked in without knocking — old habit — and
startled Laura at her desk. It had been over a year since I'd seen her.

There were new lines in her face—from weather, I thought, not worry. She rose to hug Emily, then me.

"How good to see you both. Can I get you some coffee and some *korppuja*?"

"No, thanks. We came from *Äiti's*. When is the funeral?"

"Tomorrow. But Jussi doesn't know yet. He's caretaking up at Skidway Lodge. I thought we could drive up to Basswood now and get him."

I looked out the window at her truck. "Let's take my car," I said.

Laura laughed. "There's nothing wrong with my truck. Johnny's been keeping it fixed up."

"Where is he?"

"He's around. He's been staying here."

"Does he go to school?"

"No."

I dropped the subject.

"Let me make a thermos of cocoa and some sandwiches and then we can go." She went into the kitchen. Someone came in the back door.

"Johnny!" Emily ran back to see him. I followed more slowly.

"Hi, Dad," he said. Emily was hanging on his neck. "Thought I'd run up to Basswood with you."

"How are you doing, John?"

Johnny sat down and looked at the floor.

"I'm fine," he said.

"Load up," Laura ordered. "I'm ready." She looked us over. "Is that all you people have to wear?" She rummaged in the closet and threw out snowpants, hats, scarves, and mittens. Emily bundled herself up. I added a scarf. Johnny stayed bareheaded and barehanded. Laura made another attempt. "It's only ten below but the wind might be bad on the lake." Johnny grinned and stuck the tips of his fingers in the pockets of his jeans.

We took my car. The new county boat landing was built on Frank Silvola's place. Had they burned down his cabin? The road ran right off the landing on to the ice.

"Ice is two feet thick, Andy." Laura said. She'd sensed my hesitation at the shore. The road was much smoother over the ice. Plowed clean, perfectly level.

Emily bounced around on the back seat.

"Driving on the ice!" she said. Laura looked at me. We'd lived our winters on the lake. How could things be so different for my daughter?

The road ran down the middle of Wabeno Lake, curved away from the falls, and disappeared into the woods at Four Mile. At the end of the portage smoke curled from the little store.

"It's just a winter caretaker, but he'll sell cigarettes to the desperate," Laura said.

"There's a huge locomotive wheel right off the landing there, under the ice," Johnny told Emily.

"Logging train," I said. Johnny knew.

The road dropped to the ice again. I still knew Basswood Lake as well as anything in this world. The road branched out occasionally to this resort or that.

"This will be the last year for most of them, Andy. I think only Hubachek will be left after '61."

"I know." The government had banned the resorts. Some would be moved, others burned. I asked Laura about their fates. Beautiful buildings—two stories of white pine logs—had already been burned. I felt sick at the waste.

Jussi's little caretaker cabin smelled of fried pancakes, coffee, and the damp wool socks steaming dry by the stove. Laura gave Jussi the news.

"Antti dead!" He sat down. We all sat. "Well, he was sick now, for awhile. But dead." He rose and set out heavy chipped mugs, coffee, and a can of condensed milk. "He saved his suit for the funeral. It's at his shack. I know where."

"You were together a long time," Laura said.

"I was in his first logging camp, just after he came over from Finland. Yah, we partnered off and on for almost fifty years. Logged, trapped together. That's all done now. All done."

"What will you do next year, Jussi?" I asked. Next year Skidway would be ashes and pine seedlings.

"Time to hang my teeth on the nail."

"Antti wanted you to have his cabin," Laura said.

"Nah, I'll stay in town." Jussi picked up the mugs and put them in the dish pan. "I gotta fix up some things here, then I'll come with you guys, show you the suit."

"Let me take Emily out driving on the ice," Johnny asked.

"Please, Daddy?"

I considered whether twelve year old Emily could control her brother. "Okay."

Laura and I walked up to the little point of rock overlooking the great frozen lake. Five hundred miles around if you paddled next to the shoreline, half of it in Canada.

"Who will see it like this anymore?" I asked Laura. I remembered how we would snowshoe from Sawyer on Friday night, often as far as the Canadian ranger station, and go back home on Sunday. Fifteen or twenty miles each way, in all kinds of weather. For the glory of the frozen world.

"People will always find a way," Laura said.

"What were there, twenty resorts. Twenty-five? They could have just banned new building and left these until their owners retired." How welcome was that first scent of smoke and glimmer of lamplight in a far off window on those long treks from town.

"That isn't the way they do things, Andy."

Far below us on the ice Johnny was whipping my car in circles. We watched as the car came to a stop and Emily and Johnny walked around it, switching places. Emily's first time at the wheel. There wasn't a car in sight. Little danger of a collision. She'd have to run it up on shore to do any damage. The car started in jerks, then traveled slowly along the ice road. Emily kept carefully to the right.

"Are you ever coming back up here, Andy?" Laura asked. I knew she meant move back home.

"It's too late, Laura."

Below us, Jussi opened his cabin door and threw cold pancakes to the Canada jays.

"He always cooks extra," Laura said.

We started back to the shack. Jussi was putting on his coat.

"I'll show you Antti's suit now."

We hailed the children back from the dock. Emily drove up sedately, precisely, and stepped from the driver's side grinning. She and Johnny climbed into the back seat with Jussi. Old Jussi was melancholy.

"Used to be life on this lake," Jussi said. "There were some characters in those logging camps. Yah, and there were still Indians when we got here. Antti partnered up with that Charlie Boucher for years. He almost married Charlie's sister, too. Used to be three, no four villages on this part of the lake. Used to trade furs with the Canadians right here, but before my time. Government took all the Indians. Now it takes everybody. Antti's better off, dead."

No one said said a word on the rest of the trip to Antti's cabin. On Wabeno Lake we had to jump the snowbank but the snow wasn't deep and the car drove through it easily.

It was colder inside Antti's cabin than it was outside in the sunshine. Jussi went to the bed and pulled a torn cardboard suitcase from underneath. We all stood and watched expectantly. Inside was a heavy wool suit, once black, now tinged with green.

"Last time he wore this suit he danced on the boat from Liverpool," Jussi muttered. He lifted it from the suitcase.

"Look!" cried Emily. Three little books—bankbooks—had dropped from the folds of the suit. Emily picked them up. Three different banks.

"Look at this. Look at all the money he had," she said. I took the bank books from her. Frequent and regular deposits were listed from 1912 through the 1920s in all three books. Apparently Antti hadn't trusted banks well enough to put all his money in one account.

"Lots of beaver pelts," said Jussi, looking at the figures. All the entries stopped in 1929. I totaled the figures in my head. Antti had lost more than three thousand dollars. It was a lot of money for an immigrant worker in 1929.

"He used to talk about going back to Finland to find a wife," Jussi said. "He almost made it."

"Can't we get out the money, Daddy?"

"No, Emily. The banks failed a long time ago. There is no money."

"What happened to Uncle Antti's money. Who got it?"

"It was the Depression, honey. No one got the money. It was just gone."

We took the suit. Johnny pocketed the worthless bankbooks. We looked around at the few dishes and pots, then went up to the woodshed. An old kick-sled lay on its side, a half cord of split wood spilled from its pile, and rusty traps hung on the walls.

"Anything you want, Jussi?" Laura asked.

"Nah."

"You can stay at my house overnight," Laura told him. "I can take you home after the funeral."

"Nah. Take me back now. Dead is dead. What's a funeral?" I followed him back into the cabin. He looked around, then picked up a mug from the shelf — an ordinary coffee mug with one line painted near the rim. "I'll take this."

We drove Jussi back to Skidway. He got out of the car without looking back. I shut off the motor and watched him climb the hill to his cabin, shoulders stooped under torn mackinaw, coffee mug dangling from bony fingers. I had never seen him look so small or lonely.

The trees along the lake shore were silhouetted against a red-streaked sky as we headed back to Sawyer. Two trips to Basswood in one day. I wondered over it to Laura.

"Do you remember the time we showshoed home in the wind, wrapped in blankets from the ranger station? It took us fourteen hours. I've never been so cold."

"I thought we were dead," Laura said. "Can I make you some supper?"

"No, *Äiti's* expecting us. Want to come to the farm for some pea soup, John?"

"No thanks, Dad. You can let me off here."

I dropped him off on the road to Vermilion.

"Will you be at the funeral, Johnny?" Laura called out her window.

"Sure. One o'clock, right?"

"Right."

He stood, hands in pockets, back hunched against the wind, waiting for a ride to town.

I pulled up behind Laura's battered pickup. I wanted to talk to Laura, but Emily understood Finnish so we had no privacy.

"I'll see you at the funeral, then," Laura said, hauling out the shabby suitcase with its ancient suit. She closed the car door, then opened it again.

"Antti had a good life. He was a free man. Don't grieve."

I said nothing. All I felt was grief. Emily spoke.

"He had a good life, *Täti* Laura. It was the best."

The air had grown bitterly cold. Emily and I drove home to *Äiti's* warm kitchen.

Lynn Maria Laitala

THE BIG WEDDING

J USSI AND KORVA were patching the roof of Rautio's boarding house. Jussie began to slide and bumped into Korva. Korva grabbed him around the middle, and in a great bearhug the two men rolled off the roof, knocked over the ladder, crushed through the scaffolding, fell three stories and landed in a pile of sawdust. They lay still for a minute, then slowly rose. Korva knocked the sawdust from his pants.

"Jesus Christ, Jussi," he said. They set up the ladder and climbed back on the roof.

I saw it all from the railroad tracks. I'm not going to marry a Finn, I thought.

Mama often said to Papa, "Matt, you're a rare man." That was probably true, and he was certainly a rare Finn.

What were the others like?

Einard Saari was the most timid man in the world. If he went up to the lake for the weekend and the weather was splendid Friday night he would decide to start right back home because there might be a storm on Sunday.

Then there was Eino Wirtala. If you said to him that it was a beautiful day, or look! the bluebirds are back, or the Sippola's have a new baby, he said, "Yah, yah."

It seemed like my parents were the only Finnish couple that still talked to each other. If Mrs. Maki walked to town pulling a wagon with four full milk cans and Mr. Maki drove by in his new Chevy coupe he wouldn't stop to give her a lift. Wouldn't even slow down for the dust.

Then there were the drinkers. Finns are never happy drinkers like Slovenians and Italians. They sit and drink in silence until they are drunk, and then they weep or start a fight. One or two in town didn't dare fight a man so they went home and beat up their wives. Then the other men would beat *him* up.

Mrs. Tuurila shored up her front porch with big timbers. Mr. Tuurila stood by and watched. "Hurry up, dinner will be late," he said.

There is a legend that once a Finnish man loved his wife so much that he almost told her.

Why should I marry any of those men who put salt in their coffee?

Rose Stepanovich invited me to her house for Christmas Eve. Rose and I were friends in Junior College.

"Christmas Eve?" I asked her. Christmas Eve is a quiet time at our house. We eat lutefisk and light the candles on the tree. There is a little more life at Rautio's boarding house where the boarders go out drinking. Usually they bring home some stray drunk who is sleeping it off in front of the stove on Christmas morning.

But I never heard of anyone giving a party on Christmas Eve. Mama was disappointed because Laura had come home for the holidays, but I went to Rose's house anyway.

It was an odd party—kind of an open house, I suppose. The six Stepanoviches were out visiting everyone they knew, and everyone they knew was visiting the Stepanoviches. Rose and I went down the street for a glass of wine and baked treats, and when we checked back at the Stepanoviches' house it was full of guests but no hosts. No one cared. Everyone was having a good time. Rose's brother Sam broke off from a bunch of guys and started hanging out with Rose and me. We caroled all the houses in McKinley Location. Sam and Rose drove me home after midnight mass.

Mama was waiting up. She looked worried when I said goodnight and stumbled up the stairs.

Sam came over the day after Christmas. I introduced him to Mama and we sat in the kitchen, talking about our teachers at the junior college and drinking coffee. Sam kept looking at me and grinning for no reason at all.

"Do you want to go out with me on New Year's Eve?" Sam asked.

"Go where?"

"To the dance at the Community Center."

I stopped to consider, but just for a minute. I had planned to snowshoe up to Basswood with Laura and her gang.

"I'd love to go to the dance with you, Sam."

That's how it started. We were still seeing each other when Laura came home for Easter. She was alarmed.

"Clara, are you getting serious about Sam?"

"He's more fun than anyone else I've gone out with."

"What does his family think?"

"His folks are nice enough."

"They probably hope it's just a passing fancy. Mama is worried, you know."

"What should Mama worry about? It's not like I'm behaving like Ida."

Laura let this reference to our middle sister pass.

"Clara, the Stepanoviches are Catholic."

Well of course I knew, but there it was. I said nothing.

"How serious are you, Clara?"

"I'm serious."

"Will Sam leave his church?"

"No."

"Will you convert?"

"I don't know."

"You'd better know. Can you go to Latin Mass, give up meat on Fridays, raise your kids Catholic, never use birth control?"

"I've been thinking about it."

"You'd still be an outcast in both churches."

"Laura, I've been *thinking* about it."

I thought about it. And then, for Sam, I decided yes. Mama and Papa took it well. Better than Laura had thought.

We told Sam's folks that we wanted to get married. We explained that I would become a Catholic. His mother tried to talk us out of it. She said that that kind of mixing wouldn't work. Then one day she threw up her hands and said, "Well, then you be my new daughter." She walked across the kitchen, grabbed me by the shoulders and kissed both my cheeks.

Father Petrovich was more skeptical.

"You convert to Catholicism not from the heart but for the boyfriend," he said.

"It is my heart's deepest desire to please God and to please my husband."

Father Pete taught me the catechism and converted me.

Then came the hard part.

Sam and I got his folks together and explained that we would have a quiet, private ceremony.

"That's not a real wedding," said Mother S.

"Sam is our first child to marry. We've looked forward to his wedding since he was born," added Pa S.

"Clara's folks can't afford a wedding," said Sam.

"How not afford a wedding! Once in a lifetime!" said Pa.

"I really can't ask them. They have troubles now," I said.

"I've heard about you Finns. You think a big wedding celebration is drinking black coffee in a green church basement. No. My son and my daughter will have a first class wedding."

Laura was my maid of honor. I had five other bridesmaids. I wore a beautiful gown of lace and satin with a full train. The whole town

drank and danced for three days.
We'll be paying off the loan for years to come.
And worth every penny.

Pierre Delattre

KORRIGAN'S TREE

Pierre Delattre was raised on the farm of his Finnish grandfather Herman Kanto, on a lake near Phelps, Wisconsin. He is strongly influenced by Finnish story telling. "Korrigan's Tree" is a section from his unpublished novel, Korrigan's Wedding, *in which he deliberately uses a kind of melodrama and realism he often heard in Finnish story telling.*

*H*ALF WAY UP the large tree that leaned over the lake at the bottom of the lawn beneath the farmhouse was a hole where three slick limbs parted. At the joining of these limbs, birds and squirrels had nested. Eggs had been hatched there. Rodents had slept there.

But now the matting of twigs was deserted. The crusted dry grass had not held an egg since the summer four years ago when Korrigan's father shot a nesting bird from the bedroom window.

He'd killed the bird from rage at his woman; had murdered this female for no other reason than to arouse the female in his own nest, even if only to arouse her to pain.

The sound that his wife made the night that he shot it, winged the white, gold crested bird in the tree, was ledged in the spine of Maggie's blond daughter.

Korrigan still heard the shrieks that followed the blast of the shotgun. Her flesh still remembered how the bird had exploded in the nest of the maple, the swamp maple her mother most loved of all trees; how her mother had run down the lawn, seized the dead bird and lifted it, dancing, showed it to the sky, dancing insanely in circles on the grass that blazed around her ankles as if fire were being kicked from its roots.

"Punish him! Punish him!"

Korrigan remembered, not in the memory of mind but of body. Her nerves and her blood and the hum in her ears remembered the explosion that started the real fighting, that started his boozing and his swollen up swagger; and started the shrinking down of her mother.

From that day to this her mother had withered while her father had filled his muscles with menace that ignited his eyes with the kind of light you see in the embers when the howl of a storm has blown down the chimney and snuffed out the flames.

No longer did Korrigan's father soothe his daughter. Only on certain rare nights did he hold her except when, in one of his rages, he snatched a fistful of her dress, pulled her up hard, thrust out his other fist toward the basket of eggs she'd fetched from the henhouse; a finger suddenly snapped out rigid, pointing to a crack in one of the eggs— "Can't you be careful!"; or when, as he whacked the windows, windowsills and chairs with the fly-swatter, swatted the table just before dinner was to be served until the knives, forks, and spoons were all splayed out in disorder, milk spilled from the pitcher and dead flies with that yellowy stuff smashed out from their bottoms . . . even when a delicious stew was about to be served, he'd be cursing Korey for being too lazy to close the screen door behind her so she'd filled the whole kitchen with their goddamn buzzing; and he'd finally catch her in a headlock under the smelly sweat of his arm and sting the back of her legs with the swatter.

And, if Korey's mother was out of the house, he'd seize Korey for almost any small reason, drag her to the chair on his side of the table, turn her over his knees and pull down her pants. Then he'd smack her bare bottom with the flat of his hand, sting her and sting her while she wiggled on her belly, kicked her feet, wailed for him not to hit her again.

Korrigan tried to stay clear of the house when her mother was absent. And when Mag was there she so clung to her skirts that her father, as on this particular morning, berated her:

"Don't cling to your Mommy. Can't you see you annoy her? Go out and play somewhere with your dollies. Can't you leave us alone for a time? She's my wife, see? I'm her husband. I'm not just your father. She's not just your mother. She's my lover, if you must know, and I have to have her alone with me, Korey. Surely I can tell you the truth in these matters. There are times like this, kid, when you're a pain in the ass. So why don't you just go vanish for awhile. Go down to the boathouse. Go out to the barn. Go up to the highway and wait for the mailman. Go play with the chickens, go talk to the bull. You say the stones on the beach are your friends? Well, go visit the stones."

Then she'd go get her two favorite dolls. They were monkeys her mother had made of very soft fur and stuffed with rubber so they wouldn't drown when they went swimming. His name was Fred. Hers was Matilda. She'd carry them outside and walk down to the shore to sit on the raft that was beached on the rocks, and gaze at the water and wish that her father wasn't exactly dead, but that she and Matilda and Fred could climb into bed with her mother and console her because her poor Daddy had rowed the boat across to Charlie's forest and, like some of the poachers who had ventured over there, never returned, could never be found. Poor Mommy.

Her father, reading Korrigan's thoughts while he argued up in the house with her mother, would feel a strange panic in his flesh and wonder where she'd gone, as if he had never sent her away, but was angry she'd left.

When she heard him call from the front porch, quickly she'd run to hide behind the boathouse.

"Korey! Hey, Korey! Where are you, goddamit!"

Then his voice would tighten. He'd whine. "Come up here, I'm sorry. Come play with your Daddy. Come hug your Mommy. Korey? Come inside, baby."

The way that he shouted, she knew he'd started drinking. She knew he had snatched the jug from the top shelf and was swigging to work up the rage at her mother because her mother wouldn't let him even hug her. She could see how he sucked the fat lips of the jug (lips like those of a sucker fish washed up on shore and gasping for life); how he tilted his head back, eyes bulging as he held the jug up and sucked those sucker lips and the whole neck of the bottle down into his throat, gulping while the brown juice gushed from the corners of his mouth.

She felt so sorry for this Daddy she hated.

Disgusting as he was, if she were her mother, she'd hug him, she'd change him with love. She'd let him brush her hair and she'd cook him fine dishes, not just fried fish or stew. She'd go raspberry picking and fill the bowl with cream, sprinkle on sugar, sing to him sweetly, fill a silver Sunday spoon with the luscious ripe berries ("Open your mouth wide") and she'd slip them inside while he mmmd and then grinned as he chewed them.

She'd bend to his whims. She'd dance to the record player in the parlor. She'd help him with the outdoor chores and not just stay in the house or hang around the garden all the time. And she'd mend all his clothes. She'd bake him lemon pies and brew him fresh coffee. She wouldn't ignore him and sneer and shrug at him, and push him away when he tried to reach for her.

She'd forgive him for shooting the bird in the tree and not always use that one time long ago as a reason for refusing to go laugh with him under the covers.

When her father had given up shouting her name—"Korey! Hey, Korey! Where in hell are you?"—she threw Fred onto the roof of the boathouse. Then she threw Matilda. Then she fitted her feet into the chinks where the logs met and climbed up to join them.

She stuffed Fred's hand and Matilda's corduroy ear in her mouth, clamped her teeth shut on them and, like a cat with her kittens, crawled across the shingles.

Where a thick branch of the big tree swayed over the roof, she threw a leg over, straddled it and squirmed her way along, dragging the monkeys to the hole at the juncture where the three main limbs formed a kind of hollow covered by the dead nest, the nest no bird dreamed in, where no egg had hatched since the long ago shooting; where squirrels and mice once had played until Korey took over the nest and transformed it to what it was now: the secret lid covering the place she could slip into when the misery was in her, when her father and mother were in their room fighting.

Korrigan laid Fred on his back on one of the large limbs of the tree, with his legs crossed. She admired his brave, ever smiling face staring at her. She laid Matilda on the second limb on her stomach with legs spread across it and face turned sideways so the corner of her gentle, her patient mouth showed she was peaceful as always despite the tussle of being thrown and dragged and bitten. Her tail curled from under her dress in a spiral. Her outsticking ears listened for instructions.

On the third limb sat Korrigan. She lifted the dead nest and set it aside, then looked down to make sure her hiding place was empty. From the gut of this ancient swamp maple an odor blew upward that was fecundly hot and so urgently pungent that Korey succumbed and fully inhaled it.

The odor of rot, of bat dung and beetle, the perfume of mulched leaves; a mixture of smells like her father's tobacco when he sat by the fire at times of contentment after her mother was asleep and Korrigan tiptoed downstairs to go to the bathroom and saw him there blowing out circles of smoke aimed at the andiron toward which they drifted and tilted and sometimes settled over the brass handle that stuck up next to the little broom in its wrought iron stand . . . this odor of her Daddy's playful, private contentment welled up and filled her.

Usually he'd not even notice her passage, but on rare occasions as she returned to the stairs he's murmur, "Come sit on my lap."

With her face over the hold in the tree, Korrigan smelled his smoke and his sweat. She closed her eyes and saw him set the pipe in the ashtray on the little round table. He patted his knee. She put a hand on his rough, sunburnt neck and pulled herself into his lap. He placed a hand on her stomach and pulled her up close, rubbing his beard against her hair. For a long time they were silent, staring at the fire, then he chuckled softly.

"What?" she asked.

"I was thinking of how I stink."

"You don't stink."

"Yes, I do. I spent the whole day splitting wood. Mag says not to bother to come to bed until I take a bath. I don't know. Sometimes I like the smell of my own sweat." And the slow chuckling started again.

"*What!*"

"I was just remembering what a dumb kid I was in the logging camps."

He told about a night when he was packed into a shack with a bunch of older men. They were stacked four high in the bunks, drugged by the stench of their own bodies and the clothes hung out to dry and the vapors from the oil stove. The men on the bottom were complaining of the cold, but he was on top where the risen heat was making him sweat, and he said so. Then one of the old timers remarked what a precious thing sweat is and that he should learn to collect it by stuffing a bandanna under his arm. The others all joined in to tell stories of how you only had to waft a sweat soaked bandanna under the nose of a woman and she'd go weak at the knees and start panting and beg for some loving.

"They all swore it was so," Korey's father told her. "So I swung my axe all the next week with a red polka dot bandanna stuffed under my arm. And if you think it's easy to swing an axe that way, you just try it sometime, kid."

"And?"

"And then on Friday I go into town. Well, the rest ain't so funny because I was in love, see? Not with your mother but with a girl named Ruth. This Ruth had eyes like ripe cherries, and all I had in mind from morning til night was how some day I was going to marry her and build us a place here on Sleepy Lake and live happily ever after."

"You didn't love Mommy then?"

"Your Mommy came second. She was my second choice, I hate to tell you. Hell, her butt was still stuck to the seat of a desk chair in front of a typewriter high up the trunk of a Chicago skyscraper when I was courting Ruth. Ruth Väinämöinen. So, anyhow, we had dances at the Town Hall just like they have now, except people came from much farther away. The place was packed with folks who just had to dance to that music, that beat, because it made them so happy they nearly went crazy. It was still being played on the *kantos* and sung by the blond haired Indians from the Reservation. The music they made wasn't even human. It was pure magic. I can't describe it except you couldn't sit still when you heard it. You were worked up into a kind of frenzy that raised you to your toes and started you spinning. Hell, I think you were there the very last time the Indians played, but I'm sure you don't remember. You were only about three years old – yep, it was six summers ago they walked down to their canoes and never came back. All saving Charlie died of some disease we gave them, or were shot or poisoned or had themselves sung back up to their star, which is what I happen to want to believe. Anyhow, just you and me snuck off to that dance and I don't much remember whether I took you inside to look at the Indians. Probably not, there was such a crush."

"I remember."

"You probably just think you remember because I'm pretty sure I never took you inside. You may remember the music. Once it gets into you, you're not likely to forget. You remember in your bones."

"I don't remember the music, but I remember dancing."

"You danced with your Daddy? Not likely, kid. I never danced after that time with Ruth. That time with the bandanna under my arm? I was whirling around with this Ruth Väinämöinen, see?, holding her close while we spun and we spun, with her head hanging farther and farther back, her face just laughing and laughing and laughing, her eyes flashing, cheeks all rosy red like apples, you just want to bite . . . This Ruth who was just as pretty as . . . pretty as you are, Korey, only black haired, and I was loony about her, and she suddenly just kind of fainted back over my arm and I picked her up and carried her out to the porch. The fresh air revived her and she woke up and looked at me real peculiar and I knew she was in love with me like I was with her. And I carried her down near the shore and laid her out in a soft bed of pine needles and then . . . "

Again the chuckling began and went on for a long time, growing more and more bitter.

"Tell."

"I shouldn't."

"Daddy!"

"I can laugh at it now, but it was tragic what I did. How can anything so funny be so tragic? I reached my hand into my shirt and I pulled out the bandanna I'd been keeping all this time under my arm, and I did what those loggers all said I should do.

"I pressed the bunched up bandanna over her nose and her mouth like this—hey, no, stop kicking. I'm not really going to do it to you—and I held it there. She tried to raise up. She fought real good, but I held it there thinking it was going to make her go wild with desire.

"That wasn't the case, kid. That was not the case. All she did was get a knee up into me where it hurt, and I rolled over, sick to my stomach, and she sprung up and run toward the two-holer outhouse which I'd just built and set up the day before, so I kind of felt in my confused state like it still belonged to me; and I managed to stand up, bent over, and I charged after her like the dumb, laughing, lovesick drunk lumberjack I was and still am, and I barged right into that two-holer outhouse, and there she was on her knees vomiting into one hole, which made me feel sicker, so I fell to my knees and started to vomit into the other."

"And what?"

"And that was the last thing we ever did together was puke into those side by side pinewood holes. She wouldn't let me get close to her after that.

"Now, enough of such stories. Let me tell you about Barefoot Charlie's people when they were still alive."

Korrigan turned her face against his shirt and secretly sniffed that smell that was supposed to excite Ruth Väinämöinen, and at the same time she loved him and loved his smell she was kneeling with her face over the hole, and then she realized where she was and raised up from the hole in the tree and opened her eyes.

Way out on the lake, spinning his boat, was the boy who lived on the farm next to theirs through the woods at the east end of the lake— the boy her father forbade her to play with.

He was showing off for her again.

Pierre Delattre

THE SPIRIT OF
THE WATER

"The Spirit of the Water" is a chant piece, used especially for readings. It is an epiphany within the dramatic context of Delattre's unpublished novel, Korrigan's Wedding, and is based on a story motif from the Kalevala.

*I*NTO CHARLIE'S BAY rowed Arthur, so captured by its sparkle that he turned his boat around and rowed by pushing on the oars. Stern first, parting the water slowly, smiling, feeling so delicious with the sun now on his face and chest, Arthur moved into the bay while he watched the sunlight dancing.

Such a white light played across the waters, such a gold flecked light sang out in streaks and streams of sunburst that it seemed as if a billion minnows were jumping, that the surface was alive with schools of breasting fishes.

But these were schools of light.

Schools of light were flitting right and left and towards him, veering away back to the shore, bursting from the boatsides. It seemed to Arthur that life was as beautiful as it possibly could be when it was simply sunlight blown across the surface, when every instant its excited schools, its herds and tribes and flocks and crowds took patterned forms of light to dance and die together without ever having had to feel the weight we carry in our flesh.

He wished that he could turn to light. He would have liked to graduate to schools like theirs, to leave his flesh behind and mingle with those flashes on the water, to play with them, learning and unlearning forms in such swift flashes the forms could not be seen before they'd changed again to other forms and forms and forms of things realized and then dissolved before they ever could be seen, could be seen, could be remembered or forgotten.

Entranced, he pushed his boat into their midst, broke them apart, became creator and destroyer as he aimed for the mouth of the fiery, flame streaked river.

Moving nearer, he could see the river's mouth exploding with eruptions of white light. Its waters were so eager, they were leaping toward the lake, there over the rise of sand before the spreading.

Arthur pushed across the wavy greenness, the pale translucent glow of the weeds in Charlie's Bay. They were thick as grass in places. His stern could hardly part them. He pushed the heels of his hands against the oars until he found himself delivered from the weed bed into a clear channel.

With the waters from the river rushing to each side, he positioned his boat directly in front of the river's mouth perhaps fifty yards off shore, held it there by working the oars back and forth in pulses, in and out like gull wings hovering while he leaned forward and looked to see if any bears were there.

In the marshy meadow with the bright green razor grasses and the stunted jackpines behind them on the dunes, in the clearing around the river's mouth just before the forest started, not a bear or moose or deer in sight. Only the swooping songbirds whose music seemed to take its pitch from the splash of waters there where the river had its last fling before it spread out to the lake with the birds above it darting at the insects, where the waters swam away in flat, long whirls that trailed bubbly memories from their passage through the forest.

Now he found himself in a place of curious swirlings. These first swirlings of the water after their long passage through the earth up into the churning hole and out into the air there at the source where the river issued from the rock deep inside the meadow beneath the great oak tree in Charlie's refuge. . . the first wide, sinuous swirlings after their release from the forest channel, where they'd gathered all the rivulets of melted snow, pulled Arthur's boat into the center of their motion.

He shipped oars and let the waters do what they wished with himself and his boat. He and the boat were taken on a spin that seemed the spinning of the world. He folded arms, surrendered to the force that whirled his boat around. The sky was turning. He slid back off the rowing seat until seated on the boat's floor on his piled-up clothing, leaning on his elbows while the boat spun down, yet at the same time; down into the whirlpool but up into a blinding light that seemed to lift him right into the sun until a brightness in his brain exploded with a shower of sparks cascading all across the inside of his skull. He started giggling.

The wetness in the gladness of his eyes, the whitegold sun that glowed in them, blinded him. Tears streaked across his cheeks. The whole world got to spinning so fast that he was like a top upon the waters of the universe, his hair ablaze with the billow of the fire inside his head; and, up above, the sun's hair too was flaming.

But then the sickness welled up as the boat spun out of the center and the spinning slowed and stopped.

He grabbed the sides of the boat and pulled himself back into the seat. His ears were ringing, his skin was clammy. He shuddered violently. It seemed to him the boat was about to be sucked down into a whirlpool and carried underwater and that, in the very echo of his laughter, he was about to scream a sick farewell to air and sunlight. He lurched to the side of the boat. He felt ashamed before the very face of nature to be seen so sick. Even by the animals, even by the trees and birds – that they should see him hung there over the edge.

He wiped the sweat from his brow and sat up as the warmth returned slowly to his body. After the boat had drifted for a time, he bent over the side again, washed his face and gargled and then looked about, feeling pleasantly relieved, tingly inside with only a slight ringing in his ears now.

The ringing died away. He looked about. Not a bird in sight.

He could hear the river tumbling from the forest to the bay. He leaned forward, closed his eyes and listened. He could feel the clarity returning as the grey-green swirls in his brain dimmed and dissolved. His ears burned in a pleasant way. The drops of water coursing down his chest and stomach felt alive, like living creatures eager to get on with the game. He bent to splash more water on his face and thrust his arms into the cold lake down to the elbows.

The birds resumed their chirping there in Barefoot Charlie's forest; and the river from its heart could be heard thumping as it sent all its pressure through the big vein to the lake. Charlie's forest was feeding the lake's body, Charlie's lake and Arthur's, their common water body, this oceanic person upon whose presence north and south shore people, townsfolk on the west side, Arthur and his family on the east, all loved and dreamed and fished and swam, in whose depths their visions waited patiently to rise.

Arthur was close to shore now. He could smell the moss, the shore-washed stones toward which he'd drifted while he'd been dozing. His chin was pressed against his chest. For some time, he must have let exhaustion draw him down into a dream from which it felt delightful to awaken. Utterly relaxed, he pulled his arms out of the water, yawned and opened his eyes. There she was.

He saw her plainly.

Not her fleshly body, but her gold white sparkling presence. She was dancing in the waters not very far away, beneath the river's mouth. In the bottom of the bay upon the submerged sandbar directly in from where his boat was floating he could see her figure dancing, her leaping, playful figure waist deep in the water.

Her gold white hair. Her laughter. She was like a fountain in the lake, like something there cascading.

What else could cause this moving fountain with its many arms and legs? With its flying hair, but a person in its midst? Right there where everything was calm around it except the waterfall, the giant riffle where sometimes bears fished for big trout, there she was amidst the sparkle. She was playing, leaping up with both hands, fluttering.

He stood and threw his anchor out, sprang full length from the boat.

His body smacked the water. Swiftly he swam towards her.

Anselm Hollo

GIG

Thick clouds of smoke we roll up to the terminal
they're burning old planes our host is there
Inanna too is there we drive through a flickering landscape
post-Holocaust Ernst to the Hotel Splendide

a refurbished relic from the Booming Forties
where our host has reserved two chambers for us
at astounding expense to be borne by us
the visiting poets the Splendide

sits all by itself in a rubble-strewn landscape
in the piano bar Mars & Venus await us
pleasantly high they cheer us up when the desk clerk
won't take our checks while on the other hand wanting

shekels up front relents after phone call decides
to take a chance on these weirdos & then
it's out in the murky rain for some grub
& a Byzantine film about the end of this planet

Tomorrow we'll perform in the Muses' Temple
next to the burnt-out Pic 'n Pay

FASHIONABLE SECOND PERSON SINGULAR PRESENT TENSE BIRTHDAY POEM FOR JANE

> You are not the kind of guy who would be at a place like this at this time
> in the morning. But here you are, and you cannot say that the terrain is
> entirely unfamiliar, although the details are fuzzy. You are at a nightclub
> talking to a girl with a shaved head.
> —Jay McInerney, *Bright Lights, Bright City*

You *are* the kind of guy who would be at a place like this
at three o'clock in the p.m.
& here you are & you cannot say that the terrain
is anything but familiar
although the details are still a little too clear

you are at a table in a Fells Point bar
talking to another aging expatriate post-Beatnik
who believes in even quainter Utopias
than you do
& whom you haven't seen for going on twenty years

you are in the presence of two friends of his
two wise and beautiful women
neither of whom you have met before

one of them is the love of your life

to whom now, in the present present
you say thanks

for the bright lights in her eyes
still gracing your life in this movable city—

Oh, Many Happy Returns!

15 Oct 87

LA VIDA

for Janey, mi vida

Through swirls & eddies of footfalls
converging, diverging

some soft, some percussive
she walks to work

thinks of the two
happy young people

glimpsed in the car behind her
& how they *glowed*

among thousands streaming along in their shells
under big plumes of dark smoke under heaven

Later says "if I wrote poems

those are things I would write about"

& I say, well, that—that's a *movie*—
but later think, no

it isn't, it's *life*
It's life, all right

CRICKET POETICS

"Here   here"
the crickets again

the real thing
not young friend Kevin's

hi-tech alarm clock
in the trunk of our car

in the Moab Desert
strongly proposed

(by myself)
as mysterious

Desert Cricket

well   investigation
oftentimes proves us wrong

but "here   here"
an invisible legion

& that's what we are
the poets

an invisible legion

almost as audible

sometimes

206/Sampo: The Magic Mill

DIRECT ADDRESS

Bright sun   double yellow
line down the middle   a red one
on the far curbside   drums on the radio

Man in too-short check pants glides by like a daffodil

& I sit here thinking the Vice President

then thinking the Vice President
needs a new job & a *bandido* mustache

Who's speaking   "The Finnish-American Poet"?
no no   the poet of the precise non sequitur
in his middle years
in the days of the Great Condom Revival

Hello how are ya   Ça va, ça va

*Every*body's a genius at least once a year

THE MISSING PAGE

It was a poem, the jittery sort

"about" struggling through rush hour
traffic in downtown Baltimore

then, seeing you

there, on the far side of the river

of steel & plastic & sentient bags of water

cloaked & hatted   smiling

perhaps in disbelief at seeing me pass
the second time, in midstream, unable
to pull ashore to let you embark

(it also had some quote from a Godard
—just clumsy artifice)

The thing, the thing was

"how do you say?" immense

yearning & delight

ALLA PETRARCA

Downtown
Madison, Wisconsin at night
is pretty quiet. Returning

from the dinner for scholars of Finnish
in black plastic boots that seem to be shrinking
I listen to their heels on the pavement and feel like

a German Romantic Poet
a hundred and fifty years younger, enveloped
in my sense of missing you, oh fairest of ladies!

back home in Boulder,
Colorado. It is storybook time, as when we saw
that gown in the window in Stockholm Old Town

yesterday? Or the day before?
We who are of this gender, what can we do—
we know it must be a burden to you

to appear in our visions as the *summum bonum*
the great female sun our souls do yearn for
but at least you don't have to do it in person

every time. My feet hurt but I am so glad

(receding footsteps)

THINGS TO DO AT 453 SOUTH 1300 EAST, WINTER '86

Read ten thousand lines
by the poets of Finland

translate two hundred and twenty-six

then sit & stare
across to where sky meets dead sea
out beyond the *polis*
of this valley

Think of SIERRA PLUG "The Ecological Chaw"

see hundreds of erstwhile
(*very* erstwhile) trees go up in smog
from the assholes of fast little vehicles

get up and eat some fast little vehicle

That mixed choir's really raving away on the radio

Now contemplate the wish baskets in the Xmas tree
slow down past the speed of light

see them go up & down up & down
floating across the desert & over the mountains

Feel gentleness invade you with the thought of her
who brought you here

& here she is   no need to write now

Jane Piirto

BLUEBERRY SEASON

THE LONG GRASS yielded as if with wet surprise as she cut through it, its tangles never having been brushed by a human leg. Her walking shoes were wet by now, but white buck shoes are sturdy, and very good for walking in the woods; these had, for years, and didn't look to collapse now. The blueberry bucket, a plastic aqua gallon wash pail with a twisted coat hanger handle, had seen its years of service also, and had carried from these woods and fields many treasures, including her first *Boletus edulis*, which she recognized after taking the mycology course last winter. When she brought the mushroom to class, the instructor and the rest of them had had to give her the crown, the honor of having found the most edible field mushroom that month.

She walked through a stand of white birches and searched for the two trees that formed a sort of arch, where the path would be found. Few people came into these woods these days, too busy watching television, but the path was still there, reappearing after every winter as if by magic, for it wasn't a wide path, nor a well-traveled path, but it had been here ever since she had lived near these woods, forty years now since they had moved to town after working in the Navy Yard in Virginia during the War.

They said, though, that the path the people on the Oregon Trail had taken with their covered wagons was still visible on the prairies of South Dakota, even after the harsh winds and weathers of Dakota winters for over a hundred years, so maybe woods and fields received paths much as rock or marble received a sculptor's chisel; even on alpine tundra, the path the Ute women and children used to take over the 12,000 foot mountain passes in Rocky Mountain National Park was still visible, and the weathering there had to be immensely severe. If you didn't know the path was here, between these two birches, you'd never see it from the field below. One winter, cross-country skiers had tied fluorescent ribbons on the trees to mark the path, but they were all rotted now, and she was glad.

As she ambled along the ridge she almost called for Greta, and had to stop herself from looking back or to the side for the sleek black creature, who would be ranging by now, exploring animal holes and dens, but Greta was most likely dead by now. Eight months since she disappeared into a Christmas Eve snowstorm down at her daughter's place in Lower Michigan, and people kept saying that dogs have a homing instinct and appear on the doorstep after months or even years, but she felt the dog to be dead, a black Labrador velvet lump frozen in some snowbank next to I-75, and she couldn't imagine how the dog would get across the Mackinac Bridge without having someone notice; she had told the people at the Bridge to be on the lookout for a female lab when she had crossed back after the holidays, and nothing had been heard.

"Greta?" she said out loud when the image got too strong, or the memory. Her voice was rarely used these days, except to talk to the mailman or to the neighbor down the road, or to a friend on the telephone, or to sing in church. She thought about her voice and its use over the years, how it had been used in crying, laughing, soothing, yelling, cooing, gasping. Such a good thing, a voice, and so taken for granted, as she knew that she could speak if she wanted to, even if it had now been two days since she had used it, to answer a wrong number on the telephone. Her daughters and son chided her, told her to get another dog, to have a person come and live in, after all you're getting older now, Mother; but she'd said I've had animals—pets, children, people with me, living with me all my life and I want to see if I can live alone with my own self. Loneliness isn't the worst thing in the world, you know. Just to see if her voice would still do it, she let out her Tarzan yell, the one that she used to amuse the grandchildren with. Fine. That voice worked fine.

Still, it would be good to have a dog—Greta—a pet—as a companion, especially on these walks in the woods. Last year Greta had turned fierce and had dashed into the underbrush after something—a bear?—right around here, just about this time, blueberry season, though she'd never seen a bear out here. The newspaper said just the other day that the bears were coming out of the woods into the towns; several had been sighted outside Marquette, because this is such a bad year for blueberries, not enough rain in July, and too much in June. Well, we'll see, she said to her old aqua blueberry pail. We'll see if our secret spot has any berries.

Mother, her daughters have said, leave a note when you go out for a walk in the woods, so people will know, at least, which woods you're in, and she had said, who'd find it? Nobody would miss me for a few days, and by then it'll probably be too late, anyway. But Mother, you could sprain an ankle, or break an arm, climbing up those rugged hills; or fall over a log, or drown in a lake, anything could happen to you, and who'd know? I don't know, she'd said; I'll have to take the risk, and she saw herself on that ridiculous bicycle again, learning how to ride a bike at fifty, imagine, and she'd taken the pickup out to a country road, one lane paved in blacktop, and had put the bike in the back, so she could practice.

When she was young, she'd never learned how to ride a bike, and so she'd gotten on it, wobbling but going; finally going, and the blacktop was being eaten up in front of her eyes, peddling so fast as she was, and then there'd been the hill and the curve, going down that hill so fast, and the bicycle had gone right over the edge of the curve, and she'd tumbled down into the ditch, and got scratches and bruises, and a twig had pierced her right cheek, near her eye, so she was bleeding pretty much, too; this was before Norm died, and when she finally got home, the beat up bike and the beat up woman in that old clunker of a pickup, he'd shrugged and asked her, just like the kids; why do you go into the woods alone? Something is crazy about you.

Why indeed? Her thighs were brushing ferns now, a soft caress of bright green ferns, almost waist high in places, with soft green grass and the slight click of stiff aspen leaves in the slender breeze, the smell of balsam, and her feet sure on the footwide path.

Down from the grove of birches and ferns, into a swamp, with black and spongy but not sinking wet, and the slap of high swamp bushes. She used her arms like a swimmer's, to break through, the path faint but still there, winding a little, to take advantage of the least wet terrain, and the hum of mosquitoes after her, as she stooped to tie her shoe, warning her to keep moving or they'd pounce, sweating now in this moist ravine, and then to another small bluff, scrambling up and across a large exposed granite rock face that slanted down into the swampy place, wiping the sweat from her forehead with her sleeve, wiping her hands on her jeans, setting the blueberry pail down for a minute while she caught her breath.

Apple trees here on this mound, the fruit green and small yet; sour too; her mouth reverberated inside when she tried a bite: another few trips here in the fall, though, when they would be ripe and crisp, would give her apples enough for canning apple sauce and apple butter to last the winter; she'd need a new food mill this year because she'd lost the spring on the screw on the old one, and the man at the hardware store downtown said it was so old they couldn't order a screw or spring. He said the new one would cost about twenty dollars; and she had to decide, is it worth it? Could she afford it, with heating prices the way they were and the electric company just raised the rates again? She couldn't afford to get new insulation for the drafty house, either; paying the heating bills would be cheaper; for how long? But she wasn't going to live there many more years, she supposed, and she wanted to manage on what she had, even though the company cut down her pension, they cut widow's benefits when the widows turn seventy; well, maybe she'd have to make applesauce the old way, peel the apples and core them, and mash them with the potato masher, white applesauce even though the russet color of the food mill applesauce pleased her so, and was healthier. Well, it was a decision to be saved for later. Now for the blueberries.

Her eyes turned downward, ground bound, scanning the grade and the grasses and the bushes on this mound of rock and birch and apple trees, looking for a patch. There, on the reindeer moss, the small bushes she sought. Crouching, she saw the clusters of blueberries, tiny as a doll's pearl necklace, and her practiced fingers went to work. The patch of bushes had so many berries she finally had to sit down, picking within her arms' lengths, crushing the moss with her bottom, feeling the dampness filter through her jeans and underpants.

The old ritual of August, performed by her grandmothers in Finland, and then here in this land, the women going out to gather the berries. When she was a girl, they'd all go out, her mother and her sisters and her aunts, and then the children had to clean them; she sat under a tree with a huge galvanized laundry tub full of blueberries, and she and Laina picked out the leaves and the twigs and the raw berries, careful not to crush the ripe ones; they started cleaning them in the afternoon, after everyone had picked since early morning, breaking through dew, and the cleaning lasted, under the tree, until dark set in. Now her own daughters and granddaughters lived in cities with malls and freeways, and they couldn't pick blueberries, nor clean them, but they could buy them at the supermarket, those awful domestic ones that tasted like mush.

Her fingers worked in a plucking motion, gently, and she separated the ripe ones from the green ones by just the right amount of pressure, glad to have the use of her fingers still, for such delicate work; his mother had had arthritis near the end, and had been angry when she couldn't pick the berries anymore; she saw the old woman queenly in the middle of a burnt-over scrub pine blueberry field, sitting in a patch and feeding blueberries to her youngest grandchild, chuckling at the blue-faced boy. Dead now. Concentrating so much on the picking, she barely noticed when the sound of the berries dropping into the pail turned from the plop of drumming, the quick dull sound of berries hitting the bottom of a plastic pail, to the silence of the second and third layers, berries hitting berries.

Four cups for a blueberry pie, one cup for blueberry muffins; she used to make her children pick one cup each, at least, when they'd go blueberry picking as a family, and she'd tell them that if they ate the berries, no pie, no muffins; they had to save at least a cup each, and could eat the rest. They'd pick their cup and then go to the car and beep the horn for her and Norm, just sit in the car with the mosquitoes and the black flies beeping to the wilderness: that was when they had hated blueberry picking, the stage every child goes through until it becomes a happy ritual. She herself had disciplined herself to only eat a few, just to whet her taste, but it was harder for the children; her grand-daughter, when they'd come here a few years ago, to this secret patch, had eaten every last berry she'd picked—Grandma, they're so good! Mmmm! She smiled and popped a few berries into her mouth, rolling them around on her tongue before biting. If she came out here enough times, maybe she'd have enough for canning; nothing like blueberries in the middle of winter, as a side dish with the thin Finnish pancakes she made herself for Sunday breakfast, royal purple in the snow.

Wandering from patch to patch, the next one under some cedar trees, the next in long grass where she could barely see the berries; and then there was the one in the cracks of the gray face of rock and she sat on a crust of lichens,the pail half filled, enough for a batch of blueberry jam at least, even if she stopped now, which she wasn't about to do. A full pail or nothing. She wondered what time it was, and looked up at the sun, but it had turned cloudy without her noticing it, so intent had she been, and she had no idea which direction the sun was in; everything in the sky was gray-white and she couldn't get a bearing on north or south, east or west.

She reached into her jacket pocket for her compass; never go into the woods without your compass, and a whistle at least, Mother, her son had said, and she promised she wouldn't. She saw exactly where her compass was; right on the kitchen table, right next to her whistle, right where she'd left it when she went to the bathroom before leaving. Well, no matter; she'd know her way around here blindfolded, she'd been here so much, and only a couple of miles from home if you cut through the woods near the lake instead of taking the trail. Lots of daylight left; it looked to be about four in the afternoon by the amount of light in the gray sky, though she couldn't tell where the sun was. More patches of berries, and she wandered farther and farther afield, closer to home, though, in an erratic semi-circle; she had a feeling about these things.

In the middle of one patch, a black pile. Large and sausage shaped. Bear droppings? Human? She tried to remember what bear droppings looked like; she could only remember deer droppings, and rabbit, and fox. She shrugged, pausing from her picking to listen to the wind and be quiet and receiving; to watch the chickadees on a nearby spruce as they scolded a squirrel. Sometimes thoughts got in the way of observation.

She bent her head to avoid hitting a low branch, and turned along a rock cut, and found herself in a wild raspberry patch; nothing so fragile as wild raspberries—the globules separated and fell into her palm, miniatures on a doll's plate; she had to be even more deft than with blueberries in order to pick them whole, but her practiced fingers quickly loosened the berries from the stem, and she had a layer of raspberries on top of the blueberries. A sugar plum tree had some ripe reddish-purple fruit also, and so she put a few sugar plums into the bucket too, but even more into her mouth. This feast of wild fruit, with a few chokecherries for cleansing her palate, and they wondered why she spent so much time in the woods? Her fingers were quite stained by now, deep red and purple, and she licked them, and wiped them on her jeans.

They say you can smell a bear before you see him, that he smells like a horse barn. Farther into the raspberry patch, more droppings, and a long oval of trampled grass, as if a creature had slept here. She had been so quiet in her luxuriating over raspberry treasure, and the wind was blowing into her face, so her smell wasn't that obvious, that she was not really surprised when she met him.

They were right about the smell; it was awful, worse than any horse barn. The creature was up on the rock face, about twenty-five feet away, and it looked as startled as she as their eyes met, and held. Black bear, range northern United States and Canada, 5 feet tall, 300 pounds, can run as fast as 25 miles an hour; worshipped by ancient primitive tribes as a life-giver, where did she know that from? A constellation in the sky. Taunted in the city square, caged and dancing. Her mind snapped from reverie to fear and back again, as she stared unblinkingly at the dark brown bear with matted fur hung with thistles and burrs, and in her mind she saw him running across a northern meadow in a fast lope, crossing his territory; standing on the shore of a stream tipped on a large flat rock, waiting for trout, nosing into garbage cans and ripping tents, being captured and brought to wilder wilderness with broader range.

Motionless, their eyes held each other's for—forever—and they were entranced, as lovers who meet at the airport after not having seen each other for a long time; she stood still, as loosely poised as a dancer preparing for adagio, and then she swept her arm towards him slowly, hissing softly in the back of her teeth while he stood above her on the slanted rock face, looking down at her from the angled perch, while she offered him her bucket of berries. She was surprised to know that she was not afraid now. Still hissing softly, she held his eyes and set the bucket on a bed of moss; then she backed up slowly, still holding his eyes.

When he turned and glided in a smooth gallop, up the rock and away into the cedar stand, she almost wept. She had not meant to fright him out of his place.

She waited, motionless, for a very long time, hoping he would come back and eat her berries, but he didn't, and soon she wondered if he had even really ever been there, or whether she had conjured him, imagined him and that horse barn smell; whether she had summoned him by legerdemain, her deftness.

The bucket seemed very heavy as she made her way in the direction she assumed was home; she had lost the place of it, stumbling a little, and had to slide down steep hills, smashing through stands of ground pine and through swamps of cattails and through fields of blue harebells and the tansy that seemed to grab at her fleeing feet with its stink that they used to say would bring on an abortion to a girl who needed one. She missed Bear; she wanted to touch him and comb his hair; her daughter called her up the other month and told her to get a pet, she said this show on Nova said without touch you shrivel up, Mother; you need to touch and be touched, and she had replied I touch the trees, I touch the grass, I touch the plants and the fruit, as if it were a joke, but now she longed for a bear, and she was unable to find the path to home. In one of the cedar swamps she plowed through, she kept her eyes on the slick and dark ground, and she saw a pile of black feathers, raven feathers from their size, but no bird and no remains — just feathers, a bird caught by a fox or skunk and eaten up, just like that.

It was almost dark when she finally recognized a familiar crook of maple trees on the next bluff, to her left. Yes, she had been on target again; her instinct for home, her internal compass, right again, an old woman of the woods. It was dark by the time she got home, and she almost forgot, as she sat in her kitchen cleaning the berries, smelling the muffins that baked in her oven, listening to the public radio station's chamber quartet program.

Eeva-Liisa Manner

Selected from
COLLECTED POEMS, 1956-1977
(Translated by Ritva Poom)

Spring is raw, birth savage.
Death comes lightly as the first snow.

You rise and go, no crossroads, no sign,
not a trace in the snow, not even the touch of your hem.

* * *

And the plundered star, divided by lot
among great armies as by the gods of yore,
sheds its beauty for man, who is blind.
Playing, dancing, singing animals,
swift, fiery, narrow-muzzled mountain goats
die. Birds in the forests grow silent,
the forests grow silent.

Desolation. Snow falls on the mountains.
The rivergrass does not remember.

There, beyond, stars turn.

* * *

(translated by Ritva Poom)

Christ, resurrected,
the women thought him a gardener.
Probably he still smelled of flowers and rotting leaves.
On the journey to the country village
he appeared to others as well,
one said: that was he,
another: no, it was a gardener,

and a pupil implored him: "Stay with us,
for evening comes and the sun is already setting."
And he stayed and ate and they knew him.

But the gardener returned to his garden
and changed into a tree,
and even the tree is no longer, only a warm shimmer
a very old, weary light.

* * *

The roads are long and hot.
The sky is white. Crows fly
and curse, a hoarse shrieking cloud.
Windows are eyes. My shadow a cross.

Where would I go, my house
is filled with strange tales, phrases like traps,
pregnant words, which burn like tin
and predict, casting shadows on the walls.

I am pregnant, from my wound grows a tree
of moth-eaten leaves.
The white-hot sky shimmering through,
my understanding does not reach there.

* * *

(translated by Ritva Poom)

The paths turn red, the forests yellow,
mountains darken in the distant rain,
the haze of autumn leaves burning in yards.

An ax rings with stronger echoes than before,
deeper voices of the forest tell
of the woodsman's journey to the slope of Hawk Mountain.
An echo travels along the opposite shore, sharp and bright,
as if, on empty banks, someone unseen were felling
imagined trees.

Now and then they greet each other,
this one and the other, the man of echoes,
and they call out something
across the still forest lake, deep and cold.

* * *

STRONTIUM

Why is our joy sorrow, our heart mute,
our spiritual home afire?
Seeing a falling petal, I recall
that the city was built a thousand years,
the cathedral was adorned with stoneroses
when the army came and shattered it in an hour
like a clock

* * *

My forest-scented room
gleams red ever earlier
with the sunset,
the heart of the pine darkens,
the refracted light, cold.
Evening is red and old
as the spectrum of iron.

* * *

(translated by Ritva Poom)

Childhood, wild grain. A deep forest of presentiments.
Secrecy. Change. A time of slow ripening.

Death conceals itself, it has the eyes of a mask.
Everywhere the mask's silence breathes.

I sleep in a garret. A horse: its eye like a deep pool
comes to the window, prophesying the dark of entrails.

Someone sets foot on the heart of the forest.
Someone is always near, and the vervain blooms.

* * *

I set out on a journey.
I never reached there, I grew old on the train.
I watched as fields withered,
my heart crumpled, crumpled
like an ash leaf.

* * *

Dreams wade slowly up the river.
They bring dream food to the cabin,
tansy and sorrel,
the wolf's track and the cry of a wounded crane
and a letter written in iodine.

They want to take me along
to where gravity is dead,
where, drowned like a woman, shadow has no luster,
where there is darkness and empire.

Eeva Kilpi

Excerpts from

A WOMAN'S DIARY

(Translated by Inkeri Väänänen-Jensen)

A HUMAN BEING needs to keep in touch with relatives, with the family, with parents and with children, even though during a lifetime she makes many new friends and receives much love.

I feel that a person who carries love within herself radiates that love no matter where she is. There has been so little love in my life recently that I have just not had the energy to spread it around.

* * *

I have now been divorced for ten years and am still alone. And that was the intent. Divorce was what I chose. My dog has died. The children are almost all gone. As I did at first, ten years ago, so do I now lie awake during the nights, wracked with pain and anguish. From this I can only conclude that suffering is a part of my life, regardless of my circumstances.

* * *

I complain about my loneliness here. I miss a lifelong partner, a spouse, a human being beside me along life's winding paths; but what do I see as soon as I go into town, even into this small country town? Bored looking wives, sour men sitting in their automobiles waiting for them.

* * *

It is true that a person does not know anything about life until she has experienced middle age and has seen, for example, that the under-valued or ignored observations of her parents are proved in the long run to be true. (I got this idea while sweeping the floor.) When my mother has said from time to time, "There are no friends like old friends, the friends of one's youth," I did not consider her words to have any value. But now I realize how true they are. Later on, one just does not become close friends with new acquaintances. And then my mother said, "If only one had this experience and then could live her life anew." Only now do I realize what this means. We live our lives without experience, and the whole consuming task of caring for and raising off-spring is accomplished with little preparation, without our understanding the whole picture, an understanding which would help us to see relationships more clearly and would help us to keep matters in balance.

* * *

At the moment I am very depressed. Perhaps a person comes to this during the course of a lifetime as a result of countless separations. And at the end, only a multitude of the dying stand before one. One person after another grows old and dies. Life is nothing but separation.

* * *

(The writer is now in her parents' cottage watching them moving about outside.) Without question, I still receive strength from my parents. But little by little I am moving toward becoming their mother, their caretaker, their support. Nature has surely intended this to be a part of human behavior. The child must, in time, change into a parent for her parents.

My mother is not well. I draw strength from her; that is why she is weak. During the time I am here, I feel well, I relax. Father also draws strength from Mother. We are both under her care, regardless of how we try not to be a bother to her. However, help from us or a sharing of the home tasks does not change the situation, for she carries the whole burden of the household, just as I have to carry it at home. Almost without exception, this is true for a woman, regardless of her situation; it is true for the modern woman, the liberated woman. This is her burden. Someone ought to be a mother to my mother so she could conserve her strength. Everyone should have someone as a mother. That is why I was so tired out last spring—I did not have the energy to be a mother—the source of strength. A remarkable thing, this mothering.

Knowledge has given me some courage so that perhaps I have a little bit of the strength of spirit which my mother has—and this spirit has remained with her into her old age even though she has received little recognition during her lifetime.

* * *

When I traveled last Wednesday night to Orivesi to speak on Thursday morning about documentary writing for television, a fair-haired young woman, who appeared oblivious to her surroundings, withdrawn, sat across from me on the train. She had placed her high leather boots in the middle of the floor between us and had also spread her legs so that I had to sit sideways with my feet crossed and had to be careful during the whole trip not to disturb her boots. I was provoked, but did not say anything. Suddenly, just before we reached Orivesi, she murmured, as if talking to herself, "I have not liked any writer's books as much as I have liked yours." I said, "That's good to hear," many times. Then we talked. She was a student and was looking for summer work; her major was sociology, but she didn't know yet what sort of work she would go into. Her parents were Karelians. As I left, I said, "Best wishes to you."

When the conductor handed my ticket back to me, he said, "Thank you so much for your stories about Lapland."

I was dumbfounded but managed to say, "I'm glad to hear that somebody remembers those old stories."

I should remember this when in need of self-esteem.

I felt elated and shy at the same time.

* * *

An editor telephoned and asked if I would write a short article on "How I Would Live During the Last Day of My Life.". . . I have thought about this matter for several days and now I know. For the last time, I would perform all my familiar tasks. I would like to spend most of the day alone—as I usually do. I would make notes all the time; I don't know why; that is just my way of living. I would clean at least one closet. I would probably wash dishes and vacuum. I would go to visit my parents; I would listen to them, but talk little. I would eat food that my mother prepared (perhaps it would be herring baked in cream, good, strong smelling food, food familiar from my childhood). I would look at my parents carefully. I would prepare a good meal for my children, perhaps an oven casserole with various kinds of meat. With it I would serve turnip pie, Karelian rice pasties, lingonberries, and pickled cucumbers. I would look at my children, examining my feelings for them. Perhaps just at that moment I would understand something about life. I would no longer grieve that many books would be left unwritten but regret that so many books would be left unread. I would still read some short story by Chekhov and a little of Kafka to experience the remarkable truthfulness revealed in Kafka's sentence structures. Perhaps I would even have time to read one unfamiliar short story, possibly one by Hesse. But in no way would I burden my day excessively. I would look at trees. There is something universal in their shape and reach; they resemble nerves. I would use every moment to gather new impressions. That is the greatest joy. I would not drink alcohol nor would I spend my time with any man, no matter how attractive, because that would disturb my thoughts. Yet, I would recollect briefly my sexual life. I would call my two sisters, one friend from my childhood, and one colleague, but I would not talk for long. In the evening I would clip out interesting articles from the newspapers; maybe in eternity there would be plenty of time to read them. I hope my hand would hold my pen until the very end. I would want to write to the very last moment, like this.

Or perhaps I might just go for a walk in the woods.

Lauri Anderson

HUNTING HEMINGWAY'S TROUT

COUSIN TOIVO and I bucked the empty truck along a two-track log-ging road that one of the Vainio boys had bulldozed out of the forest in late spring. In June Toivo had selected the largest birch trees for cutting. After he dropped them and limbed them, I dragged them by tractor to the roadside. At the end of each day Toivo cut the trees into four-foot pulp logs which I piled along the road. Now we were loading the truck in sticky hot July but at least the heat kept most of the blackflies swarming down in the coolness of the swamp.

Toivo used a clear patch in the forest to turn around and then parked the truck beside our twenty-cord woodpile.

We were in our work togs—jeans stained and stiffened from tree sap, flannel shirts ragged at the elbows, baseball caps sweat-blackened at the bands, leather swampers saturated with bear grease. Our faces were streaked with mosquito dope and dirt. As Cousin Toivo often said, "If you look ugly, you feel ugly, and in this kind of work a man ought to be ugly."

Both of us were feeling particularly ugly that day because we had load-ed and unloaded the truck by hand three times a day for ten consecutive days. I knew a change was coming, though, because Toivo had bought a pack of Stroh's on our return from the mill yard for this final load.

The truck radio was playing a song about driving daddy into an early grave, then another about the back door always being open. Toivo placed two open cans of Stroh's on the truck hood and we commenced loading the logs. First the two of us wrestled upright the thickest butt ends and leaned these against the empty truck bed. Then Toivo climbed onto the bed, his body bent and his birch hook ready. From the ground I hooked the base of a log and heaved. Toivo caught the top end and pulled. Straining together we somehow managed to lift and twist the huge logs—most with girths three or four times greater than our waists—onto the bed, our bulging back muscles as taut as snagged fish line. As soon as we had covered the bed with these monsters, Toivo climbed down and joined me at the front bumper where we sat in ex-hausted silence and drank the Stroh's.

This was the third straight summer I had worked in the woods with Cousin Toivo and God how I hated it! The pay wasn't much either. However, it saved me from looking for another job and it made my Finnish father happy. Toivo was the difficult child of Aunt Ellen's first marriage. Toivo and I were the same age but while I had spent my childhood in my room reading books and staying out of trouble, Toivo was out smashing up half a dozen bikes, accidentally stepping on dozens of nails, picking frequent fights with kids who were bigger and stronger, and unintentionally setting several brush fires while learning to smoke in someone's back field. Toivo was book dumb and undisciplined but I admired his practicality and his *sisu*—his bulldog courage. I also liked his wife Ann and their three boys. Ann was a secretary at a furniture factory. The boys were all school age—the oldest would be going into the fourth grade and the youngest into the second. The youngest was already like Toivo—willing to work hard at anything except book-learning.

After the beer break, we both worked from the ground. We took opposite sides with heavier logs, spaced our legs for maximum leverage, swung our hooks into the wood and, at Toivo's count of three, heaved upward and outward together. Occasionally a log missed its place in the growing load and slammed back to earth, gouging a deep hole. We'd leap back, curse, leap forward, slam in our hooks anew, and once again heave against our straining back muscles. I could feel the bones in my spine about to snap at the moment when we released each log and sent it bedward.

"It's a good thing you're not like other loggers," I said, streams of sweat stinging my eyes. "They all have jammers to load their trucks. They miss out on the real pleasure that comes from loading by hand—the torn back muscles, the sore leg and arm muscles, the sweat, the sawdust in the eyes, the dirt and grime."

"I don't need a jammer," said Toivo. "All that fancy machinery for hoisting a log is expensive and I've got a dumb college student who's cheap."

As the pile grew, it became impossible from the ground to fit each new log snugly against its neighbors. Cousin Toivo climbed onto the load and, as I tossed logs skyward, he caught each deftly with his hook, scrambled aside, and guided it in flight to its proper spot. As the load grew to completion, Toivo was twelve feet in the air and doing a sort of clumsy dance since footing was notoriously unstable among the smaller logs that filled out the top. These thin final logs felt like matchsticks compared to the monsters that formed the base. Now I chose one of the smallest logs, stepped several paces back from the truck, rushed forward and, as if throwing a fat javelin from my knees, propelled the log with maximum velocity toward Toivo. Somehow at the last moment he pirouetted out of the way, caught with his hook the weighty missile in flight, and guided it to its chosen place. The next log failed to reach the top but Toivo's hook caught it anyway. He let go before the weight of the log could yank him off the truck but he lost his balance and fell awkwardly to his knees, crunching one against a knot. I leaped back as Toivo's falling hook snapped loose and narrowly missed my face. The point buried itself three inches into the hard-packed earth between my spraddled legs.

"Are you all right?" I asked as I retrieved the errant hook and tossed it back onto the load within easy reach for Toivo. Toivo rose slowly and tested his bruised knee against his own weight. He unsheathed the gutting knife he always carried on his belt and lopped off the offending knot. Then he swore loudly, took up his hook, and motioned that we should continue.

In Gaylord, Michigan, in July the sun doesn't set until after nine, so we still had a few minutes of daylight remaining when we completed the loading. As the air cooled the flies rose in a black cloud off the swamp and headed our way. We could hear their approach. It sounded like a hundred chain saws all roaring at once. Toivo and I retreated to the truck cab just before the swarm turned the air into a seething mass. All around us the forest began to waver and shimmer as if we were undersea. Part of the cloud settled an inch deep onto the warmth of the hood. Another part coated the windshield with an insect curtain so opaque that we had to use the wipers in order to see the road.

We each drank two more Stroh's before Toivo turned the ignition and drove for home. By then it was dark and the insect swarm had spread itself throughout the forest. "When they first come out, they'd eat a man right to the bone in minutes," said Toivo matter of factly. "I've seen it before. They caught one of my dogs last year and drained him of blood. There were flies covering every inch—his eyes, nostrils, the inside of his ears. I had to shoot him."

"A good thing we can hear them coming," I said.

"And the worst days are coming," said Toivo. "These recent rains started a new cycle. Another batch of flies will be hatching in the next couple of days."

I knew from the tone of his voice that Toivo had just found the excuse he needed to take a day off. Tomorrow we'd leave the forest to the black flies while we sought pleasures elsewhere.

"You ever read Hemingway?" asked Cousin Toivo as we turned from the two-track onto a gravel road that would lead to the paved road that would take us home.

"Sure," I replied. "I've read lots of his stuff. I enjoy his writing a lot." I was a graduate student in English at the state university and I'd taken several American literature courses in which we studied Hemingway. I worked with my cousin only during summer vacation, thank God, because three months at a time was all I could take of life as a logger. Felling trees wasn't too bad but Cousin Toivo insisted on doing that himself. He said I was too educated to be trusted with a chainsaw. I peeled bark when we were cutting softwood, and always I loaded and unloaded the truck. Always I worried that I would snap my back and instantly become a cripple for the rest of my life. That had happened with my father. Years ago he had bent over while standing on top of a load of maple. That's all he did—just bent over. It took two guys to get him off the load. He couldn't move. He couldn't even sit in the cab when they finally got him down. He rode to the hospital still bent like an old clothespin. I guess he rested his forehead on the dash and his knuckles on the floorboard. After that he couldn't do much of anything, so he clerked in a shoe store. Permanently bent like that, he could put shoes on people's feet without changing posture. Another clerk had to get the shoes off the shelf.

"I've only read one Hemingway story," said Cousin Toivo, "but I liked it a lot. Did you ever read 'Big Two-Hearted River'?"

"Sure," I said. "That's one of my favorites."

"It takes place north of here in the Upper Peninsula," said Toivo.

"In Seney," I said.

"That's right," replied Toivo. "I've wanted to go there ever since I read about it. I'd like to fish where Hemingway fished. I'd like to go for trout in the Big Two-Hearted River."

My twenty-five-year-old cousin Toivo loved to fish, especially for brook trout and rainbows. He was the outdoor type but I was surprised he'd ever read anything by Hemingway. He'd only gotten to the ninth grade before they'd expelled him for punching a teacher. At fifteen he was already working full-time in the woods with his stepfather. At sixteen he had his own horse named Diablo and drove his own car—a fifteen-year-old black Oldsmobile with four-inch red dice dangling from the rearview mirror. I couldn't remember ever seeing him read anything—not even the newspaper. Somewhere though, he'd read "Big Two-Hearted River."

"'Big Two-Hearted' is my favorite story," said Toivo. "I've read it twice."

"No kidding," I said, rather intrigued. "Where did you read it?"

"We had to read it in eighth-grade English," said Toivo. "Don't you remember?" I had forgotten. "That old bitch Mrs. McDuffie gave us a big fat book full of really boring stories, but I liked that one. It was the only one I read. It made me want to be fishing with Nick. That was the name of the guy in the story."

"I know," I said. "There are other stories about Nick. A whole lot of them."

"Oh yeah?" said Toivo. "Maybe someday I'll read another one. What I'd like to do tomorrow, though, is go to Seney and fish the Big Two-Hearted River."

"How far is it?" I asked.

"It's farther north than I've ever been," said Toivo. "I checked a road map. It's at least two hundred miles. We'll have to get up really early and make it a two-day trip. We can take a tent and camp out just like Nick did."

"Sounds great," I said. I didn't tell Toivo that the Big Two-Hearted River wasn't in Seney. Hemingway conveniently moved it for his story. I didn't care if we never found it. I just liked the idea of a day off.

By the ungodly hour of four a.m. the next morning we were driving north along I-75 toward the Mackinac Bridge that links Michigan's two peninsulas. When I told Cousin Toivo about the bridge – that at five miles in length it was the world's longest suspension bridge – he immediately became agitated. At the bridge approach he pulled over and parked underneath a huge NO STOP ON BRIDGE sign and ordered me to drive.

"What's the matter?" I asked.

"I can't trust myself on the bridge," said Toivo. "I don't know if I can hold the lane. What if I drive right over the edge? We'd drown for sure."

"That's impossible," I explained. "I've been over it before. There's a curb on both sides and an island in the middle."

"You drive!" insisted my cousin.

Cousin Toivo is one of those guys who are completely in command in their own environment and completely displaced in someone else's. A couple of years ago my uncle drove Toivo into Detroit to take a three-week training course for future insurance salesmen. Toivo spent all three weeks in the hotel – ate in the cafeteria, shopped for souvenirs in the little shop off the lounge, and drank Stroh's in the bar. He saw nothing wrong with that – said proudly that the hotel contained everything he needed. "Besides," he said when my uncle picked him up for the long drive back to Gaylord, "Detroit is full of crooks and black people." Cousin Toivo knows nothing about black people. I'm not even sure he's ever seen one. He just knows they're different and Toivo doesn't trust anyone that's different. If he had his way, everyone on Earth would be a Finn.

Just for the hell of it I stopped the car squarely in the middle of the bridge. "Isn't that a great view?" I pointed out as we swayed back and forth.

"Yeah!" said Toivo as he clutched at the dash so hard that his knuckles were turning blue.

"Just think. We're halfway between Hemingway's Walloon Lake and Hemingway's Seney."

"Yeah!" grunted Toivo. "It's great. Now get me off this goddamned bridge because you're already halfway to a punch in the nose!"

After we crossed the bridge Cousin Toivo insisted on driving again. "You never know what you'll find on these Upper Peninsula roads," he explained. "Some of these unknown drivers are apt to be strange." We drove along the top of Lake Michigan past miles of empty beaches and past the edge of the Hiawatha National Forest to the north. We stopped for a breakfast of coffee and smoked chubs in the little fishing village of Naubinway.

An hour beyond the bridge we came to M-77, a secondary road that would lead us to Seney twenty-five miles to the north. "There weren't any roads like this when Hemingway came here to fish," I said.

"Oh yeah?" Toivo replied.

"His family used to take a ferry boat across Lake Michigan from Chicago in order to get to their summer cottage near Petoskey," I explained. "Up here there weren't any paved roads then. People reached the nearest point by boat and then hiked overland. If they could afford it, they took the train."

"The fishing must have been great," replied Toivo.

Soon we passed a whole town for sale—homes, a store, a cocktail lounge, tennis courts. Down a small grade we passed Lake Anne Louise and began to climb. We passed a MOOSE CROSSING sign which caught our attention. Michigan had only recently imported moose into the Upper Peninsula from Canada.

"Keep your eyes open," said Toivo. "Seney's not far now and we may cross the Big Two-Hearted River around any bend. Hemingway didn't say which direction the river was from the town."

Soon we passed a Mennonite church surrounded by old junk cars, then the Mead Creek State Forest Campground. A trailer sat beside the creek. Further on we passed a canoe rental and then a huge sign on a tiny bar that proclaimed GOOD FOOD. Soon we entered a small settlement made up of two Mormon churches, the Eagles Nest Family Dining, and a ramshackle store whose sign proclaimed BOOK BARGAINS,

JUNK, AND APPLIANCE REPAIR. Toivo was getting nervous. "Christ!" he growled. "Where's the river? Where's the wilderness? Where's the great fishing?"

"Time changes everything," I said. "Hemingway's Nick was here way back in 1919 or thereabouts."

"Rivers don't move," growled Toivo. "The Big Two-Hearted still has to be somewhere around here."

We were only about five miles from the town of Seney when we passed a huge green sign for the Seney National Wildlife Refuge Visitor Center. This was soon followed by the Wigwam Picnic Area, Holland Creek, and then Seney itself. In the boom days of the lumber industry in the nineteenth century, Seney was full of hundreds of lumberjacks. Bars and whores were everywhere. I knew what we'd find now — a virtual ghost town. Seney was so small it hardly qualified as a community. There was a gas station, a small store, and a motel. The street was deserted — no pedestrians and not even a parked car.

Toivo pulled in at the store and the two of us went in to ask directions. The clerk, the only person on the premises, looked at us as if we were crazy. "I've lived here all my life and I never heard of a Big Two-Hearted River," he said. The clerk was a very old man. "You sure you don't want the Fox? Most folks around here fish the Fox."

"I can fish an ordinary river like the Fox any time," said Toivo. "The Big Two-Hearted is special. Ernest Hemingway fished there."

"He wrote a story about it," I added.

"Never heard of it!" insisted the old clerk. "Who's this Hemingway anyway? He from around here?"

"He was from Chicago," I explained. "He came here to fish right after World War One."

The old man stared at me distrustfully and then turned in upon himself. I could see a distance in his eyes as he searched back through the years. "I think it was 1919," he said at last. "There were three of 'em. Young guys from Chicago. One was just a kid. They fished the Fox for a week and caught a lot of brookies and rainbows — maybe two hundred in all. Two of 'em were about my age — maybe a little older. I'd've been twenty. The town was different but already small. Folks back then still remembered the lumbering days."

"How could you remember that?" I asked. "It was so long ago."

"Sure it was," said the clerk, "but I spent some time with them. We didn't get many visitors in Seney back then. They came in on the train. I'd been working in the woods that summer, but I was my own boss, so I took a day off to show 'em the best stretches of the river for trout. One of 'em — I don't remember which — asked a lot of questions about the old days, about the times the town burned, about the lumbering, and so on. If I remember right, the one with all the questions was a newspaper man. I remember telling him about one of our local characters—a guy who took a pocketful of frogs to the bar every night and bit the heads off 'em for free drinks."

"That couldn't've been Hemingway," said Cousin Toivo with conviction. "He didn't write newspaper stuff. He wrote stories—like in books. The one I read was about the Big Two-Hearted."

"That's right," I added. "We both read it. He tells about fishing the Big Two-Hearted right here in Seney."

"Maybe he did but it must have been in a different Seney," said the old man vehemently. "There's no such river around here. Anyway, none of those fellows that I remember was named Hemingway."

"Do you remember any of their names?" I asked.

"Nope," said the old clerk. "The names escape me. I think one of 'em may have begun with a w—Wemedge or something like that. An odd name." I sort of gasped at that revelation. Wemedge was one of Hemingway's nicknames when he was a young man yet unknown to the literary world.

"Let's get out of here," said Toivo. "I just drove a couple of hundred miles to fish the Big Two-Hearted and I'm going to find it."

"I'd try the Fox," said the old clerk.

Toivo stormed angrily out of the store and back into the car. He sat behind the wheel fuming, wondering what to do. Seney's single street remained empty. I sat on the passenger side and waited. I didn't want to interfere. After all, it was Toivo who had suggested this trip. It was he who had chosen to drive two hundred miles in order to fish for Hemingway's trout. I wasn't much of a fisherman myself. I'd rather read Hemingway's books than go fishing with him. I liked the clean polish of Hemingway's sentences—the way they seemed to recreate the actual emotions that accompanied an action. That re-creation was enough for me. I didn't need reality. Reality always included mosquitoes, wet feet, sweat, and dirt. I'd take the fictional fishing world of Hemingway every time over the reality. In reality Hemingway seemed to be an arrogant bastard who drank too much. If Hemingway were with Toivo and me right now, he'd've turned our fishing trip into a competition—into a race to see who could catch the most fish and the biggest fish in the shortest time. I'd read enough about him to know that. So I just sat and said nothing. I was happy we'd met the old clerk though. He'd make a nice cameo portrait and a lovely literary anecdote for the other graduate students back at the university in the fall.

Finally Toivo made up his mind. "Maybe the river is west of here. Let's try that."

"The old guy said the river doesn't exist," I said as Toivo swung the car westbound onto Route 28.

"What in hell does he know?"

"He's lived here all his life," I answered. We sped westward on a paved road that must have been laid down by a surveyor's rule. We drove 26.5 miles in an exact straight line on a road that never once went up or down. Beside the road flowed a perfectly straight muddy canal with banks so level that the grass almost seemed to have been mowed. "Maybe that canal's your river," I joked.

"Shit," said Toivo. We approached a container truck. Tailgating the container and hidden by it was the local sheriff. We were doing ten miles an hour over the speed limit. In seconds the sheriff had swung around, had put on his flasher, and had pulled us over. He gave us a forty-dollar ticket—payable immediately. As Toivo dug into his wallet the sheriff noticed our fishing gear on the back seat.

"Any luck?" he asked. Toivo and I just shrugged.

"Been fishing the Fox?" asked the sheriff.

"The Big Two-Hearted," I said.

"Never heard of it," said the sheriff. "That around here?"

"I guess not," I said.

We drove back toward Seney. "Your friend Hemingway is a liar," said Toivo bitterly. "I really believed in him but he's no different from all the rest."

"All the rest?" I asked.

"Everybody," said Toivo. "Like the guys who work in the mill yard. I have to keep double checking their measurements so that they don't cheat me."

"Hemingway was a storyteller," I said. "They're all liars. That's what storytelling is."

"Hunh," said Toivo.

"Maybe Hemingway just invented the river," I said. "Or maybe he moved it from somewhere else. Maybe it's north of here. Or east. Writers do stuff like that."

"He was a liar," growled Toivo. "We'll have to fish somewhere else. And not the Fox! Let's try that lake that we passed south of here—the one that's by the town that's for sale."

"Lake Anne Louise," I said.

We'd been fishing beside M-77 for about two hours. M-77 sat on fill that cut Lake Anne Louise in half and so we were standing on the bank of the road and casting into the weeds along the two shores. We were hoping for bass but all we'd caught were two tiny yellow perch and a blue gill. Toivo was so disgusted by the prospects that he was beginning to mutter about giving up fishing for the rest of his life. "Maybe we should go back to that nameless bar with the GOOD FOOD sign and get ptomaine poisoning," I said.

"Why don't we just get drunk?" he replied.

A little Japanese car came over the crest of the hill behind us just as a moose suddenly blundered out of the forest and into the middle of the lane. The driver had no time to brake or to change direction. Toivo and I both sensed that something was about to happen. We swiveled our heads simultaneously only to watch helplessly as the little car slammed broadside at sixty-five or seventy miles an hour into fifteen hundred pounds of meat, bone, and guts. The impact ripped the moose open from front to back and flipped the massive carcass onto the hood. In a split second the full weight of the beast smashed into the windshield, scattering beads of glass onto the floorboard, the front seat, and the laps of the two occupants. All the gore from the split moose burst from the carcass to drench the occupants in moose muck—lungs, stomach, bowels, pancreas, everything.

For several seconds the car skidded dangerously, tire rubber screeching, as the driver froze the brake to the floor. The car shuddered to a halt no more than fifty feet from where Toivo's car sat by the side of the road behind us.

The driver and his wife were probably in their sixties. The car plates said they were from Ohio. Tourists. Their vacation was over—their car was a wreck, they were a wreck. Clothes, shoes, faces, hair—moose muck saturated everything.

The old lady stumbled out and stood in the road in a daze. Remembering my boy scout training, I led her to the lake shore and lay her down on a level grassy spot. I wiped her face with a handful of grass, elevated her feet, and wrapped her up in an old blanket Toivo kept in the back seat.

The old man kept circling his wrecked car, saying nothing. Toivo picked up our fishing gear and tossed it into the back seat of our car. Then he opened the trunk, unsheathed his gutting knife, and advanced upon the old man, who began to whimper as he backed down the road, terror growing on his face. I left the woman and ran toward Toivo, grabbing his shoulder and twisting him toward me. "What are you doing?" I shouted. "You're scaring this old guy to death!"

Toivo stopped and looked down with dawning comprehension at the long knife in his hand. "I just need his permission," he said. "He hit it. It's his goddamn moose. But in this state they give every DOR to a state institution."

"What are you talking about?" I asked.

"Dead on the Road. The Department of Natural Resources gives every hit deer, bear, or moose to a local hospital or jail or old folks' home. That's fifteen hundred pounds of meat we're in danger of losing. I just need to ask this old guy if he wants the hind quarters, if I can have them."

The old man was still backing down the road as if he were deaf and blind to everything except Toivo's long knife.

A car approached from the south, slowed, and stopped. The driver rolled down his window. "You need help?" he asked.

"You could call somebody at the nearest phone," I replied. "We'll maybe need an ambulance too."

"I'll do that," said the driver and he continued north.

"Damn! He'll call from that place just up the road," cried Toivo. "Come on and help me!"

Toivo rushed to the dead moose and began to slice at the hind quarters. His razor-sharp knife quickly severed one haunch and then the other. He and I together carried the meat to our trunk and heaved it in. The two haunches filled it.

"Let's get out of here," said Toivo.

"Are you sure?" I said.

"Help will be here shortly. These old folks will be ok," said Toivo. "Besides, what more could we do to help? I'm a damned good woodsman but not a doctor."

We drove east toward the Mackinac Bridge and home.

"Well, we got some moose meat anyway," I said.

"Yeah," Toivo said. "If Hemingway hadn't invented that goddamned Big Two-Hearted River, I guess we wouldn't have gotten it. You know, maybe he was right to move that river to Seney. That place is so damned dead that it needs some new geography just to liven it up."

"It's a good thing you read that story," I said.

"Yeah," said Toivo. "The moose meat'll sure help with the food bills. My three boys will be able to eat it for a couple of months. They can take moose sandwiches to school and impress their friends."

"Maybe you ought to read another Hemingway story," I said.

"Good idea," said Toivo.

"Maybe somehow we'd end up with another moose haunch," I said.

"If I could get a freezer full of meat for every story, I'd read every damned word Hemingway ever wrote," said Toivo.

"Hemingway has some stories about Spain and about Paris, France," I said. "Maybe you should read those and we could go to Europe next."

"Seney's far enough," said Toivo. "Too far."

"Maybe we'd get a bear haunch on the Champs-Elysées in Paris,

France," I said. "Or maybe we could get some bullshit at the bullfights in Spain."

"Go to hell," said Toivo and began to laugh. "I'll leave the bullshit for you smart-assed college kids who can ask for it in Spanish."

"I'll drive the bridge," I said.

"You're goddamned right you will," said Toivo. "And you won't stop in the middle! And tomorrow morning you'll be up at five to take that load to the mill yard!"

Lauri Anderson

PICTURES

T HE PICTURE is an enlargement of an old photo that my mother gave my younger brother Stuart when Stuart last made a rare visit from California to the homeplace in northern Maine.

In the picture my father is a young man—younger than I am now—posturing with a dead bear. My muscular father fills the right half of the picture. He has one knee on the ground against the left rear haunch of the bear while the other supports his left forearm. The right forearm rests on the dead bear's forehead.

The dead bear dominates the lower half of the picture. His front shoulders and head seem to be curled against my father's knee and forearm as if the bear were an overgrown pup asking to be rubbed. In reality a wooden stake supports the bear's forebody. One point of the stake is driven into the ground. The other is driven into the bear's neck.

The background brings faint memories. It's the barn at my grandfather's farm—the barn that fell down over thirty years ago. Before it fell, Uncle Leon threw open cans of red paint at it, decorating the weathered boards with huge red circles that ran toward the ground.

The picture pulls me deep into the past, into a world that preceded my existence. That distant world is Finnish. My grandparents speak only Finnish. Somewhere outside the closed narrow box of the photo, Matti and Louise converse in their incomprehensible language. The words are unknown to me. So is the subject matter. My grandparents speak of the farm—of working with horses, of drying hay, of canning, of gardening, of milking, of berrying. They have strange ways of doing things. They make yogurt of the milk. Americans of my generation do not make yogurt. They slaughter their own animals and salt the meat. Americans of my generation do not salt meat; they can get thick steaks daily at the super market. My father knows how to do these things. He grew up on that Finnish farm and can create his own hog's head cheese, blood sausage, flatbread. He traps bear and coon and shoots deer and rabbit. My father makes gloves and moccasins from the deerskin and a rug from the bearskin. He eats the meat. My father will eat anything at least once.

Did my Finnish-hating mother take the picture? I have difficulty imagining her as a visitor at the Finnish grandparents' farm. My mother is DAR. Her roots and the country's roots are the same. Long before the revolution some unknown ancestor crossed the Atlantic to the British colonies in the New World. One of them founded the town of Lee, Maine, before Maine existed as a state.

My mother's family has always known with absolute certainty that they are right. In all things. My mother knows this. She knows that Finnishness must therefore be wrong because it is not part of the rightness of old New England.

But my father is a very attractive man. My mother the photographer will marry him. Maybe has married him. It's her great opportunity. He's handsome, strong, thirty, terribly shy, has his own business. She's done with school, has begun to teach, is no one's idea of beauty. She has a soft round body as lumpy and bumpy and oddly shaped as an old potato. Her eyes are bulbous, her hair frizzy. In addition she has a violent temper, prejudiced judgment, and a long list of phobias. Frightened of much of life, she will blame these fears on my father. He will become, until he dies, the eternal scapegoat, the root of all bumps in the night.

Why will he marry her? Is it her berry pies? She can cook. Surely that is not enough. He shouldn't do it. In the picture he looks proud and happy. He has shot a bear and had his picture taken.

I want to warn him. I stare at his picture, implore him not to do it—not to conceive five children in the womb of old New England.

Years later, when I am yet a tiny child, he will give his in-laws the money to buy a farm. They will never repay him. He will bring the New Englanders sides of beef and whole pigs and lambs. He will package the meat for them—slice the tenderloin into steaks, saw the ribs for barbecues. They will never acknowledge his gifts, his talents. They are inside a wall two hundred years old, inside a wall erected long before his Finnishness ever existed in their geography. My mother is inside the wall. My father is not.

Later still we children—locked out from our father's world by our mother—will choose to reject our mother's world. We will stand alone in a wilderness—not Finnish and not old New England. What are we? We are nothing. We are America.

Our father will drive too fast. He will carry my mother over a woodpile. That will be the first accident. In the second he will take her into a telephone pole. She will shatter her leg. They will insert metal screws and plates. The trauma will bring on diabetes. The diabetes will eat her legs and take away her sight. She will become a sort of vegetable—physically helpless but with her keen mind still intact.

My father will die of a stroke. But in the picture he is intensely alive. All the little deaths lie ahead. I lie ahead. Detour, father, detour!

My mother sits helplessly and hopelessly in a nursing home in old New England. She cannot see the picture of my handsome young father-to-be. She has no eyes. Diabetes. The picture is in Michigan's Upper Peninsula in my living room on the piano. The father in the picture is surrounded by Finnishness. In every direction the street signs are in Finnish. The population is Finnish. The names of surrounding towns — Tapiola, Toivola, Paavola — are Finnish. Even the bread we eat — rieska — is Finnish. The college where I teach is Finnish.

Father, you've come home.

And I?

Still nothing. America.

Timo Koskinen

DEAD WEIGHT

T HE MORNING that Mary left for the weekend to visit her sister,
Budweiser dropped dead in his stall. Eino stood leaning against
the stall-divider, smoking a cigarette and staring down at the old work
horse covered with blue-tailed flies.

"You hadda go and do it in your goddamn stall, didn't ya?"

It would cost a good hundred to hire a payloader to drag the hulk
out and dig a deep enough hole. A hundred dollars was one hell of
a lot of money.

Eino kicked at the dirt bed of the stall. "Could bury you right here
and now, myself," he muttered. "Take a day maybe."

After breakfast he began picking at the hard earth around Budweiser's
body. He worked steadily, propping sections of the body with four-
by-four beams, and then threading three strong ropes underneath the
horse to serve as a makeshift sling. As the morning became hotter, he
would often rest on the threshold, wiping his forehead and cursing
softly at Budweiser.

"You been a good horse, though," he said once.

Budweiser was even bigger than the horses that pulled the beer wagon
all over the place, in the beer ads. But he never was that fancy! He had
been just a mongrel horse, not high-strung at all.

When the hole was deep enough, Eino crawled partially under the
body and slid in extra boards for braces. Crouching down on his knees,
he was able to begin digging deeper.

"You didn't last long, though," he shouted at the horse when the smell
began to bother him.

Eino left the hole long enough to feed the other animals and to take
a six pack to the barn. He began working again, often bumping his head
and elbows against the large, soft belly over him.

"Should have hired a goddamned miner!"

The deeper he dug, the harder it was for Eino to throw the dirt out
from under the horse. He muttered incessantly to himself when he
spilled his shovelful before he could throw it clear of the hole. His shirt
and underwear became soaked with sweat. Budweiser's wide dangling
hooves constantly fell in his way.

Eino opened a beer and sat down under the horse. He stretched his
legs out comfortably and sighed. He had to figure out how he would

raise the money to buy a new horse. He was chewing his lip and trying to do addition in his head when two ropes and a brace snapped, spilling the horse onto his lap.

"Oh Jesus jumping Christ!" Eino shouted. The soft, broad belly had him pinned in the hole. The blue flies swarmed angrily and then settled again around the open eyes.

"Now you done it!" Eino snarled, trying to yank his legs free.

After struggling for awhile, Eino decided there was really nothing he could do but open another beer and lay back and wait. Somebody might come by for a Saturday visit. Luckily the cigarettes in his breast pocket hadn't been squashed. If he continued wiggling his feet, his legs wouldn't become too numb.

Eino was nearly asleep when he jerked his head up to see Gust standing in the doorway, grinning down at him.

"When did ya get a dead horse, Eino?"

"Plopped over this morning," Eino mumbled. "Hey listen, Gust, I think I finished my beer, but there's a good fifth in the cupboard over the sink. Bring it up here, will you, and the smokes on top of the icebox."

Gust disappeared, whistling as he followed the path down to the house. When he returned, he filled two coffee mugs with brandy.

"Thanks," Eino said, cradling the mug against his chest. "What time is it anyway?"

"Close to four, I think."

"Jesus, my legs are sure numb, you know."

Gust squatted on his heels and squinted down at the horse. "Startin' to smell."

"Don't take them long at all to smell in this weather."

"Burying 'im right there?"

"Trying to Gust." They gulped down their brandy.

"Well, 'spose I got time to help you some before I go to town," Gust said, refilling his mug.

"Just if you dig a little to help me loose, that'd be fine."

"I can see what you did wrong."

"Goddamned rope broke, is what I did wrong."

Gust stroked the stubble on his chin. "And that board there, too."

Eino settled back to drink more of the brandy while Gust began digging around the ass end of the horse. Gust wasn't too smart, and he was certainly lazy, but he worked steadily at burrowing underneath Budweiser.

"You on your way to town?" Eino asked.

"Yup." Gust groaned as he lifted a shovel full.

"Drinking?"

Gust smiled in reply. After threading new ropes under the belly, he sat in the hole next to Eino and lit a cigarette.

"Need a break," he gasped.

Eino studied the clumsy knots Gust had tied. "I think we better get me loose, quick," he said a moment before the knots slipped and Budweiser settled on their laps.

"Oh Christ!" Eino said, grunting with the weight once again solid against his thighs.

Gust looked puzzled, staring first at the horse in his lap and then at Eino. "Holy shit," he muttered. He began struggling to pull himself free.

"Don't bother," Eino said. "You'll never do it." He reached up behind him, feeling for the bottle. "This calls for a drink, and a big think on what the hell we do now. Shit. Maybe somebody will stop by."

"Mary's shopping?" Gust asked.

"Gone for the weekend. How about your missus?"

"Wouldn't look for me. You know I never go home on Saturday night." Gust looked suddenly frightened. "You don't suppose we'll be stuck here 'til then?" He began to struggle again. "I think I'm getting all numb!"

"I tole you that don't do no good! Just wriggle your toes a lot, like you hadda do in the army standing at attention. Remember? Only don't just do it with your toes, but with everything on your legs that you can."

"A man could loose his legs," Gust whined. "Then what good would he be?"

"You ain't gonna *loose* your goddamn legs," Eino snapped.

They sat quietly, listening to the flies and the clucking of the chickens. It was beginning to get dark.

"Feeding time, ain't it?" Gust asked.

A cow was bleating somewhere in the barn. "Henri wants to be milked," Eino said. "Guess we're in for some of her complaining."

As it became darker, Gust grew more restless. Eino was content with trying to fall asleep. The six pack and the brandy had numbed his whole body.

"You're not gonna sleep on me," Gust said.

Eino groaned and lit a match. Gust was sitting stiffly, staring straight ahead. He blinked from the sudden light.

"Are you awake, Eino?"

"Of course I'm awake."

"I got something to tell you," Gust said.

"What's that, then?"

"I think I gotta piss, you know."

"Christ Gust! How're you gonna do it?"

"I haven't figured it out yet."

"Well, you just better hold it. Don't drink any more, and try not to think about it."

There was a long period of silence. Eino imagined Gust sitting erect in the darkness, trying to hold it. Poor bastard. Now all he'd do is try not to think of it, so all he'd be doing is thinking about it.

"Oh shit," Gust said softly.

Eino struck another match. Gust was staring again, his eyes open wide like he'd seen something scary.

"I think I went," he mumbled, his eyes watering.

Eino blew out the match. He never could stand seeing a grown man cry.

"Did you hear me? I think I went!"

"Oh Jesus, Gust. Don't cry now. Jeez, you better never tell your missus."

"I swear, Gust."

There was another long silence, broken only by tree frogs and the sound of Gust's Adam's apple bobbing as he gulped down some brandy.

"Eino?"

"Ya."

"When do you think you'll gotta go?"

"Gust, you always ask such stupid questions. I think cause you drink too much."

"Ah, go to hell."

"Now's as good a time to tell you as any. Gust, you ain't a bad sort, but you never were too hell-of-a-smart."

"Fuck you, Eino. Just fuck you! Here I been shamed, and you start calling me stupid. Well, I hope you shit in yours, you bastard."

Eino felt as if the barn was starting to spin. "This is my barn!" he shouted. "I can swear in my barn. I can say anything in my barn. But I don't need a dumb bastard neighbor coming here cussing me out!"

"I hope your legs go dead, you son-of-a-bitch!" Gust snarled. "And they gotta cut 'em off at your waist."

"I'm telling your wife that her husband pisses in his underwear," Eino said triumphantly.

Smack! Gust had landed a good punch, even though he couldn't see his target. Eino felt the blood trickle down from his nose, over his lips and chin.

"I'm not hitting you back, now, but when we get free you better run like hell."

They sat through another moody silence. Eino began thinking about how long it had been since he had taken a piss. "Bah," he muttered, shaking his head and trying to think of other things.

Eino awoke with Gust's sweaty hand on his arm.

"Eino!" Gust's voice sounded whiny. "I don't think I'm gonna make it."

"I want to sleep. Lemme sleep."

"I'm gonna be as dead as this horse," Gust insisted.

"Then I can finally sleep."

"I'm serious, Eino. Help me, please. I'm sorry I hit you. I am dumb. But I'm numb from the waist down. I think I'm getting blood clots."

Eino considered how numb his own thighs were becoming. Sharp pains were stabbing at his crotch. It would be impossible to hold it much longer.

"You remember, Eino? Mrs. Evans died cause one of those blood clots traveled to her brain and stuffed it all up. Please hand me that brandy." Gust choked on the brandy. "Oh God," he moaned. "Save me please."

"Calm down, now. It's getting light soon. It's kinda gray already."

"Oh, if only it was daytime."

"We'll make it, Gust."

"Here, the missus thinks I'm in the drunk tank again. Oh, if only she knew, she'd be praying for me." Gust began sobbing.

"Rather have her shovelin'," Eino said, knowing the piss would gush down his leg at any moment.

When it finally came, it was a relief, warming his left thigh. Eino rested his head back against the dirt and slept.

Eino opened his eyes when it sounded as if Henri and the chickens were about to demolish the barn. The bright daylight stung his eyes.

"Wake up, Gust. It's morning."

Gust looked terrible. He moved his fingers slowly, staring at them as if he was amazed that they still worked. "Maybe we can get out," he mumbled. "If only that bastard was a little lighter."

"I'll put him on less feed," Eino said, feeling cheered by the morning sunshine.

"We could cut him apart," Gust said suddenly. "You gotta knife or something?"

"You're nuts!"

"We could maybe cut the guts out, or maybe a leg, or his head."

Eino glared at Gust. "I'm on this end, and I ain't cuttin' ole Budweiser's head off, I'll tell you that!"

"Just an idea." Gust looked around the stall. "Can't reach an axe or anything, anyway," he grumbled.

They sat quietly, staring down at the flies. It seemed as if all the flies in the world had come to eat Budweiser.

244 / *Sampo: The Magic Mill*

Eino heard light footsteps near the barn. "Hey, over here," he shouted. "Gust, there's somebody here."

They turned their heads to see Joey standing behind them.

"Well, hi Joey," Eino said.

"Hi Joey."

The boy looked down at his torn sneakers. With his toe, he made a small groove in the dirt.

"Joey is kinda shy," Eino said. "Aren't you, Joey?"

"Ma said I gotta borrow some flour," Joey said, slurring his words and still staring down at his foot.

"Why sure, Joey. Can't get it for you now, myself, but it's in the cupboard to the right of the sink. You got something to carry it in?"

Joey pulled a folded paper bag from his jacket pocket.

"Well, you go and get all you need, okay?"

Joey nodded and turned to leave. At the door, he turned around. "Is your horse sick? He sure smells." And then he darted out of the barn.

"The horse is dead!" Gust shouted after the boy. "Eino, he could tell his pa!"

Eino whacked himself on the forehead. "Oh Jeez. Hey Joey! Hey Joey!" he shouted, but the boy had disappeared.

"Hey Joey!" they yelled together, over and over until they were hoarse.

Gust began giggling. "You're as stupid as me," he said joyfully.

"Ah, the boy will bring help. He's a bright boy."

"Bet he don't."

"How much?"

"A week of corn picking."

They shook hands.

Eino took a sip from the little brandy left. "You cock-sucker!" he said suddenly, leaning forward and staring into Budweiser's dead eye. "Now you're really starting to stink!"

"Oh my damn yes," Gust said, making a face before he finished off the bottle.

They sat looking at the empty bottle. Eino was feeling pain from the constant weight. His kneecaps felt as if they were slowly bending in the wrong direction. Gust was lucky. He'd fallen asleep again. The poor bastard would sleep all day, hung over and tired as he was.

Eino smoked his last cigarette, blowing smoke at the flies. He felt ashamed and disgusted, imagining the terrible scene when Mary would return to discover two fool idiots pinned under a dead horse. When Budweiser was finally lifted, everyone would see the wet, piss-stained overalls. And Mary would have to live with a man who didn't even have a horse to pull the plow.

"I'll hitch the bitch to it, if she says one word," he grumbled.

And poor Gust! The goddamned fool didn't have much respect to lose, but he'd probably make matters worse, blabbing to anybody who would buy him a drink, about how he had pissed in his pants under Eino's dead horse.

"Eino did it too," Gust would tell the men.

With talk like that spreading through the town, Eino would never get a loan for another horse.

"Can't lend the money to a man fool enough to use his stall as a grave," the banker would say.

Eino sighed and tried to blink back the tears that were forming. "Jesus. Now I'm bawling like a kid."

Eino realized that he was ruined for life. He considered the knife in his pocket, but that would only make it worse. Christ! They'd really talk if they found him trying to hack apart his own work-horse with a jackknife. There was no way out. He could try praying, but even God probably figured him to be a fool. Maybe it would be a blessing if their legs were crushed and useless. Then, it would only be a bad accident.

Eino patted Gust's shoulder. "Poor bastard," he said sadly. "Look what I got you in. We'll have to stick together, you know."

Gust groaned in his sleep.

Eino woke up suddenly in the pitch black barn. A light blinked on, and he could hear Mary scolding Henri.

"Be quiet, cow, for God's sake. I can see he ain't milked you yet." Her shrill voice cut through the quiet barn.

It seemed as if hours had passed before Mary discovered them.

Eino! Eino, is that you? What in God's name are you doing under that horse?"

Eino smiled weakly and prayed that he'd never walk again.

Sheila Packa

MINNESOTA STEEL 1975

at Minnesota Steel
there were guards
at the gate

and the General Foreman wore a green hard hat
the foremen who told us what to do
wore yellow hard hats
they had captains called labor bosses
to make sure we did it
they wore white hard hats with a yellow stripe
and our hard hats were a dirty white

the Agglomerator's labor pool
was made up of two hundred men
and seven women
my first day in hot June
I shoveled and wheeled
taconite pellets, small stones,
up the slanted, pellet-lined roof
the second day the General Foreman
had me called to his office, he said
some day there will be two wage scales
one for men and another for women
who can't do men's work
he said, you remind me of my daughter
and we may have an opening in the Admin Building,
can you type?

in the labor pool
the men watched us work, watched us walk
to the dry where we came in
where we put on our workshirts and coveralls
our steel-toed boots, hard hats,
safety glasses with side shields
they watched us as we rode the elevators
reading graffiti
like Sandy sucks cock

scrawled on the walls
they watched us all the time, said
you've got nice legs, said
do you wear a bra? said
would you like to go on the balling floor?

general labor
was hosing mud that was two feet thick
off of the concrete,
keeping the screeching conveyers clean

we climbed into
empty railroad dump cars
carrying bails of hay
to stuff into the gaps
in the bottom

we wore asbestos suits and face shields
and emptied the showering hot pellets
from metal ducts
black pellets are 400 degrees
red even hotter
both stick in the flesh and
leave a crater in the skin
just like an open pit mine
on the landscape

when a balling drum went down
we ate salt tablets and went inside
the stilled furnaces,
in fifteen minute intervals,
to shovel the jack-hammered brick
into wheelbarrows and push it out

you work just as hard
as a man, I was told,
why don't you ever smile?

HE WALKS

A man from another
        age, my father, who is still
                        taller than me,
walks along his fence line.
            I can see his lank, dignified mien
            as he treats a horse's lacerated leg
            with a balm
            of balsam pitch
            and likewise
        stitches his own wounds.
    I love his remedy.
He drives a tractor in the fields,
pulls out potatoes, weeds and
    fixes all the daughters'
    cars. Works on all our cares
                in such a way.
            Father, with so few words,
we are overcome.

SUMMERS AT GRANDMA'S

summers at grandma's
her black dog Sparky followed me
down the dirt road
where no dust rose

frog eggs grew green in the ditches
brush crowded the mile-long drive—
I don't remember
any birds—

up the concrete steps
into the dark house
the clock ticked in the kitchen
the coffee perked queerly slow

grandma sighed
the rooms were like rooms
suddenly empty
we ate dry biscuit
and waited

RUMORS

i.

the furnace operator assistant
job
she bid on
but the foreman didn't want
no pregnant
much less woman
on the job the
furnace operator
worthless
said his job
was to stay as far away from her
as he could
sorry
the plant supervisor
finally decided
the doctor had to sign a form
she did

ii.

you get called back after
five years
and you don't keep your rights
you're just like you're new

a pregnant woman on the call list
got called back in August
then her baby came in November
E.A. was put by her name at the plant

means extended absence
what do I have to do when I want to
come back she went to ask
the office told her she's not

takes 60 shifts to get in the union
they can't help oh god
where was the number
of the Human Rights Commission

where's the phone

iii.

they need a cop in Buhl
they aren't looking for a lady cop

look at me, how I draw my finger
across my throat,
when the *applicant* filed suit they claimed
she was denied for immoral conduct in the community

two women lawyers from the cities came up
gathered documentation

asked what's immoral but the witness
he went and died

REGRETS

that warm smell of roasted beef
the steam rattling the lids of pots
a set table
and you with the paper

and me, who flew the vacuum
across the rugs and hid
the mess
I took care

to conceal the disarray
I lived with
I keep the closets shut
and made the bed

a wife who mothered you
and kept the two
of us
together

until this—
a sodden trap
you love and
it isn't even safe

I took your beat-up suitcase
half the cash
the couch
and left

I left
my regrets
and you
standing at the door

later
I cried
because I had
set the table

Eeva Kilpi

AT THE COTTAGE
(Translated by Kathleen Osgood Dana)

W HICH BOOTH is free, please?"
"Number three."

She crammed herself with her bags into telephone booth number three at the telegraph office, lowered her burden to the floor, took a seat on the round stool which seemed to overwhelm the small space needed by the telephone user's physical self, and after a moment's hesitation dialed the number from memory. Was that the right area code, she had time to think before her mother answered at the other end of the line.

"Well, you were right there," Soile said. "It's me. Soile."

"Yes, your father and I were right here on the porch eating. Where are you calling from?"

"The telegraph office. I'm in town. The animals were running out of food. How are you two?"

"We're none too well," said her mother. "Your father is still having those heartburn attacks. And I woke up at four o'clock in the morning again today and couldn't get back to sleep even though I had a drink of water, and now I'm worn out. And my stomach is in such turmoil that all I can stand to think is that death will put an end to it all soon."

"How about things in general? Did you work something out with that person?"

"Oh yes, that got worked out all right. We have a little miss who comes two or three times a week, whenever we see her – carries the water and does the dishes and heats the sauna. Your father tried to heat it himself, but it was no use. His legs would hardly hold him up. His head is like that. He just gets so dizzy sometimes."

"Anyway, it's good about that girl. Excellent, that it all got worked out."

"Well, we couldn't manage here otherwise."

"I suppose not."

"Oh, I wouldn't have dared be here with your father. What with me waking up at dawn now. It's this feeling of suffocation that wakes me up. Everything seems to worry me and weigh me down. Even though I bless myself every night and mention each of you by name, every single one of you, I still wake up with such a frightful feeling of anxiety. It's so frightful I can't stand it no matter what. And I don't know who to talk to about it. It's something no one would understand."

"I know it from times in my own life, even though I don't talk about it much. Even to family. You just have to endure it. Try to think of it as a tax we have to pay to life."

Her mother chuckled as if the thought helped, although she could as easily have said that she had already, in her opinion, paid enough tax in that sense too in her lifetime. She had never attempted to avoid pain or spiritual pressures, Soile knew quite well, as did the other daughters. They had all inherited that tendency from their mother, the daughters especially. In the boys, the brothers, it was not apparent. Perhaps they too suffered from unnamed anxieties, but they didn't discuss them, at least not with their family. The daughters, on the other hand, talked such things over among themselves and with their mother. It was frequently a great relief. However, it sometimes seemed that their mother dominated the territory, assumed for herself the prerogative of complaining the most. The prerogative took time. Sometimes it took the very minutes, as it did now. As Soile grew older she noticed some bitterness in herself about this, or perhaps not bitterness but impatience: she couldn't stand to listen, always to play the role of the listener, to which she was more and more often relegated. She would have liked to complain herself. Or at least to talk about things. And she thought with frank jealousy: Mother maintains the uncontested right to complain, to describe her slightest feelings in detail every day, and we have listened; she's had four daughters to listen, she can tell every story four times and every time she gets sympathy. No one has dared do anything but listen, approve and sympathize for years now. The youngest sister, Terhi, had once said in a period of depression toward the end of her student days, "I'm terribly afraid our parents will die right now when I don't have the strength to give them any of myself, but I can't do anything about it." And their mother had been offended that Terhi had not managed to be as sympathetic as the other daughters. Such approbation was not expected from the boys. Whenever the boys called or visited, their mother was as surprised and proud as if she were receiving unanticipated, rare and desirable guests.

"I don't know, all sorts of trivial things worry me, things I know I shouldn't bother myself over worry me," her mother was saying. "Like the shopping and cooking, everyday things like that. It's just that your father's stomach can't take anything. And all the pleasures of life we've had to give up. We can't go out in the car. Can't get around any more. Can't go shopping. Your father won't hear of taking a taxi. We can't go fishing, he doesn't dare get in the boat because of his dizziness. I've been tossing the fish trap in from the rocks."

"Have you caught anything?"

"We surely have. I was just saying to your father, look at us—God's looking after us, all right. This very morning there were two perch in the trap, pretty decent-sized ones. I cleaned them and baked them. We were just eating them here now. My, they were fine! I brushed them with butter and bread crumbs before I put them in the oven, but before that I had them in salt a couple of hours. Their flavor's a lot fuller that way. And I fixed a casserole of grated potatoes in white sauce to go with them. Potatoes are so miserable right now—they're better like that. I was just telling your father that we're pretty lucky. If only our stomachs were in better shape! And I was talking about you right here at the table just before you called—it was a premonition. I said, isn't it true what Soile says about how it's strange that your stomachs are in such bad shape when you're people who haven't taken alcohol, haven't drunk coffee, haven't smoked tobacco; what can it be that's wrecked your stomachs, when other people have drunk red wine, white wine, had drinks with their meals and Madeira and coffee and cognac to top it off and smoked tobacco and stayed up all night and eaten all the indigestible food in the world and traveled abroad, and yet their stomachs are fine till the day they die. Maybe if we'd lived badly, I was just saying to your father. But we've struggled to save, we've eaten wholesome, pure, nutritious food, we've paid attention to our vitamins and trace minerals and now fiber too, and still our stomachs are ruined. It just goes to show. How do you figure that one out? Maybe we've just had everything else too good. When you stop and think of all we've made it through—we should just fold our hands and thank God that we've had it so good. And that we have fine grandchildren."

"Have the others been in touch with you? Did any of them come visit last Sunday?"

"No one's been here for a long time, except last Sunday Terhi came with the children. That was when Kerttu drove us out and spent the night and raked the yard a little. Eila called yesterday and cried on the phone again."

"Why? Was it Teppo again?"

"Yes."

"Hasn't she gotten over it now Teppo's fever is gone and all the doctors have assured them. . ."

"Well, what with the diagnosis not being completely satisfying, they still have to keep an eye on him. And Eila just isn't up to it. She says she's afraid she won't be able to cope. I told her a person must have faith. Besides praying a person must have faith. Always whenever the parasite of disbelief tries to enter me, I fling it away. 'Begone, demon!' I say."

"Mother," Soile said, "when Eila calls you again, would you give her my love? Tell her I'm bearing this pain with her—she doesn't have to bear it by herself, we're all supporting her. Tell her I've thought about Teppo every day since I was first told about him, and every time, often during the day and at night when I wake up and first thing in the morning, I've prayed for him to be cured, unconditionally and completely, and that this not be anything serious. I've sent him spiritual strength every day and from now on I'll send it to Eila too. . ."

"Eila says we don't need to pray for her, just Teppo, and she asked us to pray for him as much as we could."

"Tell her we already are. I will demand this of God. He has his responsibilities to people too. He uses people to fulfill his own intentions. He appears through people. We bear the burden of his wish to appear. It's a heavy burden, and because of that God must take care of us, he's responsible for us, he must defend and support and help us. . ."

"You mustn't talk like that. I'm going to ask you something now. Tell me if it's true you've left the Church."

"Yes, Mother. It's true."

"Why didn't you tell me?"

"I felt it was my own business. And I knew it would upset you no matter what I said. I thought maybe you didn't need to know. Nothing about me has changed because of this."

"I just can't help it. This shocks me, it's a horrible shock. How can I accept it?. . .It's too much to bear."

"Mother, this is just what happens when people are close. Feelings get hurt, it's that tax we pay when we're so. . . Mother, don't cry. . . How will I be able to end this call?. . . Mother dear, could you try to understand, I feel I do live near God. It's as if I lived in the midst of God, within God. I don't need a mediator. . .And I do believe in prayer, I believe in prayer unconditionally, I just don't use that method very often, there's such enormous power in it. But now I've told God to take my share of strength and give it to Teppo. I need so little of it at the cottage, I have enough to give away. And all the while I get strength from nature and the animals, that's what tells me about God. It flows through me, God flows. . ."

"I'll try to think of it that way. Maybe I'll get used to the idea. But right now it hurts."

"Mother, please rest after we hang up. Promise me you'll rest. I don't have the strength to call Eila and the others, but give them my love when they call you. Be absolutely sure to tell them that they should feel we're in touch with each other and that I'm thinking about them, especially Teppo and Eila. And could you call my boys tonight? Tell them Mother sends her love."

"What time do you think they'll be home?"

"Around six or seven maybe. Thanks. And my love to Father. I'm going to hang up now and I'll call again next time I'm in town. Take care of yourselves. Goodbye."

"Bye," her mother said, as cheerily as possible in order to leave Soile with a favorable impression.

Each minute could be the last, each farewell eternal, Soile heard herself think before the connection was broken. That thought never lost its edge. Without being spoken, it was always present when they said goodbye or parted, and it tyrannized their relationship.

Throughout the entire telephone call she could almost see her mother standing and talking near the small table on the porch, and in the background her father eating at the long table, picking the fishbones from his teeth. It was impossible to envision the world without them.

The image disappeared and the phone booth closed around her. It was filled with the heavy odor of the pet food. The ventilator hummed uselessly and disturbingly.

Once on the street, as she lugged her packages to her station wagon, she thought, Let them live. They belong to our lives, to all of this wholeness. Give them strength. Cure Teppo. Completely. Unconditionally. Do your duty, God. And take care of my children. Support them. Protect them. They have the right to comparative happiness. Just like everyone else. I need all of this, all of this.

For the first time in her life she thought: Prayer is an imperative, it takes the form of a command. And that was quite right. She had never understood that immoderate humility which religions demanded. It wasn't natural, she thought. Even the most wretched specimen of plant life in the wild deliberately held on to its life as long as it could possibly hold up and held up as long as it could possibly hold on. A wounded bird chooses life. I've seen it with these eyes. A fledgling thrush, its throat ripped open by the cat, pecked my fingers in fury as I took it to the woodshed to put an end to it, but before I got there it had wriggled free from my hands and flown to a tree branch. My parents don't need anything in the end except being itself, nothing more.

A feeling like the fatigue of journey's end washed over her; for some reason her last thought helped alleviate it. Maybe all I need is to be, she thought, as she opened the back door of her car and began to shove in her packages.

She had two dogs, three cats, a couple of turtles, six ducks, and some chickens. Recently a goat had joined the flock. In general she came to town only when the animals ran out of food. Her two sons lived in a former apartment house in Vantaa in some kind of *kolkhoz* or commune, to which an ever-changing crowd of people belonged.

I won't get tangled up in this moment. The moment won't wait. Living won't stop. I choose this course, this motion, this is the way I am flowing. . .

She was already on the highway and could feel the town sliding away from her. She wiped off the sweat that had trickled down her cheek. She always sweated in town.

Bernhard Hillila

HAIL MARY

With all the chutzpah
of a fly lighting on the swatter,
God assumed a human body.

He knew what he was getting into—
dust recycled on its way to dust—
he knew that loads a cross
the shoulders make a body weary,
that skin is torn by thorns
and flesh is pierced by spears.

And yet, on the wheel of eternity,
the potter entered the clay.

That was hard, very hard,
even for an angel to explain to Mary
that extraterrestrial day
in dusty Nazareth.

SUPPLY-SIDE THEOLOGY

Does God think riches trickle down and that
the plutocrat, with glut and gorge of gift,
soon shares his capital and spends his thrift
on indolent poor and fribbling bureaucrat,
that milk and wheat flour filter from our fat,
fat land to thin Third World, that shirts down-shift
from mannequins to men, that doctors lift
the curse of pestilence before too late?
Who in the world but God would pour down grace?
As barn-born baby, battered man, he cast
his lot with the down and out, not counting cost,
abdicated his throne for the human race—
so prodigal a father that he'd waste
the highest and best on the least, the last, the lost.

WILLOW WATERWAY

*(A tree receives water from the ground up,
processes it both upward and downward,
exhales it to the sky. So go with the flow
and read this poem from the bottom up.)*

leaving leaves for outer space.
scraping skies in outmost twigtips,
rising up the Xylem)
(flowing down the Phloem,
solar-powered food factory,
and twig to the blown crown's
welling artesian through branch
currents defying gravity, -
flowing down the Phloem)
(rising up the Xylem,
to sun-seeking emerald sails
from underground anchor
manifestly destined for higher things,
traveling the grand trunk,
sluicing to life and lofty limbs,
rising up the Xylem)
(flowing down the Phloem
percolating through capillaries,
streaming in arboreal arteries,
unbounding dun ground,
leaving juicy sod,
flowing down the Phloem)
(rising up the Xylem,
coursing between earth and heaven,
water osmosing, soil to root,
my willow is a waterway—
in the blue-sea sky,
to its spreading delta
of the deep, damp ground
From the headwaters

Kathleen Osgood Dana

MIDSUMMER

The midsummer North now quickly moves
    Raising the sun to fire the dawn.
The sun rises carefully,
    Veiling its splendor
        in old wisps of rose,
        baby tan clouds
        and its very own vanity.

The lakes so sketched
        in ink shades of blue,
The rivers outstretched
        in ribbons of mist.
The black forests etched
        in midnight cold blue.
The roads coiled crazily
        toward the sun.

Through a windshield of warmth
    I'm in Finland again.
Apart from the picture,
Legs light with dancing,
Face warm from laughing,
My body alive with friendship and love,
I sit in a car.
                Midsummer 1971
                Orivesi, Finland

Aale Tynni

ON MANY A WINDY NIGHT

(Translated by Richard A. Impola)

On many a windy night, the boat
breaks free from the end of the blue dock,
jerks loose the tie-rope wound around the birch trunk,
and drifts off, the rower asleep,
toward the sound, between the crag and the island,
beyond which the broad, open water swells,
beyond which the gulls, like miniature sailboats,
rock on the rolling waves.
The wind turns it aside before the island.
As always, it bobs toward the west,
colliding with treeless crags, running into rocks,
sliding off shelves into the water,
drifting along toward the familiar cove,
where the rower finds it among the reeds
when the cool, windless morning comes.

So I awake in the morning, now you are gone,
cheeks wet on the pillow, about me rootless emotions,
torn loose, wound around each other
like mangled reeds.

THE LAKE

(Translated by Richard A. Impola)

A veil of dawn lies on the lake.
Shredding, lifting,
The wind carries it away.

Waters reflect
Round island images,
Sketching spruce spires
Shapes of black alders
In deep and lucent green.

Stretching out his neck
The loon dives, splashing.
Sitting on the dock
The finch flirts his innocent tail.

A ripple stirs on the channel.
Spreading, it moves toward shore.
A wind rises,
Waves shimmer, catching a new light.
Day's colors. Pearl-gray,
Transparent as a dragon-fly's wing,
Slants across the surface.

Night has come; the lake is calm.
Clouds swim, sparkling with snow.
Waters assume
Iridescent colors of Capri:

Cornflower blue, violet, and rose adjacent,
Where the sun slides over the island,
Dropping below the line drawn by sky and water.
Darkness covers the reeds and iris.
Under the alders, the water grows black.

Suddenly in the night
The lid of heaven opens.
A milk-white gleam floods the waves.
Selene!
The dim gray maple and the aspen,
Where day breezes stir incessantly,
Hold their breaths in stop-action.

On the sauna shore
The lake is a pool of light, deep-shining.
My soul absorbs the hue
Of light and intuition
Inexpressible in words.
Eadem nocte
accidit ut esset luna plena. . .
Reeds rustle on the shore and a mist rises from
the lake.

Morning again.
A breeze moves over the land,
Life impelling,
A loon and a finch.

Heikki Turunen

Excerpts from the novel

CHILDREN OF THE LAND
MUSTARINNAN LAPSET

(Translated by Richard A. Impola)

The novel, Children of the Land, *is one in a series dealing with the lives of the* uudis-raivaajat, *resettlers granted land on easy terms by the Finnish government after the wars of the 1940s. The settlers were refugees from Karelia and combat veterans, probably the last of the rural pioneers.* Children of the Land *has been described as the swan song of rural life in Finland, before the advent of television and technology. One of the children describes his developing consciousness in a natural world so vividly that ordinary objects and events turn into moving poetry.*

A TIME OF DREAMING

ONCE AGAIN the picture came suddenly into his mind. The blue tin plates with the white spots were laid out on a low flat rock between them, and the tin mugs grated harshly against it. The summer sun, seen from the base of the pines, was a bright region somewhere beyond the glowing green of the boughs, and the warm air smelled of clay and ants and cold stone. The ground under his bare feet was extraordinarily dry and rough and cutting, and there were untrampled tufts of hay around the rock. It was awkward to eat without being able to put his feet under the table. Father sat barefoot by his side to help him with the fish stew, and the insects swarming around had everyone in a bad mood. A part of the picture was a small, light-colored stack of lumber. A shadowless, insubstantial shimmer playing over it made it seem in part a creation of sunlight reflected on the water. The direct, jagged shafts of light piercing the fragrant boughs stood out against the smoke of the campfire, impressing him as somehow fearful and solemn, while they themselves were small and helpless in the lofty light.

Perhaps other later discoveries had blended into the picture. At any rate, ants always seemed to be an important part of it. Their silent stop-and-go progress everywhere over earth and rock, over the line of stumps along the fence nearby, over the piles of brush. A nasty, thick ring of ants around a birch sapling, scores of dead ants trapped in the reddish, frothy sap of a birch stump. He could still see vividly a line of ants on the dried bark of a big birch tree, clearly visible on its lower trunk, even to their thin, reddish-brown midriffs and their cross-striped rear sections. Nearer the tree-top, their line narrowed, they shrank to dots against the white, moss-flecked bark, their destination and point of return invisible in the dizzying height of the top branches, as if the thinning and ending of the tree-top had no meaning for them, as if their silent, patient, ghostly progress began on earth and went on to the heavens and eternity. And if you looked at the tree in a certain way, it seemed to lean over and fall toward you. The sound of the river was a part of the scene too, seeming to have gone on forever, but audible only when he listened for it. In the steady ceaselessness of the sound, there was something fearful, approaching and spreading independent of them. When he looked at the river, its deep black surface yawning below a steep bank seemed suddenly to be moving toward the lake with frightening speed. At this point, the picture always dimmed and vanished, and he would remember nothing of it for a long time afterward. It was as if the new environment had been so strange and raw that the mind of a two-and-a-half-year-old had been jolted into wonder, and having made the necessary explorations, had slipped back into a dream-like state.

And since all that had happened to him earlier in life was completely gone from his mind, he began to feel as if a flat rock by a certain lake was his first perspective on the world. Everything had begun to take shape in relation to it, as if his entire life had begun at that point.

BUTTERFLY MEMORY

It was the time of day when Father had already stopped in at the house for his afternoon coffee. There was still a long wait before the others came home from school, and Mother had nothing in particular to do around the house. A sunny and fairly warm day following a frosty morning, so bright it almost hurt the eyes and made seeing difficult when you stepped outside.

In the dazzling brightness of sun and snow, Father was driving the manure sled with its load of odd-smelling muck to the sloping garden plot in back of Kettunen's woods, to spread it around on the hill they used for sledding and skiing in the winter. The sizable colt running around loose scared them a little. Occasional drops of water fell from the eaves on the sunny side of the barn, but the shady side beyond the manure shed was chilly, and tarnished icicles hung there. He and Kimmo were riding their one-runner kick-sled down the slope near the barn. It had a small, blue factory marking on the back of its faded seat. It ran faster in that kind of weather than in severe cold, and when you leaned backwards, the runner began to bend. It was fun too, to ride downhill on Father's long, gray logging skis, sitting on the front part of them. They ran best in the slippery, rust-stained tracks of the sled runners, the hummocks of snow thumping their rears. Sometimes they would send the skis alone down the hill in the sled tracks. Standing on the rise by the big rock where the stamping of the horses had turned the snow brown, they watched tensely to see whose ski would go farther. In the heavily trampled snow, there were brown hairs from the horse's coat and tail.

On the same kind of bright day in early spring, with Mother busy between sink and table, they were playing in a corner by the wooden sofa near a patch of light shaped like a window with one side indented by the shadow of the stove. At its edge, you could plainly feel the difference in temperature between the sunlit spots and the other air in the room. They had big, battered cardboard cartons filled with junk of every kind: pieces of wood left over from building, tin cans and containers, tin hoops and tangles of wire, wooden trains and trucks made for them by Hannu and Father and Red Uncle, worn out from use in playing. These they arranged in a carefully planned manner in cardboard cartons lying on their sides on the floor. When the structure of goods filled a carton completely, they would toss pins and other small objects inside and listen laughing as they fell from one level to another, plinking unseen for a long time as if proceeding on their own once given a start. It sounded like a machine to them.

The close sunlight was reflected from the metal sides of the stove as a soft, shadowless red glow throughout the room, casting a strange sheen over their box of scrap. Merely looking into it as he lay stomach-down on the floor, he was enthralled and fascinated, imbued with an extraordinary sense of satisfaction. He had no idea why, but he always longed to create new and more skillful arrangements of things, differing planes and hollows at the outer perimeter and labyrinthine passages and pockets within, alleyways that disappeared into infinity. The small recesses between objects had an appeal of their own, luring him to enter, but thwarting him by their size. The rearmost objects loomed dimly, a scrap of metal unrecognizable in the gloom shining mysteriously as if it were another, more precious thing. Cheap, coarse, dusty objects there in the reddish glow under the torn surface of the smelly cardboard, his own small and secure world to imagine and shape as homey as he pleased, without inhibition.

Among other things that were springlike, what most impressed itself on his mind was the woodshed at one end of the barn and the place before it that they all called the "Chip-Pile." It was a particularly pleasant spot for them on sunshiny days, and it felt and smelled of spring when alder poles hauled in during the winter and stacks of firewood first appeared from under the snow, drying on the side exposed to the sun, with streaks and patches of light in their recesses. Around the scarred sawbuck was a hard-packed layer of chips and sawdust that hid any sign of snow. There was an odor from the fresh logs and bark and from the littered area near the wall that was wet by water dripping from the eaves. They could see pale, withered grass under the storehouse and a dry place beneath its ramp. It was colder at the shady end of the shed: the gap between wall and woodpile breathed an air of frosty, grayish-blue chill.

He was leaping and playing there with Eero and Kimmo, wearing a snowsuit brought by Santa and given to him for everyday wear by Mother before he outgrew it. It was made of a soft, warm fabric with a metal zipper down the front, and it had a checkerboard pattern in small squares of a brilliant yellow and black, with bright red borders at the wrists, pockets, and collar. Everyone always said how nice he looked in it, and that made him even more fond of the garment. He was lording it over Eero and Kimmo as they went leaping from the woodpile into the snowbank, waving their arms like the wings of birds. In his snowsuit, he felt, he could make longer and more stylish jumps than the other two in their commonplace jackets and knee-pants: he could almost fly. Then, as he was leaping in all his glory from the woodpile, the suit caught on a sharp, protruding end-stake, tearing such a large, ugly tongue of cloth from its side that he knew it could never be restored to its former state.

Through the fog of a mood now quickly changed to a sense of unreality and dismay, he could hear the malicious laughter of Eero and Kimmo as if they were somewhere far away. His own weeping was like that of another child, receding in the distance, and he could still hear it when they went into the woodshed to play. As if it were another, quite unrelated matter, he was aware of the pleasant atmosphere in the half-empty, earthen-floored structure, partly owing to the still-thick cover of snow outside, while here the deep layer of shavings was as unfrozen and dusty-dry as during the summer, and the sunshiny area near the open door was broodingly warm and calm, the reflected images of water-drops from the eaves flickering translucent across it. The sun shone through cracks in the board wall onto the dusty ends of the blocks, into the shadowy hollows between them, onto the dirty debris from the cookstove woodpile. In the slanting beams from the cracks, tiny bright flecks hovered in slowly wheeling circles. They were like thin partitions of light in the cool gloom of the shed, and running through them, he could almost feel their faint touch and the alternation of brightness and shadow on his tear-stained cheeks. Toward evening, more light entered the irradiate gloom smelling of dry alder from cracks between wall and framing and the ice. A cold luminescence seemed to filter up from some miraculous source of subterranean light. It began to seem that a treasure trove lay buried there, of golden ornaments and pearl necklaces and glittering coins, like the one under the fearsome black stump of a fallen tree on the cover of their book of fairy tales.

Searching for it, they grubbed deep holes in the litter at the spots where the light came through. After he tore the snowsuit, the thought of finding the treasure seemed even more compelling and consoling, so he dug more furiously and desperately than ever. In a panic at not finding it immediately, he kept on probing and prodding in a blind and growing frenzy, tiring hands groping convulsively through blind alleys, back stooped in exhaustion, and weeping. He was oblivious to every-thing around him, time and place lost their meaning, there was only the moment, and the heat, compulsion, and desperation of the search. Yet all the while his mind kept exulting, visualizing the discovery they would make under their common, ordinary woodshed, something unat-tainable until now, something rare and stupendous. He had found nothing yet, not yet, but he was so certain of finding it at any moment that it seemed already there. A beautiful, incredibly precious chest, gleaming with dull yellow gold and pearls there in the twilight, with a heavy handle and an arched lid reinforced with iron, almost tangibly real to his trembling, seeking fingertips. He wept and laughed; it seemed the spring of childhood.

The snow would no longer bear their weight, and before midday, icicles would break off and fall from the eaves with a clinking sound. They would find the bright, round bits and pieces in the deep troughs worn along the walls by the dripping water. They licked and sucked at them with mouths numbed by the cold, pretending they were candy canes. They were glad when they saw a good-sized strip of wet shingles exposed to the sunshine along the eaves. The thawed band widened and the tempo of the drops quickened toward evening. Before the drops fell, the sunshine radiated tiny, slow-moving patterns of light from them onto the wet drip-board. There was an almost conscious urgency in their splashing onto the hay-littered ground ice along the steamy wall. When Eero returned from school, they would arrange tin cans and battered pots to catch the falling drops. Each sounded a different note, and played a cheerful, far-off spring melody as they squatted to trench out brooks from the puddles along the sloping path that was now turning to slush. The best tool for the task was a sturdy, short-handled little shovel, which always reminded them of Father saying he had brought it back with him from Rukajarvi. Their largest brook ran down the well-slope. Bright, symmetrical riffles appeared on its surface, just like those on a real river, and were mirrored on the bottom in patterns of color. They were silent as they listened to its faint rippling as it dropped over a ledge. They took it to be the pathetic little voice of the water, happy at the coming of spring.

"The water is whispering to me."

"No, to me!"

* * *

When the spring waters receded, the ice was still thick on the high, jutting rocks near the former sauna shanty. As it melted away, little volcano-like protrusions developed in the hollows. Through deep clefts in the slabs of ice, the familiar outlines of the rocks could be seen in the greenish-blue chill. The murmur of the waters flowing from the meadow in the swamp and from the woods, faint in the winter, grew in volume to a gushing sound that could be heard far off, while the thawing patches around trees and rocks seemed to expand visibly as they watched. Every new patch of exposed ground, every extra wet strip on the margin of another was cause for joy, and they would race each other toward it, leaping and shouting as if celebrating their own and summer's conquest.

"My summer! Mine, mine, mine!"

"No, it's mine, mine, mine!"

As he grew older, his picture of summer grew progressively clearer. Everything about it seemed familiar, but as things seen earlier and enjoyed in a superficial and childish way, before he could understand them properly. They looked and laughed at the gently rippling lake as at a friend long unseen and partially forgotten. The very form of the waves, of particular features, of the bottom seen through shallow water along the shore began to feel like summer.

Their favorite places for playing during those first summers—the crossroads, the gate at Onnela, the pit in Jessipäinen's woods—

nearly strangers during the winter, seemed new but yet familiar enough so that they knew from memory what would be the most fun there. The shadowy recollection of a good time from the preceding summer added to their enjoyment in leaping and playing. The wood pitch they had deposited on the high, round rock near the gate at Onnela the year the house was built had hardened into black, tacky patches and streaks. They looked to see if the ants that had gotten stuck in it were still there. They did not remember seeing a small pine shoot growing from the debris in a large cleft of the rock.

Sometimes they stopped to listen to the little birds chirping in back of Jessipäinen's new picket fence, and suddenly a cuckoo would begin to call from the direction of Jukkoniemi. They looked at each other wide-eyed, a smile overspreading their faces. Eero would count the calls, nodding his head with each number.

". . .two, three, four, fi-ive, seven, eight, ni-ine. Ha,ha, we still have nine years to live."

"Let's go and jump off the lumber pile!" shrieked Heino.

They went dashing across the field in their rubber-soled, canvas-topped low-cuts, ankles bare, howling and yipping with joy as they saw themselves bounding on the springy, protruding ends of the boards and heard the distant echo of their oscillations.

As a basic part of summer, the mood that went with fishing from a boat began very early to etch itself into his mind. A calm pocket of rocky shallows close to a bed of reeds. Details of the boat, its tar-black bottom, its curving sides and its seats, dirty and fish-scaly, water near the drain-plug at its stern, the smell of boat tar and fresh fish and the warming summer lake. The rocking of the boat and the waves splashing gently against it, the banded sides of perch and their spiny, contracting back fins, the color of their gill fins against their bright scales. The twists and turns of the long, white fishing poles made of fresh aspen, the chunks of sinkers torn from toothpaste tubes sliding along between the bottle-cork float and the hook when the line was jerked, the resistance of the worm to being threaded onto the hook, its breaking and the resultant strange, wet, clayey smell. Their tension as they watched the cork bobbing on the pollen-pale waves, watched as the always-deceitful roach drew it under by pulling on the worm without getting hooked, the feeling when it was pulled deep under with a jerk and the struggling weight of a big perch as the rod was lifted, their alarm and enthusiasm, the growing rapture of life and summer.

Along the road that led to the meadow, near Jessipäinen's small hill, was a landmark they always stopped to look at, an unusually tall, thick-limbed spruce tree, which stood where boulders bulldozed from the

road lined the fence, and where arctic brambleberry bushes grew from
the pale soil among the still-embedded roots of an overturned stump.
The tree always reminded them of Erkki Karuvaara, who had been
climbing it with Hannu and had fallen from high up in its limbs into
a smaller spruce growing nearby without being hurt. They played there
every summer between the roots of the stump and the rocks, with board
remnants and boughs and branches to serve as a roof. One of their
games was "storekeeper," with Hannele pretending to be the merchant
Sysma. They used pine cones and pretty little pebbles as money. Then
Hannele would pretend to be Mother, washing real cups, chipped
kitchenware with handles missing, as she sang "The Vagabond's Waltz."
Eero would loll around on a rock with a stick in his hand, looking angry.
Heino and Kimmo would be their children.

"Since you're so young, Kimmo, you can get the water," Hannele
would say.

"Since you're so young, Heino, you can get the wood," Eero would
command.

"Don't yell at me, old man," Hannele would say angrily to Eero.

"Shut your mouth, slut," Eero would say.

Then they would all break into giggles.

Before the heart of summer arrived, with its haying and the lake warm
enough for swimming, Midsummer's Day was a kind of high point for
them. His developing mind-picture of it was colored in by the small
birches Heino and Father fetched for either side of the stoop, their rustling in the breeze and the fragrance of their drying leaves mingled with
the odor of sweetbread and rice pastries from an open window, an odd
happy holiday mood, calm and yet restless at the same time, intensify-
ing with the approach of evening. "The sky of blue above me,/ Happy
dreams around me,/ I dance my waltz of destiny," Mother sang as she
did the evening milking. Father and Mother went to the evening dance
at the Community Building, she in a light summer dress with broad,
padded shoulders, a bell skirt, and a pattern of multi-colored flowers
on a blue background; he in a brown, striped suit with bell-bottomed
trousers, wearing both a belt and suspenders. To the children too, it
seemed somehow pleasant and festive to spend the evening together
after their parents' departure. Dressed in their best clothing, they wandered along the shore throwing stones and watching the people from
the Korpijärvi side rowing to the Midsummer dance over the still, open
waters. While they were busy with something near the twin-trunked
pine of the point, so oddly vivid that it seemed intended as a pattern
for such Midsummers in his memory, he heard the music of an accordion from the village far across the lake. Hannele turned over a piece

of sod, looked under it and said she would meet a rich, dark, and hand-some sweetheart when she grew up. The call of the cuckoo from the dense green woods across the river was especially resonant.

But their real anticipation of summer, what they missed and dreamed of most often was the berries. As soon as the plants began to flourish in the spring, they took time off from running and throwing stones to search them out and to predict the measure of their good fortune by the number of buds. Unusual amounts of arctic brambleberries and strawberries had begun to grow along the roads opened by bulldozers, among the stumps that bordered new clearings, and in the ashes of burned brush piles. On both sides of a pile of poles by the Onnela road, over heaps of rocky debris, a patch of raspberries spread more luxur-iantly every year. In time, they knew all the best spots for berrying, even the ones far out in the woods. Familiar places nearby, a small clear-ing in Jessipäinen's woods near the bottom land, a field bordered by cherry trees in the Tahaslahti woods, details of particular rocks and stumps by the roadside impressed themselves indelibly on his mind only because of the phenomenal amounts of strawberries and arctic brambleberries growing there. After Midsummer, they would follow the growth and reddening of individual berries, keeping an eye on one another and quarreling over them as they began to ripen. At haying time, when the first strawberries were ripe enough to eat it seemed the high point of summer and the fulfillment of life.

Many a summertime happening, at home, among neighbors, or out in the world, was like a subdued commotion in the background of life, soon forgotten, but certain powerful sights continued to open before his eyes, stirring him to wonder: luxuriant hillocks of arctic brambleber-ries along a row of rocks in the last field to be cleared, the dark little blood-drops of their buds against the ground-rock gouged by the blade of a bulldozer, then, in the calm, radiating warmth of the sun, the glow-ing sea of their blossoms against the sullen gleam of the charred stump remnants, their purplish tinge seemingly bleached by its rays. The peculiar soft green tint of the strawberry, pretty and more delicate, its sharply indented leaves, the gentle glow of its white petals with their core of yellow out in the pasture where the cowbells clanked.

Large arctic brambleberries grown in the shade of bushes could be sweet and soft even when green, the incipient red on the side toward the sun blending neatly with the pale green of the firm fruit. But the large berries ripened to a deep red were even better when already a little past prime, their skins swelled to bursting and quiveringly fragile from the pressure of juices, all their lives in the sun and grown by its warmth. And best of all were over-ripe strawberries, the fruit beneath the dark red flame of the surface a ruddy translucent pink as if it were laced with tiny blood vessels. The greatest numbers grew on the distant, dry willow dunes of Rasi Meadow and on the rental land at one end of Tiura Marsh, where stiflingly hot patches of field remained among willow thickets running wild and birch trees at the edge of the woods. In the summer, during the very hottest spells, even when the heavy air simmered with heat before a thunderstorm, the sweet, gentle breath of the strawberries seemed to blow in among the odors of hayfield and meadowsweet and the fresh fragrance of warm birch leaves. Whenever Kimmo saw strawberries in a difficult cleft blocked by stinging nettles, and could not get at them immediately, he would throb with agitation. When he squatted to eat the berries, he seemed to tremble, and his heavy, familiar skull bobbed up and down. Even late at night when they were exhausted from a hot, eventful, exciting day of haying and were finally settling down to sleep, as if the image were burned into his soul, there rose to haunt his eyes, revealed in the more open patches of meadow bleached almost white and weightless under the hot, open space of the sun, the dusky, melancholy, severe glow of huge, old strawberries.

It was a mood of the kind that follows a bitter quarrel. They must just have come from haying on the most distant enchanted ground of Rasi Meadow, their minds still filled with the willow-thicket darkness in the yard around the collapsing little barn, their fingers covered with the stinging, bloodless gashes made by the dark-green, bitter-smelling sedge grass. Aune Tiainen had come by to go swimming with Hannu, and Mother was cleaning small bream and roach in back of the sauna. He and Kimmo joined her to explode the fish's air bladders. Mother said nothing and did not look at them. They were delighted at the sight of the big, bulging air bladders of the bream, where they lay mixed with heads cut off at the gills in the blood-smeared pile of fish guts. The bladders were in two sections, one of them longer than the other and curving a little, their covering a transparent, grayish membrane, the fragile lightness of their inflated hollows somehow pleasing to hold. They would always put a bladder on a rock and burst it with a quick pressure of the foot, laughing at the loud pop it made. Suddenly he saw Mother's cheek puff out and the side of her face pucker as she bent over with her back half turned to him, saw sharp little lines appear on her temple near the eye, as if she too were beginning to choke with laughter at them, and it made him feel good. But no sound of laughter followed, and then they saw Mother's head sag, the bloody hand holding the scaly knife drop into the entrails on the slimy board, her back and shoulders shaking.

"Our life seems to have come to nothing," Mother said, her voice a whimper of misery in the midst of her sobs.

"Go for a swim now," Hannu, on his way to the shore with Aune, whispered into his ear from behind.

And somehow the moment took possession of him, an inexplicable feeling that seemed to have colored their summers from the very beginning, a strange, persistent shadow even among their very best memories, the dark side of a progressively clearer and more pleasing reality, for some reason especially accentuated in the summer. So much so that later it was difficult for him to remember summer without it, for when past summers came to mind, it rose compulsively with them, as if it were an integral part, a constituent element of them.

Nor was it always associated only with quarrels and Father's harshness. On occasion, it had no regard for time or the relationships among them, or to his state of mind. It had no effect on his behavior, for the others never noticed it. Sometimes it seemed to arise when least expected, when everything was at its best and his satisfaction at its height, in summer and in the finest weather. It could bring a sudden and senseless tremor to his mind at the very heart of summer when he heard the strangled, gravelly cawing of a baby crow being fed by its mother, broken off at intervals when its throat was choked with food. He heard it as a jarring note even in the drone of horse and houseflies, in the sporadic buzz of a bumblebee burrowing into a flower in the heat of summer.

It seemed to lurk in the rush of a barn swallow's wings above the yard and in the hungry chirping of its young in their nest under the eaves. Because of it, he vividly remembered a moment when Mother had called them in from the hayfield to eat. Father was swinging a scythe near the gravel pit, and Kimmo was sitting motionless in the shade of a willow thicket, Father having upbraided him about something or other. It was hot and smelled of mown hay, and a small bird was chirping in the willow thicket, a bird whose name he could never remember, but whose song always sounded of haying time to him. And it flooded his mind with sudden force as they swam the mud-crawl in the sun-warm shallows along the shore. It was always as if nothing had occurred in the interim, as if one moment from the summer when the house was built had persisted on some dream level of his mind. In the wink of an eye, everything was instantaneously unreal, it all seemed a dream, he was unsure of his existence, into a happy summer mood something as fateful and ominous had intruded as the cry of a hawk before a thunderstorm. The fear of some disaster haunted him stubbornly, the imminence of death seemed startlingly real, until the hope of awakening, of ordinary life, the sense of its approach, came to relieve him.

Diane Jarvenpa

AFTER THE CONCERT

It's as if you become more careful
walking through a room
where music is playing.
Don't make the record skip,
the earth is tipping already.
You step slowly
like wading through an island
of white campion,
sky misted with a low wind
sea birds.
The world is now understood.
And beyond the sound that opens
the body into weightlessness—
a shadow lingers
suffused in the region of the heart
that can't retreat,
a burning reflection of a storm
bursting hot,
leaving behind silent flowers
heavy with hunger.

TUULA's NETTLE SOUP

For Tuula Besse

The night opens her body
to the May earth,
lays a long dark sash
across the screen porch.
Guests sit around a table,
small candles burn like
tiny flames of monarch wings.
Conversation hangs quietly
in the air, swaying with the
lilies-of-the valley,
their bells holding a power
inside each creamy light like

some small death we all share.
The long tail of early summer
sweeps its clean, dry threads
around the porch, around the table,
and at each place with its white bowl
filled with nettle soup.
Each bowl unfurls a sweet fragrance
like the head of a fern, each bowl
filled with bits of cloud, sea foam
and forest.
As we eat, the language of grass and
of flat arctic woods becomes clearer
in the moonlight, its beam as bright
as the rims of our bowls.
Syllables grow in our mouths,
familiar movements of reed and water
on the earth's floor
spin in the spoon
that softness there.
Our friend weaves her mother's magic
turning nettle fire into glacial water,
its stinging leaves cooked into
silky pieces of broken emerald.
Our friend has given us new words
with which to feel a spring night.
As we learn to speak our lines,
the earth once more gives up
a little more of itself.

VESUVIUS

There is a time you reach
when you begin to remember,
when all the cities of your youth
stare at you in the blur
of freeway lights.
It is a time when
you smell the old secrets
as if you were trying them on
like an old woolen coat,

seeing how many of the lost buttons
were saved.
A time when familiar names
swim to the surface of the bar,
rising to the pitch of voices
and the low moaning of the jukebox,
those young faces that touched
your body with dark stories,
waking you with the play of the sun
through a torn shade.
It is a time when you find yourself
driving in the moonlight,
idling under a pair of windows,
once more hearing girls turn
in restless sleep,
murmuring like mayflies
of hunger and love.
A time when you pause at spaces
where buildings once stood
that pulled deliberately at your life,
like the invisible thread
that pulls the skydiver
closer to the insistent ground.
Some things you do find the same
in spite of the wide dispersal
of your friends and the
missing neon lights.
The old bridge still shakes
its iron and cement over
the wet seam of the river,
and the golden lights still rim
the forehead of the bandleader
as he smiles at a woman in pearls,
gesturing in a new song.
These are the static features
seen through the open window,
through the haze of couples
on the crowded dance floor,
as the world hurls itself by you
leaving you in its after-light.
The light of memory
seen over and over,

seen riding a stream of purple ash
that streaks the sky,
recalling the fever
of an old volcano.

WINTER SUN

Here in this northern country
the small winter sun
shines like a slice of amber.
I want to take it;
hold it in my hands,
select out bright gold threads
to keep in a drawer for another day,
a day that hangs like a wet sheet.
But it isn't mine to hold.
I still don't know enough of its face,
its equatorial flame salting
the back of my neck,
distant flashlight beam of
Antarctica barely reaching my shoulders.
It has much to teach of personal silence
as it cracks its shell on the sea's wet stone,
watching the planet turn
over and over again.
It can fool death,
shaking its hold with a touch of hot silk;
luring a string of bodies on shore,
glistening like small gifts.
I want to learn more
yet know I'm not ready.
I can't give in to the control
in the long wave of its fist,
the power in its lost music
hanging behind a drape of cloud,
soaking a day black.
I'm unable to follow
the pointed arrow of birds,
butterflies ripping through the winds
led on by its constant robe of yellow ash.
So I wait for the return of its

slow summer descent over the edge of the bay,
watching its seasonal flux
like a map of Venetian waterways
that you experience,
but never come to understand.
To some day know its flame
not as a distant thing,
or just an endurance.
Not as a breathing out and over
of an endless star,
but also as a breathing in.

SOMEWHERE SOMEONE IS DRINKING BRANDY

Here under the bridge
that swings across
the frozen water
nothing is as it seems.
The blue smoke from the factories
rides up, each stream set in a row
slicing the air with activity
but looking as lifeless
as just blown candles.

Sitting at the lip of the river
empty soup cans and wine bottles
emerge from the snow crust
like tips of early crocus buds.

You feel the bridge rumble on your back
as cars and buses
push through lights,
endless exhaust of evening.
The rolling of tires from above
floats down,
low waves breaking
on a cracked sea wall.
You hear a distant dolphin scream.

Every day the years
burn out of sight

but remain forever suspended
in the bird's nest,
tracks of the old man walking the dog,
pausing to stare
at the opposite shore.

As you feel
the cold vapor once again
walk around inside you
with the thud of a German boot,
you look at the city,
at the lights strung like pieces
of colored velvet,
turn to strike a new match,
open a new can.

BEGINNINGS OF SPEECH

You sling your voice
over the edge of the crib.
It trembles like a fish
falling to the watery floor
with the penguin and plastic rings.
Your hands, curved pink shrimp,
reach for the stain of sleep,
rubbing the dust from your eyes,
dreams of rabbits running at the moon.
You swim through grass,
wade through kelp beds
as the curtains undulate
across silent windows,
soft green waves.
The warmth of salty baked bread
rises in the dim light
with your voice,
vowels long and deep.
You pitch them like pennies
waiting to hear the echo,
the long arms of morning,
as you stamp at the rim of the canyon.

Jussi Stenvall

THE LAST SWIM

S IXTY-EIGHT YEARS! It was hard to believe they had crept up on him so stealthily and in such numbers. It seemed only yesterday that his father, with tears streaming down his face, had announced to an unbelieving family that their assets had been wiped out that Black October Tuesday; and that the family had gathered round the radio in a moment of national crisis to hear FDR's urbane voice reassure the nation that the only thing it had to fear was fear itself; and that cold, gray December Sunday when he heard the airwaves crackle with the news of the attack on a naval base half a world away; and the action-packed war years, flirting with death in the flak-filled skies of Europe; and the post-war years with his marriage to the love of his life—sweet Emily, tall and lissome with ash-blond hair and delicate features who selflessly dedicated herself to him and their children; and settling down to a career to provide his family with the needs and comforts they so richly deserved; and it seemed only a twinkling of an eye that the children were up and gone and he and Emily were left to enjoy the golden years together. But that was not to be, for his beloved was struck down by a massive coronary, sundering their thirty-eight year love affair.

The suddenness of her death numbed his grief, but as he became fully aware of the enormity of his loss, the pain reached deep into his soul and so eroded his health that almost a year to the day of Emily's passing he was felled by a stroke. He had now recovered from most of its debilitating effects; his speech and ambulation were virtually restored—only his closest friends could detect the slight slur in his speech and the absence of spring in his walk. However, he knew full well that the first stroke was only a precursor—he would be hit again with even more devastating effects. He was "turned off" by the prospect of spending his waning years as excess baggage with either of his daughters and their families or in the stultifying environment of a nursing home playing parcheesi or viewing television with his peers of the "scrap heap set"—better to go out quietly and with dignity at a time and place of his choosing. Emily and the girls had always taken him in jest—but he had been in dead earnest—when he said he'd make a last, long swim in the sea rather than play out his days in a nursing home. He recognized that now was the time for him to carry out his "final plan," as he was in the habit of calling it, while he still controlled his own destiny.

Yesterday morning he had gone to the cemetery to lay a last rose on Emily's grave. He was an agnostic, for nothing in his long life-experience or considerable readings had confirmed or denied an after-life, but as he knelt at her headstone he vowed he would soon be laid in the plot alongside hers so that their remains would experience eternity together. Later in the day he joined his daughter and her family for Sunday dinner. He had always been proud of her grace and beauty – the spitting image of Emily in her youth – and now he saw both of them replicated in five-year-old Ashley. This confirmed for him his concept of eternal life that had taken seed during his college years: so long as a man's children lived and the children's children lived, the man lived also, and so it would be until the end of the world.

When he mentioned his plans for a brief sojourn to the coast, his daughter couldn't hide her anxiety, "But, Daddy, do you think you're up to going away like that by yourself?"

"No problem, Hon, never felt better in my life," he lied. "Besides, it'll do me a world of good; you know how invigorating that sea air can be."

Later that evening he telephoned his out-of-state daughter and spoke with his grandson. The boy had reached an age of sophistication and self-involvement that made it difficult for him to relate to a grandfather half a continent away, and he could hear his daughter in the background coaching him to say "I love you, Grandpa." No matter, he loved the boy even if he found it difficult to express his affection for a grandfather he seldom saw.

He awoke with the first light of dawn, as was his habit, enjoyed a leisurely breakfast, and after cleaning and putting away his dishes called his favorite motor-inn on the beach to reserve the suite he and Emily were so fond of. It was a top floor corner with a balcony providing an unobstructed sweep of the Gulf as well as the ship channel into Gulf City. It was their pleasure to spend hours reveling in the broad expanse of the sea with its changing moods and watching the ships rise out of the horizon and wend their way between the channel markers into port. He didn't anticipate any problem because it was now in-between seasons – most in-staters had used up their summer vacations and the "snow birds" wouldn't be coming for another month or so – but it would be reassuring to know that the suite would be waiting for him. He laid out on the dinette table his will, insurance policies, and other papers he felt the children would need to settle his estate. He included a final note to each of his daughters. As he gave the house plants their Monday morning watering, he was thankful that he no longer had a pet to make provisions for. He slipped an overnight bag—more for appearance than need—into the trunk of the car and made one last slow walk around the yard. It reflected his fastidious nature: shrubs neatly trimmed and hardly a blade of grass out of place. The flowers were a riot of color—the bougainvillea, especially, had never flamed more brilliantly. Before starting the engine, he savored once more the attractive home he and Emily had shared for most of their union, dwelled on the many pleasures it held, then turned the key and backed out of the driveway for the last time.

He joined the interstate on the southern outskirts of town, set the cruise control at fifty-five miles per hour, for he had no need for haste, and settled down for a relaxed two-hour drive. The road was a twin ribbon that slashed through rich farm and ranch lands, still verdant save for brown stubbled fields where harvests had been made. Ubiquitous whiteface cattle, heads lowered, were cropping the grasses while here and there a maverick, head stretched between barbed strands, searched for greener stuff on the other side.

The day couldn't have been more beautiful; while autumn was making incursions in the North, the Gulf South was still clinging to summer. The sky, a blue dome, was host to cotton boll cumulus that cast passing shadows on the land. The highway bridged a broad but shallow lake, the northern limits of the reservoir for Gulf City, its waters a haven for the vanguard of waterfowl on their southward migration. All that he viewed as he motored along represented the panorama of life, and he was pleased that he had been given the opportunity to have been a part, albeit a microscopic one, of this continuum of life.

Soon the high rises of downtown pierced the skyline and he took the off-ramp that would bypass the city completely and connect with the causeway to the Gulf islands. The rich farmlands were now replaced by tidal marshes, and the roadway, raised beyond the reach of all but the highest floods, looked out over a sea of marsh grass interlaced with a network of waterways. From the height of the causeway, he could see the blue-green gulf stretching to the southern horizon, and he savored with slow, deep breaths the sea air that flooded his car.

The desk clerk at the motor-inn, remembering him from earlier years, extended him more than the usual commercial welcome, and looking at the lone piece of luggage asked, "Any bags in your car we can help you with?"

"No, thanks, traveling light this time."

Up in his room he drew back the drapes and the sliding glass door to the balcony to allow the sweep and the smell of the Gulf to flood the room. The sun was in its southern declination keeping the balcony bathed with its light and warmth all the day long. "Without that solar furnace," he thought, "the earth would be a barren place indeed. It was easy to understand why so many ancients revered it as a god." He kicked off his shoes, removed his shirt and sat in the recliner to soak up the sun's warmth.

In late afternoon he ordered through room service the Gulf shrimp dinner which was the hallmark of the inn's cuisine, together with a decanter of chablis, and dined leisurely by the rays of the waning sun. The wine flooded him with warmth, inducing in him a comfortable lethargy. The prospect of ending his life in the sea did not frighten him; rather it was the hastening of an event that was inevitable – the time and place would be of his choosing rather than leaving it to chance. He had planned his last swim for the twilight hour free from inquisitive eyes. When the last pink tip of sun slipped below the horizon, he stepped into the dressing room and donned his swim trunks. As he adjusted the fit in front of a full length mirror, he noted with sadness how youth had fled his body – a body once upright and strong that had propelled him faster and farther than his peers – and left him a bent and flaccid shell. He covered his nakedness with a terry beachrobe.

Prior to exiting the room, he left a note with an emergency number on the dresser together with a tip for the maid; he felt certain she would find it when she cleaned in the morning. He was grateful that the inn had an exterior elevator that bypassed the lobby and provided direct access to the pool and beach area. Facing other humans at this time was the last thing he wanted.

As he walked toward the water, he was amazed at the acuteness of his senses – they seemed to have acquired a special awareness for the occasion. The sights and sounds of the night were truly part of his existence: the intermittent flash of the lighthouse on the point, the play of heat lightning against towering cumulus far out on the horizon, the squeak of sand underfoot, the swoosh of surf against the shore, the gentle breeze caught in a moment of hesitation between onshore and offshore. Before stepping into the surf, he removed his robe, folded it neatly and laid it on the sand. The water was comfortable – the Gulf retained its summer warmth late into the fall. It was slack low tide, forcing him to wade far out before reaching swimming depth. Finally he struck out in an easy breaststroke, for it was as effortless and natural to him as walking. As he pulled through the gentle swells, he marveled at the Gulf's calm, for he had seen it, abetted by hurricane winds, sweep the beach sands far inland and carelessly toss homes half a block from their foundations. Then he felt a change in the water's movement – that perceptible moment when the tide begins its inward flow. The waves now surged higher, and he felt an exhilaration in topping each crest and coasting down its backside. It was as though he had been flung back through time to the years when, with youthful bravado, he had challenged and bested many a high running surf.

He stopped swimming and turned on his back and floated, not so much to rest but to measure his progress from shore. Rising and falling with the sea, he saw it as a jeweled string against a black velvet backdrop. "No doubt about it," he thought, "man was something special, for of all creatures he was the only one who could adjust to his environment so ably." He maintained headway with a flutter of his feet and an occasional backstroke. He raised his face to the heavens, now rapidly approaching full black, allowing the stars to take their nightly positions. "There's a mystery out there that's unsolvable," he mused, "if only from the sheer size of it." Finally, he turned over and resumed his smooth, steady breaststroke. From the remoteness of another memory, far beyond his conscious recall, arose an awareness that he was once again in his element and he was one with the sea. "Now is the time," he decided. He stopped swimming, hesitated a moment, then exhaled and allowed himself to slip under the waves.

Stephen Kuusisto

PENTTI SAARIKOSKI: OUTSIDE THE CIRCLE

*I*N AN EARLY DIARY entry Pentti Saarikoski wrote that "the *Kalevala* is unendurable—though it does, for the most part, have a historical significance." His argument is emblematic of a generation of poets that emerged in Finland in the late fifties—there was a new willingness to break with tradition and to look beyond Finland's cultural and political boundaries. The publication of *Mitä tapahtuu todella? (What is Going On?)* in 1962 earned Saarikoski instant recognition both in literary circles and the media. The book established modernist poetry in Finland by combining found poems, dada collage, imagistic and lyrical impressions, palimpsestic allusions from the ancients, and directed political statements.

Any single book by Saarikoski will contain hundreds of voices— each belonging to a liminal figure—a threshold persona who has stepped outside the ritual circle. His early training in ancient Greek, as well as his interest in twentieth century Anglo-American literature, helped him to synthesize several traditions. Like Eliot, Pound, and Joyce, Saarikoski loved dismantling given identities in his poems—the narrator is usually an isolated figure whose guide is language. That language may have the purity of Homeric Greek or the freshness of recent Helsinki street slang. His importance to Finnish literature was well established by the time of his death at 46 in 1983.

Pentti Saarikoski

Selected poems from

THE DANCE FLOOR ON
THE MOUNTAIN
TANSSILATTIA VUORELLA

and

INVITATION TO THE DANCE
TANSSIIN KUTSU
(Translated by Stephen Kuusisto)

Today I go by another route
arriving at the meadow from the west
I want to see the mountain in a different light,
        the ocean's light
The air is tissue—

the trees' shadows are faint against it
I walk in the meadow
I'd like to be a poet whose song
gets stones moving
constellating
into city walls—
the trees walking to the carpenters
who build homes for people

The emptiness that comes with grief
is a hard burden,
but still, still I want to see
everything in a different light,
the ocean's light

                * * *

(Translated by Stephen Kuusisto)

You couldn't see through the snow squall
as I pulled on my boots
and slowly skied down the road
to the ocean
I veered off and entered a meadow
that borders
those summer cottages
they're starting to build
They're the color of shit
from a regular and well fed man
A light was still burning
in a construction shed
I looked through a window—
a sugar packet was on the table
and they'd left the refrigerator open—
the telephone was on the floor
Today was Sunday
I skied around the place
and looked through a second window
A poster on the wall said "Love Not War"
I headed back. Now the sun was setting behind me
Ships on the bay shrieked like frightened birds
My skis froze
I finally knew
who I'd been searching for
when I sat back at my kitchen table

* * *

Snow melts
I get sauna water from a rain spout
All day there's a hymn in my mind
Strange—I'm just searching for my fatherland
Soon time will take care of it
I sit on a bench
reading
Gyula Illyes' book
and throw water on hot stones
I learned a new thing—
even books can sweat
I wash, rinse, and go out to dry
I put on clean clothes
and think of Homer—
they started saying he was blind
because he saw it all
so clearly

* * *

Here's a fine stone where you can sit
Ezra—
it's beside an apple tree
and a pine
Each grows according to its nature
Cats would spring into your lap
as the sun goes down
You'd take a leaf
from the bearberry
and hold it up
to study its veins
Its odor is like papyrus
You'd talk in a leisurely way
to Eliot
and to all of us

Stephen Kuusisto

PAPYRUS & STONE

in memoriam
Pentti Saarikoski

I'm reading
in the early hours before dawn,
and my hands are shaking
from too much coffee,
too many cigarettes
until I must get up
and go outside
to walk it all off.

But my thoughts
curl
around the weight
of this obsession

* * *

How easy it is
to write
when water stays close
to the ground,
when we love each other
without ambition:
this simple desire
to suckle
and not go hungry.

You can read anything
after that. . . .

* * *

Teacher comes along:
Hipponax,
pale, fiery hair
sorry old Greek. . . .

His poems are
instinctual
like the desire
for a glass of water
or the sleep
that circles
around the very old.

His poems are
the sounds of tide
on crushed stone,
or hay
scratching hay.

* * *

Sunlight!
No hymns!

Pentti—
the apple tree
and the pine
are growing
side by side!

Now,
when you lift
your hand
to study
its veins
up close,
it's scented
like papyrus.

It's so early . . . .
It's morning.

And you've given me
these murmured
consolations—
the only things
we can
give away . . . .

Shirley Waisanen Schoonover

Excerpt from

MOUNTAIN OF WINTER

*T*HE DAY was intensely clear, making Old Big look deceptively close and mild. They ran through the pasture, galloped up the sloping turf and slid under the barbed-wire fence. Free of the farm now, they entered the outlying fringes of the black woods, walking beneath the few silver poplars that stood just at the edge of the wood. They followed the old lumber trail, going in and out of the early sunlight that already burned the dew off the grass. Following the trail made the walking easy and they chattered back and forth, certain that they would climb to the top of Old Big by nightfall.

"How'll we come back down?" Piss-ant asked.

"Well, you nut. It'll be a lot easier coming downhill. We'll just run all the way back down." She was confident that she'd know the way down, for wouldn't it be easy to see the lights of the farm from the top of Old Big?

The trail ended in a patch of torn-up bushes and tree stumps that Ava's father had cut down. The children went past this place into the deeper shadows of the black woods. They walked in knee-deep moss that held sweet and jeweled water, the drops glittering in the half light. Ava stooped down. "Hey, look at this." She touched a small plant that stood six inches high.

"What?"

"Pitcher plant. It catches flies and eats them." She demonstrated by running her finger down the slender green throat of the plant. True enough, the plant was shaped like a small pitcher of water inside. "It doesn't grab at bugs. See, it has water in here and the flies and bugs come to drink. But they can't get out again because these little hairs point down at them." Ava stuck her finger down into the pitcher's bottom, stroking the silver hairs that lined the green throat. "That's the flower part there," she said, holding her other hand out to a flat green blossom that had leathery, almost crisp petals.

"Why don't the flies just fly out?" Piss-ant asked.

"They can't. Dumbhead, they walk down on the hairs and slide into the water. Flies can't fly if their wings are wet, and these hairs point down so they can't get ahold with their feet."

"Mphm." Piss-ant wasn't impressed. "Rather see a real mean plant that grabs at things. This only sits around."

"Well, it gets its bugs that way."

"How'd you know? You a wizard or somep'n?"

"No. Mummu read about it to me in her Nature Book. You know. The one in the fancy glass-door cabinet. Know something else? She read me a long story-poem about the heroes of *Kalevala*. I bet they live up on Old Big. I seen their lights in the sky last winter, those Northern Lights." She whispered, "That's why we're going up Old Big. I wanta see them up close."

Piss-ant's eyes grew big and serious. "You mean it? Heroes? Like giants?"

"Yeah. Väinämöinen was the best one. Boy, he had all kinds of adventures."

"Did he fight any monsters?"

"Yeah. Kalma. He was a bugger that lived under the water of Lake Tuonela. He's always trying to kill Väinämöinen."

"Jeez. What'd he look like?"

"All black." Ava was inventing now, to keep Piss-ant interested in the long walk ahead of them. "All black with a gray face. And no eyes, just deep holes in his head. And he's cold. Clammy, you know, like a dead fish."

Piss-ant shuddered appreciatively. "He's up there, too?"

"I don't know. I guess."

"Oh." He regarded her with suspicion. "How'd you know that other guy lives up there?"

Ava curled her lip scornfully. "Where else would he live? In a house? He's ten feet tall, I bet."

Piss-ant scratched his head and looked around. "My feet are cold and wet. Ain't there no better way to go but through all this wet stuff?"

"Yeah. But I got a little lost. We'll find the dry part soon."

They set off again, looking for dry ground. A flock of crows flew up sharply, startling them until Ava waved an arm in recognition. "Noisy old crows," she scolded. The crows called to one another and flew off, their racket fading with distance. Ava found a rabbit trail and they turned onto it. "Rabbits know the fastest way around in these woods." They came to higher ground and left the moss, now walking amid the black-green shadows. The ground here was soft, ankle-deep with pine needles. Ava paused beneath a tree and picked up a small furry object, holding it out to Piss-ant.

"What's that?" he asked.

"Owls live around here. This is a kind of cud that owls spit up. When they eat a mouse or rabbit they almost eat it whole and then spit up the fur and bones. This must've been a mouse."

Piss-ant took the dry, fragile cluster of fur and tiny bones, "Jeez, that old owl must've had a big belly to gobble up a whole mouse in one bite."

"Oh, that's only a snack. You should see the rabbits a big owl can stuff away. Pa said he bets a big owl could take a fifteen-pound rabbit easy."

"Don't the rabbits scratch awful, though?" Piss-ant was remembering the large jackrabbit Ava had caught last summer, and how that rabbit had clawed her arms when she had picked it up by the ears.

"They don't get a chance to scratch. The owl flies down real quiet and just grabs them on the back and flies away. The rabbits scream so bad it hurts your ears."

Piss-ant urged her on. "What else do they do? Do they peck out the eyes?"

"Ah no, the owl takes the rabbit to its nest up in a tree and just kills it." Ava glanced upward, trying to find the sun. "Let's eat our lunch and get started. Don't wanna fool away any more time gabbing." They munched a sweet roll apiece and set out again. They jogtrotted along the firm ground, not talking, saving their breath to work up the side of the mountain. When they came to a clear place Ava went up a tree to see how much farther they had to go.

"Well?" Piss-ant asked when she came down.

"I don't think it's very far anymore. I couldn't see the top any from here. But that's because of the trees in the way." She paused for breath, eyeing the sun that was sliding over the western shoulder of the mountain. "Remember, when we started we knew the top was just on the other side of this woods? Well, I bet we only have a half mile to go and we'll be there."

But she was thinking that they could go straight up the mountain as a crow flies. She didn't realize that they could not go straight up but would have to work at an angle, turning back and forth to work up the side of the mountain. It would take an adult on horseback days to climb that side of the mountain. But she didn't know this, so they began walking again.

By the time the sky had turned a citron green of sundown, the children were tired and cranky. They had eaten the last of the sweet rolls and had drunk from a lake they had found. They kept walking, although Piss-ant complained of blisters on his heels, for Ava was sure that once they came to the upper edge of the black woods they would be within reach of the summit of Old Big.

"Hell, Ava. When're we going to get out of this woods?"

"Any minute. Shut up and keep walking." She was impatient and beginning to wonder about the size of this old mountain. She didn't want to spend the night in these black woods, and she hurried Piss-ant along.

Night fell suddenly. All the light went out of the sky and the forest was truly black now, full of silence. Ava walked uneasily, wishing they would come out from this dark place. At least a clearing wouldn't be so full of blackness, she thought, biting her lip.

Piss-ant crept up behind her and grabbed the belt of her pants. She squalled and twitched around. "Don't grab at a person like that!"

"I got lonesome all of a sudden," Piss-ant explained.

"Oh. Well, I know." She let him hang on to her belt, relieved by his physical nearness. They walked along for some distance, skirting the darkest places in the woods. Piss-ant kept crowding up behind her and tripping her heels. She took his hand and they walked side by side, staring into the darkness, listening now for any sound. But it was all silence upon silence, for no bird sang, no crow shrieked imperiously from the treetops. Ava's hide began to prickle with apprehension. She had not wanted to be up here at night, not in these trees, she realized; and her chest shriveled so that breathing was hard. She hunched her shoulders and peered ahead, avoiding the darkest shadows.

Piss-ant said, "Wait a minute. What's that up there?"

They had come into a small clear place. As she looked, the moon flew up out of the treetops, thin as a curved needle but infinitely bright.

"Oh, it's the moon," Piss-ant said, disappointed. "I saw a light coming from those trees. I thought it was home."

"Couldn't be home," Ava said, a little scornfully. "Home's back down there."

"Well, why don't we go back? I ain't in the mood to climb this damn mountain anymore."

Ava, too, wanted to go home. She thought a minute. "I'll go up one of these trees and see where it is. Then we'll just run back downhill." She went up the tree in a hurry until she had come to the place where the tree swayed back and forth like a pendulum with her weight. She shimmied around to look down the side of the mountain and strained her eyes to see the lights from home. There were none. She caught her breath and looked harder. She scanned the entire horizon of black treetops and could see no glimmer of light. Only stars were there and they looked coldly back at her. She let herself cry a little up there in the tree so Piss-ant couldn't hear her, then she went slowly back down to the ground.

Piss-ant had cuddled up to the tree trunk, waiting for her. "Is it far?" he asked anxiously.

Ava was silent. She sat down next to him in the soft needle cover beneath the tree.

"Huh, Ava?"

"I couldn't find any lights."

"Did you look hard?" He searched her face to see if she was lying.

"Yeah. My eyes almost fell out of my head. I looked so hard."

They were quiet for a moment. The forest drew close to them and they could feel an immense breathing go through the trees. Piss-ant snuggled up to Ava, burrowing his head into her chest. "What'll I do?" he asked.

"Well, let's yell for Pa. He might be looking for us already. And he'd hear us." Ava put her hands in her mouth and yelled, "Pa-ah!"

The breath of the forest carried her voice out and down, spinning it along through the trees. An echo came back to them, Ah-Aah!

They took turns calling; calling and then listening. The echo always answered, eerily coming from some place deeper in the forest.

Then a sound came to them, the shrieking laughter of a loon, and it shattered the night around them. Both children flinched and grabbed each other. "What was that?" Piss-ant whispered.

"A loon, I think."

The echo laughed mockingly through the forest and Piss-ant said. "Let's don't yell anymore. I don't like it."

Ava agreed and they sat together under the tree, staring out at the dark around them. The moon made too many shadows and the forest breathed too chilly and close. Ava said, "Let's find another place to sit. Where it's lighter." Piss-ant followed her and they stepped into the small clearing. They walked a few small steps and paused while Ava squinted around for a place. From behind them a loud thrumming, beating sound started. Ava half turned and yelped. A huge, tall black something flew at them, was on top of them, clawing at Piss-ant's bald head, pummeling Ava's face with harsh wings. All Ava saw was a dark shape with glowing hollow eyes. She squawked and broke for the woods. Piss-ant, clutching her belt, ran blindly after her.

They fell down under a low-branched pine tree, huddling together, too scared to move. "It got me, Ava. I'm bloody." True enough, the owl, for that's what had attacked them, had scratched Piss-ant's head, leaving deep cuts. Now the blood trickled into his eyes. Ava wiped his face with pine needles. "Boy, that was a monster—*hey*, like you were telling about!"

"*Shh*. Let's sit quiet until it's gone for sure."

They sat motionless, staring out from their cover; silence had returned to the black woods. "I'm gonna yell for Pa again. Maybe it can't find us in here." She began calling in a soft, high voice. "Pa-ah!" She made her voice stretch the sounds so that they would fall a little longer on the waiting air. She imagined that she could throw the words so lightly that they would cast a thread of sound through the darkness, and that that sound would loop and fall over her father (who was surely looking for them now). She listened for the echo to come back before she called again, afraid if she broke the silence too often that from somewhere in the alleys of these black trees the loon would be aroused to shouting its vindictive laugh. Or that the dark shape would find them. But the loon was still. Ava called and called, listening always for the echo, and for some response from down the mountain.

Finally, as she began to fall into a half dream that held only her outgoing voice and the darkness, the night changed around her. A flickering, swinging light came along the floor of the forest. She called, loudly, to bring the light nearer. "Pa-ah!"

It was her father, carrying a lantern; the yellow circle of light advanced and stopped as he listened, then came straight toward her.

She flung herself at him, glad to hang on, smelling the warmly familiar tobacco-sweat scent of him. He put the lantern down and hugged her, then hugged Piss-ant. "You shouldn't of come up here so far," he began to scold.

"Boy, I'm glad you got here!" Piss-ant yelped. "That Kalma guy chased us. He got me all bloody!"

"You been telling him scarey stories, Ava."

"No, I never. Look at the cut on his head."

Juha lifted the lantern and looked at Piss-ant's skull. "Owl did that. Saw that fuzzy head 'n' thought you were a rabbit." He took Ava's hand. "Hold on to Ava, Joel. Get you home before any more owls grab you."

At home in the snug kitchen they were fed, washed, spanked and scolded. "And you don't set foot past those fences, understand?" But they were asleep at the table and Old Big was far away.

Gladys Koski Homes

WHILE DRIVING TO WORK

On a January Minnesota Monday
children dance at the edge of the highway
keeping warm in pale air
so thin and crisp it crackles like cellophane
in light so early
it lays tints of mauve on snowbanks and tree frost.

Young children made fat by mothers forcing layers of clothing
old children wearing only short short jackets
and big big gloves
have stalked out stiffly
to stand bravely rigid in cutting cold.

They queue up in mouths of driveways
in ragged lines of first out, first on;
white vapor escapes fresh good-bye kissed lips
encircling heads and leaving hover-marks long after
chugging buses shaped like yellow loaves
have vacuumed up their charges.

Mary Jokela Eichholz

MAIA TO ORION

You may write me a poem,
say I resemble a faun —
subtle, elusive,
delicate, shy.

I will not believe you.
I will turn and lift my head
wary of praise.

You may give me a handful
of sweet meadow grasses.
I will quiver gently
at the unfamiliar scent
of your hand on my hair.

I will wear a beige silk shift
as smooth as skin.
I will not let you in.

CAVITY

We look furtively at each other
only the nurse is cheerful
I pick up the scent of old fear
that clings to the chairs
in the waiting room
My tooth has stopped hurting

I re-read last year's *Glamour*
as if it were a foreign language
The paper sticks to my hands

The office chair is contoured
holding my head
I lie back, closing my eyes
in this small death
a white Kleenex like a flower

My dentist is young and kind
proud of his skill

That didn't hurt, did it

He doesn't know
I am nine years old again
    the old slow drill
    no novocain
    the dental clinic
    where I sat for hours
    my mouth full of cotton
    my eyes tight as fists
not even time can be relied on

You can rinse now

My eyes creep open
I can't believe it's over
relief bubbles up
from its underground hiding place
I spit my fear out
into the swirling water

Oili Mäki

LANDMARK
MAAMERKKI

(Translated by Aili Jarvenpa)

It was an especially joyous day
when I discovered my hands,
academic hands that, at their best,
tapped on the typewriter – not to mention
household tasks and the baby's laundry.
But for my hands to do professional
work!I had already discovered my eyes,
my eyes grafted to my heart,
with which I can see more
than can the eye of a camera.

John Piirto

SPUR

*I*AM A TWELVE-YEAR-OLD boy standing on our back porch. My mother, weeping hysterically, has ordered me to wait here and think about what I've done while she takes my father to the hospital. What I've done is to sink an arrow into my father's left shoulder. Tiny icicles drip above my head. A half mile off the railroad spur track climbs toward the mineshaft; the meadow, once spring green and fragrant and filled with gypsies picking dandelions, has been smashed down by the cold rains of October. I have heard my mother say that the winter will be a bad one and I have heard my father tell her to be quiet about such things.

* * *

There were only six or seven houses in our neighborhood seeing as how we were so close to the spur track. Most people couldn't take the noise of the railroad cars, I guess, and other homes were never built. Lanny lived three doors down and he was my best friend. He was a tall boy with black hair and shiny dark eyes, and his good-natured grin assured me we were buddies even though he was so much older than me, sixteen, able to drive. His family didn't own a car but his uncle did. Whenever his uncle would visit, he'd let Lanny take the car up and down the street. One day I spied Lanny driving by and ran out to the front porch.

"Hey, kid," he hollered, "you wanna lift?"

Proudly, I sat in the front seat next to him. The seat was soft and the interior of the car smelled like our attic on a warm day. A '52 Chev – the speedometer went up to 100 miles per hour!

"Will she do a hundred?" I asked.

"Course, kid, if I could get it out on the highway."

Lanny drove about a quarter mile up, to the north end of the street where the road ended in a field, made a clumsy Y-turn, and then headed south. The south end was wider, to accommodate a cross street, and Lanny made a U-turn and we drove back north again. We went up and down the street how many times? I lost count. I do remember Lanny stopping once at the south end and staring at the cross street.

"I go this way," he said, "cut down Main, cross the tracks and we're on the highway, kid."

"To do a hundred!" I shouted, filling in the dream for him.

"No, to escape."

"What?"

His grin faded. "Three minutes and we're outa this hole."

"What hole?"

"You gonna stay here the rest of your life?"

No answer came. I must have looked confused because he punched my arm and grinned again. Then he made a U-turn and we headed north, up our street to the field, then south, then north, south, north, and so on until his uncle finally came out and hailed us.

My mother didn't like it that I hung around a boy as old as Lanny, but she didn't keep me from him either. Our end of town was pretty desolate. Besides a ball game I'd invented next to the garage, there wasn't a lot to do. Sometimes I must have looked so lonely out there, banging the ball, that my mother would actually come out and play with me. The Tigers were my team and I was Al Kaline. She'd be the New York Yankees. Trouble was I would always win because she didn't know the mechanics of catching and throwing.

One day I decided to teach her the proper way to play and something remarkable occurred. I was in the midst of showing her how to throw when my father came out on his way to the garage. (Since the mine had closed, that's where he spent a lot of time, "thinkin and tinkerin," as he used to say.)

"Dad, show her how to throw like you showed me," I said.

"I don't have time for something like that." Immediately he seemed to regret the remark and he looked at my mother like I hadn't seen him look at her in a long time. The corner of his mouth smiled, a gleam came to his brown eyes. "Whattayou wanna learn something like that for, Lee?"

The cool wind blew my mother's hair back. "Why I'm going to be a major leaguer," she said, and threw the ball at him.

He caught it. "Not if you throw like that. You step with your wrong foot, Lee. You throw with your right hand, step with your *left* foot." My father stepped and threw. "See?"

My mother caught the ball and threw it back.

"That's better. Now use your shoulder, the shoulder."

My father threw to me, I threw to Mom, Mom to Father. In short order our game of three-cornered catch became garage baseball and I made my father a member of the Yankees too, Mom and Dad, Mantle and Berra. I showed him the rules and soon we were bouncing the ball off the garage, keeping score with pebbles on the concrete, yelling and laughing, me against them. Then suddenly my father stopped. I turned and saw Lanny leaning at the corner of our house, watching. We all stared at him.

"Need a fourth?" he asked.

To me this idea sounded terrific.

My father looked angry. "How long you been there, boy?"

"Couple minutes."

"I don't like people sneaking around here."

"I wasn't sneakin, Mr. Haukola," Lanny said. "Honest, I wasn't. It looked like you was havin fun."

The scene then must have seemed pathetic to my father—the entire family playing fake baseball against the garage on a cool Saturday in September while he was out of work. His eyes softened. "No, I'm sure you weren't sneaking, Lanny. I apologize."

"I wisht my father'd play ball. He's downtown drinkin." Lanny looked at his feet. "He's . . . he's a drunk."

"Don't you say that, son," said my father. "He's just out of work. The strike's done it. We strike, the mine closes for a spell, but soon it'll open again and we'll all be happy." Lanny eyes were yet downcast. The four of us stood stock still as the wind blew over us, around us, past us out toward the railroad spur. A thatch of my father's dark hair blew down over his forehead, into his eyes, and I wanted to go put it back in place. But before I could move he tossed me the ball underhanded and went into the garage.

* * *

When my father told Uncle Ev we might be moving, Ev's face went blank as a sheet of paper. Evert was the eldest of my father's three brothers and four sisters, a machinist not dependent on the mine for work, the wise man of the Haukola clan.

"You can't mean it," Ev said.

He and my father sat at our kitchen table in front of beers Ev had brought with him. He'd even brought me a cream soda and I sat with the men.

"I do. Lee and I have been discussing a move since July."

"That mine'll start up again."

"Might, probably will," my father said. "Then it'll close again too."

Ev took off his steel-rimmed spectacles, rubbed his eyes, and put them back on. He gave my father a disgusted look. "You and your goddam union."

"Not the union's fault."

"Hell it isn't." Ev had a quick sip of beer and set his glass down. "Anyway, moving isn't the answer. You got family here. It's out of the question."

My father then took my hand in his; he *buried* my hand in his and gave it a squeeze. "No use talking about it then," he said.

Over the next few weeks we had more visitors than I ever remembered. Aunt Helga brought two apple pies one day and spoke of her "loved ones," meaning father, mother, and me. Uncle Dutch came down from Marquette with my two cousins and their BB guns. Dorothy dropped by. Sunday afternoon Aunt Lynn and Uncle Martin and Uncle Davey knocked on the door hollering, "Surprise!" The surprise was Gramma Haukola in her wooden wheelchair out on the walk, a light snow falling around her. My father knew what was up. My mother too. *I* knew.

"Look," my father told the group that Sunday. "If the mine was going good, leaving would never have occurred to me. But I have my own family to think about."

Gram said, "*Me olemme sinun, perhe. Sinun isäsi muutti Suomesta asumaan tänne.*"

"Country's a big place, Ma."

"Oh, *poika.*"

No one said anything for awhile. The snow was supposed to get harder but the storm had petered out. In fact, from my chair by the window I could see a white ball of sun behind the fading clouds. The room was quiet. No one looked at my father, but he was definitely the center of attention.

"Okay." My father nodded. "Okay . . ."

* * *

Lanny appeared at the door just after supper one evening. He had with him one of the most beautiful things I'd ever seen: a brand new bow. It was narrow and made of blond wood and had a thick shine. Lanny's hand caressed the red wood handle which was larger on one side to hold the arrow. He then put his leg between the string and the bow, bent the wood into a powerful arc, and notched the string up top. "Whattayathink," he said.

I was speechless.

"Let's go shootin, kid."

"Can I, Mom?" My mother and father had come to the door to see for themselves. *Brand new* didn't exist often in our lives.

"You know how to use that thing, son?"

"Yeah, Mr. Haukola. There was a booklet with it my father had me read first."

"Your father buy that for you?"

Lanny's grin disappeared momentarily. "He's been feelin pretty bad about me I guess."

I felt my father's had on my shoulder. "You be careful."

We were, too. Lanny was amazingly careful. Maybe he had to be because there were only four arrows and if they were broken or lost, that would be it. We started taking the bow regularly out to the spur, using the steep incline as a backdrop for target practice. Our target? An old tire which we filled with clumps of dead grass and dirt clods all bundled up in a gunny sack. Lanny would make sure I stood to the side as he shot all four arrows, then it would be my turn. I wasn't as strong as Lanny, of course, but I could pull that string back far enough to feel its coiled power, string digging into my fore and middle fingers. I held my shoulders and arms steady, kept my eyes focused, and let the arrow whistle through the air where it would miss or *thunk* into the target.

After a few weeks we got pretty good and the garage wasn't enough. Lanny sharpened the arrows to razor-like points for the hunt. Animals. We were after game. And we were successful. The day came that I actually killed something and at the time, I considered it a turning point in my life.

We were walking along the rusted tracks of the spur when up ahead a rabbit leaped over a pile of ore and disappeared. As suddenly he hopped back in our line of vision. We froze. I had the bow. Though Lanny was a better shot, stronger, there was no time to give it to him. I notched an arrow and pretended the small brown animal was the gunny sack. My heart pounded as Lanny whispered something. I let go and watched the rabbit bound away. But he wasn't running. He rolled to a stop with the arrow sticking upright, out of the back of his neck.

Lanny let me keep him. When I showed the rabbit to my parents, they looked aghast. "It's dead," my mother said.

"Course, here's the hole where the arrow went in. I shot it."

My Dad said, "You shot that thing?"

"Yessir."

"What do you expect us to do with it?"

"Eat it. I'll clean it. Lanny says you can make a stew."

Still, they looked aghast. They looked as if I'd just told them we should eat it raw, pass it among us right then and there. Lanny helped me clean it. We washed the carcass off with the hose and I wrapped the meat in wax paper and put it in the fridge. Next night my mother indeed made a stew with carrots and potatoes and celery and . . . rabbit. I never tasted better food in my life. I was no longer a mouth to feed, a child who needed tending. In these times when we had little or no money, when father was out of work, when the future looked as bleak as that silent railroad spur out back, I could provide.

A quiet rain enveloped Upper Michigan over the night and by morning the air was misty and icy cold. My day at school passed as slowly as if I'd spent the day in church and on my way home, the heavy gray clouds seemed to descend in front of my eyes, hurrying the dusk into darkness.

Uncle Ev's pick-up truck was parked in front of the house and I hoped he'd brought me a cream soda. He had. He'd also brought along some beers, though from his speech he didn't seem to be needing anymore. He and my father were at the kitchen table. My mother, her back turned, was cooking something on the stove, maybe leftover rabbit.

"Ya little squirt, whadja learn in school today?"

I told Uncle Ev I couldn't remember and watched my father, hoping he, too, wasn't drunk.

"Ya gotta pay attention ya little squirt, or you'll end up in the mine like your daddy. You don't want that, do ya?"

I was silent.

"Ya can't speak either?"

"Ev, leave the boy alone," my father said.

Ev tilted the brown beer bottle and we couldn't help but watch his lips and neck suck the liquid down. Clutching the empty, he leaned across the table toward me. "Turn around young fella. See them groceries?"

I turned and saw two boxes of groceries next to the refrigerator.

"That's what learning a trade'll do for ya. Learn welding, learn about machines like I did, learn how to fix a watch, by God. Anything." He leaned back. "I been telling your father here, if he'd a learned a trade like me he wouldn't have the family bring him his food. But that's all right, that's what family's for." His head fell back further. "Right, Lee?"

"Ev," Father said, "you better go now."

"What for?"

"Because I'm telling you to."

"I bring you groceries and you tell me to go?"

"Take your groceries with you then."

"By God . . . " Uncle Ev shook his head sadly. He stood with difficulty. "Learn how to do *something*," he said to me. Then he looked at my father once more. "I'm goin . . . "

We all kept our places as Uncle Ev walked from the kitchen. We heard the front door open and close, heard his truck rev and start, then the low whine of the engine as he drove off.

School was in session only until noon the next day and I came home with nothing to do. The weather was the same, gray, wet, cold. Snow would have been better. My mother sat in the kitchen, writing a letter to her sister in Detroit. She told me my father was in the garage and not to disturb him.

For lack of anything much to do, I went for a hike along the spur, looking for game Lanny and I could later shoot. I also came up with an idea that would make us better marksmen. Lanny wasn't around, so by myself I hauled the tire back to our place. I got an old piece of rope from the basement and after struggling for a half hour, finally succeeded in hanging the tire from the metal clothes pole by the garage. I pushed it. The tire swung. Now we had a moving target!

I hurried down to Lanny's place to see if he'd come home yet. His father came to the door and I could smell the beer on his breath from three feet away. He wore a T-shirt and his trousers were open at the belt.

"Lanny here?"

"Naw, he ain't. Bet you want his bow, though."

The idea hadn't occurred to me but my face must have brightened.

"Yeah, that's what you want, okay." With that he went to the closet and got the bow for me. "He says you shot a rabbit, must be learnin you good how to shoot this thing."

"Yessir, thank you. Tell him to come on over when he gets back."

By the time I returned home and set things up, a combination of snow and rain was falling but I couldn't let that stand in my way. I was too excited. I saw myself firing arrow after arrow into the swinging target, getting so good that every day I would go out to the spur and bring home rabbits and squirrels and during season, pheasant and deer. I would be our family's source of meat, a hunter at only twelve years of age.

I gave the target a shove and marked off twenty paces. The bow felt solid and lively in my hands, the arrow light and ready to fly. I pulled back the string, my left arm straight but moving with the target, leading the tire slightly like a quarterback leads a receiver. Just as I let the arrow go, expecting it to thunk into the gunny sack center, my father emerged from the garage and in that instant the tire swung up, the arrow glanced off it, and my father was hit in the arm. Stunned, he staggered to his knees and looked at the arrow like he looked at my dead rabbit. I ran halfway to him, then back into the house screaming for my mother. I was bawling. "He's dying. He's dead."

My mother flew past me and I hurried with her. My father still had the arrow embedded in his shoulder, right through his light jacket and flannel shirt.

"Oh, my God," she said.

My father tried to get up but fell back to his knees. I was sure he'd topple over dead in the wet gravel any second. He'd lie there like that rabbit, watery eyes, blood oozing from his mouth. But he didn't die. He looked at us like he was trying to figure out who we were. Then his eyes burned and he set his mouth. He rose from the gravel, rose solidly to his feet, and told my mother to get him to the hospital fast. My mother, crying at this point, told me to get on the porch and think about what I'd done. Then they both went into the garage for the car and left.

What did I think about while they were gone? I have no idea. My view included the spur, the moist gray skies, the tiny icicles that began to form on the eaves directly above my head. The target still moved ever so slightly in the wind, rope twisting. Lanny's bow lay in the wet grass. For awhile I though Lanny would show up—what would I say?—but he never did. I waited on that back porch hoping my parents would never return and hoping harder that they'd drive up that minute.

They finally did. They drove past me for an instant into the garage and I waited some more. I heard their car doors close. They appeared together in the cold dusk. My father's arm was in a sling and though the light wasn't good, I could see that he still had that burning look in his eyes.

"I'm sorry, Dad." My face was so cold I could hardly get the muscles to move. I wanted to say more. But what?

He nodded at me.

"I'm really sorry," I said again.

"It's all right. It was an accident," he said. "You ready to work?"

"Yessir." I had no idea what he meant.

My mother then came up the porch too. She had a sack of hamburgers for us all and we went in to eat. It was one of the happiest dinners I've had to this day. Hamburgers and shoestring potatoes and cole slaw and cream soda and lots of exciting conversation. After eating we worked most of the night packing. The next afternoon a truck came for our things. Two days later we were living in a fine-looking town called Neenah, Wisconsin, my mother working at a bakery, my father overjoyed with his work at a paper mill, I attending sixth grade at Franklin Delano Roosevelt Elementary.

Carol Staats

LAPLAND BEAR SONG

Ancient beast,
Beast of magic,
Magic old one. Hai! Ai!
Hai! Ai! Karhu!
Karhu, magic one,
One who first begins,
Begins and lasts forever,
Forever known to all my people.

Bierdne, fierce one,
I will cleanse with juice of alder,
Cleanse from hand your magic blood,
Cleanse your blood from hand with alder,
And your sacred soul atone.

Ancient beast,
Beast of magic,
Magic old one. Hai! Ai!
Hai! Ai! Karhu!
Karhu, magic one,
One who first begins,
Begins and lasts forever,
Forever known to all my people.

WHERE SALT WIND RISES

I come from where the wind
sets all things dancing,
not cyclone dervish whirl,
nor channeled in the flow
of wind-honed stone forever.

I come from where sea wind
sets all things dancing,
and rises with the rising tide,
and ebbs, and sets
green birch kites flying.

My home is where salt wind
sets all things dancing,
and shadows, in the morning
fill with light, and sun,
bronze dancer,
pirouettes, and smiles.

THIS SEED OF YOUR OWN SOWING

Reap then the bitterroot, wild parsnip,
pottage nurtured by the salted
early rain of innocents
you left behind.

Roll now the bitterroot upon your tongue.
Taste now the tea of baneberry and say,
"How sweet! The sweetest!"
this, the crop of your own sowing.

Now reap the bitterroot and berry,
and know that earth cast up
the fruit of seed, and salt
will never grow sweet fruit.

Carol Staats

THE RITUALS

*A*NJA SALMINEN sat in the comfortable living room as she had so many times before. From the tile floor, the light reflected upward across the round-log walls, darkened, mellowed now by age and the smoke from the wood fire.

Between the narrow monastic windows were the wall hangings, tangible evidence of her friend's legacy. Here were Saani's ryijy weavings of the Lapland Saan, granite fault-block, under Northern Lights, and the golden wheel of the sun chariot whirring in the night-blue sky.

Like the summer tundra, the walls bloomed with color, form. Intricate tapestries depicted country scenes of weddings, harvests, dancers under Midnight Suns, a reindeer drive bright with Lapp folk dress, mosses, flowers, ferns, and birds, and berries.

Laughing, singing Lapland joiks, the little songs, weaving magic with her flying hands and mind, Saani had sat before the loom, now silent, still, in the pale light of early spring.

Now, momentarily silent, too, was the living room. The sudden stillness startled Anja out of her reverie. She looked around at Saani's family, all of the Heikkiläs.

There were Martta and her brother, Juhani, the middle children, so like their mother, short, wiry, swart. Then, their sister, Maija, the "baby," and Heikki, the elder in his clerical collar, both tall, lithe, fair like their father, Erkki, who sat rocking, plummeted into despondency by his wife's death.

Juhani's fist slammed the table. Stubbornly, sullenly, he persisted, picking up where the argument had ended. "It was her wish. That's all I know. None of your fancy theology—just her wish."

Heikki's collar seemed to be choking him. "She was my mother, too, and a simple Lutheran burial is what is necessary." His point was made in a harsh, insistent whisper. "A simple country woman, however dear and lovable...a simple Lutheran funeral...that's all."

Martta turned to Anja. "Look," she said, "my two brothers arguing over what to do with my mother's poor bones!" She looked at Heikki scornfully. "Why any question? What did she want done?"

They sat, silent again. Erkki rocking aimlessly, Maija wringing her hands on her lap.

Anja brushed her skirt, waiting.

Finally she said, "Your mother was my friend, like a sister to me. Your father has been as a brother, and you are all my friends. And I know you, Heikki, are used to taking charge in such matters as these, and I don't want to interfere. But, never would I want it on my shoulders."

She shivered and crossed herself. "Never would I ignore the wishes of the dead!"

"But, Anja, the wishes are nothing but superstition!" Heikki was adamant, and Anja could see her words had only reminded him of his position.

"Barbarism! Paganism!" he said. "*Lappalainen* ritual, indeed! This is the twentieth century, a modern world with ways that are modern, not a village of Lapp *kotas*, moving with the seasons, full of charms and superstitions. A sauna is a bath, nothing more. Next to Godliness as cleanliness is next to Godliness. Preparation for church, a bath, nothing else!"

Anja, though she was a Christian, gasped. Such blasphemy, to dismiss the sauna ritual so!

Quietly she said, "Perhaps for you. But your mother was born in a sauna. She gave birth to you all in the sauna. And she wanted to be prepared for the grave in a sauna. . .made ready by loving hands, not shipped off to the city like a carcass to be pumped full of wax and handled and molded by strangers. It has been the custom. Surely you can see that."

Juhani and Martta nodded.

Then Juhani, watching Heikki's expression, said, "Well, we'll talk more of that later. What of the plain pine box, and her own coverlet?"

Martta nodded again.

Heikki frowned. "And what would the villagers think," he asked, "if we, who could buy a bronze or copper casket lined with velvet and satin, buried our own mother in a pauper's box? Think, brother, think! The family's reputation!"

Juhani's lip curled. "Ah. . .now where is the simple country woman's simple funeral?" He laughed. "The fact is that the box must be ordered from Kuusisto if it is to be ready. He will build it, but we've got to decide."

Maija, still wringing her hands, went to fix coffee, a simple decision. The rest of the family sank back into their private thoughts, and Anja returned to hers.

What could she say? She would sing a lament in the Karelian tradition, a song of mourning, regardless of these decisions. She dwelled on the memory of Saani's face, ruddy and glowing after an afternoon of skiing; of her eyes when she spoke of a scene from her childhood, the spring drive of the reindeer to summer pasture; of her delight when the southern winds signaled the return of birds and gypsies. The wanderers of the earth she understood, even the seeds on the wind, and the flowing of streams. . . how strange that her learned son should call her a simple country woman!

Maija brought in the coffee and offered some to her father, who shook his head and rocked furiously. The others moved to the table, helped themselves, and ate of Maija's good rye bread.

"Heikki," Juhani said, "we must decide. You and Maija have your ideas, and Martta and I only want to respect Mother's wishes. Anja, good friend though she is, has no vote. So, it is up to Father. . . if we can get him to say."

Anja saw a brightening in Heikki's face, a certainty that his predictable, scholarly father would side with him and Maija, and all this nonsense would be over. He took Erkki's hand, which had been clutching a beloved book, in his.

Erkki drew it back and stroked the embossed binding. Although he scarcely seemed to know what it was, and hadn't read a word, it yet anchored him somehow to reality.

Heikki spoke softly, slowly, explaining everything patiently, as if to a child. He tried to look in his father's eyes, but could not bear to see the pain. He focused on the hands and book, and spoke on.

"Then, what do you say, Father? What is it to be?"

Erkki's glance darted right and left like a wounded ferret. "To be? What. . .what?" As though he had heard nothing. Then, looking at Heikki as if he were a stranger, his voice echoed heavily. "How should I know what to do? Leave me alone." He shrugged. "Do what you will. . .anything." His head drooped and he started rocking again. He suddenly shook his head, his grey hair falling across his glasses. "No. . .no! Do what she said. Everything. . .just as she wanted."

"But the family, think of the family. . ." Heikki started.

"Leave me alone! She's gone. . .left. . .now leave me alone."

Martta put her arm across Heikki's shoulder. "Let him rest. It is decided. We will only honor her wishes and have done with it all."

"All right, then," Juhani said finishing his coffee. "I'll talk to Kuusisto. He'll hurry to please us."

"I'll stop by the *kuppari's*, if you like," Anja said.

"*Kuppari?*" Heikki questioned.

"For the *Lappalainen* ritual," Martta answered.

"Oh..." He seemed lost in thought.

"What about Pekka?" Maija asked.

"Pekka?" Heikki echoed. "The dog?"

"She wanted the dog at the service," Juhani said.

"The dog?" Heikki couldn't believe he'd heard it. Anger rose in him. "Then you, Juhani, should lead the cow, and Martta you take the dog, and Maija can carry a chicken under each arm. She loved them, too, you know. Martta, you take the dog, and your husband can lead the pig, with a ribbon on, a fancy one around his neck. And Anja can bring her goats, then all we need is a horse and a couple of lambs. And a judge from the country fair!" His laugh was bitter.

"Or maybe we should hire the inn and a band. Everyone can get drunk and like the Poles, or Czechs, or some Slavs, we can all dance with the corpse!" He laughed at their expressions, and shrugged. "Why not? If it is to be a farce, make it a good one. . .complete." He subsided into a cold silence.

"I'll go to Kuusisto's," Juhani said, finally, getting up for his jacket and cap.

"Wait, wait," Martta said. "Let's check and see that everything is covered, so we don't waste trips."

To Anja she said, "See the *kuppari*, then, and we'll want the lament. You should come tonight with the women. Juhani can see Kuusisto, and I'll go tell the old aunt, in case she wants to come. And she knows the others. . .Pietists, Orthodox, those who knew Mother." She looked at her list.

"Pietists? Orthodox? And what else?" Heikki asked, his eyes blazing.

"Your mother was a friend to them all," Anja said. "And she wanted them to know that she wanted them to come, if they liked."

"And why not the people at the asylum? Let them all come. The whole world. . .beggars, crazies. . .animals. . .kings!" Heikki's eyes rolled behind his lids. He turned away and his steps were like a child's marching, playing soldier, his words garbled.

Anja listened closely. "Dear Heavens! He's speaking in tongues! Heaven help us!"

Maija screeched and sank into her chair, while Martta and Juhani exchanged glances. Heikki's head was jerking, and he marched in place, his feet making erratic circles before they stomped on the floor.

"Not tongues," Juhani said, helping Heikki to the couch. "It is only a fit. He has them sometimes when he gets too excited." He loosened Heikki's collar. "Didn't Mother tell you?" he asked Anja, who shook her head.

On the couch, Heikki's voice stopped sounding. The spasms stopped and he lay quite still.

"Is he all right?" Maija asked.

"Juhani checked his brother's breathing and nodded. "He'll come to in a minute or so. He's all right."

In a few minutes, Heikki sat up. He looked at Juhani, the mute question in his eyes. Juhani nodded and Keikki's neck flushed red. He rubbed his face and arms, massaged his knees, then without a word he rose and put on his overcoat. His fingers fumbled with the buttons and, in the end, he let it hang open. He nodded to them all, and put on his Homburg.

To Martta he said, "I'll prepare the regular service."

"But you'll come tonight, won't you?" she asked.

He shook his head. "Tomorrow, with the family." They barely heard the great back door close.

"Maija, you keep an eye on Father, and start the cooking for the wake. I'll be right back, as soon as I see Old Auntie." Martta pulled on her sweater and left with Anja and Juhani.

Anja sat on a stool in the dark corner of the sauna. The *kuppari*, midwife, was there also, head in hands, deep in meditation or prayer. Only the small bulb in the dressing room shone. The wooden buckets were clean, turned upside down until they were needed. The whisks of cedar stood in the corner, and the old wine barrels, filled with clear spring water were on their rack. The sauna room was redolent with the evergreen fragrance, a faint wine smell from the barrels, and a wisp of smoke from the birch fire which heated the stones on the fireplace.

On the high bench, nearest the low ceiling lay Saani's body. How many times they had taken a sauna, Anja thought, each time enjoying the heat, the burning birches lending the heat of the summer's sun to the coldest winter; the white granite rocks, stones of the earth heated by birch, and the steam bursting in great puffs off the stone, the clear spring water cleansing, purifying. A mortification of the body, leaving the mind clear, the soul free.

Then a brisk slapping with the whisks to hurry the blood racing beneath the skin, hastening the sweat streaming from every pore, carrying off the poisons, the residues, accumulated debris of daily life.

And often they had spoken of the sense of belonging, of the sense of the sauna ritual. Many times the women went together, sometimes women of one family and sometimes of many. There, these people known usually by only their faces and hands, were their naked selves, unadorned, enjoying the same ritual. They were the generations, ailing, ancient, expecting. The sagging breasts and buttocks, the beauty and the flaws, the strength and weakness of the human body all made plain. The strange and natural oneness in all its ages and variety, the perishable flesh, house of the soul.

And Saani, born in a sauna, was made ready for the grave. It took but a few minutes for the midwife to cleanse the body. At each side of the neck, she made a small cross with her straight razor, placed the cow horn over it, and made the mark of the sun's wheel. On each wrist, inside, she did the same. On each foot. And then over the heart. She invoked the spirits of the sun, the moon, the stars, the sky, the wind, the earth and all upon it, all good things upon it, and the waters of the seas and great oceans, lakes and rivers, streams and spring.

Then, with linen sweet with cardamom and cedar, they wrapped her. Anja wept, wondering at the dignity.

And she vowed to sing as sweetly, full of heart, as sadly, as she had at her own mother's grave. "My friend, how I will sing! And then I'll ask you on your journey to give greetings to Our Father, and finally, to speak our love to all our own beloved dead!"

Sara Johnson

MIXING

Poised on the brink of memory, it is
so hard to tell at thirty, the feeling
of being full and empty precisely
in the same moment. Childlessness and
childhood bisecting each other in a
round fat scary respectable number.

Two perfect syllables that rise and fall,
The sound of someone breathing in their sleep.

Thirty is the lamprey that attached
itself to your worn out orphan doorway,
the mold that lives on memory, a tear
under your sleeve you didn't care to mend.
Poised on the brink of desire it is
so hard to tell, at thirty there is no truth.

TAPPIO (DEFEAT)

Who is it that comes to me
bruised, broken,
looking like death warmed over
as I pace through the
halls and rooms of this
burning house?
He has a bandaged head
and walks among us
with a crutch
while we frantically search
for car keys,
windows,
anything to get out.
Who is it that goes
quiet between us
day and night
till I dream of wolves

ripping off our limbs
And he is gone,
and cannot help by
looking for thread to
stitch up this catastrophe
of houses
of holy water
where we are required
to cleanse our dead.

PRAYER FOR A HERMIT

Do you hear me?
I am desperate.
You surround yourself with
black spruce, winter darkness,
dead rams and beer
while I thrash through Colorado
in spastic wonder.

I see cows,
lean pastures, drift fences,
ranches going to rot.

The broad basins and
thin air begin to
get to me.
we stop the car at
the top of a pass,
In a querulous wind
under furious skies,
I pull down my pants
and take a piss
on one of the highest spots
in America.

Every white pine and blue spruce
talks.
They spew the atmosphere

with a torrent of words
above my numb head.
Short of breath
matter collides,
I am desperate,
Do you hear me?

Roberta Christine Kulma

THE IMMIGRANT'S GRANDCHILD REMEMBERS

G ROWING UP in the 1940s in the village of Fairport Harbor in Northeast Ohio was idyllic in many ways. Fairport had lush green tree-lined streets, neat well-maintained houses, a sense of community, and the relative safety and security of life where houses were rarely locked and crime nonexistent.

Fairport was called "Finn Town," although nearly half of the population were Hungarian, Slovak, and Slovenian immigrants with a smaller percentage of Irish and Italian families. These latter groups comprised the Catholic half as opposed to us Lutherans. Also living in this Lake Erie waterfront town were families who migrated from the Appalachian Mountain area and were known as "hillbillies."

My parents' experience was somewhat different from my own. My mother recalled that Finnish women were stereotyped as highly prized domestics who couldn't accomplish much more in life. Finns were scrupulously clean. They even tore the house inside out each spring. My job was to wash the "good" dishes, polish the silver, and replace them in the cupboard only to take them out for Thanksgiving and re-wash and polish all over again. Many of my American contemporaries find it incredible that we annually washed all the walls, ceilings, re-moved all carpeting or rugs, and followed similar procedures with the basements, garages, and attics.

These stereotypes extended to dating practices, too. My uncle, for instance, was dating an "American" girl whose father forbade her from seeing a "foreigner." There was even mention of his being thrown out of her house, literally or figuratively, I am not sure.

I vividly recall my mother recoiling whenever an "American" re-minded her that Finland was the only country to repay its war debt to the United States. She felt that the conciliatory tone which accompanied this "compliment" only masked intolerance or prejudice.

Despite the adjustments my parents had to make, my mother was ex-tremely proud of being a Finn and often used the expression, "I have the map of Finland on my face." Her name was Aini, and during adolescence she probably acquiesced to the American pronunciation and adopted "Ina." But that didn't last too long. Following her years at Suomi College, she reaffirmed Aini as her name and corrected anyone who insisted upon Ina. My father opted for George during his school years, but he was always Yrjö to my grandparents. I recall my father's periodic statement, "We're American now," and I regret never talking to him about his feelings on assimilation. There was, I think, a common need to blend in, not to stand out, not to feel different. Despite "being American now," my parents were active in a Finnish singing group who performed the *kansallis* (patriotic) songs of the old country, always ending their performance with "Finlandia." I grew up hearing the folk music which is still deeply rooted in my soul.

Because of the Russian invasion of Finland in 1939, and the phobia about being identified with anything related to Communism, the color red was forbidden in clothing and in the home. My mother, who worked for a chemical research firm which had government contracts, was investigated periodically by the FBI. These agents would come to town and question the pastor about her church attendance, and would talk to people in the community and at her work about her loyalty. She believed their invasion of her privacy was due to her being Finnish, and she greatly resented these inquiries. It was the 1950s, and the era of McCarthyism, and she was, in a lesser way than some, a victim of this mass hysteria. As a result of these investigations my parents overreacted to anything or any color which might hint of Russian Communism or challenge their loyalty to the United States. My father once burned a pair of my shorts which were fire engine red. He loved the music of the Russian classical composers but strongly objected to my recording of the Red Army chorus singing Russian folk songs. To this day I never wear bright red, and the color doesn't appear anywhere in my home.

I cannot recall any forms of overt discrimination as a child. Ethnic slurs within our community were not absent, however. Finns were stereotyped as stupid partly due to the accent where the "th" word sounds became "duh, dem, dat." Local humor referred to suicides as "the Helsinki rope trick," and there were multiple references to the problems related to alcohol. During adolescence the teenagers from the next city called us "Fish Eater," "Dumb Finn," but I don't recall ever feeling hurt or defensive because of these taunts. I think we merely dismissed them as unimportant and unworthy of reaction. Our church sponsored a basketball team, and it was common to see our high school athletes wearing "Suomi" jackets as well as the local school colors. In my mother's day, her high school teams were entirely Finnish. It was a favorite story that by calling out plays in Finnish they outwitted their American opponents.

In Fairport, the two primary cultural groups (Finnish and Hungarian) peacefully coexisted. But there were large differences between them. The Finns thought the Hungarians were too gregarious because they enjoyed parties and dancing; their houses (primarily in nearby Cleveland) were painted green and red, which was considered loud and in poor taste; they expected their children to quit school and work rather than acquire an education. I don't know what they said about us, our houses, our lack of parties or dancing, and the sedate Finnish wedding receptions held in the church basement with fruit punch, petit-fours, and canapes, but we Finn kids couldn't wait to crash the Hungarian receptions where they served real food and alcohol, and danced on far into the night. They definitely had more fun.

Probably the first thing a Finn kid learns is not to talk back, especially to your father whose word is law. My father's voice was often heard in the higher decibel range. He was obviously someone to be deferred to, but it was really my mother who ran things. She would eventually win out whether the issue was a decision or a disagreement. Given this initial rule, the Finnish child was given a strict code of respect for parents and grandparents. This respect carried over to other people in general. You learned how to act in public, you learned how to be well-mannered, and rudeness to anyone anywhere was not tolerated. If necessary, physical punishment was used to keep the child in line.

Money, politics, and religion were taboo topics relegated to a status of nondiscourse. It was impolite to ask anyone about his or her business affairs. You could never ask an uncle, for instance, how much his new car cost. I was told to never pry, or put my nose where it didn't belong. You never asked anyone how much money they had or earned, how old they were, what religion they practiced, or how they voted in the last election.

The child quickly learned not to ask too many questions about things that weren't his or her business. I never knew my parents' income, never knew how much they paid for household items, how much they gave to the church, or how much insurance they had. When overhearing any discussion concerning money, I was told to forget what I heard and never repeat it. My father was fond of saying, "That (information) stays in this house." They were hardpressed to keep things from me, because I understood Finnish and they couldn't hide behind their primary language. They never knew where my comprehension ended, and I often translated their private conversations into English. It gave me wonderful feelings of power.

Finnish families were also known to keep secrets and to never talk about anything unpleasant from the past. Once the skeletons were hanging in the closets, the doors were locked and the keys thrown away. If a member of the family acted in an unacceptable manner, his or her name disappeared from conversation. If, by chance, this individual was discussed, the "incident" was ignored. There were so many things "we just didn't talk about," like the cousin in Chicago who ran off leaving his wife and five children. I was middle-aged before I knew my grandmother had several children who died in infancy. She would never have shared such personal information. And no one ever talked about it or mentioned the graves on Memorial Day.

Major and minor crises were repressed and swept under the carpet. In my extended families, the only emotions ever witnessed were joy/happiness and grief/mourning. We were never an expressive group—even the emotions of joy or grief were controlled. You would seldom see a Finnish male dancing center stage during a wedding reception, or a Finnish mother shrieking with pain over the loss of a child. We keep much to ourselves, perhaps too much.

Another valuable lesson learned was the philosophy of pragmatism. "You should only buy what you need" and "You only get what you pay for," were my father's two favorite pronouncements on the art of managing money. I probably heard these words of wisdom a million times, and I can't argue the worth of repeating them. He watched his accounts like a hawk, read the *Wall Street Journal* daily, thought Sylvia Porter was a genius, and when buying a new car did months of research before making a decision. And pity the car dealer who had to deal with him—my mother later refused to go along because his wheeling and dealing embarrassed her. Some people see this behavior as cheap or frugal, but he understood the system and played his cards with great care and foresight. I don't think the Finns are great risk-takers or gamblers, but they are careful where they put their money.

Growing up in Fairport Harbor had its downside. As a teenager, I felt I had to walk around town on eggshells. You could never be a target for gossip and had to live an exemplary life. The phrase, "What will the neighbors think," became an obsession with my parents. Disgrace of any nature could not be tolerated. My father would come home with stories of someone (never identified) who "mentioned" to him that I was seen in a place with so and so. There was rarely any point to these "stories," but they did lend to creating a certain amount of paranoia that the whole town was watching everything you did. This feeling also generated an amount of normal rebellion and even strife between Father and me. It may have influenced my decision to live my adult life in metropolitan areas where the "neighbors" hardly know me. Looking at it from that perspective, I would have to regard the "fishbowl" childhood experience as being positive in getting me out into the world.

We grew up with multicultural events celebrated on the Fourth of July. The Finn kids paraded in their costumes, as did the other groups. We danced the native folk dances and even danced in the other camp. I think I could still do a modified Hungarian czardas. Intermarriage between the groups, much to the chagrin of the grandparents, spawned a new breed of children who were labeled "Finngarians." These bicultural (actually tricultural) children lost a part of both heritages to some degree, but gained bits and pieces of each others'.

Language was a dominant binding force for the Finnish-American child. The children of my generation who spoke Finnish with their parents probably felt a deeper sense of Finnish identity. We were also able to communicate with grandparents who either spoke no English or used it sparingly. We were sent to *kesäkoulu* (summer school) to learn Finnish from Suomi College seminarians. I used the language fluently as a child, but rebelled during my school years and refused to speak it at all. Family members spoke Finnish to me and I answered in English. That didn't always work, as *Mumma* (grandmother) spoke no English. Despite my rebelliousness, my Finnish identity was foremost, and I don't think any of us ever really thought of ourselves as American first — we were just Finnish. In Fairport a child probably suffered if he didn't have another cultural identity. I asked a college sorority sister what she was. She looked at me blankly and said she didn't know but assumed she must be Scotch-Irish. I replied in all sincerity that I felt sorry for her. Obviously I didn't comprehend an American identity as being adequate, one had to be something else.

The Church, which played a vital role within the entire community, was another binding force. Both the Lutherans and Catholics preached to their young the evils and pitfalls of the other. We were told marriage to a Catholic would require all children to be signed over to the Pope and Catholic Church. In turn the St. Anthony nuns warned against dating "those Finn kids," and probably threatened possible excommunication and untold years in purgatory. Perhaps if someone had taught a course of the psychology of a taboo, fewer intermarriages would have occurred.

The "Suomi" Church (the name was later changed, much to my disappointment) was the center of both social and religious life. The children's choirs sang in English and Finnish, family dinners were sponsored by the women's group, the teenagers took part in Luther League and went to Camp Luther in the summer, and the boys played on church teams.

Next door to the church was Sippola's Public Sauna where we went to sauna parties. Many people loved the sauna so much that they built them in their basements or adjacent to their homes. I will never forget my grandmother sitting on the top rung telling me to pour more water on the stones, while I held my head over a bucket of water in order to breathe.

By the time I approached my mid-twenties, I finally made it to the Old Country for the first time, the only grandchild in my family to get there. I traveled alone believing my bits and pieces of Finnish would get me where I wanted to go. Amazingly the words came back, though my vocabulary was vintage 1880 and probably peasant in origin. I loved Helsinki and spent days going up and down each street, taking the street cars to the ends of their lines, and talking to students who gathered near the train station. I met young women who invited me to meet their parents and even attended a wedding outside of the city in an old country church. It amazed me that everyone looked like my father, an uncle, a cousin, a neighbor in Fairport—I was really among my own people and all these strangers in the street were related to me. It was as if I had returned to Fairport Harbor, now located across the ocean.

I took the train to Tampere to see an old friend from New York City, and then rented a car to drive to the family home sites in Jalasjärvi, Seinä-joki, and Soini to meet the many members of my two families. The Tör-mäs in Seinäjoki wouldn't let their cousin stay in the local boarding house, so I had to check out and move in with the "family." I drove to Mantila to meet the many Väiniönkulmas, then on to Soini to my mother's relatives. The Haavisto family welcomed me warmly. I was home and these were my people. Liisa *Täti* (aunt) and I sat in her kitchen one evening drinking her apple wine and singing *kansallis* songs; my meager Finnish and knowledge of the music surprised my family. I was, after all, a third generation American Finn. Since that first trip, I have been in Finland several times and have formed close relationships with cousins there. One night in 1984 as we cousins sat in a Seinäjoki *ravin-tola* (restaurant), I remarked, "Here we are, the three grandchildren (Raimo, Rainer, Roberta) of three Väiniönkulma brothers, Isaac, Arvi, and Thomas. I wonder if our Pappas are up there watching us."

Marcelle Doby-Williams

SOUL FOOD

Thin boned
fair daughter of the north
as a child
I was slight.

My grandmother fed me Rosettes:
deep fried batter butterflies
    and flowers
sprinkled with white powdered sugar
to make my blood sparkle
    and bloom flesh.

Later I grew plump
skin stretching like succulent cooked chicken.
Now I search through the dough
of over-risen flesh
looking for those thin bones
searching for my marrow.

RENEGADE BLOSSOMS

Fresh cut along the freeway
Fragrance rising high inside the nostrils
Prairie grasses falling under the blade
thatch after thatch falling
sleepy bodies rolling
fields growing toward release
like aroused flesh
finding it in a single "AHHH"
fast swish of the sickle

An aftermath of strewn hay
bleeding the dew green smell
up, up, into the air
where I take it in
in deep

deep into my lungs
and on
on to the blood
where it rushes through my heart.

INFIDELITY

Moonlight puddled on my bed,
Poured over my flesh like buttermilk.
After many nights of being alone
I took the moon for my lover.
She loved every inch of me,
Turned me into silver globes
That rolled into the night
Glancing off the edges of things
With blue-white laughter.

In the first splinter of dawn
I opened my eyes.
The stars were fading,
Drops of milk on a grey felt sky.
Caught in my hair, a cricket,
Tired finally, of making his tiny legs sing,
But humming a last faint melody
A parting love song learned from the moon.

Marcelle Doby-Williams

THE GIFT

*T*HIS STORY is not about my childhood, although much of it takes place during that time. I had a mother and father, no siblings, and all the other standard kin; but this story is about something else; the real thread is between her and me. It is about my aunt and how she tried her best to give me something she believed that I needed very badly. It is also about persons who live and die and are not really noticed properly, and about the debt we all owe to such persons in our lives. It is about family secrets that should never be told but are too important not to be.

And I think that basically we are much the same: you and I, the rest of the people in the world. That is why we must speak to each other as truthfully as possible, so we will not be lonely. This may also turn out to be the moral of my story, but it is too soon to tell.

I hold in my hand two photographs. One is a photograph I have not seen in many years, the other new to me — found at the bottom of a shoe box full of old family items. These are important, and in a way they tell the whole thing. Yet, for all the absolute information they give you about the people in them, the shape of their flesh, how the bones direct muscle, the eyes that gaze back at you with every intention of carrying on with their lives despite what you may have understood about them at first glance; yet for all this, you must know more, and that is what I am about to tell you. I see the familiar picture of my Aunt Margie with my grandfather standing behind her. Her hands are apologizing for her imperfect gift to those who seek ideal proportions. Her face is startled, vulnerable to what the camera is searching out: the relationship to the man standing behind her. He stands grimly, but confidently behind her. He knows what is his. The deep shadows are cast from the walls they live in, from their lives.

The stuff of life, my aunt's life, was made up of mundane things. She was born in Superior, Wisconsin, in 1916, the second child and only girl in my father's family. My father was the oldest. Two more boys were born after her. The family was poor and they lived on the wrong side of the tracks in a big way — the railroad yards in Superior were the largest in the world for many years. The earliest memories I have of my grandmother's house include the forlorn locomotive whistles and the hollow thud of boxcars switching tracks. The name of the area was Billings Park, and it was a Scandinavian/Polish ghetto.

The cement of Billings Park was a strange shade of gray – the usual gypsum color but altered by a thin veneer of black coal dust. Along the curbs and in the many cracks grew uncut grass and weeds, homes for grasshoppers singing noisily in the summer sun. Together they created a curious blend of city and meadow. In the winter the snow would drift as high as six feet and had to be laboriously shoveled to make walkways. Not far away Lake Superior allowed the St. Louis River to cut inland with a series of fjord-like inlets that were beautiful throughout the four seasons. On these cedar banks, families came to picnic on Sundays; young boys explored the magnificent pine woods and wildlife lurked shyly in the shadows, waiting patiently for the noisy humans to go back to their workday homes to toil for another week. And toil they did, for this was the first generation of immigrants fleeing from forced conscription and bread laced with sawdust. Though often confused by the emptiness of this New Land, they were quick to draw to them what trappings of civilization they could and re-created what comforts they remembered from the countries left behind. With hard set jaws and determined hearts, their feet marched straight ahead through the days, the years, toward the dawn of a better day for their children. And in this great army of life it was inevitable that some lives and dreams would fall by the way.

My grandfather was a miner in Colorado and then in Montana. After my father was born, they moved to Superior where grandfather got a job at the Stott Briquette Plant, and he worked there the rest of his life. My grandmother raised the family. Her father had come from Cornwall, England, to be a baker in Victor, Colorado. Grandmother completed high school, knew something about music, and taught her children to read and to make change before they were old enough to attend school. I suspect she had secret ambitions toward culture of sorts but little chance to pursue them in the Billings Park of 1915. By the time I arrived on the scene, she had become a permanently large woman. Her black hair, streaked with grey, was worn in two long braids wound round and round her head. When she undid them, her hair came cascading down to her knees and I thought it was the most beautiful, the most wondrous thing about her, how in a few seconds she could be transformed from my Grandma to an almost magical being (whose real name was Sarah) with such magnificent hair!

Of the family, my father was settled down with our small family, 600 miles away in Michigan. Being a professor, he was able to take summers off and bring me, the only grandchild, back to Wisconsin for the summer. My Aunt Margie was still living at home, as was the youngest son, my Uncle Ray. The other brother, the in-between one, was an alcoholic and was prone to turn up only when he needed money. I barely remember him, and he died of TB in 1946 in Walla Walla, Washington.

Although my grandfather had light skin, and by the time I knew him, sparse hair, I only remember him as dark and always foreboding. When he was younger, my aunt told me he used to go to Finnish dances on Saturday nights — perhaps he would smile there. My grandmother did not go with him for reasons unclear. Either she was not invited, or perhaps she did not feel comfortable in the company of women who spoke mainly Finnish and belonged to a tight kinship system.

The other picture is the namesake picture. I never saw it until my Uncle Ray died a couple years after my aunt. She never showed it to me or mentioned her name, though it was "Marcelle," the same as mine. This "first Marcelle" was the only, and doted-on, child of my grandfather's only sister. This was the part of his family that stayed in Houghton, Michigan, or the "Copper Country," as it is locally known. What the inspiration for that particular name was will forever remain a mystery. It is an unusual name, not the more common Marcella of Raggedy Ann and Andy fame, but definitely the feminine form of the French Marcel. But there she is, the first Marcelle, and holding a bisqued china doll, dressed in satin as she is. She looks about six years old, and she could not be any older for she died at age seven. Presumably this must have been a terrible tragedy for the family. Several years later Harry O. Dobie would name his first and only daughter after his sister's dead child. Yet my Aunt Margie was always "Margie" in the family, although she designed stationery and book plates for herself that bore the name "Marcelle" on them. Her friends called her Marcelle too. A generation later, I was the next Marcelle and afterwards heard reference to "Big Marcelle" and "Little Marcelle." Yet, in the family, Aunt Margie was Aunt Margie and I became "Marge" to my father. But that picture and the story with it was a surprise to me, and it started me thinking and remembering.

Of my aunt's childhood, I have only her accounts and some brief comments from my father. I can never remember my grandmother giving any of those childhood anecdotes about her daughter although she told stories of all the boys. Poverty was freely acknowledged, and the most often quoted fact by my aunt was that she never even had a doll. And my father began buying milk for himself as soon as he got a paper route. Yet my aunt's lack of a doll seemed to go deeper, as though she suspected that it might have been possible to have gotten a doll for her from somewhere, that it was more an insensitivity to her. In her later years she lamented the fact that no one took any pictures of her as a child. It is true; I found only one. She said nobody curled her hair, and it is true that in the one picture that I found, she stands chubby and somber, looking out from under straight bobbed hair.

Is it possible that the picture of that first Marcelle, precious but lost, sat on some shelf for her to contemplate? Carefully dressed, her hair in ringlets and holding a truly elegant china doll, Marcelle was the ideal little girl. What sort of responsibility might that have been to the second Marcelle? Was she to be a substitute? Had she failed at this since she did not have the things the child in the picture had? Still, the second Marcelle was alive and no one was grieving her.

From conversations I had with my aunt when we were both older, it became clear that she was not the valued member in the family. That fell to the oldest boy, my father, and his life held a special hope and fascination for my grandmother. Though, in retrospect, I can see how oppressive it was to him, it is also obvious that my aunt suffered as much from lack of this attention. Her lot was the same as her mother's: she was there to serve in whatever capacity she might be needed. Her claim to fame in the family was the fudge she made when they were all teenagers.

Out of this circle of want came an opulence in living. Slowly, but surely, she set about to rectify her situation. Everything she touched began to shine. She worked as a public stenographer in an office where she owned her own mimeograph equipment. Her letters were written on stationery embroidered with printed designs. New appliances appeared in my grandmother's kitchen. Treats from the Fanny Farmer store showed up regularly, and one day there was a car parked in the alley behind the house.

But the most singular activity in which my aunt involved herself was her doll collection. It numbered well over 500 and each doll was something special. She had bisque dolls with movable eyes, china dolls with painted faces, old paper mache dolls and apple-head dolls. They were all sizes; one bisque doll was almost three feet high and had bisque feet and arms as well. This doll had a magnificent wig and was dressed in purple with leather shoes and silk stockings. One doll was dressed like me, with a wig made out of my hair. Her outfit was blue velvet and she wore roller skates. There was a china baby doll only two inches tall with arms and legs that moved. She had sets of "story book" dolls, contemporary to the early 1950s, and a friend of hers crocheted tiny "Southern Bell" outfits for them. Some of these dolls were very valuable and some were not at all, only gathering wealth in my aunt's eyes.

I must comment on her aesthetics because she maintained them to the end. She liked what she liked for her own reasons. If something caught her eye, it had to be gotten. If it was fifteen cents at Goodwill, so be it. If it was fifty dollars in a department store window, she managed it eventually. Her first wax doll was a display piece in a jewelry store window. In fact, it was not a whole doll but the upper half of the figure of an angel. This torso was surrounded by pleated gold foil and held two paper wings made iridescent with pearled glitter. The angel's hair was spun glass and the whole thing was about eighteen inches in diameter. Although it was not for sale, she had to have it. I learned later that it cost thirty-five dollars after she had finally wheedled it out of the store manager. That was a pretty penny in the early 1950s. Sometimes she would stumble upon something very valuable. Yet this was always secondary to whether or not she liked it. She did not disdain monetary worth, but most of the things she bought were for herself, not to resell or hoard for wealth.

Her other passion was Christmas. She planned decorations for months! She bought them, discovered them, constructed them, yearned for them. A common description for her about something she had just found was, "It's kind of 'Christmasy' don't you think?"

This applied to blown glass deer with little glittering antlers, painted wooden circus figures, or plastic Cinderella coaches. She would start setting things out about the first of December. As the holidays grew nearer, she would enlist the help of those around her to string wire across the ceiling so that she could hang snow flakes and stars from wall to wall. She lit up everything she could with the tiny lights that have become popular today, but the first time that I ever saw them was in my aunt's living room. A white plastic church played Adeste Fidelis as the stained glass windows glowed from inside. Deer stood on shelves among choir boys and angels. A double window bloomed with hand-made, oversized Christmas balls filigreed from starched string dried over balloons that were then broken to leave a sphere a foot in diameter. These were embroidered with lights, glitter and sequins, sometimes with birds and angels. Others were large styrofoam balls embellished with beaded designs cut from old dresses and filled out with more sequins and beads. Beneath these balls sat her jewel trees, styrofoam cones studded with old earrings, necklaces and bracelets, and quite Victorian in their lavishness. She never started taking anything down until February.

Glittering sentinels of Christmases gone by with nothing. Dolls upon dolls where there had been none before. The process of her life continued steadily, with few surprises, from the beginning in Billings Park, but more and more it grew richer in texture as she layered it with velvets and gold tinsel.

Although she lived in the shadow of her brothers, she did not lack attention from her father. He allowed her out at night only to go roller skating at the public roller rink just on the other side of the railroad viaduct. If she were late coming home, he would rail at her, accusing her of flirtations and worse. Eventually he would reverse his attack and begin to hug and fondle her. It was only many years later that she spoke of this. Even then it still bewildered her. "I couldn't understand it," she said. "Ma was upstairs, always. She must have known what was going on but she never said a word. Of course he never went overboard, but he may as well have, the way I felt."

It was only after my grandfather died in 1947, when my aunt was thirty-two, that she met her first "boyfriend." She went with him for a number of years before they were married. From the first, however, he was a member of the family outings that always occurred when we summered and spent Christmas "up North." When she was forty she had her only child, a son. Less than two years later my grandmother died and my aunt became the family caretaker. All through those years her closets bulged and her front porch filled with wonderful brick-a-brack. She had antique candy jars and purple parasols, blue willow china and a sterling silver phone jacket that sported a stranger's monogram. A "side room," as she called it, held her mimeograph equipment where she did small jobs for local stores. She had her own income this way. Later, when she lost her business and Insty Print came along, she sold off some of her dolls for extra money.

She was never well off, and her husband worked hard, but for mediocre pay, so that the little extra she could lay her hands on allowed her to pursue her dolls and decorations and have lunch out regularly with her youngest brother. In fact, the two of them spent many mornings prowling the secondhand stores and then taking lunch at a modest but clean "greasy spoon" near the north end of town. From the time she was forty, my aunt had diabetes and used her own money to buy her insulin. Later she began using vitamins, and she told me many times that she bought these with her own money.

Her husband had also grown up in the poorest of circumstances. Coming from The Barrens, an area outside Superior which got its name from being burned over by a great forest fire in the thirties, he was raised on venison and blueberries. Unlike my aunt, however, he grew used to sparseness in life and over the years began to quietly retreat from the overabundance of things accumulating from my aunt's projects. My aunt pointed out that he bought a new car every two years even if he had to remortgage his house, but he absolutely would not acknowledge any connection between the glint of a new chrome bumper and the silver stars twinkling on his living room ceiling. His assessment of anything that embellished the bare necessities of life was that they were frivolous and, at best, not to be taken seriously. This included insulin as well as plastic coaches. My uncle may turn out to be a villain in this piece, but, in truth, his only fault was that he had to work hard for every penny he earned and that he used this as a measure of value for everything else in his life.

My part in the story remained much the same until my aunt died. My aunt was one of my favorite playmates. Summer meant going to a small lake outside of Superior where we had a cabin. Next to ours was the cabin my grandfather built, and every weekend I would race over there at the sound of an approaching car on the gravel road. I loved it! My grandmother, Sarah, made me treats. My Uncle Ray told me stories and took me for endless walks, and my Aunt Margie surprised me with all the luxuries deemed necessary for a little girl. I still have the remnant of a Japanese paper umbrella and a kimono from that time. And how we all loved to play cards: canasta, casino, Hollywood rummy for a dime a hand. My grandfather nursed his property in the shadows and spent more time working on the boat than fishing in the boat. He silently ate the meals my grandmother cooked. No cabin fare here but solid repasts of pot roast with mashed potatoes and home baked bread. Though I laughed and chattered through those meals, my uncle and aunt teasing me, my grandmother's soft contentedness, never a smile crossed the old man's face.

When I was four years old, my grandfather took me swimming. I was crazy for the water, and he rowed me across the small lake, almost to the other side. It was hot in the boat, and he said I could go in without my clothes since I did not have a suit. The beach was sandy, and small green reeds stood up through the sparkling water. Birches and pines lined the shore, and "our" two cabins looked like doll houses on the opposite side of the lake. He sat in the boat, and the waves lapped around the oars as they rested in the water. I leaped and danced in the shallows and once looked up to see him looking at me intently, but he said nothing. Finally it was time to go. When we returned, I told my aunt and grandmother where we had gone and that I had gone swimming. Only now, years later, can I describe their reaction with any understanding. Both were chagrined, and afraid. Each was afraid alone, and neither acknowledged the other's concern. I was never alone with him again.

As I grew up, my aunt was always there with a treat, or an interesting bauble. Often I was content to admire what she had. At other times I intensely wanted what she had. When I really wanted something, it usually played into my own current interests. When I played "dress up," she gave me incredible old gowns. When I was a witch on Halloween, I wore a floor-length black taffeta dress with long sleeves and a billowing skirt. When I was interested in Lucretia Borgia, she gave me an elaborate ring. When I graduated from high school, she gave me the typewriter I took to college and after I was married, I noticed the vases and tea cups she had.

Through all this she was matter-of-fact. Generally her treasures came from the secondhand shop, and she was proud of her bargains. She did not indulge in fanciful origins for these items for she usually knew where they came from. "So and so died and the widow brought in this box" or "these drapes came from that big house up on the hill in Duluth." It was thus I learned that the stuff of fairy tales could be found close at hand.

Which brings me to the end of the story, when my aunt died. I immediately understood the consequences of the loss as I had learned about loss years before, when my father died. Yet I was unprepared for the feelings I had about her belongings. There were not many things I yearned to take home with me, but I could not bear to think of all those accumulations being scattered into unappreciative hands. I wanted to keep them all together, yet where could such a feat be accomplished? I did not know. Her husband waxed heavy under the apprehension that he had come into something valuable, yet incomprehensible. He closed the house and did not allow anyone in while he took a bewildering inventory of what she had left behind. He anguished that she had thirty pair of slacks in her closet, and he knew no one her size who wanted to buy them. At the sales he finally had, he priced them at three to five dollars each, and I knew for sure that many had been purchased at Goodwill for fifty cents and altered by hand as she needed. It became clear that if I wanted any keepsakes from that magical accumulation of stuff, I would have to buy it at one of his sales. I also berated myself for coveting those things, believing myself to be more spiritual than I felt at that time.

But, as sometimes happens to me, I had a dream that made things clear. I was sixteen or so in the dream. My Aunt Margie and I were in a secondhand store in a shabby part of Duluth. The shelves of the store were lined with a myriad of odd things, and as I looked closer, I saw that many of them were things that had been my Aunt Margie's. Why were they here? Had she sold them and come here with me to retrieve them? Slowly it dawned on me: she had, in fact, died. "Is this all that is left?" I wondered, filled with panic. The things were dusty. I had no money. I turned to ask her if all this were true, what I was thinking, and she was no longer there. I stood in the center of the empty store, a great feeling of loss upon me. Very slowly a pair of hands put a shawl over my shoulders. I could not see who had put it there. It was a soft, thin, wool shawl, brown with wool fringe. I stretched my arms out, spreading the shawl out behind me into a triangle and went to a mirror in the corner of the store. I turned my head back to see the reflection. It was plain and brown from the back too, but spelled in tiny glittering beads was my name, shining there on the back of the shawl. Then came the realization of the gift she did indeed give to me. Her own inheritance from the first tragic namesake that gave her a sense of what she might be, that she shaped into a possibility passed on to me: what she saw as magic that she felt she had missed, that she tried to make up for, to me, was mine for having been there, for passing through her hopes and dreams. And I came by it honestly. It was not a casual encounter, hers and mine, but real time was spent in those early years when the dust particles drifted through the afternoon sun and people lagged in the Superior summer air, always tainted with a suspicion of industrial waste. The colors and textures I learned there became a firm part of my own vision. I will never be able to say or write my name without realizing a bit of glitter put there by her.

There is a great deal to think about and occasionally I do just that. How on earth did they do it all those years and in those places? The extent of passion and energy confined in those small circumscribed spaces: tea cups and canasta? Where would it have gone if released? I suppose that is the answer, right there.

Aili Jarvenpa

FIRST LESSON

Back in 1938, in the depths of the Depression,
Father sent me off to the University.
With his usual Old Country wisdom,
he cautioned me to watch my pennies
and keep an eye out for city slickers.

I'll never forget that first walk across campus.
It was Freshman Week,
the September sun was warm.

I spotted him right off.
He came toward me,
tall, good-looking,
broad-shouldered in his maroon and gold sweater.

In less than five minutes
he sold me a two-year subscription
to *Harper's Bazaar*.

SOUTH OF SOUTH IS NORTH

Things aren't always what they seem.
When I was in the fourth grade at Garfield School,
my favorite teacher, Miss Magnuson,
told the class: "If you dig deep enough,
you can reach China."

Some of the kids snickered.
Jimmy Kinnunen, with some help from his brother,
dug a deep hole in the front yard
and broke the water main.
His father was not pleased.
My faith in Miss Magnuson remained unbroken.

Let's look at it this way—
when you travel far enough
in the same direction,
south of south becomes north.
You know what I mean?

And of course east of east is west.
Say you fly east from New York to Helsinki,
and from there continue flying in the same direction,
but just a tad southeast,
you could end up in Walla Walla, Washington.
About as far *west* as you can get,
on dry land, that is.

Of course Miss Magnuson was right.
And while there are Doubting Thomases
who insist the earth is flat
and the holocaust never happened,
there will always be the Jimmys of the world.
Inspired by the Magellans and the Miss Magnusons,
they will continue to seek new paths
to the east and to the west,
new pathways to the planets.

MOTHER DREAM

I roll dough out on the board
cut three strands
Never get them even like Mother did
Braid three uneven strands
smelling of cardamom into coffee bread

Braid, braid Mother's long hair
divide it in three
Weave one thick braid
down her back for the night
her back bent in her last illness

A dark strand
escaping awkward fingers
flows out over darkness
I reach out to gather it
flowing over water
edge of madness
waters black in shadows of the spruce
no stars to show the way

She cannot breathe
I cannot breathe for her
I cannot breathe
I run, escape
to another room, and another
none familiar
one leading to another
leading nowhere
I cannot find my way

A strange door opens toward the lake
I hear water lap against
an old boat moored near shore
feel oars in my hands
smell dankness of the wood
fish smell of the last catch
death smell

Row back and forth
rock back and forth, back and forth
going nowhere
nowhere

Eeva Kilpi

THE BRIDES
MORSIAMET

(Translated by Aili Jarvenpa)

1

Planes fly. Guns fire.
The world speaks with the voice it has.
But the bride stands in the snow in her small shoes
and lights a candle in the ice lantern
under the new moon.
Walls radiate. We hug. We kiss.
Happiness, happiness,
eyes well with tears.
Everyone loves the bride.
The dying lift their faces toward her.

2

Immediately after the wedding,
when the groom returns to his garrison,
the mass media announces the decision has been made
to begin construction of the neutron bomb.
It annihilates the living — as you know —
but saves the inanimate.
It destroys vermin in hand-me-down furniture
but saves the wedding gifts and the groom's rifle,
leaves the photographs to look at each other
and keeps the bride's smile.
Technology builds itself a museum of its dreams.
The public is eliminated.
Perfection is finally achieved.
From now on it is unnecessary to strive for it.
Nervous coughing,
irrelevant question

dirty feet
no longer disturb the order.

3

Don't worry: the bride is smiling.
Right above her stomach is a cloud of small angels,
and glitter rains down from her eyes onto her breasts.
With four hands she lifts the church roof
for new winds to come,
and relatives on both sides of the entrance
drink hope.
Look at the bride's face, world, and
read your fate from it as the groom does.
Don't worry as long as the bride is smiling.
She knows.
She is pregnant with joy.
She is light from strength.
She is firm and fearless in her beauty.
She has enough to create the world.
Don't worry: the bride is smiling.

4

The earth is so beautiful.
The earth is so beautiful in order to make it
        difficult to lose it,
to make us sad when it is destroyed.
It defends itself with its beauty.
It looks us in the eye and asks:
How can anything destroy me?
Nature grows to avoid death.
Growth is the only power against destruction.
Also beauty.
When the development of weapons has reached its ultimate,
and nothing can become more deadly,
beauty rises against destruction
stronger than ever before,
stronger than anyone has ever risen.
Nothing can stand up against beauty.
In front of beauty, weapons are powerless.

5

The bride is smiling.
There is nothing more beautiful than a bride's smile.
From her eyes glitter falls down upon her breasts,
right above her stomach a small cloud hovers.
She smiles victorious
and carries our future step by step
closer to us.
Against all anguish, all pain and threats,
the bride steps, smiling.
A soldier's vow now meaningless, we stop being afraid,
and soon the child kicks for the first time.
The bride is smiling.
She knows without knowing:
it may go differently,
it may go well.

The bride is smiling.
In front of her smile, weapons are lowered.
Her smile will not fade.
The bride's smile is unconditional.
it answers every moment: I do.

6

The youngest bride dances.
She has only recently stepped out of her child's shoes
but already looks a bit like a wife
as she turns at the altar, a ring on her finger.
And the groom, like a blackbird snared
in her whiteness, dances with her.
Who leads and who follows
when love, like a beautiful prey,
speeds them across the floor's meadow?

Dance, youngest bride, dance.
As long as you dance
there is hope,
as long as you dance
the world has the strength to believe and love.

May you shed your virginity slowly
so the world won't grow old.
It is young with you.
It is young as long as you dance,
a ryeflower in your hair.
Seeds of birches rain down
and the youngest bride dances,
shoes of her childhood abandoned,
and her maidenhood, with the tinge of a wife,
sheds slowly.
And the world dreams.
Its heart fluttering, it bows to you like a groom
and hopes to be accepted.
Youngest bride, dance with the world,
twirl it until it's exhausted, youngest bride.
The youngest bride dances her sisters into mutual
        understanding,
brothers as brothers to each other.
She has just been freed from a child's shoes
and already turns at the altar, looking a bit like a wife.
There is not much time.
Therefore dance, youngest bride.
The world loves you the most.
For your sake, the world doesn't want to die.
Dance, youngest bride.
There is no worry while the bride is dancing.

7

The last one to step to the altar is the serious bride
and she also says: —I do.
A wreath of roses in her hair, she wants autumn and winter
just as before
and after autumn and winter, spring
and early summer and summer,
mid-summer and continuity.
Thus the brides step forward wanting for us
the seasons of the year one after the other.
The corner of her mouth quivering a bit, the serious bride
gives her promise.
Her hip sways slightly inside the white gown

346 / Sampo: The Magic Mill

remembering its strength,
and despair flutters aside.

The unwed sit
peacefully around,
unhurried, trusting.

This is what life wants.
Life wants it like this.
A charming challenge
before death.

PART IV

A retrospective

Anselm Hollo

THE *KALEVALA*
THROUGH MY YEARS

F OR A FINN of my Helsinki generation (b. 1934), the *Kalevala* was an early obligatory task of reading and memorization. I dare say I won't offend anyone by stating that this task was an onerous, and at times, even unbearable one.

For a child raised in the midst of World War II, in a family torn by Nazi versus Human sympathies, any form of glorification of heroism, racial mythology, and so forth, was bound to be repugnant. In other words: everything my parents, one from a humanistic-Socratic view-point, the other, from a Nietzschean "will to change" vantage, enthused about that smacked of heroics, idealism, reverence of some occult "virtue" or another, was deeply suspect to me. I was an early "punk" which, at that time, took the shape of jitterbugs, Lester Young hats, pegged pants, and a generally snotty and cool attitude. (Well, if *you* have ever encountered a thoroughly likable and psychologically coherent adolescent, let me know.)

So, first encounters with the *Kalevala* were rather nonproductive of anything but the traditional schoolboy jokes about birch-bark shoes, and so forth. Hayseed stuff. Yet, not long before those forced readings of our national epic, I had perused a good German prose translation of the *Iliad* and the *Odyssey*, cover to cover, possibly due to its illus-trations: engravings of opulent gods, goddesses, and "demi" ver-sions of both. . .I had to sneak the book from a somewhat "forbid-den" shelf.

There was, indeed, something about the school system's presenta-tion of the *Kalevala* that was off-putting, even in sober retrospection. It was *hyped*, much as I imagine the *Nibelungen* was in contemporary (1930s-40s) Germany, as the greatest literary achievement of mankind, the ancients' blessed gift to us weak descendants, a fount of wisdom, essentially, a kind of bible—which it quite patently was not, any more than the haphazard historical agglomeration of Near Eastern texts known as "The Bible" is, to anyone but those regrettably renascent self-styled "fundamentalists."

Years passed, and, while living and working in London, beginning to gain some consciousness as a writer in this, my chosen language, I became aware of the *Kalevla's* story power. While not the product (at least, as we have it) of an amazing Homeric intelligence in terms of organization, it does have other charms: of The Word, the power of the word; the Osiris myth, complete, and in two versions, yet; the quest motif; and, as Paavo Haavikko has shown us in two brilliant versions, the story of the origin of abstract wealth. Plus, Lemminkäinen's amorous and martial exploits, closer to the Norse Sagas' world than to the shamanistic, ancient ambience of The Smith Ilmari, The Singer/Sorcerer Väinö, and so forth.

In fact, while engaged in a parallel study of a number of different records at that time, it struck me how bleakly secularized the Icelandic ones were compared to the *Kalevala* and *Kalevipoeg*. Not until my reading of — again, at least a decade later — Native American matter did I realize that this was in no sense an "accident," but due to the stubborn preservation of an old tradition in certain cultures, possibly and particularly in those the nineteenth century was fond of calling "backward."

Then, came my encounter with Giorgio de Santillana's astounding book *Hamlet's Mill*, which resulted in a slightly embarrassing contretemps with a Finnish ambassador to the U.S. During the ten minutes preceding my modest speculative reading of Santillana's thoughts on the *Sampo* theme, at a major American city's Kalevala Day, said ambassador delivered himself, in a manner reminiscent of Heinrich Mann's *Der Untertan*, of a speech to the effect that the *Kalevala* was simply so great that it did not, and should not, ever, require any form of interpretation. Not unlike Yahweh's tablets, though more Savolaxianly verbose, it had to be taken at, as it were, face value.

At the risk of sounding immodest, I would like to have it on record that I managed to retain my lunch, deliver the lecture, and walk away with a great glowing new-found affection for *Louhi, Kauko, Kullervo,* and all those folks.

Yet it must be said that the *Kalevala* is, possibly due to the time of its collection and compilation, a remarkably patriarchal cycle of narrative poems. No expert, I conjecture it to be a revisionist document, one of the earliest. Louhi, the powerful and from our heroes' point of view "vicious" Lady of the Northland, is Kali, the Great Mother, who is apt to devour feeble ambassadors. Her powerful and decisive presence in the epic as we have it now does seem to hark back to a time when a battle was waged between an ancient, shamanistic, matriarchal culture and upstart bands of "heroes," who must have found the approaching Judeo-Christian ideology — as in the *Kalevala's* final canto — a remarkable godsend, and that's an intentional pun.

More mundanely speaking, the *Kalevala's* translations into English, with the exception of the Peabody/Magoun version, do not seem to have spawned anything more remarkable than Longfellow's *Hiawatha*, a period piece even the recent generations of "camp" lovers have failed to put to any reconstructive use. Which is not to say that Henry Wadsworth Longfellow should be consigned to total oblivion—*Evangeline* is a masterpiece of sorts, and almost comparable to Byron's *Don Juan* as an epic that is incontrovertibly *comic, both* intentionally and unintentionally.

In a book titled *Maya* (Cape Goliard/Grossman: London & New York, 1970), I included a selection from an earlier work, *Loverman*, which had been published in a limited, elegant small press edition by Piero Heliczer from his *the dead language press* then located in the painter Hundertwasser's studio barn north of Paris, in 1968. The sections I decided to keep and title *Out of the "Kalevala"* go as follows:

HERO, RIDING

Riding
July
Mosquitoes
Trees

Birches   few holy
oaks

Forget not the spells:
oak spell snake spell
spell against dwarves
dwell in the ground
sleeping are any handful earth

Evergreens
Pines
Rocks   grow larger
Trees
low   up north
Riding thinking singing

See her turn
golden
below the charred beams

Slanteye
Bluehair
Remember how round o those daughters

Long night
9 moons dark
Nipples marshberries
far apart

    Long hair swung
    'cross buttocks
    broad belly
Surprised:
his eyes in the door
Turn golden
charred beams

His thoughts hardly
thoughts flames
in the round-cobble hearth
lick softly through

TROLL, CHANTING

Moom moom
Hear my call
Moom moom
Speak to me
Mother   father
Lands   sea
Moom moom
In your room
I   we   all
Hear my call
In you are
Toad   star
Moom moom
Are you far
Moom moom
Are you near
Moom moom
Moom moom
You are here
I will hear
Moom moom
Moom moom
Moom moom
     Moom

MAIDEN, SINGING

They say she was
this one who sang

Dawn   sunrise
set and dusk
     Come at night
     Smell my musk

Dusk   sunrise
set and dawn
Loverman loverman
where you gone

Dusk   dawn
Sun rise and set

                    *

Dawn   dusk
Sun set and rise
On eyes
lies
hope he dies

Sunrise   sunset
dawn and dusk
     Came and
     left me
     here   a husk

                    *

Who sang   was
beautiful
          His once   who sang
          sweet invocations
                    in her ear

Sara Johnson

CHICKALOON LUMBER COMPANY

The house we lived in,
hedged by verdant fantasies,
stood on the brink of
clear-cut watersheds
perpetually leaning
into a tunnel of untouched white fir.

They say these woods
were burned,
in 1929
they blew up
overripe,
and left their fragments
gasping on a vacuum
of ruined ground.

I fall face first
into the river
my thirst unequal to its flow,
leafless I roll
over blistered rock until,
at the bottom of a rotting cliff
I drown.

In a spasm of sun
you and I stand waist deep
among deadheads, battered limbs
and orphaned twigs.
Today, there are not enough
conifers spreading their comfort
over this violated dirt
to atone for our neglect.

William Lamppa

SOUDAN IRON ORE MINER

The shaft in the earth
took the bloom of youth,
and left it lingering around dark corners
of hard rock and dust.

Swollen veins and knotted muscles
beneath sturdy work clothing
knew the sinking feeling
of the bowels of the earth approaching.

Grimy cheeks had the same temperature
winter and summer, year upon year
in the insidious dust,
until one warm spring day
a wasted body was lowered into a shallower shaft
between bouquets of mellow flowers.

The mine is a State Park now,
and Finnish and Slovenian accents
no longer re-echo among unworked slopes
where weekend tourists trudge curiously.

Jane Piirto

THE COMPANY

I.

negaunee caves in.
they're moving palmer.
republic used to be a bluff.
ishpeming has no tax revenues
now the undergrounds have closed
tilden location is now a metropolis
cliff's drive is blocked off
with open pit low grade iron pellets

in 75 years
the largest gem in the world
jasper knob
of jaspillite and hematite
will be an open pit, too.
but they don't call it strip
mining.

here's to The Company!

II.

mr. mather and his friends
explored and coveted
they bought and litigated
claimed from the Chippewa

and the word went
new england and europe
to the famished of famine
cornish, irish, french,
swedes, norwegians,
finns and italians later.

poor people
second sons unmarried daughters
sailed to ellis huddled

carriage canal and railroad
boat and hope
carried them to ishpeming, michigan,
where their cousins worked.

housemaids and miners
housemaids and lumberers
housemaids and carpenters
shoemakers merchants farmers
barkeeps and miners
and miners' sons

sought respectability
in claimed cedar swamps
bearing
babies and an ethic
work and not welfare
damp mines and falling chunks
the ore to make the autos
to make America
what it is
compasses went crazy
north pointed south
at this iron red
dust soiled the sheets
hand-wrung, hung
on clotheslines frozen
stiff as walls
between workers and bosses
ore
red mud covered sensible
boots tramping trails
in mosquito-owned woods

adventurers became family men
housemaids housewives
and there were children
and hope for the children
and the Lutheran Church
and the Catholic Church

and the Methodists
and the streets of taverns
and The Company
tentacled.

III.

we are yours, Company.
you pollute with our blessing
you own the land

you hired our grandfathers
our fathers
brothers husbands
you gave us girls college
at Northern and
"teaching is a *good* job
for a woman"
you own the land

our sons go to Northern too
they live in detroit now
work for the auto companies
or hamburger franchisers

teach school
if they don't work for you
'cause The Company pays good
now there's unions
and being a miner
is a respectable job
and we work for you
whatever we do

my dad died of cancer
he worked in your shops
the noise made him deaf
The Company paid the bills
my mother is a widow

with a penion
now there's unions

my husband worked the Empire Mine
he spit taconite
black ooze on the pillow
for a year after he quit
but he made good money
saved it up for college
my cousin's your accountant

we are yours, Company
you showed us the land
your land
seduces us

trout deer waterfalls
clean water pine woods
you only pollute a little
you sent our kids to college
you helped us own our homes
we had nothing
when we came
you own the land
our homes stand on
you hire us
to move our homes
when you wish
to dig a shaft
a pit a strip

you own the land
and jobs
are more important
than land
we are yours
wrapped and fenced
we are your links
in a chain
pass it on

Paula Erkkila

ON THE ROAD TO ROCK: A SEARCH FOR IDENTITY

*I*T IS THE FARM TOWNS of Rock and Bruce's Crossing that are in my mind, islands of security and refuges in the woods and swamps of Michigan's Upper Peninsula. They are welcome and soothing reminders of the numerous farm villages of Finland. They will always be a part of my Finland in America.

We lived, not in a farm town, but in the iron mining town of Ishpeming. My father dreamed of owning a farm, my mother didn't. They fought over this for at least forty-five years. "Ma said No!" he would interject as he pounded his fist into the table. She wasn't going to take any chances. She wasn't a farm girl, but was raised by poor landless peasants from Pulkkila. Her father had been an indentured servant who fled from his servitude and hid under the assumed name of "Lehtikankaan Jussi." They were so poor that sometimes they ate bark for bread.

One branch of my father's family was fortunate to have owned the Lehtimäki farm in Mäntylä near Jalasjärvi for some seven generations. I suppose the strong desire to own a farm runs in the blood from my father's side, but it also ran strong for the mostly landless Finnish immigrants, to whom owning a farm represented independence and security. Many Finnish immigrant miners like my father hoped to save their money, and get out from under the thumbs of the bosses and the big shots by purchasing land in the Bruce's Crossings and Rocks of Upper Michigan, Wisconsin, and Minnesota.

On Sundays during my childhood my family would frequently leave Ishpeming and head south on M-35 towards Rock or Bruce's Crossing. We visited the Harsila's, the Lindberg's, the Erickson's, and the Ruotsila's, on the way to the Roini's in Rock. Every time we stopped, my parents got involved in endless conversations in Finnish which neither my sisters nor I could follow. We whined and complained and sent our little sister in to disrupt the chatter, in the hopes of persuading our parents to drive on to something more exciting. She would usually return with bribes of gum or candy.

The most exciting stop was the Harsilas' farm south of Negaunee. We merrily played for hours there, catching frogs in the creek, feeding the mud-mired pigs, and playing hide and seek in the haystack, squealing in anticipation of getting caught. Aili Harsilas' homemade butter and ice cream have never since been excelled. I remember even as a young child experiencing a sense of reverence for Matt's long rows of potatoes.

I last saw the Harsilas in 1977 or '78 at a Labor Day festival in Rock. Matt, one of those tanned Finns with a noble looking Indian face, was demented by then. I was surprised and touched to see him there. He wasn't relegated to some back room somewhere in a nursing home. Aili dutifully pushed him around in a wheelchair, with the same self-assuredness and competence she exhibited in her former cow-tending and butter-making days.

Since then the mining company has gulped up Aili and Matt's farm. I still have a hard time accepting the possibility that there may be a big gaping hole there. I've tried approaching their land from different directions, only to be stopped by settling ponds, barbed wire fences, or gouged-out open pit mines.

Further down the road, enroute to Rock, just before Gwinn, past the old Salo farm, there stands a former dance hall that always gives me a nostalgic twinge as I drive by. I never had the opportunity to attend the dances, but I look up to those fun-loving pioneers who walked fifteen to twenty miles from Rock and Ishpeming and all the outlying directions to dance and play and socialize with one another. By my time the culture was dying out. Its heyday was over after the first thirty years of this century. Gone were the plays, the music, the dances, the poetry, the politics, and the cooperative endeavors. We were becoming Americanized at the expense of our cultural heritage. Luckily, however, we did have several years of Kaleva Camp at Three Lakes, Michigan.

During my twenties I found myself in a cultural vacuum, not belonging to either culture, afraid to proceed, and afraid to turn back. I fumbled for years trying to establish an identity. My father once recounted that on his journey from Finland in 1903 his ship sprang a leak somewhere in the English Channel. He had to walk a narrow plank from his leaking Finnish ship to an awaiting English boat. He said he was afraid to turn around, and also afraid to go forward.

Now I'm no longer afraid to walk that bridge between cultures. I'm beginning to enjoy it. I'm sure I wouldn't have conquered my fears and gotten through it all, however, without the Finnish *sisu* that so many of us were blessed with—that strong sense of determination and courage and resolve to persevere and to find joy and happiness in life.

During my college years I was quite busy looking into other people's roots. I took Black economics, Native American art, Tibetan, Chinese, Tantra and American-Russian relations, anything to avoid the sterile, meaningless psychology classes that were offered. Finally an old friend pointed out to me how lucky I was to be bicultural myself. He inspired me to take a trip to Finland to explore my own roots. I spent a year there researching my family tree, perusing the collections of Finnish Americana at the Helsinki University Library, learning more about the *Kalevala*, visiting relatives, and partaking in small and sometimes unbelievable adventures that make for good stories. My appreciation and understanding of my parents began to grow.

One of the more memorable and believable stories took place on the gently sloping plains of Pulkkila. As I approached the birthplace of my mother, I could feel the tears welling up inside of me. I passed the old wooden church, which was freshly painted. Nearby was a monument that seemed to have something to do with the Finns defending themselves against the Russians. As I drove down a gravel road with my mother's half-brother, Ensio, the one with one arm (it was cut off during an accident in the woods), I remembered how my mother used to tell of her starvation years, how she and her mother would walk down the country roads begging for food at the time of the Finnish Civil War. I thought of how special beets were to her; I guess they grew around there.

My mother had been born in a large one-room log cabin, and my Uncle Ensio was taking me there to see it. It was hard to believe that this structure would still be standing after some hundred or so years.

We pulled up in the driveway to a small house with modern siding. A man as black as coal came out to greet us. He was the current occupant. No sooner were we introduced than he whisked me into the house. He had just come down from cleaning the chimney. To my surprise, he produced a violin and began to serenade me in memory of my mother, my grandmother, and my grandfather. As he played the beautiful strains of *Parempi Valssi*, I looked around the low-ceilinged room and wondered how my mother could ever have fitted in a large cigar box at birth; apparently she was premature. Her maternal grandfather, Niilo Luutinen, a poor tailor, used to brag that she could read while still in the cradle.

How I managed to suppress the tears as the blackened serenader played on and on, I'll never know. The muses had joined us for that very special moment, and the very poetic side of the frequently unobtrusive and quiet Finnish man revealed itself to me in the form of the violinist and in the soft tenderness of my beautiful uncle.

In a daze we drove still further down the gravel road to a tributary of *Siikajoki*, to the place where my grandmother drowned in 1924. There was a special bond between my uncle and me, and now sixteen years later it's still there, even though I don't even know where he is or if he's still alive.

My journey and adventures in Finland changed and broadened my perspective as my old friend had predicted. My appreciation and understanding of my parents and grandparents began to grow, and continues to grow as I heal from the hurts and wounds of childhood – the early years spent in a foster home due to my mother's tuberculosis, and the many ruined weekends of childhood due to my father's alcoholism and her co-alcoholism, two diseases that have affected many other Finnish-American households.

Now that my parents are dead, all I have left are the memories. I have discovered I can choose to put the pieces of those memories together into numerous patterns. What inspires me the most was their simple love, their humbleness, and their innocence. They were common, ordinary people caught up in their troubles in a strange new world they were never fully able to join. Unfortunately they lived out their tragedies to the bitter end.

My father was proud of having built his house, and proud of his rock garden, especially his "new potatoes." Even though he loathed the squirrels who desecrated his garden and pursued them with a vengeance, he dearly loved animals. He killed a deer once, and its head was mounted on our porch. When he was drunk, he used to cry about that deer; that was the one and only deer he ever killed. He frequently sat in his rocking chair in front of the picture window enjoying the birds, the other animals, and the seasons. He said the U.P. had everything, and there was no reason to ever leave the U.P.

He was one of the old storytellers and jokesters. You could see his mind churning out the stories and jokes in front of your eyes, as he listened to what others were saying. He bragged he could have been a minister, and once taught Sunday School in Gwinn. We always laughed at that, because he rarely stepped foot inside a church, and in deference to that, his memorial service was not held there. He begrudgingly paid the church tithes, as our forebears had been forced to do for hundreds of years in the Old Country. He became incensed every Sunday when the television evangelists came on – he ranted on and on that they were crooks who were bilking people. He insisted, "There's only one god and that's the sun. When that goes down, we're doomed!" He also insisted that the earth was flat, despite all my arguments to the contrary. He used to say that Jesus Christ was the only true communist there ever was, but in later years he revised this to socialist.

He was particularly proud of his service in the U.S. Marines; he once was an orderly for President Harding on the U.S.S. Mayflower. He refused to sabotage the U.S. government as suggested by a more radical cousin. He was buried in his 1918 Marine uniform while taps were played on a tape recorder.

His mother and father had settled in the U.P. in the early years of this century. They built a large house with a two-story barn that nestled against a steep side of Camel's Hill. They had a barn full of cows before my time; my older sisters used to go out to the swampy areas near what is now Lake Angeline to bring the cows home from their day of grazing.

They also had an old double sauna in which many guests bathed over the years. Grandma Erkkila held many blood-letting parties in that sauna. She would send for the *kupari* woman, who would suck blood through a cow's horn covered with stomach lining. A longtime neighbor of ours, Lempi Haavisto, now in her late eighties, recalls having cuts made in her legs, and being treated for some ailment by the *kupari* woman.

Grandma Erkkila was the family matriarch. She was about four feet, ten inches tall, and had thin white hair wrapped around the back of her head. She was somewhat of a mystery to me, since she never learned to speak English in the seventy or so years she lived in this country; yet she appeared to be a revered and powerful dynamo of a woman. I recall numerous visits to her small, cozy kitchen, with the old, wood-cooking stove, the round welcoming table, and the grandfather clock. Seeing her and partaking of the inevitable candies she offered produced a certain sense of security, the security of knowing that her place would always be there, and that one could count on her entrenched stability.

She read the Bible every day and was a pillar of the church. I have to admit that when I looked up the church records in Finland and found out that she was four months pregnant with my dad while working as a *piika* (servant girl), I couldn't suppress a certain glee that even my pious grandmother had succumbed to temptation like the rest of us. This was also my way of identifying with my father's religious rebellion against his mother.

Grandma Erkkila was quite a remarkable woman. She died at the Palmer Nursing Home shortly before her 101st birthday. I was surprised to learn, after she died, that she had played the stock market. It strongly contrasted with my image of her sitting in the lower part of the barn day after day, year after year, especially in her late seventies and eighties, faithfully weaving her Finnish rag rugs on her old wooden *kangaspuu* (weaving machine).

Grandpa Erkkila struck me as a quiet, gentle soul, although I hardly knew him. In his photos he looks like a cross between Abraham Lincoln and Adolf Hitler. He came to this country around 1896, several years before my grandmother. He worked as an underground iron miner for many years. He fell off the barn roof one day in 1949, punctured himself with a stick, and died.

My mother was a wistful romantic dreamer behind her facade of worry. She possessed a spirituality not understood by my father. She was an unrealized poet at heart, as well as a Russophile. She transmitted to me her unrequited love of the *Kalevala* and of the Finnish culture. She frequently apologized for her poor English, although she had a better education than my dad; she got up to the ninth grade in Finland, and he only completed the sixth in this country.

She was once a member of the Communist Youth League, as were many of the poor children of her village of Pulkkila. Her mother, who was blacklisted during the Finnish Civil War, destroyed all the records so my mother would have an opportunity to go to America and earn some money to return for a higher education. Instead she met my dad at a woolen mill in Maynard, Massachusetts.

I'm sure part of my mother died when her mother drowned in Pulkkila trying to save two young boys in 1924. She described her mother as a dreamer who visualized a better world for poor people. Her mother, who only had a fourth grade education, learned to read the works of the philosophers and was an admirer of Marx. She was also a village masseuse and healer. My mother referred to her as a free thinker.

My mother faithfully nourished, fed, and cared for me without fail. She stood by me despite all the years of acting out and anger I demonstrated towards her. I knew she loved me deeply. I last saw her at the Mather Nursing Home in Ishpeming. She gave me a farewell hug— she knew it was our last embrace.

Many immigrants like my parents learned to speak rudimentary English. As the years went by and "Finglish" crept in, their Finnish became poorer. I myself have struggled for many years to express myself in English and am still struggling. I finally have realized that this is a difficulty shared by many of us first and second generation Finnish-Americans. Even more significantly, the English language does not always lend itself to the cultural and emotional expressions of the Finnish mind and soul. I believe the Finnish mind works more like a *Sampo* grinding and churning and considering various possibilities in an attempt to integrate, similar to the oriental mind, whereas the western mind is more immediately goal-directed.

Four years after my journey to Finland and during my medical school years in Escanaba, Michigan, in the late 70s, my husband and I used to drive northwards towards Rock on Sundays. We fantasized about owning some land along the Escanaba River. We were beside ourselves with delight one day when we stopped near a farm and were invited in for coffee. It wasn't long before we found ourselves in the barn trying to milk the cows.

The stocky, dyslexic son of the farm had big strong muscular hands from years of milking. He patiently taught me to milk, as he observed my feeble attempts with amusement. My hands were strained, but my admiration for his skills increased. He looked like the eternal stereotype of generations of Finnish farm peasants with his rough-hewn hands and face.

The next morning as we cosily nested like gypsies next to the comforting sounds of the river, our cow-milking friend woke us up and invited us over for a breakfast of farm fresh eggs.

Later we drove over to the Finn Hall in Rock. It was being restored as an historical building. I fought back tears of gratitude, mixed with nostalgia and sadness for those immigrants now gone, whose voices and laughter once filled the now empty, cold hall. My heart was heavy with grief and appreciation for their struggles and achievements and their courage in moving to a faraway land.

I know a part of me will always be on that road to Rock. It's etched into my memory along with the love and longing for the Old Country and our mother culture that my parents imparted to me and which their personal tragedies prevented them from fulfilling to a higher degree. This love and longing form a passion that transcends all the sufferings and tragedies we'd been through together. It's a passion that heals. It's endless, and I know now that my life will be filled with many journeys on the many roads to Rock that await my choosing.

Kathleen Halme

WOOL, BREAD, ROPE

And the young sit uneasily,
stiffly as wood, at the point
that the threads all somehow
insist on coming back to.
                        Alan Williamson

1. VISITING POET SUIT

The man who wore that suit to visit us—
a weave that's loose like long ago.
A suit of antique wool, but new in style.
I think he saw the ram who wore that wool.

2. IMMIGRANT IN SUBURBIA

Pentti in the kitchen cutting up a chicken.
The knife slits quick and sure and nice.
His past: a trans-Atlantic crossing,
a boat of mute people with their bundles,
babies, two English words. Sick of the sea.

His children will try to make the past
be more than wheels of bread hung up to dry:
a gypsy man as dark as bread (Pentti said)
at midnight in still light lifted the latch,
grabbed the live chicken and ran.

3. THE NEXT IN LINE

No form, no past, no brooch for me to wear:
as if tying a rope between my feet,
trying to learn to walk a certain stride
would teach the rules that intuition wants.

SAUNA

When people, cars, and Kelvinators
still had rounded sides,
first married couples,
then anyone, uncoupled,
of one sex,
steamed and beat themselves
with spicy birch—
brusque crustaceans who lived
to dance out of the pot alive.

They met the others in a house to drown in vowels
I didn't know,
to sit around a table
set with Lutheran coffee
and seven kinds of sweets—
the only excess they allowed
that didn't suffocate or sting.

Glad to be mute,
I vowed to marry soon.
I'd be done with the melting widow women
who weren't embarrassed anymore,
who would search my skinny body
for signs of spring as I popped
bubbles in the metallic paint
on the dripping sauna door.

I loved the place;
I didn't have to talk,
still, the woods around
the sauna and the house
urged dark and foreign words,
an angry-sounding tongue.
In bed, at night,
I made up words to use some day.

This is no plan for nostalgia.
My grandfather's gradually
losing his mind.

Is it because of a pay-day gal
he met in the twenties
in an Alaska sawmill town?
He never learned English;
he keeps his stories home.
His wife married him because he asked.
She left her house in the woods—
the table set, the closets full.
I go sometimes to see
what else has fallen apart.
The measure of memory is her first
husband's coat still hanging stiff
in the tilting porch.

They have stopped asking,
"Marry?"
And poetry, to them, is no husband,
but they let me sauna alone.
Their past is all necessity and work.
Kalle will slip on the sauna floor and die.
Esteri will mumble in a nursing home
where no one will speak Finnish.

Love and luxury have no claim here.
Only words that work.

Paula Ivaska Robbins

IMPRESSIONS
OF FINLAND

I HAVE A SPECIAL ADVANTAGE as a Finnish-American visiting Finland. Although I was born in the United States, my parents raised me in the traditional Finnish way. My first trip to Finland brought many excited thoughts to mind. "Why that's the way I behave as I do—I am Finnish!" On the other hand, my education was American, and I have lived and absorbed that culture all of my life. Therefore, I look at Finland from an American perspective. So that at the same time and in the same person I am both a Finn and not-a-Finn. I can both question and understand.

The heightened perception which living in a strange environment evokes has a ripple effect which touches many other aspects of life. Because my mind is more alert, my research goes more smoothly, and I'm in touch with new insights and can see more connections between concepts and theories. I can delight in the aesthetic, from the combination of natural and man-made beauty of Saarinen's Hvitträsk or of a painting by Kimmo Kaivanto, or a Sibelius symphony. My body is awake to the physical pleasure of a mushroom hunting tramp through the mossy sun-dappled Finnish forest of autumn-gilded birches and lichen-covered firs. I enjoy the challenge of a strenuous folk-dancing class and can usually get my feet to move the right way despite the fact that I am twenty years older than the next oldest person in class. I struggle to unlearn old habits. The American polka and the Finnish polka are just sufficiently different to throw my partner off balance.

THE FINNISH CHARACTER

Some people may question the existence of a national or regional character that determines personality traits, but it is clear to me that it exists. There also seems to be a relationship to geography. People who live in cold countries with long winters tend to be shy and quiet. In the United States, the Finnish temperament is not that different from that of the down-East Yankee from Maine. I can watch the young couple shushing their two children in the tram and understand why so many Finns speak softly and almost in a whisper. All the eyes in the tram look disapprovingly toward the shouting and laughing young people or the visiting tourists. "They are so noisy!"

I am reminded of the pastor who ministered to my father in the hours before his death who later spoke of my father's gruff inability to express emotions. "Well, of course," said the pastor, "He was a Finn!" Finns have such an urgent need to grasp out and communicate with other people. Put three Finns in the same room and they will soon form a club. But on the other hand, they have such trouble staying together that each organization soon divides into splinter groups and factions. They want to come together, yet put twenty Finns in party dress in a living room, and after the initial introductions and handshakes, the first five minutes will be spent in agonizing silence with no one knowing how to break the ice. Yet, Finns do not seem to be shy when it comes to making a speech, reciting a poem, or singing a song. Somehow, the Finn seems to need a formal structure and accepted rules of behavior in order to be socially comfortable. It's with new people or in new situations in which the norms are unclear that he or she becomes shy and unable to communicate.

Perhaps this is because the Finn is a contradictory combination of the old-fashioned peasant and the modern sophisticate. *He* is still the country bumpkin from the log *tupa* in the forest living in the sophisticated world of computers and Marimekko design. The transition has been too swift. He is still partly the shy peasant who's overwhelmed by the big city and who feels *he* must sit politely and not talk too loudly lest someone discover that he doesn't really belong there after all.

Finnish men, especially, seem to be constricted by this national feeling of not being good enough. Is it the result of generations of being the battleground for the wars between the neighboring giants and always having to look on impotently, unable to effect any real difference in the outcome? The Finnish man had to bow to the Swedish or Russian ruler who governed him in a foreign tongue and exacted tribute.

And yet, as with many other groups of underdogs, this forced acceptance of second class status has its rewards in a certain creative vitality— the *sisu*, the ability to persevere and to stand firm despite all odds against whatever a foreign ruler or a cruel northern nature dishes out. It has also resulted in the Finnish eagerness to be cultured and civilized. Finns spend more time and money on books, theater, music, art, and education per capita than do the people of almost any other country. There is a desperate need for the farm boy from the woods to be as good as the other folk, whether running or driving faster or creating a more beautiful building or piece of sculpture.

There seem to be two sides to Finnish manners. On most occasions, Finns are exceedingly polite to the visitor, with always the requisite coffee table, loaded with three kinds of cakes—each of which must be sampled. But sometimes they are ill-mannered and oblivious to the stranger's needs, as if to say, "We're as good as you foreigners and don't need to put on any airs." At times I miss the comfort of the breezy informality of American manners, which seem to give the feeling of "We'll gladly share with you whatever we have, but don't expect us to put on our Sunday-best."

This same polarity seems to be at the root of the Finnish problem with alcohol. Because the Finnish man seems to believe that he must sit up straight, mind his manners and behave properly all the time, he can only express his emotions under the artificial stimulus of alcohol. In Leningrad it is no wonder that hotel employees are so surly when the Finnish "vodkatourists" come there for the week-end to buy cheap alcohol, get drunk, and behave like boors.

While many more sophisticated Finns have learned to enjoy a glass of wine with dinner without having to get drunk, there's still an air of furtiveness and disrespectability about alcohol. The Friday evening shoppers at the Alko hurriedly wrap their bottles and sneak out of the store with eyes straight ahead lest anyone see them.

However, Finnish laws governing drinking and driving are admirably tough. Taxis are plentiful, and people plan to use them to get home after an evening of drinking. At one country inn, before taking the order, the waitress asked who the driver in the party was, and when the others in the party were served wines, he was given fruit juice of a similar hue.

There are obvious advantages to living in a small homogeneous community. It is easy to know how to behave in public. And if one should try to break the rules, there's always an elderly woman's voice crowing forth, *Älä polta tupakkaa täällä* (Don't smoke here) or some other such stern admonishment. I didn't know whether I was more embarrassed or frightened when, one day, I inadvertently crossed the street against a red light, and a speeding car almost ran me down. The old lady standing on the other side of the street, rather than sympathizing with me, shouted that I should not have crossed when the light was red.

As a result of the consensus of behavior, the streets of Helsinki are amazingly free of litter, and everywhere in Finland things are neat and tidy, flowers are grown in the summer, the trains run on time, and the mail is delivered promptly. At night one has no fear of walking alone in the cities. There are standards, and they are kept.

The other side of this is that Finns are very serious. Everyone on the streets walks very fast as if late for an urgent appointment, and lunches are bolted down as if the food were about to be taken away.

FOOD

Food in Finland, while simple, is of high quality and usually well prepared. There is a growing concern with proper nutrition and a balanced diet. Almost every school and workplace of any size has a well-run, attractive cafeteria or dining room where a well-cooked dinner is served in the middle of the day. Finnish bread is probably the best in the world, with many varieties from which to choose. Pastries, too, are good, and not too sweet. Fish dishes and cheeses are also excellent. Special delights in the summertime are the many varieties of berries and mushrooms that can be gathered in the countryside.

LANGUAGE

Finnish was my mother tongue, and I didn't learn English until I was three years old. However, I haven't spoken Finnish for forty years and have seldom heard it spoken, nor did I ever study Finnish grammar until recently. I have never been so motivated before to learn a language. I look forward with eagerness to each class and am disappointed when the hour is up. I practice saying Finnish sentences in my head and play a game each time I go into a store. I try not to let the clerk know that I am a foreigner. My pronunciation is good enough so that, unless I make a grammatical mistake or don't know the proper word, I sound like a Finn. Each time that I can conduct my business without revealing that I am an American I count as a minor triumph.

However, the language is so difficult that I am constantly frustrated. Not only are there sixteen cases of nouns, but many words change their spelling four or five different ways depending upon the case or tense. Everything must be memorized, and that is a process which is harder for me now. As an adult, I learn by organizing and classifying my experience, but this complex language often defies categorization.

I find it disappointing that most Finns speak their language so sloppily. I admire the Finnish of a native Swedish-speaker like former Foreign Minister Per Stenbeck, whom my cousins disdain as having "too perfect" Finnish.

I am reading all of the Finnish prose that I can find in English translation and have started to read some simple stories in Finnish. I am struck by the themes of nature which are treated so differently from the New

England Transcendentalism which I have grown to accept as my own philosophy. For the Finns, nature is a much more mystical and less benign force. Despite the harshness of their winters, New Englanders generally seem to expect nature to be caring and loving and full of beauty. The Finns, in contrast, cherish a beautiful summer day as a rare surprise from an ordinarily hostile and mysterious force. They are less likely to see order and continuity in nature. There is a constant feeling of man's struggle against capricious elements.

Even the language reflects the closeness to nature. There are many words and expressions describing weather, for example, several different words describing snow. The months of the year are related to the land and farming; for example, July is "hay month."

The importance of nature to the Finns is reflected in city and town planning. Buildings are sited so that a view of forest or water is preserved. One can't find anything like an American subdivision in which everything has been bulldozed to develop rows of single family houses each on its half-acre plot. In Finland, every city dweller wants to have his summer cottage on a lake or the sea shore, and fortunately, Finland is sparsely populated and big enough so that there is enough land available on its thousands of lakes and rural forest land to make this possible.

THE SAUNA

Only the people of a cold Nordic country could have invented the sauna, that temple for the worship of the far-off sun god. Roasting heat becomes a real value when the climate is never too warm and almost always too cold.

I love the freedom with which Finnish women accept the sensuality of their own bodies and sit unashamedly enjoying the heat of the sauna, like the young mothers who come and fondle their naked babies on their laps, or the three middle-aged women who chat and laugh together as they scrub each other's backs. Once I saw a beautiful blond young woman murmuring softly to her three-year-old daughter caressing her full firm breasts and delightedly taking the opportunity to suckle again at the nipples which brought her such pleasure as a baby.

RELIGION

Ninety or more percent of Finns are nominally members of the state church, which is Lutheran. But churches are almost empty on Sunday mornings, and most Finns clearly don't give religious experience an important role in their lives. The church maintains the function of registrar of births, marriages and deaths, and for many Finns serves only in this capacity of ceremonial marker of life transitions. The church is generally politically conservative, and is seen by many Finns as a bulwark against the left and, therefore, to be protected at all cost, even if they do not believe in its teachings. The state radio broadcasts prayers and sermons during morning prime time, sandwiched between the news, weather, and music. While I find it shocking that a Finnish author was convicted of blasphemy less than twenty years ago, Finns find it equally shocking that American courts can convict equally serious authors for pornography. Each society defines differently that area of behavior which is only to be regulated by the individual himself.

GOVERNMENT AND SOCIETY

As an American liberal Democrat, I admire the Finns' clear definition of where the dividing line should be between public and private ownership. In the United States, the decision to limit taxation, particularly by states and municipalities, and to encourage spending by individuals has led to a situation in which the quality of life, even for the very rich, is jeopardized. Even a ride in a Cadillac is bumpy and unpleasant if the street is full of potholes.

In Finland, public facilities of all kinds are built with great attention to quality, durability, workmanship, and design. There are sufficient public swimming pools, sports facilities, public transportation, and the like, for everyone so that there is little need for the individual to invest in those goods and services for himself. Public buildings are so well and tastefully constructed that it is usually a pleasure to be in them. This is in contrast to much of the shoddy workmanship seen in American public buildings, where the prime motive is so often to produce a public facility at the lowest possible cost. Twenty years later extensive repairs must be made on a building that never did function adequately. In Finland, whenever a new public building is proposed, there is often a competition for the best design. Architecture and city planning rank among the best in the world.

Still, Finland is clearly a capitalist country with a strong entrepreneurial spirit. The advertising signs atop every building in Helsinki's main business district, the signs on the buses, and the advertisements in the newspapers attest to this. But my Eastern Bloc neighbors living with me in the Education Ministry's guest house would agree with me that in Finland there is an ideal mix of socialism and capitalism. Unlike the Swedes, the Finns have not dedicated such a huge percentage of Gross Domestic Product to the socialist state that it threatens to overwhelm the private side. The balance seems to me to be as close to perfect as possible. There are no slums in Finland, and while there are rural poor in the North, basic social services are guaranteed. On the other hand, there are no very rich people either. Finns have all of the goods and services any modern society can offer, but in reasonable amounts. They do not waste things in the ways that Americans do. In the grocery store there are six kinds of salad dressings or cereals to choose from rather than the preposterous fifty of an American supermarket. There's also an admirable concern for helping poorer countries and strong support for the United Nations and for preserving international peace.

Unfortunately, this generosity does not extend to foreigners living within their boundaries. Finland is in many ways like a small town. People are much more locked into occupations and living arrangements than are Americans, simply because the country is small and can only provide a limited number of options. It is clearly very difficult for a foreigner to break into this closed society. And, shockingly, the laws governing the behavior of foreigners are more stringent that in any other country of western Europe. Foreigners have virtually no civil liberties. They aren't allowed, for example, to own property or join a trade union or even walk on a picket line.

My four months in Finland provided me with a wonderful "roots" experience in which I was able to get to know the culture and language of my ancestors and, in the process, to learn more about myself and my country. Despite its faults, there are many things that I like and admire about Finland, and I'm sure that I will return.

Mary Jokela Eichholz

SPINSTER

In a thicket of knick-knacks
spin and knit
braid your long loaves
kneaded with fists
scrub the upstairs toilet twice
hide the toilet paper roll
in a crocheted ante-bellum doll
stretch the attic curtains tight
nail by nail across the frame
your mother stretched her curtains on
iron the cotton underwear
the sheets, the towels
the starched print dress
polish again the mirrored floor
dust the dustless walnut chest
clutch the neatly lettered lists
    this week bind the crewel heart
    next week stained glass classes start
surround the house with garden gnomes
arm it with windmills
rows of ducks
straight edge the beds
until the grass lies cowed and neat
cut stark red tulips
sharp as tongues
and when night comes
wear your hair long
and weep

HAPPY BIRTHDAY, MOTHER!

(Your gift this year is for both of us.
I am learning Finnish.)

If you can know a people
by their language,
I am learning Finns.
It isn't easy.
They expect hard work,
persistence.
You must want to know.

Complex and logical,
I think they spend
the endless Arctic evenings
drinking, making compound words
and polishing new cases
for the nouns.

They travel light
behind their reindeer,
economize on consonants,
using the same ones over.
The air is filled
with the soft fall
of vowel sounds.

A word is said exactly
as you see it,
no subterfuge, precise:
sukka is stocking,
suukko is kiss.
The difference to a Finn
is very clear.
My ear and tongue are slovenly.
At least I like both
kisses and warm feet.

The second generation in America,
we learned to count to five,
to say, "Good Day," and one mild curse.
I am ashamed to be so ignorant.

It's good to be reminded who I am,
to touch in a real way
those Finns I never knew,
who persevered by their own warmth
in that cold land,
keeping alive this language
unlike any other.

Onnellista syntymäpäivää, Äiti!

Hazel M. Koskenlinna

"TALKING STORY" – FINNISH STYLE

W HEN THE STUDENTS in my course on "Ethnic Literature in the United States" were discussing Maxine Hong Kingston's autobiography/novel *Woman Warrior*, I asked them if their parents had "talked story" to them as Kingston's mother had. Rarely did they say yes. Is it a practice that died when TV was born, except as rendered by Mama on *Golden Girls*?

My parents "talked story." Along toward bedtime I would say to my mother or father, "Tell me a story," and they always had a story to tell.

Sometimes the story was about the *Hölmöläiset*. They were so funny, these *Hölmöläiset*, that I never tired of hearing about them.

Much later, when I was searching for material for a Bachelor's thesis on "The Beginnings of a Finnish-American Literature," I discovered that Toivo D. Rosvall had written a charming children's book, *The Very Stupid Folk*, who were my old friends the *Hölmöläiset*. So other Finnish-American children, sitting on their fathers' laps in the evening or being tucked into bed by their mothers, had pleaded "Tell me a story" and giggled about the *Hölmöläiset*. What a good feeling of community arose from knowing that there were people all over the United States who shared this warm childhood memory.

Väkevä Matti was another favorite. More brawn than brain, perhaps, but a lovable hulk, Powerful Matt often sent me chuckling off to sleep.

A story that evoked not smiles but question marks was the tale of *Susi-Tuomo*, Wolf-Tom. Was *Susi-Tuomo* real or was he a legend? He was renowned for his unfailing marksmanship. The local folk rejoiced that *Susi-Tuomo* kept them and their animals safe from the wolves who drew nearer to the villages as the cold and snow of winter grew deeper. They always had a place at their fireside for *Tuomo*, a good meal, and something warming to drink.

"Tell me how to be as good a hunter as you are, *Tuomo*," one young man pleaded. The hunter told him:

"At communion, take the blessed wafer but do not let it dissolve in your mouth. Only pretend; secrete it in your hand and keep it whole.

Then, as soon as possible, go alone into the woods; nail the wafer to a tree, at the height of your eyes. Then walk away in a clear straight line until you can just see the circle of the white wafer. Sighting along your gun barrel, stare at the holy wafer until it becomes the figure of Christ on the cross. Then shoot. If you can hit the wafer then, you will never again miss your target."

Whether the young man followed the wolf-hunter's advice I do not know, but soon after the next bitter snowstorm *Susi-Tuomo* was found frozen in the snow. He lay face downward as he had fallen. There was no mark on his body, but his arms stretched outward. He looked like a body thrown from the cross.

What does that story mean? None of the stories were interpreted for me. Either the significance came immediately, or later, or, in this case, not yet or maybe never.

Sometimes I asked, "Tell me what it was like when you were a little boy (or girl, depending) in Finland."

My father told about reading the Bible to his grandmother as she sat knitting before the fireplace, and about putting whiskey in the grain to feed his grandfather's prized rooster while the old man was at church one Sunday. How bewildered and dismayed his grandfather was when he returned from church and saw the strange behavior of his usually dignified, lordly rooster!

In my father's catechism class one day the minister called upon a boy (named Matti?), who stood up in properly respectful manner when his name was called. The minister asked, "Who is the mortal enemy of mankind?" Matti, hesitating, was befriended by the fellow in the seat behind his, who gave Matti a sharp poke in his butt. "*Per-r-r-kele*," Matti said, with force and a good trilled *r*. "That's right," said the minister, "but you didn't need to say it with such feeling."

My father told about running away from a harsh master to work in the forests of Sweden, and what life was like there. I heard about the compulsions of Finnish hospitality—it almost killed him, he said, when he was taking the census and courtesy required him to drink the coffee offered at every household on his assigned route.

My mother talked about her days as a cowgirl (definitely not in the style of the Old West), when she carried her lunch of a chunk of bread and a forbidden piece of sugar broken from the loaf in the larder ("A *loaf* of sugar?" "Yes, that's how it came in those days.") when she took the cows out to pasture. The cows had names like *Mustikka, Sinikka, Mansikka* (Blackberry, Blueberry, Strawberry). Did all the cows have names ending in *ikka*, or was that the memory of a little girl who had been too often hungry?

That little girl was hungry for more than food. When she was six she was an indentured servant. Too many mouths to feed at home. The contract specified many details—how much yarn she was to receive for knitting so many pairs of stockings, and how many pairs of shoes. But apparently it said nothing about education.

When the minister paid his late summer visit to the family on whose farm my mother worked, he asked each of the children to read for him. Little Hulda wanted to read for him too, and she was permitted to do so. She read so well that the minister said to the family, "You must send this child to school also."

But when the first day of school came, the lady of the house (the *emäntä*) said, "No, you can't go. We need you to help around here."

Hulda watched the other children go off to school, and then she silently did her household and barnyard chores as usual. But that night, when everyone else was asleep, she took some bread, crept out to the barn, and hid herself under the hay.

All the next day she heard cries of "Hulda! Hulda!" echoing in the farmyard and from the woods, but she stayed hidden under the hay. That night, when all were again asleep, she stole back into the house and into her bed atop the kitchen fireplace.

Astonishment and relief greeted her reappearance the next morning. "Where have you been, you naughty girl?"

"The minister said I was to go to school with the other children. If I can't go to school, I won't work."

Defeated, and perhaps fearing disgrace in that small community, the *emäntä* said, "All right, but you must do your work before you leave in the morning and when you return in the afternoon." Hulda agreed to those terms, and the little girl who listened to the story rejoiced in her mother's victory.

Stories of the emerging Finnish nationalist movement were among those my father told. The Finns would gather in the forest and raise a makeshift banner on a flagpole created by lopping the branches from a tall, straight pine. They talked about how to free their country from the Russian yoke. Sometimes a lookout would come running to warn that the Cossacks were on their way into the forest. Down would come the banner, and when the soldiers arrived they found in the clearing merely a crowd on a Sunday afternoon outing, singing some incomprehensible song—must be a hymn—in that gibberish of a language spoken by the common folk.

My father liked riddles and riddle-stories. There was the one about how you would manage to transport safely across the river a goose, a sack of grain, and a fox, when your rowboat could handle only one of them with you at a time. Another: A surgeon was called to the hospital to treat a boy badly injured in an accident. "Good God!" cried the surgeon, "this is my son!" But the doctor was not the boy's father. How do you explain this? The doctor was the boy's mother, of course.

Not so many years ago I heard the same riddle-story from a feminist friend. "That's not a new story," I said. "My father told me that story when I was a little girl. I could answer the riddle, but I didn't know what he was really telling me."

That was true, I see now, of the meanings that underlay many of the tales I heard in my childhood.

The stories changed as I grew older. How did the storytellers in the olden days—the *really* olden days—tell their stories? Two men astride a long wooden bench began:

> Let us link our hands together,
> Let us interlock our fingers.

That's from my memory of my father's voice quoting the old translation of the *Kalevala*, not from the newer (1963) translation by Francis Peabody Magoun, Jr. Through the *Kalevala* I heard the stories of my people of the distant past, men and women who believed in the magic of words and whose very names roll on the tongue and come out like the sounds of Sibelius: *Väinämöinen, Ilmarinen, Lemminkäinen, Kyllikki, Louhi, Kullervo.*

Seitsemän Veljestä, Laulu Tulipunaisesta Kukasta, Isänmaan Parturit, Tuntematon Sotilas were read and discussed in our house. Later, when the Mike Waltari novels (*Men from the Sea, The Egyptian, The Roman*) became available in English translation, what pleasure they gave.

Listening to stories told and then reading stories made me aware that words are created by human hearts and minds, spoken by the human voice. When you once learn that, you feel the human presence and hear the human voice even in the printed word. You come to know that words are powerful magic.

The literature in the Finnish language gave me a sense of deep roots in the past, and the contemporary literature in Finnish or in English translation, or written by Finnish-Americans, made me aware that this literature is alive and growing; like a healthy tree with its roots deep in the earth and its branches growing upward and outward, like the oak trees of the Old World and the New, and with a life outlasting the oak and the redwood.

Aili Jarvenpa

THE SPRUCE

Kangasniemi, Finland   August 8, 1978

> *Harken to the spruce*
> *in whose root is thy home.*
> *— Finnish proverb*

The old house is gone
like you said, Father,
but the dark spruce stands tall
spreading its green
above the lonely field,
empty barn.

If I had the voice, Father,
I would tell you how it is for me,
always knowing of this home
called *Puusteli*,
yet standing here for the first time
beside the tree you planted as a child.

It is so tall now.
It holds the summer sky
filled with rain.
Its roots go far, as far as yours,
into the soil,
rocky hills of *Kangasniemi*,
to birds calling their lament,
deep to arctic winds, to the core of hunger.

They go back to an August day like this
when, at eighteen, you said goodbye
and left alone
for a place called Minnesota.

Yes, Father, it is tall now,
and its wide branches reach far
across the waters and the darkness
to a new warmth and light.

(In memory of my father who died
June 15, 1978, at the age of 86)

TO GRANDMOTHER'S HOUSE

Multia, Finland   September, 1984

We are of the same generation, Hilja and I,
she a grandmother, widow of my cousin,
mistress of this big house.
I am the American guest in her home.

The old Finnish farmhouse sits high on a hill
as it has since the 1500s,
nine generations of the same family.
The maples are ablaze with September colors.
The potato crop has just been dug.
It could be Indian Summer in Minnesota.

I study Grandmother Kristiina's portrait on the wall.
I never knew her—just a small, dim picture
that Mother brought to America in 1913.
Mother seldom talked about her. It was too painful.
Hilja points out the pictures of Grandmother's sisters—
Erika, Johanna, Maria.
Kristiina was the prettiest, Hilja says, as though
to please me.
It is all so strange, so long ago.

I feel a chill. Hilja urges me to rest,
brings me a blanket.
I lie down on the couch,
begin to feel young, protected.
Hilja grows older as I listen to her bustling sounds
in the kitchen.
She is becoming my mother.

We have a light supper,
for dessert a warm rice pudding full of plump raisins.
We talk late into the night.
Hilja says, yes, she understands my Finnish.
She laughs a lot, her cheeks rosy like Mother's,
her eyes a crystal blue.

She promises to reheat the rice pudding for breakfast.
I keep growing younger.

In the morning Hilja wakes me up gently.
She is my grandmother.
It is my first visit to my grandmother's house.

Arlene Renken

REUNION AT
LAKE SUPERIOR

In midsummer
we sit like seals
on sun-soaked rocks
that hold in their granite
the signs of an ancient past.
Browned bodies of our grown children
and grandchildren
dapple the pebbled shore before us.

Once in a brief youth
it was we who searched expectantly
for agates
and nimbly braved
the clear and icy waters
of Lake Superior.
We picked thimbleberries
along cliff-ridges
and built bonfires
on wave-washed shores.

Now united with our Finnishness
we are gripped by remembrances
of other times
that came and went before;
of golden summer jaunts
of *Juhannus*
and the Fourth of July;
of our parents
who fashioned a heritage
in our childhood season.
The past is never really over.

CONTRIBUTOR NOTES

JUHANI AHO (1861-1921), perhaps the best known and most popular Finnish writer of his time, began with short stories, most of which first appeared in newspapers and later as collections. His first stories were half-humorous descriptions of country people; later ones were ironic sketches of certain socially representative types; some were portraits of contemporary personalities. He remained a dispassionate resigned observer. He also wrote successful novels, among which were *The Clergyman's Daughter, The Clergyman's Wife, Panu,* and *Juha,* with the first two representing some of his best writing.

LAURI ANDERSON was raised in the Finnish-American community of Monson, Maine. He has degrees from the University of Maine, Michigan State, and the University of the Pacific. He has studied at the University of Nigeria, Universidad de Guadalajara, and Indiana University and has received research grants from the National Endowment for the Humanities. He was a Peace Corps Volunteer during the Biafran conflict. Currently he is Chairman of Language and Literature at Suomi College. He edited *Small Winter Wars,* a collection of short fiction, and has published stories and criticism in journals. A fanatical Red Sox fan, he believes that only baseball makes sense.

MAVIS BIESANZ was born on a farm near Tower, Minnesota, in 1919. She attended Winona State Teachers College and the University of Iowa, from which she graduated *summa cum laude* in 1940. Mavis and her husband, Dr. John Biesanz, have shared a successful teaching and writing career. They have traveled extensively, often with their three children. Since John retired from university teaching in 1971, they have lived in Costa Rica. Mavis continues to write and travel. A portion of her memoir, *Helmi Mavis: A Finnish-American Girlhood,* is used by permission of the publisher, North Star Press.

REBECCA CUMMINGS grew up as a third generation Finnish-American in Maine. She has also lived in Thailand and Brazil. As the winner of the 1985 Maine State Commission on the Arts and Humanities short fiction prize, her first book *Kaisa Kilponen* was published by Coyote Love Press. She is the author of *Turnip Pie,* Puckerbrush Press, a collection of short stories. Her stories have appeared in several anthologies and magazines. She lives in Maine with her husband, John Thompson.

AINA SWAN CUTLER (Mrs. Henry H.) was born in Gardner, Massachusetts, of Finnish immigrant parents, John M. and Edla Aaltonen Swan. Aina attended public schools in Worcester and has studied languages and writing at University level. She is a member of the New England Poetry Club. Her collaboration with Heikki Sarmanto, Finnish composer, began in 1975. She has translated and written original English lyrics for over 200 songs, mostly for Sarmanto. More than half of these have been published in Finland. She has also provided English texts for 60 percent of WSOY's collection: *Song of Finland — Tuhansien laulujen maa.*

KATHLEEN OSGOOD DANA got her nickname, Kati, on one of her many sojourns to Finland to study or work. Kati spent her senior year of high school at Oriveden Opisto, where she taught later one summer during college. Another college summer she worked in Finnish Lapland. After marrying, she studied at the University of Helsinki and explored the hinterlands with her husband, Tad. Kati and Tad live in Northfield, Vermont, with their two children, where Kati teaches composition at nearby Norwich University. She was recipient of the 1981 PEN/American Scandinavian Foundation Translation Award.

MARCELLE DOBY-WILLIAMS has been involved with image making of one sort or another for as long as she can remember. In 1973 she earned a B.A. degree from Montieth College (in Detroit) and the University of Minnesota, with a major in studio arts. Ten years ago she was a founding mother of WOMANSWORK, an organization dedicated to preserving and uncovering the woman's tradition in art. She now owns and operates, with her husband, a Rainbow Taxi. She also does free lance art work. She lives in Minneapolis and is a member of the Greater Midwest Literary Association.

PIERRE DELATTRE is the author of two novels published by Houghton Mifflin: *Tales of a Dalai Lama* (1971) and *Walking On Air* (1980). His stories and poems have been published in some fifty magazines, among them *The Atlantic, Harper's Bazaar,* and *The Village Voice.* He received a Bush Foundation Fellowship in fiction writing in 1985 and is currently writing near Santa Fe and exhibiting his paintings in New York City and Truchas. He was raised by Finnish grandparents near Phelps, Wisconsin, and has been strongly influenced by the *Kalevala* and by music of the *kantele.*

MARY JEAN JOKELA EICCHOLZ was born in 1932 in Menahga, Minnesota. All four grandparents came from Finland. She graduated from Central High School, Duluth, Minnesota, and Goddard College, Plainfield, Vermont, where she studied poetry, Finnish, and Loren Eiseley. She is divorced and has three sons. She owns a 200-acre farm in the northern Berkshires of Massachusetts, where she lives with her youngest son, his wife, two horses, a German shepherd and 14 wild turkeys. She is addicted to knitting, yard sales and book stores.

PAULA ERKKILA is a second generation Finnish-American who practices as a psychiatrist in Astoria, Oregon. She was born and raised in Ishpeming,

Michigan. Her father, Swande Erkkila, who emigrated from Jalasjärvi in 1903, worked as an underground iron miner for forty years. Her mother, Hannah Saisa, who emigrated from Pulkkila in 1923, was a housewife, proud mother of five daughters, and a long time member of the Ladies of Kaleva. Her husband of 25 years, Richard Knight, enjoys his profession of nursing. They are loving parents of Melissa and doting grandparents of Manzanita and Wayland Bittick.

CARL GAWBOY was born in 1942 at the Cloquet Indian Hospital to his parents, Robert Gawboy and Helmi Jarvinen Gawboy. His mother taught on the Vermilion Reservation near Tower, Minnesota. When Carl was small, they moved to the farm that Helmi's father had homesteaded near Ely. Carl earned his B.S. in Art from the University of Minnesota, Duluth, and his Master's from the University of Montana. He is well known as an artist of the Lake Superior region. He teaches at the College of St. Scholastica and lives with his wife, Lynn Maria Laitala, and daughter, Anna, in Bennett, Wisconsin.

M. EKOLA GERBERICK, M.F.A. City University of New York, is a visual artist and poet from Bath, Maine. She has had many major one-woman exhibitions in the New York City area, Colorado, Maryland, and Michigan, including one in Kuopio, Finland in 1987. Various grants in 1983 and 1985 enabled her to do research in Finland. She has received considerable support for her U.S. projects. She has been a successful guest lecturer at colleges, universities, museums, libraries. Her poems frequently appear in U.S. literary magazines. A sequence of her Taava Miina (healer) poems will be published by A.K.A. Press in 1989.

KATHLEEN HALME is the daughter of a Finnish father from Lappajärvi and a Finnish mother from the United States. She grew up in the Upper Peninsula of Michigan. The family moved to Milwaukee where she attended high school. She studied French and Anthropology at the University of Wisconsin and earned an MFA in poetry at the University of Michigan. She teaches writing and literature at Virginia Polytechnic Institute and State University. Her work has appeared in *The North American Review* as well as many other small journals. She has received several awards, including the Hopwood Creative Writing Award.

ERNEST HEKKANEN, who lives in Vancouver, B.C., is the author of two short story collections, *Medieval Hour in The Author's Mind* and *The Violent Lavender Beast*. He has been published in a number of literary reviews, including among others, *Canadian Fiction Magazine, Prism Internal, Malahat Review, Literary Review,* and *Canadian Literature*. He earned a B.A. degree in Sculpting and Painting from the University of Washington and a Creative Writing Degree (M.F.A.) from the University of British Columbia. He works as a renovator, accomplished at plumbing, framing, drywalling, plastering, painting, and electrical jobs, and runs his own business.

AARO HELLAAKOSKI (1893-1952), as a young poet, was opposed to the then current trend of Finnish poetry—learned, aesthetic expressions of melancholic dreams—and, instead, wrote simple, forceful poetry, often using satire as a weapon. He earned a Ph.D. in geology and wrote a number of geological papers. His literary career was marked by two distinct periods, the first from 1916 to 1928. He renewed his writing again in 1943. After World War II his creativity was finally recognized. *Hiljaisuus* (Stillness, 1949) was one of his best collections. In his later years he was considered Finland's greatest living poet.

BERNHARD HILLILA, Professor Emeritus of Education at Valparaiso University, has been pastor of Lutheran churches, president of Suomi College, dean at Hamma School of Theology and California Lutheran University. He has translated Olavi Kaukola's *The Riches of Prayer* and authored *The Sauna Is---* and *History of the Indiana-Kentucky Synod, Lutheran Church of America 1970-87.* His poems and articles in Finnish and English have been published in numerous books and journals. The fall 1988 issue of *The Haven: New Poetry* is devoted entirely to his poetry. Married, father of three, grandfather of three, Hillila's hobby is tight-rope walking.

ANSELM HOLLO was born in Helsinki in 1934. His father was a noted translator, and young Hollo grew up in an internationalist milieu, becoming fluent in several languages. In 1951, he spent a semester at McKinley High in Cedar Rapids, Iowa, on an American Field Service scholarship, subsequently studying modern languages and literature at the University of Helsinki and the University of Tübingen, Germany. Since 1967, Hollo, renowned as a translator and poet, has lived in the United States and is frequently engaged as a visiting professor by literature departments at many American colleges and universities. He lives in Salt Lake City, Utah, with his wife, the painter Jane Dalrymple.

SIRKKA TUOMI HOLM was born in Minnesota of Finnish immigrants, Fanny and Werner Tuomi. They were active on stages of Finnish halls in Minnesota, Massachusetts, Ohio and Maryland, where Sirkka also performed from childhood through adulthood. She studied drama at Peabody Conservatory, Carnegie Tech and American Theatre Wing, performing in professional summer stock several years. Currently she is completing oral histories of Finns and writes a weekly column for *Työmies-Eteenpäin*, frequently drawing on her memories of stage doings amongst the Finns. She lives in New Hampshire with her husband, Taisto, who is also involved in projects concerning immigrant Finns.

GLADYS KOSKI HOLMES, a second generation Finnish-American, finds that all creativity springs from a common source in each individual, but may find different paths of expression. This visual artist and writer lives in rural northern Minnesota with her husband of 38 years. All but one of their five children and their families live on the same land that was once farmed and logged by her husband's family, thus carrying on the Finnish tradition of sharing what one has with one's children.

RICHARD IMPOLA was born in 1923 near the village of Ahmeek on the Keweenaw Peninsula of Upper Michigan. He attended Calumet High School, served in the U.S. Army (ETO), was graduated from Columbia College in New York City, and ultimately earned a Ph.D. in English Literature from Columbia University. He is now retired after more than thirty years of college and university teaching. One of his main activities in retirement is the reading and translation of Finnish literature. He believes that Finnish writers deserve to be better known outside their own country.

AILI JARVENPA was born in Winton, Minnesota, of Finnish immigrant parents. North Star Press has published two books of her poetry, and her work has appeared in various literary publications. In 1983, New Rivers Press published her anthology, *Salt of Pleasure: Twentieth-Century Poetry of Finland*, which she edited and translated and for which she received a translation grant from the Finnish Literature Society. Her translations have also appeared in *Milkweed Chronicle*, *Great River Review*, and *World Literature Today*. A graduate of the University of Minnesota and retired Minneapolis high school teacher, she lives in Minneapolis with her husband, Oliver.

DIANE JARVENPA is a third generation Finnish-American. She has been published in *Sing Heavenly Muse!* and in 1988 was awarded the first prize in the poetry contest of the American Association of University Women, St. Paul branch. She is a vocalist, musician, and composer, and was a member of *Koivun Kaiku*, a Finnish-American kantele group. She has studied at Macalester College and the University of Minnesota and is currently involved in further studies in music and literature. She lives with her husband in Minneapolis.

EEVA JOENPELTO, born in 1921, is a prolific novelist in the front rank of Finland's prose writers. Her work is valued by both a large readership and by critics and scholars. She has received the Government Prize for Literature four times. She was a well-known, successful writer long before her renowned Lohja trilogy appeared in the 'seventies, a trilogy to which she added a fourth novel in 1980. Her portrayal of people is fresh and full of life. In her historical novels she describes events honestly, without stripping her characters of their worth.

JIM JOHNSON was born in Cloquet, Minnesota, and is a graduate of the University of Minnesota, Duluth, and University of Wisconsin, Superior. His first book, *Finns in Minnesota Midwinter*, was published by North Star Press in 1986. He has been part of Dovetail Corners, a poetry and photography collaboration exploring the Finnish immigrant experience in Minnesota, and has given readings at numerous locations, including FinnFest '88 in Delaware. Currently he is teaching in the Duluth public schools.

RUTH PITKANEN JOHNSON was born in Oulu, Finland, in 1908, the daughter of The Reverend Matti Pitkanen and Elin Durchman Pitkanen. She came to the United States in 1912 with her parents, who were called by the Methodist Episcopal Church to minister to Finnish immigrants in the Upper Peninsula of Michigan. She has a B.A.E. degree from The School of the Art Institute of Chicago and an M.A. from the University of Iowa. She was an assistant professor in the Department of Art and Design, University of Illinois, until her retirement in 1971. She still paints and exhibits.

SARA JOHNSON was born in the Upper Peninsula of Michigan and has lived in Idaho, Iran, Turkey and Alaska, her present home. She is an artist as well as a writer and holds a degree in Comparative Literature from Alaska Methodist University. Leisure time activities that she enjoys include gardening, skating, and collecting and listening to reggae records. She is an accomplished cross-country and alpine skier. She states: "In Alaska we ski to die."

MICHAEL KARNI earned a Ph.D. in American Studies at the University of Minnesota and wrote his dissertation on the Finnish American labor movement. He is currently on the faculty of the Scandinavian Department at the University of Minnesota, where he teaches courses on Scandinavian immigration. He has edited *Finnish Americana*, a scholarly journal on Finnish immigrant culture, since 1978. He has also published numerous articles and edited several collections of articles on Finnish immigration. He has been awarded two Fulbright grants to teach and to do research in Finland.

GLEN KARTIN, a third generation Finnish-American, was raised in the then predominantly small Finnish farming and logging community of Gowan, Minnesota, located almost half-way between Duluth and Grand Rapids. After graduation from high school in Floodwood, he attended the University of Minnesota (Duluth branch). His English professor encouraged him to submit his "fresh, humorous short stories" to publishers. Glen's boyhood experiences with his family and Finnish neighbors have been fictionalized and illustrated in short stories appearing in *Good Old Days* magazine and other periodicals.

ILMARI KIANTO (1874-1970) was born in Suomussalmi, Finland, in the northeastern border of Kainuu. He won fame with his novel, *Punainen Viiva* (The Red Line, 1909), which deals with the beginnings of political activity among the poor peasants of the region. In 1978 it was made into an opera by the composer, Aulis Sallinen. It received international attention and was performed at the Metropolitan Opera in New York City in 1983. Among his many later writings, the most celebrated is *Ryysrannan Jooseppi* (1924), the naturalistic account of a peasant and his family.

EEVA KILPI, respected as an author both inside and outside Finland, was born in Karelia in 1928. Her novel, *Elämän evakkona* (Life's Refugee, 1983), is the epic of uprooted Finnish Karelians forced in the last war to find new homes, including Kilpi and her childhood family. She often writes of the single-parent household — a middle-aged woman facing problems alone after a divorce, as in her novel *Häätanhu* (Wedding Dance, 1973). Her themes in short stories and poems often center around homeickness, women's varying relationships with family members, and their relationship with nature — a source of renewed strength.

HAZEL M. KOSKENLINNA was born in Kenosha, Wisconsin, of parents who came from southern Finland. She earned her Ph.D. at the University of Wisconsin, Madison, and taught for a number of years at the University of Wisconsin, Stevens Point, where she is now a Professor Emerita. One of the classes she most enjoyed teaching was Ethnic Literature of the United States. Earlier she was employed in a number of governmental positions, including Chief of the Air Force Fiscal Unit, U.S. Army Finance Office. She is a member of MELUS (Multi-Ethnic Literature of the United States).

TIMO KOSKINEN was four years old when he was sent alone to this country. His childhood consisted of winters in Florida and summers and fall in the U.P. pulp-bush and iron mining towns. In graduate school he earned a degree in English/Creative Writing. Currently he teaches at Suomi College. He and his wife recently completed a log home, where they live with their three sons. Lynx House Press published his novel, *Bone Soup and A Lapland Wizard*, and he has several published short stories. He received the nationally esteemed Pushcart Prize for his short story, "Dead Weight."

ROBERTA KULMA grew up in Fairport Harbor, Ohio. Upon graduating from college, she moved to California and later to New York City, where she completed post-graduate studies. She has worked in the field of medical social work for 15 years, was former director of social work at Mt. Sinai Medical Center, Miami Beach, and on the graduate school faculty of several universities. Her writing includes editing a state hospital newsletter and published pieces in medical and women's publications. She currently writes for a national newspaper. She resides in Florida with her husband, a cardiologist, and her son, Kevin.

STEPHEN KUUSISTO was born in Exeter, New Hampshire, in 1955. He attended the Writers' Workshop at the University of Iowa, where he received an M.F.A. degree in 1980. He has been a Fulbright scholar in Finland, and he currently teaches in the English department at Hobart & William Smith Colleges in Geneva, New York.

LYNN MARIA LAITALA spent her early years in Winton, Minnesota, where her grandmother lived in the old boarding house, and in Superior, Wisconsin, where her father worked for Central Cooperative Wholesale. In 1968, she graduated from the University of Minnesota with high honors in history. After graduate school, she worked as an oral historian and taught history at the college level. She lives on a small farm in northern Wisconsin with her husband, Carl Gawboy, and daughter, Anna, where she indulges her love of animals, particularly horses. She now writes full time on projects in history, current events and fiction.

WILLIAM LAMPPA was born in Embarrass, Minnesota, in 1928. He was educated at the University of Minnesota and lived for a number of years in New Brighton, Minnesota, with his wife and two sons. He has been a teacher, and since 1958 was employed as a social worker in Minneapolis. He retired in 1987 and returned, with his wife, to live in Embarrass. He has published three books of poetry: *The Crucial Point, In Familiar Fields With Old Friends*, and *The Ancient Chariot*. His poems have also appeared in a number of literary publications such as the *Cardinal Poetry Quarterly*.

LAURI LEMBERG (1887-1966) was one of the most talented actor/director/ playwrights in the history of Finnish American theater. He wrote more than 15 plays which range from proletarian dramas to romantic comedies and musical folk plays. Among these is the immensely popular *Laulu Vaaleanpunaisesta Silkkipaidasta* (The Song About the Pink Silk Shirt), one of the all time favorite farces of the Finnish American stage. Lemberg earned the distinction of being the only Finnish-American playwright to belong to the Dramatist's League of Finland. *St. Croix Avenue* is the only novel he ever wrote.

JAAKKO LIUKKONEN was born in 1947 in Virolahti, Finland. He received formal art training at the Ateneum in Helsinki and, upon graduation, helped found an art cooperative. In addition to the *Karhu the Bear* stories, Liukkonen has retold and illustrated other animal stories (*Karhusatuja, Eläinsatuja I* and *Eläinsatuja II* published by Osuuskunta Käyttökuva, Helsinki).

EEVA-LIISA MANNER is one of Finland's leading writers. Her book of poetry, *Tämä matka* (This Journey), 1956, became one of the most influential books of poetry for the Finnish modernist movement of the fifties. She has written nine other collections of poetry and has translated into Finnish from English, German, classical Greek, Spanish, and Swedish, the most notable being *The Iliad* and the works of Shakespeare, Herman Hesse, and Ben Johnson. She has received numerous prizes for her original writings and translations. She lives in Tampere, Finland.

NANCY MATTSON, a third generation Finnish-Canadian, was born and raised on the Canadian prairies and spent childhood summers at her grandparents' farms in New Finland, Saskatchewan. She researched and edited a history of this community, *Life in the New Finland Woods* (1982). Her poetry has appeared in numerous Canadian periodicals and on radio in Canada and Finland, and she has received grants from the Alberta Foundation for the Literary Arts and the Canada Council. Her first poetry book is *Maria Breaks Her Silence* (Regina: Coteau Books, forthcoming 1989). She is an editor at the University of Alberta, Edmonton.

OILI MÄKI, Finnish textile artist, learned her handicraft skills in her childhood home in a part of Karelia ceded to the Soviet Union after World War II. Her major sources of inspiration are national themes: Finnish music, landscape, literature—especially the *Kalevala*. She is the first textile artist in Finland to be awarded the honorary title of "professor." She has displays in many public buildings, including the largest tapestry in Nordic countries, "The Sea of Silence," in Bank of Finland's Vaasa Branch, and another, "The Creation," in the United Nations "Palais des Nations" in Geneva. She is also a poet.

EARL NURMI is a second generation Finnish-American. His parents were both immigrants. He has published well over 100 poems in periodicals and a chapbook, *A Diverse Gathering*, and a full length book, *My Nation, The World*. He is a chronic schizophrenic and has spent probably a total of four years or more in mental institutions. Other than that, he lets his poems speak for themselves. By Christmas 1988 he expects to have published another chapbook, *Enemy of the State*.

SHEILA PACKA was born in 1956 in Eveleth, Minnesota, the grandchild of Finnish immigrants. She grew up in northeastern Minnesota and has a bachelor's degree in Social Development from the University of Minnesota, Duluth. She lives near Chisholm with her husband and son and works as a child protection social worker for St. Louis County. Her poetry has been published in literary magazines such as *Sing Heavenly Muse!*, *Loonfeather*, and *Women's Times*, and also in a collection of poetry, *Across the Fence*. She contributed poetry to the Iron Range Documentation Project. In 1986, she received a Loft-McKnight Award for Poetry.

ANNA PERKKIÖ is the pen name of Anna A. Anderson. She was born in Oulu, Finland, in 1903, the daughter of Maria and Karl Gustav Kiiskilä. Her pen name is in honor of her maternal grandmother, Anna Perkkiö Yliniemi, who told her stories. She attended public schools in Oulu and graduated from Oulu Business School in 1921. She came to the United States in 1922 and in 1925 married Gustaf E. Anderson of Ossining, New York. They had four children. Now widowed, she lives with a son in South Carolina.

JANE PIIRTO is an Associate Professor at Ashland College, in Ohio. She is a native of Ishpeming, in the Upper Peninsula of Michigan, and has been an educator in Michigan, Ohio, South Dakota, and New York City. She has published many short stories, poems, and scholarly articles. Her novel, *The Three-Week Trance Diet* (Carpenter Press), won a first-novel award. She has completed a second novel and is at work on a third.

JOHN PIIRTO teaches in the writing program at the University of Colorado. He lives in Boulder with his wife and two children.

RITVA POOM has studied Uralic languages at Columbia University. Her translations of literature and ethnography from Finnish and Estonian have appeared in numerous publications. She has translated Mati Unt and Paul-Eerik Rummo (Estonian) and Paavo Haavikko (Finnish). In 1988, her bi-lingual chapbook of poems by Eeva-Liisa Manner, *Fog Horses* (Cross-Cultural Communications, 1986), received the Columbia University Translation Center Award. She is currently translating and editing *Kalevala Mythology*, to be published by Indiana University Press. It has received the support of the National Endowment for the Humanities.

ARLENE RENKEN, born and raised in a Finnish farming community in Michigan's northern peninsula, is a descendent of Finnish immigrants, a teacher of art, and coordinator of the K-12 art program for the Stevens Point, Wisconsin public school system. In 1986 she completed a doctoral thesis at the University of Wisconsin, Madison, on symbolic ethnicity in art. The focus of the study was the rag rug weaving craft among descendants of Finnish immigrants to the United States. She has authored articles for professional art education magazines. She and her sister, Viola Nixon, co-authored a cookbook, *Finnish-American Folk Recipes*.

TIMO RIIPPA, a graduate student in Scandinavian Studies at the University of Minnesota, works as a Research Assistant at the University's Immigration History Research Center. He has taught Finnish in the Department of Scandinavian, served as associate editor for *Finnish Americana: A Journal of Finnish American History*, and been involved in numerous Finnish American activities, including the Salolampi Finnish Language Villiage, where he served as curriculum writer and staff member. He has translated and written a number of published works on Finnish Americans, among them the chapter on Finns and Finland-Swedes for *They Chose Minnesota*, published by the Minnesota Historical Society (1981).

PAULA IVASKA ROBBINS was born in the United States, but spoke Finnish as a child. She received her B.A. from Vassar College, M.Ed. from Boston University and Ph.D. from the University of Connecticut. She studied Adult Education in Finland in 1981, sponsored by the Finnish Ministry of Education. "Impressions of Finland" was written in 1982, when she taught for a semester at the University of Helsinki under a fellowship from the Finnish Academy. She is the author of *Successful Midlife Career Change* (New York: AMACOM, 1978) and the Assistant Dean of the Graduate School at the University of Lowell, Massachusetts.

ANNIE RUISSALO (1884-1987) was a Finnish-Canadian writer whose novels, short stories and articles appeared for close to sixty years in the Finnish American women's newspapers, *Toveritar* and *Naisten Viiri*. She began writing from a farm outside of Fort Frances, Ontario in 1917. Most of her fiction, especially her early novels serialized in the *Toveritar*, depicts life in Finland and Karelia and is characterized by a bucolic romanticism. Her later autobiographical writings clearly follow in the grand Finnish literary tradition of *korpikirjallisuus*, literature describing everyday life in the backwoods.

PENTTI SAARIKOSKI (1937-1983) was a major poet and brilliant translator of postwar Finland. His writings have been received with critical acclaim, and collections of German and English translations of his poems have proved his work to be internationally recognized. The turning point in his career came in 1962 with the publication of his poetry collection, *Mitä tapahtuu todella* (What Is Really Going On). He translated into Finnish Homer's *Odyssey* and James Joyce's *Ulysses*, among many others. He was the recipient of several State Prizes for literature. A symbol of unconventionality during his lifetime, the whole country mourned his early death.

SHIRLEY SCHOONOVER was born and raised in northern Minnesota of Finnish parents and grandparents. She holds a Master's degree in English and is author of several novels. Her novel, *Mountain of Winter* (1965), has been translated into eighteen languages. An excerpt from it is included in *Sampo*. She has received O. Henry awards for some of her short stories. She now lives in the East and works in Manhattan. She is currently writing another book about growing up, maturing, with a Finnish background.

UNTO SEPPÄNEN (1905-1955), a Finnish novelist and short story writer, was born in Helsinki although he was of Karelian origin. His novels and short stories tended to be set in the Isthmus of Karelia between the Gulf of Finland and Lake Ladoga. Seppänen is particularly well known for stories of that area, such as that of old-time country life in which he described half-humorous situations which might occur in a small village. His lively fancy and talent for storytelling keep them entertaining, such as his story, "The Knitting," translated by Reino Virtanen, which is included in *Sampo*.

EILA SIREN-PERLMUTTER is a Professor of English at St. John's University. In 1985 she received a Fulbright award to write and lecture at Jyväskylä University in

Finland where she completed her novel, *Sirkka*. That work elicited the encouragement of the late John Gardner at the Breadloaf Writers' Conference in Vermont. Dr. Perlmutter is Finnish born, and emigrated to the United States at the age of five. Growing up in a wilderness outpost on the Minnesota-Canadian border in the late 'thirties provides the unique background for her stories. "Karhula's House" appeared in *Finnish Americana* and *Finnish American Writers*.

CAROL RUOTSALA STAATS, Alaskan poet and author, was born in Seattle, Washington. She grew up in southeastern Alaska and was educated in the old Territorial schools, later studying at the State University of Washington at Pullman and University of Alaska at Anchorage. She and her husband, Willard, live on a farmstead near Wasilla. Her poetry has been published in literary publications such as *The Raven* and *Finnish American Writers*. Working with Alice Countryman, a number of her poems have been set to music. Her work reflects the influence of the Alaskan scene and people and her Finnish-American heritage.

JUSSI STENVALL is the son of Finnish immigrants, father from Rauma, mother from Pyhäjoki. During World War II he was a B-17 Navigator with 28 combat missions over Europe. He graduated Magna cum Laude from the University of Tampa in 1949 and did graduate work at New York Graduate School of Business Administration. After a successful career as Director of Purchasing and Property for a large public agency, he has taken up writing as a hobby during retirement years. He has won honorable mention in several nationwide writing contests. He and his wife, Irene, have six daughters.

HEIKKI TURUNEN, born in North Karelia in 1945, is a powerful narrator whose first novel, *Simpauttaja*, created a sensation in Finland in 1973. One of his later novels, *Kivenpyörritäjän kylä*, examines how a small town reverts back into wilderness. Turunen boldly uses rough language seasoned with rich dialect. Due to his expansive form and fresh style, his novels become broadly sweeping epics of working class life.

AALE TYNNI, well-known poet and translator born in 1913 in Ingria, the Finnish-speaking province near Leningrad, has spent most of her life in Finland. She is the widow of the late Martti Haavio (P. Mustapaa), poet and internationally renowned folklorist. Tynni has published numerous collections of poetry and also translations, including Shakespeare's *Sonnets* and Ibsen's *Brand*. In her earlier poems, she speaks of love as the condition for the continuity of life. Her collection, *Lehtimaja* (The Arbor, 1946) reflects the difficult war period during which it was written. In recent years her poems praise joyful acceptance of life.

REINO VIRTANEN (1910-1987) was the son of Finnish immigrants. He spoke only Finnish until he entered school at the age of five. After he left home, he lived in communities where no Finnish was spoken. Nevertheless, he retained a love for his first language and translated numerous short stories, poems and articles from the Finnish. He earned a Ph.D. at the University of Wisconsin. He taught his speciality, French literature, at the Universities of Wisconsin, Tennessee, Minnesota, California at Los Angeles, and since 1954, at the University of Nebraska, Lincoln. He was married to Sylvia Bernstein. There are two daughters.

K. BÖRJE VÄHÄMÄKI, born in Vaasa, Finland, joined the faculty at the University of Minnesota in 1975. He currently serves as chair of its Department of Scandinavian Studies. He has taught at Åbo Academy and the Universities of Oulu and Stockholm. Professor Vähämäki's opus magnum (Ph.D. thesis), *Existence and Identity*, was published in 1984. In the area of Finnish literature, he has written, for example, the Introduction to *Salt of Pleasure: Twentieth-Century Finnish Poetry*, published by New Rivers Press in 1983. He is also co-translator of *Finnish Short Stories*, 1982.

INKERI VÄÄNÄNEN-JENSEN is a student of Finnish language and literature, with degrees from the University of Minnesota. In 1982, as Nordic Translators, she published a book of translations, *Finnish Short Stories*. She edited the 1986 book, *Women Who Dared*, published by the Immigration History Research Center and is preparing a book, *Finnish Proverbs*, for Penfield Press, Iowa City, Iowa. She has finished a manuscript, *Inkeri's Journey*, about her life as a child of Finnish immigrants. She is collaborating on a *Helmi Mattson Reader* and serving as a co-editor of a book of Finnish American and Finnish women writers.

ACKNOWLEDGEMENTS

Mavis Biesanz: "Introduction" and "June 1928" from her memoir, *Helmi Mavis: A Finnish-American Girlhood*, by permission of the publisher, North Star Press.

Rebecca Cummings: "The Hair Brooch," originally published in *Yankee*, August 1986. Reprinted by permission of the author.

Kathleen Osgood Dana: Translation of Eeva Kilpi's short story, "Mökillä" ("At the Cottage"), originally published in *Scandinavian Review*, No. 2, 1983, the original Finnish text published in Kilpi's collection of ten short stories, *Se mitä ei koskaan sanota* (*That Which Is Never Said*), WSOY, 1979, reprinted by permission of the author and translator. Translated *Karhu the Bear* stories, originally retold by Jaakko Liukkonen and published in Finnish in *Suomen kansan karhusatuja*, Osuuskunta Käyttökuva (Mechelininkatu 8 A 7, Helsinki), 1979, by permission of the author and translator.

M. Ekola Gerberick: "Language and Grandma Ekola" and "Vanha *Iso-äiti*," originally published in *Finnish Americana*, Vol. 5, 1982-1983. Reprinted by permission of the author and publisher.

Ernest Hekkanen: "In the New World," originally published in *Cutbank*, No. 9, 1977. Reprinted by permission of the author.

Bernhard Hillila: "Yrjö Kaarto," originally published in *Finnish Americana*, Vol. 6, 1983-1984, reprinted by permission of the author and publisher. "Hail Mary," originally published in *The Cresset*, December 1983, reprinted by permission of the author. "Willow Waterway," originally published in *The Christian Science Monitor*, July 26, 1985, reprinted by permission of the author. "Supply Side Theology," originally published in *America*, 1986, and *Anthology of Magazine Verse* and *Yearbook of American Poetry*, reprinted by permission of the author.

Anselm Hollo: "The Kalevala Through My Years," originally published in *Kalevala 1835-1985, The national epic of Finland*, a special 1985 issue of *Books from Finland*, reprinted by permission of the author.

Sirkka Tuomi Holm: "Stage Recollections Among the Finns," originally published in *Finnish Diaspora II: United States*, edited by Michael G. Karni and published by the Multicultural History Society of Ontario, Toronto, 1981. Reprinted by permission of the author and publisher.

Richard Impola: Translated excerpts from Heikki Turunen's novel, *Mustarinnan lapset* (*Children of the Land*), WSOY, 1985, by permission of the author and the publisher. Translated poems of Aale Tunni, "On Many a Windy Night" and

"The Lake," originally published in Finnish in *Kootut runot* (*Collected Poems*, WSOY, 1977) by permission of the author and the publisher.

Aili Jarvenpa: Translated excerpts from Chapters One and Two of Eeva Joenpelto's novel, *Vetää kaikista ovista* (*A Draft From All the Doors*), WSOY, 1974, by permission of the author and publisher. "*Morsiamet*" ("The Brides"), from Eeva Kilpi's poetry collection, *Ennen kuolemaa* (*Before Death*), WSOY, 1983, in translation, by permission of the author. "The Spruce," originally published in *Tuohela*, North Star Press, 1982, reprinted by permission of the publisher. "Mother Dream," originally published in *View From the Loft*, July 1980. "To Grandmother's House," originally published in *Sing Heavenly Muse!* No. 12, 1985. Translation of excerpt from Oili Mäki's "*Maamerkki*" ("Landmark"), *Eripainos Horisont-lehdest*, 8/73, p. 47, by permission of the author.

Jim Johnson: "Getting Off the Train at Brimson," "Skeletons," and "Mojakka," originally published in *Finnish Americana*, Vol. 6, 1983-1984, reprinted by permission of the publisher.

William Lamppa: "Finns of the North Country," originally published in *Työmies-Eteenpäin*, March 10, 1971, reprinted by permission of the publisher. "Soudan Iron Miner," originally published by *Finnish Americana*, Vol. 7, 1986, reprinted by permission of the publisher.

Nancy Mattson: "Writing" and "Kanadalainen," originally published in *Canadian Woman Studies/les cahiers de la femme*, Vol. 9, No. 2, Summer, 1988, reprinted by permission of the author. "Matt Breaks His Silence" and "Maria Learns Resentment," originally published in Canadian Forum, October 1986, reprinted by permission of the author. "*Tietäjä*," originally published in *Prism International*, Vol. 26, No. 2, Winter 1988, reprinted by permission of the author.

Earl Nurmi: ".25-36 Caliber Rifle," originally published in *My Nation The World*, Guild Press, 1981, reprinted by permission of the author. "Trapping Weasel Near Duluth," originally published in *A Diverse Gathering*, West End Press, 1979. reprinted by permission of the author.

Jane Piirto: "Sauna," originally published in *Ocooch Mountain News*, April 1980, reprinted by permission of the author. "Grandma You Used To," originally published in *Images*, 1978, reprinted by permission of author. "The Company," originally published in *Sing Heavenly Muse!*, No. 5, Summer 1980, reprinted by permission of the author. "Blueberry God," originally published in *Finnish American Writers*, 1983, reprinted by permission of the publisher and author.

Ritva Poom: Translations of Eeva-Liisa Manner's poems from her *Collected Poems 1956-1977*, Tammi, Helsinki, 1980, by permission of the author.

Timo Riippa: Translation of excerpts from Lauri Lemberg's novel, *Saint Croix Avenue*, originally published in *Industrialisti*, August 3, 1967-August 14, 1967 issues.

Translations of Annie Ruissalo's "The Floating Caravan" and other sketches, originally published in *Naisten Viiri*: "The Farmer's Old Lady" from "Annie Ruissalo *Pakinoi*," August 10, 1973; "Sunday Morning" from "*Rinnastuksia*," September 18, 1970; "The Fur Coat" from "Annie Ruissalo *Pakinoi*," August 10, 1973; "The Floating Caravan" (*Uiva Karavaani*), July 22 and 29, 1966; "Townsfolk and the Farmer" (*Kaupunkilainen ja Farmari*), July 29, 1966. "Epilogue" from "Annie Ruissalo *Pakinoi*," August 10, 1973. Translation of prose piece in *Kevät*: "The Speaker at the Hall" (*Puhujaa Kuulemassa*), 1973.

Paula Ivaska Robbins: "Impressions of Finland," originally published in *Raivaaja*. Reprinted by permission of author.

Shirley Schoonover: Excerpt from her novel, *Mountain of Winter* (pp. 276-283), published by Coward-McCann, Inc., New York City, 1962. Reprinted by permission of author.

Carol Staats: "Lapland Bear Song," originally published in *Finnish American Writers*, 1983. Reprinted by permission of publisher and author.

Reino Virtanen: Translation of excerpt from Ilmari Kianto's *Scenes from Travels in Viena-Karelia*, Virtanen's translation originally published in *Työmies-Eteenpäin*, January 17, 1985, reprinted by permission of the publisher. Translation of Unto Seppänen's short story, "The Knitting," Virtanen's translation originally published in *Prairie Schooner*, Winter 1976-1977, and in *Finnish American Writers*, 1983, reprinted by permission of publisher.

Inkeri Väänänen-Jensen: Translated excerpts from Eeva Kilpi's *Naisen päiväkirja* (*A Woman's Diary*), WSOY, 1979, by permission of the author.